THE POETRY OF THE FIRST WORLD WAR

The poetry of the First World War remains a singularly popular and powerful body of work. This *Companion* brings together leading scholars in the field to re-examine First World War poetry in English at the start of the centennial commemoration of the war. It offers historical and critical contexts, fresh readings of the important soldi   war poetry of women and civilians, Georgians   ists, and of poetry from England, Ireland, Scotland, Wales and the former   h colonies. The volume explores the range and richness of this body of work, its afterlife, and the recent expansion and reconfiguration of the canon of 'First World War Poetry'. Complete with a detailed chronology and guide to further reading, the *Companion* concludes with a conversation with three poets – Michael Longley, Andrew Motion and Jon Stallworthy – about why and how the war and its poetry continue to resonate with us.

Educated at Presidency College, Kolkata, and St. John's College, Cambridge, Santanu Das is Reader in English at King's College London. He is the author of *Touch and Intimacy in First World War Literature* (Cambridge, 2005) and the editor of *Race, Empire and First World War Writing* (Cambridge, 2011). He has published in journals such as *Modernism/Modernity* and *Essays in Criticism* and is completing a book entitled *India, Empire and the First World War: Words, Images and Objects*.

THE CAMBRIDGE
COMPANION TO
THE POETRY OF THE
FIRST WORLD WAR

THE CAMBRIDGE
COMPANION TO
THE POETRY OF
THE FIRST WORLD
WAR

Edited by

SANTANU DAS
King's College London

CAMBRIDGE
UNIVERSITY PRESS

32 Avenue of the Americas, New York, NY 10013-2473, USA

Cambridge University Press is part of the University of Cambridge.

It furthers the University's mission by disseminating knowledge in the pursuit of
education, learning and research at the highest international levels of excellence.

www.cambridge.org
Information on this title: www.cambridge.org/9781107692954

© Cambridge University Press 2013

First published 2013

Printed in the United States of America

A catalogue record for this publication is available from the British Library.

Library of Congress Cataloguing in Publication data
The Cambridge companion to the poetry of the First World War / Santanu Das.
pages   cm. – (Cambridge companions to literature)
Includes bibliographical references and index.
ISBN 978-1-107-01823-5 (hardback) – ISBN 978-1-107-69295-4 (pbk.)
1. English poetry – 20th century – History and criticism.   2. World War, 1914–1918 –
Great Britain – Literature and the war.   3. War poetry, English – History and
criticism.   4. World War, 1914–1918 – Literature and the war.   5. War poetry –
History and criticism.   I. Das, Santanu.
PR605.W65C36   2013
821′.91209358–dc23   2013017433

ISBN 978-1-107-01823-5 Hardback
ISBN 978-1-107-69295-4 Paperback

In Memoriam
Paul Fussell (1924–2012)
Dominic Hibberd (1941–2012)

CONTENTS

CONTENTS

FIGURES

NOTES ON CONTRIBUTORS

FRAN BREARTON is Professor of English at Queen's University Belfast. Her books include *The Great War in Irish Poetry* (2000), *Reading Michael Longley* (2006) and, co-edited with Alan Gillis, *The Oxford Handbook of Modern Irish Poetry* (2012).

SARAH COLE is Professor of English and Comparative Literature at Columbia University. She is the author of two books, *At the Violet Hour: Modernism and Violence in England and Ireland* (2012) and *Modernism, Male Friendship, and the First World War* (2003), and she has published articles in such journals as *PMLA*, *Modernism/Modernity*, *ELH* and *Modern Fictions Studies*, as well as in a variety of edited collections.

NEIL CORCORAN is Emeritus Professor of English Literature at the University of Liverpool, and he previously taught at the universities of Sheffield, Swansea and St Andrews. His books include studies of Seamus Heaney and Elizabeth Bowen, and *Shakespeare and the Modern Poet*, which appeared in 2010. He edited *The Cambridge Companion to Twentieth-Century English Poetry* (2007), and he has recently completed a book titled *The Responsibilities of Poetry*.

SANTANU DAS is Reader in English at King's College London. He is the author of *Touch and Intimacy in First World War Literature* (2005) and the editor of *Race, Empire and First World War Writing* (2011). In 2010, he gave the British Academy Chatterton Lecture on the poetry of D. H. Lawrence. Currently he is completing for Cambridge University Press a monograph titled *India, Empire and the First World War: Words, Images and Objects*.

SIMON FEATHERSTONE teaches Drama at De Montfort University in Leicester, United Kingdom. He is the author of *War Poetry: An Introductory Reader* (1994), *Postcolonial Cultures* (2005) and *Englishness: Twentieth-Century Popular Culture and the Forming of English Identity* (2009).

CHRISTINE FROULA, Professor of English and Comparative Literature at Northwestern University, has published widely on modernist art and thought, including *Virginia Woolf and the Bloomsbury Avant-Garde: War, Civilization, Modernity* (2005); *To Write Paradise: Style and Error in Ezra Pound's Cantos* (1985); 'War, Peace, Internationalism' in the Bloomsbury circle and 'Sovereign Subjects: Stephen Dedalus, Irish Conscience, and *Ulysses*'s Utopian Ethos'.

SANDRA M. GILBERT is Professor Emerita at the University of California, Davis, and has published eight collections of poetry, most recently *Aftermath* (2011). Amongst her prose books are the memoir *Wrongful Death* (1997), the cultural study *Death's Door: Modern Dying and the Ways We Grieve* (2006) and two essay collections, *On Burning Ground* (2009) and *Rereading Women* (2011). With Susan Gubar, she is the co-author of *The Madwoman in the Attic* (1979) and *No Man's Land* (three volumes) and the co-editor of *The Norton Anthology of Literature by Women* (2007). She is currently at work on a book tentatively titled *The Culinary Imagination* along with an anthology of food writing. In 2013, Gilbert and Gubar were named winners of the National Book Critics Circle Award for Lifetime Achievement.

DAVID GOLDIE is Head of the School of Humanities at the University of Strathclyde in Glasgow. He is the author of *A Critical Difference: T. S. Eliot and John Middleton Murry in Literary Criticism, 1919–1928* (1998) and the co-editor, with Gerard Carruthers and Alastair Renfrew, of *Beyond Scotland: New Contexts for Twentieth-Century Scottish Literature* (2004) and *Scotland and the Nineteenth-Century World* (2012).

MARGARET R. HIGONNET, Professor of English and Comparative Literature at the University of Connecticut, co-chairs the Study Group on Gender, Society, and Politics at Harvard's Center for European Studies. Her interests range from German romantic literary theory to the intersections of feminist theory and comparative literature, children's literature and word-image relationships. She has edited nineteenth-century women poets and Thomas Hardy. Much of her scholarship, including *Lines of Fire* (1999) and *Nurses at the Front* (2001), has been devoted to women's literature of the First World War.

PETER HOWARTH is Senior Lecturer and a National Teaching Fellow at Queen Mary, University of London, and the author of *British Poetry in the Age of Modernism* (2006) and *The Cambridge Introduction to Modernist Poetry* (2011). His essays and reviews have appeared in *PMLA*, *Textual Practice* and the *London Review of Books*.

TIM KENDALL is Professor of English at the University of Exeter. He is the author of numerous books and articles on war poetry, including *Modern English War Poetry* (2006). He is currently editing the three-volume *Complete Literary Works of Ivor Gurney* with Philip Lancaster for Oxford English Texts, and his anthology of First War poetry was published by Oxford World's Classics. His latest monograph is *The Art of Robert Frost* (2012).

EDNA LONGLEY is a Professor Emerita at Queen's University Belfast. She is the editor of *Edward Thomas: The Annotated Collected Poems* (2008) and has recently co-edited (with Peter Mackay and Fran Brearton) *Modern Irish and Scottish Poetry* (2011) and (with Fran Brearton) *Incorrigibly Plural: Louis MacNeice and His Legacy* (2012). Her book *Yeats and Modern Poetry* was published by Cambridge University Press in 2014.

MICHAEL LONGLEY was born in Belfast in 1939 and educated at Trinity College, Dublin, where he read Classics. He has published nine collections of poetry including *Gorse Fires* (1991), which won the Whitbread Poetry Award, and *The Weather in Japan* (2000), which won the Hawthornden Prize, the T. S. Eliot Prize and the Irish Times Poetry Prize. *Snow Water* (2004) won the Librex Montale Prize (Milan), and *A Hundred Doors* (2011) won the Irish Times New Poetry Prize. His *Collected Poems* appeared in 2006. In 2001 he received the Queen's Gold Medal for Poetry, and in 2003 the Wilfred Owen Award. He was Ireland Professor of Poetry from 2007 to 2010. At present he is working on a memoir and on his next collection, *The Stairwell*.

ANDREW MOTION was Poet Laureate from 1999 to 2009; he is now Professor of Creative Writing at Royal Holloway College, University of London, and President of the Campaign to Protect Rural England. His most recent collection of poetry is *The Customs House* (2012).

ADRIAN POOLE is Professor of English Literature at the University of Cambridge, and a Fellow of Trinity College. He has written extensively on tragedy, on Shakespeare and his afterlives and on nineteenth- and early twentieth-century literature, including *Shakespeare and the Victorians* (2003) and *Tragedy: A Very Short Introduction* (2005). He edited *The Cambridge Companion to English Novelists* (2009) and is one of the general editors for Cambridge University Press's *Complete Fiction of Henry James*.

MARK RAWLINSON has published widely on cultures of war, including *British Writing of the Second World War* (2000) and, with Adam Piette, *The Edinburgh Companion to Twentieth-Century British and American War Literature* (2012). Current work includes an edition of First World War plays, a study of the Second World War in fictional narrative after 1945, and a reading of camouflage as a military, biological and representational construct; he is also involved in a number of research projects on university pedagogy. He is Reader in the School of English and Academic Director of the College of Arts, Humanities and Law at the University of Leicester.

VINCENT SHERRY is Professor of English and Howard Nemerov Professor in the Humanities at Washington University in St Louis. He has written on the literary and political culture of the First World War in *The Great War and the*

Language of Modernism (2004), and he has edited *The Cambridge Companion to the Literature of the First World War* (2005). He is currently writing *A Literary History of the European War of 1914–1918* for publication in 2018. *Modernism, Decadence, and the Literary History of Lost Modernity*, as well as the edited volume *The Cambridge History of Modernism*, are forthcoming in 2014. His previous books include *The Uncommon Tongue: The Poetry and Criticism of Geoffrey Hill* (1987); *Ezra Pound, Wyndham Lewis, and Radical Modernism* (1993) and *James Joyce: Ulysses* (1995).

JON STALLWORTHY is a poet and a Fellow of the British Academy. Formerly Professor of English Literature at Wolfson College, Oxford, he is the author of prize-winning biographies of Wilfred Owen and Louis MacNeice and the editor of Owen's *Complete Poems and Fragments* (1983) and of *The Oxford Book of War Poetry* (1984). He has published many volumes of poems, works of literary criticism, anthologies of poetry and a memoir, *Singing School: The Making of a Poet* (1998). Revised editions of his Owen biography and the *Complete Poems and Fragments* are to appear in 2014, together with a *New Oxford Book of War Poems* and a collection of his own poems called *War Poet*.

ELIZABETH VANDIVER is Clement Biddle Penrose Associate Professor of Latin and Classics at Whitman College. She has published on translation studies, Catullus, Livy and Herodotus and is the author of *Heroes in Herodotus: The Interaction of Myth and History* (1991). Her translation of Johannes Cochlaeus's biography of Martin Luther appeared in *Luther's Lives* (2002). Her current research focuses on classical receptions and British poetry of the First World War, on which she has published several articles and the book *Stand in the Trench, Achilles: Classical Receptions in British Poetry of the First World War* (2010).

JAY WINTER is Charles J. Stille Professor of History at Yale University. He was Fellow of Pembroke College, Cambridge, and Lecturer, then Reader, in Modern History at Cambridge from 1979–2001. He is the author of *Sites of Memory, Sites of Mourning: The Great War in European Cultural History* (1995). His biography *René Cassin et les droits de l'homme*, co-authored with Antoine Prost, was published by Fayard in February 2011. The English version was published by Cambridge University Press in 2013. He is editor-in-chief of the three-volume *The Cambridge History of the First World War*, forthcoming in 2014.

Figure 1 Frontispiece to *In Parenthesis*. Estate of David Jones and National Museum of Wales.

In the frontispiece (Figure 1) to the poet-painter David Jones's modernist classic *In Parenthesis* (1937) based on his First World War experience, the figure of a young soldier – naked except for a loose-fitting helmet and an army jacket thrown over the right shoulder – looms in the foreground. He is vulnerable and exposed, yet tragically upright. Barbed wire runs menacingly close to the most private and delicate parts of his body. Around him lies scattered the chaos of the trenches. Jones's intricate mesh of strokes – executed in pen, ink and watercolour – conveys the war between form and formlessness. Over the last hundred years, the image of the First World War soldier as damaged but resilient has remained etched on British cultural consciousness, partly formed and periodically reinforced by the reading of a handful of soldier-poets. More than any other genre – fiction, memoir or film – it is the poetry that has come to form the terrain of First World War memory. This *Companion* investigates the continuing power of such poetry, but is equally interested in what happens beyond the trenches: the scope of war poetry is larger and more international than that of the British trench lyric.

The aims of this *Companion* are two-fold. It seeks to provide fresh and historically nuanced readings of the familiar soldier-poets as well as examine a wider and more varied range of First World War poetry: poems by male civilians, women and non-combatants; poetry in English from Ireland, Scotland, Wales, the United States and the former parts of the British empire, as well as from England; and the afterlives of such poetry and its place in cultural memory. This *Companion* takes stock of the recent expansion of the canon of First World War poetry and indicates the reconceptualisation of the term. If poetry by male civilians and women is now largely part of the accepted canon – few serious anthologists today can ignore the war poetry of Thomas Hardy, Rudyard Kipling, Charlotte Mew, or Margaret Postgate Cole – this volume seeks to push it in fresh directions: it examines war poetry from the colonies, dominions, and the British archipelago, as well as war-haunted modernist poems such as T. S. Eliot's *The Waste Land* (1922). Inclusion of works by poets as diverse as Hardy, Kipling, Mew, Cole, Eliot, H.D. or the Indian writer Rabindranath Tagore alongside the popular soldier-poets puts pressure on the term 'First World War poetry', broadening our understanding of the war itself and the literature. Such inclusiveness calls for a more flexible frame of reference nuanced to different histories, cultures and traditions explored by critics in recent years and taking us far beyond those established by Paul Fussell in his seminal book *The Great War and Modern Memory* (1975).

Whether war poetry makes anything happen or not, one of its achievements has been to democratise poetry. Its centrality in the school curriculum means that, for many, it represents their first encounter with poetry – and not just in Great Britain. When I was a student in Kolkata, the former capital of British India, the figures of the two 'Tommies' standing guard by the city's Cenotaph-like First World War memorial always blended in my mind with Owen and Sassoon whom we read at Presidency College which claimed to have the oldest English department in the world. In India, as in many other countries, First World War poetry spoke with a British accent. And of all the literary genres, it was one that remained most tightly cling-filmed around an event, and conjured up the iconic images – trenches, barbed wire, gas, rats, mud. The anthropologist Claude Levi-Strauss has argued that the substance of myth 'does not lie in its style, its original music, or its syntax, but in the story which it tells'.[1] In the classroom, First World War poetry often ceases to be poetry and begins to look like history by proxy. This *Companion* seeks to read the poetry as *poetry*, paying attention to questions of form and how it is shaped by social, political and material contexts. Neither the transparent envelope of experience nor just language whispering to itself about itself, First World War poetry represents one of those primal moments when poetic form bears most fully the weight of historical trauma.[2] Aesthetics and testimony are often yoked together by real-life violence, leading to formal realignment, invention or dissonance. Categories such as 'pro-war' and 'protest' poetry often prove inadequate, if not sometimes soluble, when tested against the complexity of individual poems.

Is war poetry confined to 'another place', as Keith Douglas calls it,[3] or does it operate within a wider cultural, political and linguistic field? For many critics, the problem is in the name. As Simon Featherstone has noted, the label 'war poetry' may risk the 'isolation of the work within the artificial enclosures of the war years'.[4] War, as we will see in the following chapters, is crucial to the poetry and its intensities of meaning, but it is not the only – or isolated – focus of attention or analysis. First World War poetry looks before and after the war, joining past and future, and combatant and civilian zones; it speaks in varying cadences not just of combat, but of life at large – of beauty, longing, religion, nature, animals, intimacy, historical change, poetic responsibility, Europe and Englishness, race, democracy and empire, or what it is for women to have 'years and years in which we shall still be young'[5] – all touched directly or indirectly by the war. If a moral vocabulary ('truth of war' or 'adequate response') has been used in the past to understand the popular soldier-poets, then recent developments in criticism – investigations in ideas of testimony, trauma and memory, theories of gender and sexuality, and a more historically and politically nuanced understanding of the literary milieu of the early twentieth century, including the category of 'modernism' – have opened such poetry to new approaches. Moreover, during the last three decades, cultural and feminist historians and literary scholars have drawn attention to the experience of civilians – men, women and children – and uncovered a powerful body of literature. The chapters in this *Companion* register these broad shifts through their careful attention to particular poets and bodies of work, placing them in fresh contexts and amidst larger historical and cultural processes.

This *Companion* supplements Vincent Sherry's important volume *The Cambridge Companion to the Literature of the First World War* (2005) which showed some of the work being done in the field across different genres.[6] What marks out the present *Companion* is its concentrated focus on the poetry of the First World War. The poetry considered here is written in English, whether in Britain, the former parts of the empire or the United States; poems in other European, Asian and African languages belong to different contexts and traditions. These are vast and complex areas, and single chapters on each, it was felt, would not do them justice.[7]

The *Companion* is divided into four parts – 'Historical and Critical Contexts'; 'Soldier-Poets'; 'Archipelagic, Colonial and Civilian War Poetry'; and 'Afterlives of First World War Poetry' – but they intersect with each other. Edward Thomas unsettles the categories of 'civilian' and 'combatant' while David Jones is at once a 'soldier-poet', a 'modernist' and an 'archipelagic' subject. Part I sets out the overarching critical and historical frameworks. The introductory chapter investigates the term 'First World War poetry', its historical trajectory and recent reconceptualisation in relation to particular contexts and poems, and links them to the different strands in the volume. Vincent Sherry (Chapter 1) provides a map of the cultural and political contexts of the poetry of the First World War, with attention to the tradition of liberalism and traces an arc from English 'Georgianism' through the trench lyric to the modernism of Eliot and Pound. On the other hand, Peter Howarth (Chapter 2) examines the implications of the war for poetic form through the concepts of 'realism' and 'idealism': he interrogates our familiar assumptions about them and analyses the private and public work that poetry is called upon to perform at such a time. The chapters in Part I explore works by combatants and civilians, men and women, and reveal common ground.

Part II (Chapters 3–9) addresses the works of 'soldier-poets'. If these men remain inextricably connected in cultural memory, the chapters foreground the range and diversity, as well as the significant differences between them. Brooke, Owen, Sassoon, Blunden and Graves were all officers while Rosenberg, Gurney and Jones served as privates. They also came from very different backgrounds: Sassoon, the cricket-playing and fox-hunting country gentleman, and Rosenberg, growing up in the East End of London as the son of poor Lithuanian Jewish immigrants, represent almost the two ends of the British social spectrum (Sassoon was partly Jewish as well). These soldier-poets are here read in the context of the war as well as a world beyond it: classical education; Romantic, Victorian and fin de siècle poetry; modernism; or the death of rural England. Elizabeth Vandiver (Chapter 3) and Mark Rawlinson (Chapter 4) examine the connections and differences within and across the 'early' poets (Brooke, Grenfell and Sorley) and the 'later' poets (Nichols, Blunden, Graves, Read) of the war respectively, putting pressure on these very categorisations. Four chapters – by Sarah Cole, Neil Corcoran, Sandra M. Gilbert, and Adrian Poole – focus on individual soldier-poets. If a previous generation of critics alerted us to the 'literariness' of trench poetry, the chapters in Part II substantially broaden the intertextual map and relate it to a range of contexts: Sassoon's poetry is examined in terms of the 'divergent tendencies' of protest and a more 'soluble private self'; Owen is imagined as 'Keats with a camera', at once marking his intimacy with and difference from his Romantic predecessor; Rosenberg's poetry is read closely with reference to his Jewishness and a variety of poetic traditions and registers; and the delicacy and density of Jones's 'writing' in *In Parenthesis* are investigated in the light of his role as a 'maker' as well as his 'split and conjoined' identity as Anglo-Welsh, soldier-poet and poet-painter (hyphens unsurprisingly play a significant role in his style, as Poole points out). Poets are freshly connected: if Sassoon and Owen remain coupled through their famous encounter at the Craiglockhart War Hospital, Edna Longley in Chapter 8 uncovers startling affinities between Edward Thomas and Ivor Gurney, particularly in their common work of 'cultural elegy' and the 'poetry of cultural defence'.

Part III takes us beyond familiar terrain through various worlds, including Hardy's Wessex and Pound's London, the British archipelago and the far-flung former colonies and dominions. Both combatant and non-combatant poetry is explored by David Goldie and Simon Featherstone in their chapters on 'archipelagic' and 'colonial' war poetry respectively. Are poems written by writers from Ireland, Scotland and Wales necessarily different from those of their English counterparts? Is there a tension between assertions of imperial loyalty and emergent nationalism in the poetry of the First World War from the colonies and dominions? The word 'colonial' is used as a historical category in Featherstone's investigation of the poetry from Australia, Canada and India. On the other hand, the last three chapters in Part III by Margaret R. Higonnet, Tim Kendall and Christine Froula examine civilian war poetry in different contexts: women's war poetry (Chapter 12), the poetry of Hardy and Kipling (Chapter 13) and the modernist poetry of the 'London Vortex', particularly that of Eliot and Pound (Chapter 14). Civilian war poetry is often marginalised, but these chapters show how deeply and complexly the war penetrated life and writing far beyond the trenches. Part IV further enlarges the map by examining the afterlives of First World War poetry. Fran Brearton in Chapter 15 explores how the war continues to haunt the post-war generations of poets, from Vernon Scannell and Keith Douglas to Ted Hughes and Michael Longley, while Jay Winter unravels the deep connections between literary language and cultural memory through a fundamental question: how did a small group of soldier-poets come to represent the voice of the nation (Chapter 16)? The *Companion* concludes with a conversation with Michael Longley, Andrew Motion and Jon Stallworthy – three poets who over the years and in various forms have profoundly engaged with the First World War.

Finally, a brief note on the two chronologies. Because the contexts are so immediate and tumultous, the first chronology provides a timeline of historical and political events alongside which the publications of the literary works can be viewed. The focus, in keeping with the subject of the *Companion*, is on the poetry, but I have included works from other genres and fields to provide a sense of the broader social and cultural milieu. The 'Chronology of Poets', however, provides a list of poets who lived through 1914–1918. Not all of them were 'war poets' (see 'Introduction'), but all of them wrote poems addressing the conflict and not just in English. This is a rather expansive, although by no means comprehensive, list. The aim is to suggest the richness of the corpus and the sense of shared history by letting nothing but birthdates determine the juxtaposition of poets – familiar and unfamiliar, men and women, soldiers and civilians – who lived through and wrote about the Great War.

NOTES

1 Claude Levi-Strauss, 'The Structural Study of Myth' in Thomas A. Sebeok ed. *Myth: A Symposium* (Bloomington: Indiana University Press, 1985), 86.
2 Edna Longley has powerfully argued that First World War lyric poetry may be a 'quintessential case' of the 'encounter between form and history'. See 'The Great War, history, and the English lyric', in Vincent Sherry ed. *The Literature of the First World War* (Cambridge: Cambridge University Press, 2005), 58.
3 'Dead Men' in Desmond Graham ed. *Keith Douglas: The Complete Poems* (Oxford: Oxford University Press, 1979), 100.
4 Simon Featherstone ed. *War Poetry: An Introductory Reader* (London: Routledge, 1995), 47.
5 Margaret Postgate Cole, 'Praematuri' in Catherine Reilly ed. *The Virago Book of Women's War Poetry and Verse* (London: Virago, 1997), 22.
6 Also see Tim Kendall ed. *The Oxford Handbook of British and Irish War Poetry* (Oxford: Oxford University Press, 2007) and Adam Piette and Mark Rawlinson eds. *The Edinburgh Companion to Twentieth-Century British and American War Literature* (Edinburgh: Edinburgh University Press, 2012). Both contain stimulating discussions of First World War poetry.
7 See Tim Cross ed. *The Lost Voices of World War I: An International Anthology of Writers, Poets and Playwrights* (1988); Elizabeth A. Marsland, *The Nation's Cause: French, English and German Poetry of the First World War* (1991); Margaret Higonnet, 'The Great War and the Female Elegy: Female Lamentation and Silence in Global Contexts' in *The Global South*, Vol 1:7, 2007, 120–36. Also see Geert Buelens ed. *Het lijf in slijk geplant: gedichten uit de Eerste Wereldoorlog* (Amsterdam: Ambo, 2008) which includes poems from forty nations: the poems appear in the original and in Dutch translation.

ACKNOWLEDGEMENTS

It was while travelling back together from a conference that Dr Ray Ryan of Cambridge University Press suggested that I consider editing *The Cambridge Companion to the Poetry of the First World War*. In the ensuing conversation, I managed to miss my stop, but the volume began to take shape. Many thanks for his support and for reading the whole typescript at a day's notice.

It has been a pleasure to work with the contributors to this volume: I would like to thank them for their hard work and for dealing with various queries with meticulous care, speed and good humour. I am particularly grateful to Alice Kelly: during a busy schedule, she found time to transcribe the poets' 'conversation' and assist me in constructing several key years of the Chronology and compiling the list for 'Further Reading'. Jon Stallworthy has been characteristically generous with his time and advice. For their help at various points, I would like to thank Gillian Beer, Peter Howarth, Tim Kendall, Jo McDonagh, Kate McLoughlin, Vincent Sherry, Trudi Tate and Hope Wolf. Hugh Stevens was the first port of call for most things.

I am grateful to the Leverhulme Trust and to the English department at King's College London for their support. Some concentrated research time in my family home in Kolkata over the winter of 2012 enabled me to bring the project to a conclusion. And it was both serendipitous and appropriate that Abigail Williams, the great-niece of David Jones, would help me greatly in the final stages of the volume; she created the index and her wonderful eye for detail kept me on my toes. I would finally like to thank the dedicated team at Cambridge University Press, particularly Fred Goykhman, Louis Gulino, Jayashree and Marielle Poss. All efforts have been made to contact the owners of the diary of A. Reid.

CHRONOLOGY OF EVENTS AND PUBLICATIONS

Year	Historical and Political	Cultural and Literary
1890		James Frazer, first volumes of *The Golden Bough* (1890–1915) William James, *Principles of Psychology*
1892		Rudyard Kipling, *Barrack-Room Ballads*
1895	Trial of Oscar Wilde in London	Stephen Crane, *The Red Badge of Courage*
1896	First modern Olympiad in Athens Alfred, Lord Northcliffe founds *Daily Mail* in London	A. E. Housman, *A Shropshire Lad*
1898	Spanish-American War Sudan: Battle of Omdurman, Mahdist forces defeated by British Madagascar	Thomas Hardy, *Wessex Poems and Other Verses* H. G. Wells, *War of the Worlds* Oscar Wilde, *The Ballad of Reading Gaol*
1899	Anglo-Boer War (1899–1902)	Joseph Conrad, *Heart of Darkness* Sigmund Freud, *Die Traumdeutung* (translated as *The Interpretation of Dreams*) Kipling, 'The White Man's Burden'
1900	Boxer Rebellion in China First Pan-African Conference in London International Socialist Congress in Paris	
1901	Death of Queen Victoria Edward VII succeeds to the throne	Hardy, *Poems of the Past and the Present*

Year	Historical and Political	Cultural and Literary
1904	Outbreak of Russo-Japanese War (1904–1905) Anglo-French *entente*	Hardy, *Dynasts* I (II 1906; III 1908) Opening of Dublin's Abbey Theatre
1906	Liberal Party wins in British Parliamentary elections	
1907	Dominion status granted by Britain to its self-governing (white) colonies Anglo-Russian *entente*	Pablo Picasso, *Les Demoiselles d'Avignon* Kipling awarded the Nobel Prize in literature
1908	National Association for the Advancement of Colored People (NAACP) formed in America	Ford Madox Ford starts the *English Review* Rabindranath Tagore, *Ghare-Baire* [*Home and the World*]
1909		Filippo Tommaso Marinetti, *Futurist Manifesto* Ezra Pound, *Personae*
1910	Death of Edward VII and the coronation of George V	Post-Impressionist exhibition in London E. M. Forster, *Howard's End*
1912	*Titanic* sinks Wars of Balkan States (1912–1913)	*Georgian Poetry 1911–1912*, with Preface by Edward Marsh Harold Monro edits first issue of *Poetry Review*
1913		Harold Monro founds the Poetry Bookshop in Bloomsbury, London Igor Stravinsky, *Le Sacre du printemps* [*The Rite of Spring*] Rabindranath Tagore awarded the Nobel Prize for Literature Thomas Mann, *Tod in Venedig* [*Death in Venice*] Marcel Proust, *Du côté de chez Swann* [*Swann's Way*] Albert Einstein, *Theory of Relativity* Jacob Epstein, *Rock Drill*

Year	Historical and Political	Cultural and Literary
1914	28 June: Archduke Franz Ferdinand, heir to throne of Austria-Hungary, is assassinated in Sarajevo, Bosnia 28 July: Austria-Hungary declares war on Serbia 1 August: Germany declares war on Russia 3 August: Germany declares war on France and invades Belgium 4 August: Britain declares war on Germany; President Woodrow Wilson of the United States declares neutrality 11–12 August: Austro-Hungarian troops invade Serbia 13 August: Japan declares war on Germany 23–24 August: Battle of Mons 26–29 August: Germans defeat Russians at Battle of Tannenberg 6–12 September: First Battle of Marne 12 September: First Battle of Aisne; first trenches appear 30 September: The first two regiments of Indian Expeditionary Force arrive at Marseilles 1 October: First battle of Arras begins 18 October–15 November: First Battle of Ypres 28 October: Turkey joins the war on the side of the Central Powers 25 December: Unofficial Christmas Truce on the Western Front	*Deaths* Charles Péguy (4 September, in action at Villeroy, Seine-et-Marne) Georg Trakl (3 November, from a cocaine overdose) *Events* Secret meeting of writers in London for War Propaganda Bureau (2 September) *Poetry* Laurence Binyon, 'For the Fallen' Hardy, *Satires of Circumstance* W. B. Yeats, *Responsibilities and A Play Songs and Sonnets for England in War Time* *Our Glorious Heritage, A Book of Patriotic Verse for Boys and Girls*, compiled by C. S. Evans *Des Imagistes: An Anthology*, ed. Pound *Poems of the Great War* *Other Publications* James Joyce, *Dubliners* Wyndham Lewis founds *Blast* *The Little Review* founded
1915	19 January: First German zeppelin raid on England February: Allied naval bombardment of the Dardanelles begins 10–13 March: Battle of Neuve Chapelle	*Deaths* Brooke (23 April, of sepsis on the way to Gallipoli) Julian Grenfell (26 May, from shell wounds suffered near Ypres) Henri Gaudier-Brzeska (5 June, killed at Neuville–St. Vaast)

Year	Historical and Political	Cultural and Literary
	22 April–25 May: Second Battle of Ypres; first use of poison gas by the Germans	August Stramm (1 September, killed in hand-to-hand combat near present-day Belarus)
	24 April: Armenian genocide begins	Charles Sorley (13 October, shot by a
	25 April: Allied military landings at	sniper in the Battle of Loos)
	Gallipoli peninsula: Australian and	*Events*
	New Zealand Corps land at Anzac	Ivor Gurney, Wilfred Owen and Isaac
	Cove, and British and French troops	Rosenberg enlist in the army
	land at Cape Helles	Tagore receives knighthood
	7 May: Germans sink *Lusitania*	*Poetry*
	23 May: Italy declares war on Austria	Brooke, *1914 & Other Poems*
	25 May: British Prime Minister	C. J. Dennis, *Songs of a Sentimental*
	Herbert Henry Asquith forms an all-	*Bloke*
	party coalition	T. S. Eliot, 'The Love Song of J. Alfred
	31 May: First German zeppelin raid	Prufrock'
	on London	Wilfrid Gibson, *Battle*
	6–9 August: Anzac attack at Lone	Grenfell, 'Into Battle'
	Pine	Francis Ledwidge, *Songs of the Fields*
	25 September–14 October: The Battle	John McCrae, 'In Flanders Fields'
	of Loos; first use of poison gas by the	Jessie Pope, *War Poems*
	British	Pound, *Cathay*
	19 December: Sir Douglas Haig	Sorley, 'When you see millions of the
	replaces Sir John French as com-	mouthless dead' (written)
	mander of the British Expeditionary	*Lest We Forget: A War Anthology*, ed.
	Force	H. B. Elliott
	19 December: Allies start evacuating	*One Hundred Best Poems on the*
	Gallipoli	*European War by Poets of the Empire*,
		ed. C. F. Forshaw
		Some Imagist Poets: An Anthology, eds.
		H.D. and Richard Aldington
		Georgian Poetry, 1913–15, ed. Marsh
		Other Publications
		John Buchan, *The Thirty-Nine Steps*
		Ford, *The Good Soldier*
		Sigmund Freud, 'Thoughts for the
		Times on War and Death'
		Ian Hay, *The First Hundred Thousand*
		Franz Kafka, *Die Verwandlung*
		D. H. Lawrence, *The Rainbow*
		May Sinclair, *A Journal of Impressions*
		in Belgium
		Edith Wharton, *Fighting France*

Year	Historical and Political	Cultural and Literary
1916	27 January: Conscription introduced in Britain 21 February–18 December: Battle of Verdun, the longest battle of the war, finally won by the French 24 April–30 April: Easter Rising in Dublin, with sixteen people executed following the Rising, including Patrick Pearse, Sir Roger Casement, James Connolly and Thomas MacDonagh 29 April: Charles Townshend surrenders and Kut falls with 11,800 British and Indian troops after a siege of 147 days 31 May–1 June: Battle of Jutland 5 June: HMS Hampshire sunk, Lord Kitchener killed 6 June: Start of Arab revolt in Hejaz 1 July: Beginning of the Battle of the Somme, with 60,000 casualties on the first day, including 20,000 killed or dead from wounds 7 July: Lloyd George succeeds Kitchener as Secretary of State for war 28 August: Hindenburg appointed German Chief of Staff 15 September: First large-scale use of British tanks on the Somme 7–9 November: Woodrow Wilson re-elected President of the United States 7 December: David Lloyd George replaces Henry Asquith as Prime Minister of Britain	*Deaths* Henry James (28 February, following a stroke) Alan Seeger (4 July, killed at Belloy-en-Santerre in the Somme) *Events* Hugo Ball recites the first Dada manifesto at the Cabaret Voltaire in Zürich, Switzerland (14 July) *Poetry* Edmund Blunden, *Pastorals* Dennis, *The Moods of Ginger Mick* Robert Graves, *Over the Brazier [and other poems]* Hardy, *Selected Poems* H.D., *Sea Garden* Patrick MacGill, *Soldier Songs* Charlotte Mew, *The Farmer's Bride* Pope, *Simple Rhymes for Stirring Times* Seeger, *Poems* ('I Have a Rendezvous with Death' appears first in the October 1916 issue of the *North American Review*) Robert Service, *Rhymes of a Red Cross Man* Sorley, *Marlborough and Other Poems* (published posthumously) Tagore, *Fruit-Gathering* Yeats writes 'Easter 1916' *The Anzac Book*, ed. C. E. W. Bean *Soldier Poets: Songs of the Fighting Men*, ed. Galloway Kyle *Some Imagist Poets, 1916: An Annual Anthology*, ed. Amy Lowell *Wheels: An Anthology of Verse*, ed. Edith Sitwell (1916–1921) *1914–16: Eine Anthologie* (verse) published by anti-war Die Aktion *Other Publication* Henri Barbusse, *Le Feu: Journal d'une escouade*

Year	Historical and Political	Cultural and Literary
1917	31 January: Germany declares unrestricted submarine warfare 11 March: Baghdad falls to the British 12 March: Russian Revolution begins and Tsar Nicholas II abdicates on 15 March 24 March: British offensive on Palestine begins 6 April: United States declares war on Germany 9–14 April: Battle of Vimy Ridge, with victory for the Canadian Corps 9 April–15 May: Battle of Arras 13 June: German daylight air raid on London, with 162 killed and around 430 injured 25 June: First U.S. troops arrive in France 1 July: Start of Kerensky (Russian) Offensive 6 July: T. E. Lawrence and Arab forces capture Aqaba 18 July–10 November: Third Battle of Ypres, culminating in two Battles of Passchendaele (October–November) 7 November: October Revolution in Russia; Bolsheviks seize power 5 December: Armistice between Germany and Russia signed 7 December: United States declares war on Austria-Hungary 9 December: Jerusalem falls to the British 22 December: Russia opens separate peace negotiations with Germany at Brest-Litovsk	*Deaths* Edward Thomas (9 April, killed in a shell blast at Arras) Ledwidge (31 July, killed by a shell at Passchendaele) T. E. Hulme (28 September, killed by a shell at Nieuport) Patrick Shaw Stewart (30 December, killed in action) *Events* Owen arrives at Craiglockhart War Hospital (26 June), and in July, becomes the editor of the *Hydra* Sassoon's 'Soldier's Declaration' printed in *The Times* and he is sent to Craiglockhart (31 July) Owen introduces himself to Sassoon at Craiglockhart (17 August) The Hogarth Press founded by Leonard and Virginia Woolf Eliot becomes the assistant editor of *The Egoist* *Poetry* May Wedderburn Cannan, *In War Time: Poems* Eliot, *Prufrock, and Other Observations* Leon Gellert, *Songs of a Campaign* Graves, *Fairies and Fusiliers* Gurney, *Severn and Somme* Hardy, *Moments of Vision and Miscellaneous Verses* Alice Meynell, *A Father of Women, and Other Poems* Robert Nichols, *Ardours and Endurances*

Year	Historical and Political	Cultural and Literary
		Owen writes 'Dulce et Decorum Est'
		Pound writes *Homage to Sextus Propertius*
		Rosenberg writes 'Dead Man's Dump'
		Sassoon, *The Old Huntsman, and Other Poems*
		Thomas, *Poems* (published posthumously)
		Canada in Khaki
		A Treasury of War Poetry, ed. G. H. Clark
		Soldier Poets: More Songs by the Fighting Men, ed. Galloway Kyle
		Georgian Poetry 1916–17, ed. Edward Marsh
		The Muse in Arms, ed. E. B. Osborn
		Other Publications
		Freud, *Vorlesungen zur Einführung in die Psychoanalyse* [translated as *A General Introduction to Psychoanalysis* in 1920]
		Tagore, *Nationalism*
1918	January 1918–December 1920: Influenza epidemic	*Deaths*
	8 January: President Woodrow Wilson announces 14-Point Peace Program	McCrae (28 January, from pneumonia)
		Rosenberg (1 April, killed in combat in the Somme)
	6 February: Representation of the People Act 1918 allows votes in Britain for women older than thirty, men older than twenty-one	Owen (4 November, killed in combat on the banks of the Sambre–Oise Canal)
		Guillaume Apollinaire (9 November, influenza epidemic)
	21 March: Start of German Spring Offensive	*Poetry*
		Vera Brittain, *Verses of a VAD*
	9–29 April: Second German Spring Offensive	Brooke, *Collected Poems*
		Dennis, *Digger Smith*
	27 May–5 June: Third German Spring Offensive	Gerard Manley Hopkins, *Poems*, ed. Robert Bridges
		D. H. Lawrence, *New Poems*
	15 July: Last phase of German Spring Offensive, Second Battle of the Marne begins	Owen, 'Miners' and 'Hospital Barge' published in the *Nation*
		Margaret Postgate, *Poems*
	16 July: Former Tsar Nicholas II murdered by the Bolsheviks	Sassoon, *Counter-Attack and Other Poems*

Year	Historical and Political	Cultural and Literary
	18 July–7 August: Allied Aisne-Marne counter-offensive; German retreat at the Marne	Thomas, *Last Poems*
	8 August: Successful Amiens offensive supervised by Haig, 'black day' for German army	Arthur Graeme West, *Diary of a Dead Officer: Posthumous Papers*
	19 September: Beginning of successful British offensive in Palestine	*Poems Written during the Great War, 1914–1918*, ed. Bertram Lloyd (first anti-war anthology)
	4 October: Germany and Austria ask for an armistice	*Other Publications*
	5 October: Allied forces take Hindenburg line	Georges Duhamel, *Civilisation, 1914–1917*
	17 October–11 November: British troops make advances at Battle of the Selle (17–26 October) and Battle of the Sambre (4 November). German troops in retreat	Rebecca West, *Return of the Soldier*
	30 October: Turkey forms armistice with Allies	Wharton, *The Marne*
	3 November: Austria makes peace	
	9 November: Kaiser Wilhelm II abdicates	
	11 November: Armistice signed	
	14 December: Lloyd George wins the elections in Britain	
1919	10–15 January: Communist revolt in Berlin	*Poetry*
	18 January: Paris Peace Conference begins	Aldington, *Images of War: Poems*
	25 January: Peace Conference accepts the League of Nations	Eliot, *Poems*
	14 February: Draft Covenant of League of Nations completed	Gurney, *War's Embers and Other Verses*
	13 April: Jallianwala Bagh massacre in Amritsar, India – General Dyer opens fire on unarmed Indian protestors	Kipling, 'Epitaphs of the War'
	6 May–8 August: Third Anglo-Afghan War	Rose Macaulay, *Three Days*
	7 May–28 June: Treaty of Versailles prepared and signed	McCrae, *In Flanders Fields and Other Poems*
		Pound, *Quia Pauper Amavi*
		Herbert Read, *Naked Warriors*
		Sassoon, *War Poems*
		The Paths of Glory: A Collection of Poems Written During the War, ed. Betram Lloyd
		Georgian Poetry, 1918–1919, ed. Marsh

Year	Historical and Political	Cultural and Literary
	19 July: Unveiling of temporary Cenotaph in London	*Other Publications* A. P. Herbert, *The Secret Battle* John Maynard Keynes, *The Economic Consequences of the Peace*
1920	16 January: First meeting of the League of Nations 11 November: Unveiling of the Cenotaph by King George V	*Events* Woodrow Wilson awarded the Nobel Peace Prize *Poetry* Owen, *Poems*, intro. by Sassoon Pound, *Hugh Selwyn Mauberley* Thomas, *Collected Poems* ed. Walter de la Mare *Other Publications* Eliot, *Sacred Wood* Ernst Jünger, *In Stahlgewittern* (translated into English in 1929 as *The Storm of Steel*) Freud, *Jenseits des Lustprinzips* (translated as *Beyond the Pleasure Principle* in 1922) D. H. Lawrence, *Women in Love* Vernon Lee (Violet Page), *Satan the Waster* W. H. R. Rivers, *Instinct and the Unconscious*
1921	6 December: Irish Free State created, with partition of Northern Ireland	John Don Passos, *Three Soldiers*
1922	BBC founded Collapse of Lloyd George coalition	*Events* Gurney certified insane and admitted to Barnwood House, Gloucestershire and later moved to the City of London Mental Hospital at Dartford *Poetry* Eliot, *The Waste Land* Housman, *Last Poems* *Poems by Isaac Rosenberg*, ed. Gordon Bottomley *Other Publications* Joyce, *Ulysses* C. E. Montague, *Disenchantment* Woolf, *Jacob's Room*

Year	Historical and Political	Cultural and Literary
1923		*Poetry* D. H. Lawrence, *Birds, Beasts and Flowers* Wallace Stevens, *Harmonium* *Other Publications* Rivers, *Conflict and Dream* Wharton, *A Son at the Front*
1924	Ramsay Macdonald becomes the first Labour Prime Minister of Great Britain British Empire Exhibition in London	André Breton, *Manifeste du surréalisme* Ford, *Parade's End* tetralogy (completed in 1928) Forster, *A Passage to India*
1925		*Poetry* Gurney, 'War Books' Yeats, *A Vision* *Other Publications* Adolf Hitler, *Mein Kampf* Woolf, *Mrs Dalloway*
1926	26 April–12 May: General strike in Britain	*Poetry* Read, *Collected Poems, 1913–1925* *Other Publications* William Faulkner, *Soldier's Pay* T. E. Lawrence, *The Seven Pillars of Wisdom*
1927		*Poetry* Graves, *Poems* (1914–1926) *Other Publications* Martin Heidegger, *Sein und Zeit* (translated into English as *Being and Time* in 1962) Proust, *Le temps retrouvé*
1928		*Poetry* Lawrence, *Collected Poems* *Other Publications* Blunden, *Undertones of War* Radclyffe Hall, *The Well of Loneliness* Lawrence, *Lady Chatterley's Lover* Sassoon, *Memoirs of a Fox Hunting Man* R. C. Sherriff, *Journey's End*

Year	Historical and Political	Cultural and Literary
1929	Collapse of the New York stock market	Aldington, *Death of a Hero* Mary Borden, *The Forbidden Zone* Graves, *Goodbye to All That* Ernest Hemingway, *A Farewell to Arms* Frederic Manning, *The Middle Parts of Fortune: Somme & Ancre, 1916* (published anonymously) Erich Maria Remarque, *Im Westen nichts Neues* (translated as *All Quiet on the Western Front*)
1930	German Federal Election, with the Social Democratic Party of Germany remaining the largest party in Reichstag The Great Depression hits Britain	*Events* Film of *All Quiet on the Western Front* (dir. Lewis Milestone) wins two Oscars *Poetry* W. H. Auden, *Poems* Blunden, *Poems 1914–1930* Eliot, *Ash Wednesday* Owen, *Poems*, with notices of his life by Blunden (1931) *An Anthology of War Poems*, ed. Frederick Brereton *Other Publications* *The Middle Parts of Fortune* published as 'Private 19022', *Her Privates We* Freud, *Das Unbehagen in der Kultur* (translated as *Civilization and Its Discontents*) Graves, *But It Still Goes On* Sassoon, *Memoirs of an Infantry Officer*
1933	Nazis come to power, with Hitler named Chancellor of Germany	Brittain, *Testament of Youth*
1936	Beginning of the Spanish Civil War (ends 1939)	Sassoon, *Sherston's Progress* *The Oxford Book of Modern Verse*, ed. Yeats (Owen excluded from the selection)

Year	Historical and Political	Cultural and Literary
1937	Bombing of Guernica	*Deaths* Gurney (26 December, tuberculosis) *Poetry* Auden, 'Spain' David Jones, *In Parenthesis* *Collected Works of Isaac Rosenberg: Poetry, Prose, Letters and Some Drawings*, ed. Bottomley and Denys Harding, with a Foreword by Sassoon *Other Publications* Lewis, *Blasting and Bombardiering* Sassoon, *The Complete Memoirs of George Sherston*
1939	Beginning of the Second World War	Louis MacNeice, *Autumn Journal*
1940–1949	Dunkirk evacuation (1940) London Blitz (1940) D-Day Landings in Normandy (6 June 1944). Dropping of atomic bombs on Hiroshima (6 August 1945) and Nagasaki (9 August 1945) End of the Second World War (1945) Start of the Cold War India gains Independence (1947)	Keith Douglas, 'Desert Flowers', 'Landscape with Figures' (1943) *Anthology of War Poetry, 1914–1918*, compiled by Nichols (1943) Douglas killed by enemy mortar fire in Normandy (1944) Eliot, *Four Quartets* (1943) Douglas, *Alamein to Zem Zem* (1946) Sassoon, *Collected Poems* (1947) Graves, *The White Goddess: A Historical Grammar of Poetic Myth* (1948) *Collected Poems of Rosenberg*, with foreword by Sassoon (1949)
1950–1959	The Korean War (1950–1953)	*Poems by Ivor Gurney*, ed. Blunden (1954)
1960–1969	The Vietnam War (1965–1973) Irish Troubles (late 1960s–late 1990s)	Sassoon, *Collected Poems 1908–1956* (1961) Vernon Scannell, 'The Great War' (1962) Benjamin Britten, *War Requiem* (includes settings of poems by Owen) (1962) Owen, *Collected Poems*, ed. C. Day-Lewis (1963) Gerry Raffles and Joan Littlewood, *Oh, What a Lovely War* (1963)

Year	Historical and Political	Cultural and Literary
		Philip Larkin, 'MCMXIV' (1964)
		Up the Line to Death: The War Poets, 1914–1918, ed. Brian Gardner (1964)
		Men Who March Away: Poems of the First World War, ed. Ian Parsons (1965)
		Seamus Heaney, *Death of a Naturalist* (1966)
		Ted Hughes, *Wodwo* (1967)
1970– 1979		Susan Hill, *Strange Meeting* (1971)
		Michael Longley, 'Wounds' (1972)
		Jon Stallworthy, *Wilfred Owen* (1974)
		Paul Fussell, *The Great War and Modern Memory* (1975)
		Heaney, 'In Memoriam Francis Ledwidge' (1979)
		The Penguin Book of First World War Poetry, ed. Jon Silkin (1979)
1980– 1989	Falklands War (1982) Fall of the Berlin Wall (10 November 1989)	*Scars Upon My Heart*, ed. Catherine Reilly (1981)
		Wilfred Owen: The Complete Poems and Fragments, ed. Stallworthy (1983)
		James Fenton, *The Memory of War: Poems 1968–1982* (1982)
		Poet Laureate Ted Hughes unveils memorial stone in the Poets' Corner, Westminster Abbey, to commemorate sixteen poets of WWI (11 November 1985)
		Blackadder Goes Forth (1989)
1990– 2000	First Gulf War (1990–1991) Dissolution of the USSR (1991) End of Apartheid in South Africa (1994) Irish President and Queen Elizabeth II commemorate Irish dead of the First World War in Messines, Belgium (1998)	Pat Barker, *Regeneration* trilogy (1991–1995) Sebastian Faulks, *Birdsong* (1993) Heaney awarded Nobel Prize in Literature (1995) *I Remember: Soldier Poets of the Korean War*, ed. W. D. Ehrhart (1997)

Year	Historical and Political	Cultural and Literary
2001–2012	Al-Qaeda attacks on the World Trade Center (11 September 2001) Declaration of the War on Terror (2001) Opening of the Memorial Gates at Hyde Park Corner, London, to commemorate the services of the Indian subcontinent, Africa and the Caribbean to the two World Wars (2002) Huge demonstrations against the invasion of Iraq in London (2003) Start of the Second Gulf War (2003)	Michael Longley, *Cenotaph of Snow: Sixty Poems about War* (2003) *The Poetry and Plays of Isaac Rosenberg*, ed. Vivien Noakes (2004) Andrew Motion, 'The Five Acts of Harry Patch' (2008) *Edward Thomas: The Annotated Collected Poems*, ed. Edna Longley (2008) Death of Harry Patch, the last surviving Western Front veteran (25 July 2009) Carol Ann Duffy, 'The Last Post' (2009) Alice Oswald, *Memorial* (2011) Colin Matthews, *No Man's Land* (musical adaptation of Christopher Reid's 'Airs and Ditties of No Man's Land', premiered at the Proms 2011) Iain Burnside, *Ivor Gurney: A Soldier and A Maker* (2012) Tom Stoppard, Adaptation of Ford Madox Ford's *Parade's End* for BBC 2 (2012)

CHRONOLOGY OF POETS

Thomas Hardy (1840–1928)

Alice Meynell (1847–1922)

John Oxenham (1852–1941)

George Abel (1856–1916)

Edith Nesbit (1858–1924)

William Watson (1858–1935)

A. E. Housman (1859–1936)

Katharine Tynan (1859–1931)

Owen Seaman (1861–1936)

Henry Head (1861–1940)

Rabindranath Tagore (1861–1941)

Henry Newbolt (1862–1938)

Violet Jacob (1863–1946)

May Sinclair (1863–1946)

August Stramm (1864–1915)

Stephen Phillips (1864–1915)

Israel Zangwill (1864–1926)

Charles Murray (1864–1941)

Rudyard Kipling (1865–1936)

W. B. Yeats (1865–1939)

Henry Lawson (1867–1922)

John Galsworthy (1867–1933)

Eva Dobell (1867–1963)

Jessie Pope (1868–1941)

Charlotte Mew (1869–1928)

Laurence Binyon (1869–1943)

Saki (H. H. Munro) (1870–1916)

Harold Begbie (1871–1929)

W. H. Davies (1871–1940)

Ralph Hodgson (1871–1962)

John McCrae (1872–1918)

Edward Shillito (1872–1948)

Ford Madox Ford (1873–1939)

Walter de la Mare (1873–1956)

G. K. Chesterton (1874–1936)

Gordon Bottomley (1874–1948)

Robert W. Service (1874–1958)

R. E. Vernède (1875–1917)

John Buchan (1875–1940)

Robert Frost (1875–1963)

Archibald Strong (1876–1930)

Clarence Dennis (1876–1938)

Joseph Lee (1876–1949)

Edward Thomas (1878–1917)

Herbert Kaufman (1878–1947)

Wilfrid Wilson Gibson (1878–1962)

John Masefield (1878–1967)

Carl Sandburg (1878–1967)

Harold Munro (1879–1932)

Sarojini Naidu (1879–1949)

T. M. Kettle (1880–1916)

Guillaume Apollinaire (1880–1918)

John Freeman (1880–1929)

Guy Noel Pocock (1880–1955)

Aleksandr Blok (1880–1921)

Alfred Noyes (1880–1958)

Lascelles Abercrombie (1881–1938)

Herbert Asquith (1881–1947)

Rose Macaulay (1881–1958)

Eleanor Farjeon (1881–1965)

Wilhelm Klemm (1881–1968)

Alexander Robertson (1882–1916)

John Drinkwater (1882–1937)

Mina Loy (1882–1966)

Ernst Stadler (1883–1914)

T. E. Hulme (1883–1917)

Max Plowman (1883–1941)

James Elroy Flecker (1884–1915)

Gilbert Frankau (1884–1952)

Francis Brett Young (1884–1954)

Douglas Leader Durkin (1884–1968)

D. H. Lawrence (1885–1930)

F. S. Flint (1885–1960)

Ezra Pound (1885–1972)

William Norman Ewer (1885–1976)

Willoughby Weaving (1885–1977)

Georg Trakl (1886–1914)

H.D. (Hilda Doolittle) (1886–1961)

Siegfried Sassoon (1886–1967)

Mary Borden (1886–1968)

J. Griffyth Fairfax (1886–1976)

Georg Heym (1887–1912)

Rupert Brooke (1887–1915)

Ellis Evans (Hedd Wyn) (1887–1917)

Frederic Manning (1887–1935)

Edith Sitwell (1887–1964)

Edward de Stein (1887–1965)

Donald MacDonald (Dòmhnall Ruadh Chorùna) (1887–1967)

Elizabeth Daryush (1887–1977)

Julian Grenfell (1888–1915)

Alan Seeger (1888–1916)

Patrick Shaw Stewart (1888–1917)

F. W. Harvey (1888–1957)

T. S. Eliot (1888–1965)

Giuseppe Ungaretti (1888–1970)

Teresa Hooley (1888–1973)

Leslie Coulson (1889–1916)

John Munro (Iain Rothach)
(1889–1918)

John Stewart (1889–1918)

C. K. Scott Moncrieff (1889–1930)

Alfred Lichtenstein (1889–1941)

Claude McKay (1889–1948)

Anna Akhmatova (1889–1967)

Enid Bagnold (1889–1981)

Isaac Rosenberg (1890–1918)

Ivor Gurney (1890–1937)

Patrick MacGill (1890–1963)

A. P. Herbert (1890–1971)

Francis Ledwidge (1891–1917)

Arthur Graeme West (1891–1917)

Philip Bainbrigge (1891–1918)

Osip Mandelstam (1891–1938)

Yvan Goll (1891–1950)

Marina Tsvetayeva (1892–1941)

Edna St Vincent Millay
(1892–1950)

Edward Shanks (1892–1953)

Richard Aldington (1892–1962)

Osbert Sitwell (1892–1969)

Leon Gellert (1892–1977)

Hugh MacDiarmid (1892–1980)

Archibald MacLeish (1892–1982)

Joseph Leftwich (1892–1983)

Robert Sterling (1893–1915)

W. N. Hodgson (1893–1916)

Alan Mackintosh (1893–1917)

Wilfred Owen (1893–1918)

Robert Nichols (1893–1944)

Herbert Read (1893–1968)

Vera Brittain (1893–1970)

May Wedderburn Cannan
(1893–1973)

Margaret Postgate Cole
(1893–1980)

John Rodker (1894–1955)

E. E. Cummings (1894–1962)

Charles Hamilton Sorley
(1895–1915)

David Jones (1895–1974)

Robert Graves (1895–1985)

Hamish Mann (1896–1917)

Edmund Blunden (1896–1974)

Edgell Rickword (1898–1982)

Kazi Nazrul Islam (1899–1976)

PART I

Historical and Critical Contexts

SANTANU DAS

Reframing First World War Poetry: An Introduction

In some papers found in his kit after his death in the Battle of Loos on 13 October 1915, the twenty-year-old Charles Hamilton Sorley had scribbled in pencil what would become one of the most celebrated sonnets of the First World War:

> When you see millions of the mouthless dead
> Across your dreams in pale battalions go,
> Say not soft things as other men have said,
> That you'll remember. For you need not so.
> Give them not praise. For, deaf, how should they know
> It is not curses heaped on each gashed head?
> Nor tears. Their blind eyes see not your tears flow.
> Nor honour. It is easy to be dead.
> Say only this, 'They are dead.' Then add thereto,
> 'Yet many a better one has died before.'
> Then, scanning all the o'ercrowded mass, should you
> Perceive one face that you loved heretofore,
> It is a spook. None wears the face you knew.
> Great death has made all his for evermore.[1]

Repeatedly anthologised, yet forever startling. Sorley was deeply suspicious of the 'sentimental attitude' adopted by Rupert Brooke in his war sonnets, but he would nonetheless fall back on this traditional yet flexible form to rebut the dead hero's 'fine words' with his studied monosyllabic force: '"They are dead."'[2] The power of this bleak, disturbing sonnet partly lies in the way the insistent spondees and the desolate imagery of the octave reach some sort of climax in the opening lines of the sestet with the exhortation and the classical allusion (the quotation in line 10 refers to Patroclus's death in the *Iliad*, as Vandiver discusses in Chapter 3 of this volume), only to be intensified by the haunting gaze ('Then, scanning...') and the sudden, ominous, darkly comic shock of 'It is a spook'. The eeriness of the image is enhanced by the poignant circumstances of the poem's posthumous discovery. Like John Keats's spookier and chilling fragment 'This Living Hand', written a month before his death, Sorley's poem operates on that fine threshold where poetic form and personal tragedy meet.[3]

Often regarded as the 'transitional' figure between the early and later soldier-poets, the Germanophile Sorley, like his poem, was unusual for the time.[4] Yet, the poem provides one of the earliest examples of what we now regard as the classic features of First World War poetry: the lyric testimony of the broken body – mouth, eyes, the 'gashed' head – set against the abstract rhetoric of honour; the address to the reader ('you') that we associate with the poetry of Wilfred Owen and Siegfried Sassoon (see Cole, Chapter 5 in this volume), as opposed to the egotistical 'I' of Brooke; the 'pale battalions' haunting the shell-shocked dreams of veterans, limning John Singer Sargent's dream-like *Gassed* (1919) and Sigmund Freud's *Beyond the Pleasure Principle* (1920), and becoming the iconic image of the war. Robert Graves found Sorley's poetry so powerful that he introduced it to Sassoon, who in turn introduced it to Wilfred Owen. And, spook-like, First World War poetry knows no habitation or rest. Mixing cultural memory with linguistic desire, it has ranged far beyond the covers of the book. It appears on postcards, posters and in politician's speeches, in memorials and epitaphs, and has inspired every art form, from Sean O'Casey's play *The Silver Tassie* (1928) and Benjamin Britten's musical tribute *War Requiem* (1962) to the BBC TV series *Blackadder Goes Forth* (1989) and Pat Barker's novel *Regeneration* (1991). War poetry, as represented by a small group of 'anti-war' soldier-poets, has come to dominate First World War memory. We seldom *read* such poetry; it is usually a matter of re-reading, remembering, returning – with familiarity, surprise, sometimes resistance. Given its centrality in the school curriculum in Britain and much of the English-speaking world, we associate it with a part of our former selves. Today, a hundred years after the war, the poetry of the soldier-poets has coalesced, beyond literary history and cultural memory, into a recognisable structure of feeling. Here lies an undeniable part of its power and some of the larger critical problems.

As this *Companion* seeks to show, the scope of First World War poetry is far wider than that of the trench lyric. Many of the works considered here extend and sometimes disturb conventional notions of 'First World War poetry' and make us interrogate the usefulness of the term 'war poetry'. As indicated in the Preface, a 'war poem' contains much besides the war. In addition, our understanding of even familiar war poems has been largely transformed by recent scholarly enquiry into fields as diverse as cultural history, modernism, psychoanalysis and gender studies. Whereas the Preface explains the aims and structure of this *Companion*, here I examine the trajectory of the term 'First World War poetry' and the quiet but powerful expansion of the canon over the last three decades through an investigation of particular contexts and poems. This inquiry explores some of the broader frames of reference and the critical cross-currents underpinning the volume.

What Is 'First World War Poetry'?

The 'war poet' and 'war poetry', observed Robert Graves in 1942, were 'terms first used in World War I and perhaps peculiar to it'.[5] The *Oxford English Dictionary* gives examples of a number of words related to artistic representation of warfare from the nineteenth century – 'war music' (1847), 'war-ballad' (1854), 'war poem' (1857), 'war story' (1864), 'war pictures' (1883) – which, according to Matthew Bevis, show 'the perplexed Victorian fascination with warfare'.[6] However, the *OED*'s only reference to 'war poetry' from the period is telling: 'We have no such war-poetry' (*Atlantic Monthly*, 1865). Of course poetry, as Jon Stallworthy's classic *The Oxford Book of War Poetry* (1984) shows, has always been interested in combat, from the *Iliad* and *The Battle of Maldon* to Tennyson's 'The Charge of the Light Brigade'; two highly popular poetic works of the late nineteenth century, he importantly reminds us, were about private soldiers – Rudyard Kipling's *Barrack-Room Ballads* (1892) and A.E. Housman's *A Shropshire Lad* (1896). At the turn of the century, the Boer War (1899–1902) – which had the first literate army in British history – inspired poetry by both combatants and civilians, including Thomas Hardy.[7] But Graves's observation still holds true. From Anglo-Saxon times to the Boer War, war poetry in English was written largely by civilians and did not have a clearly defined identity; with the extraordinary outpouring between 1914 and 1918, it established itself as a genre and the soldier-poet became a species.

On Easter Sunday 1915, when Dean Inge read out 'The Soldier' by Brooke from the pulpit at St Paul's Cathedral, he was at once creating and anointing a secular saint: the 'poet soldier'. Over the next three years, the 'poet soldier' would morph into 'soldier-poet', and by the 1930s he had become, according to Edmund Blunden, 'as familiar as a ration card'.[8] The term 'war poetry' or 'war verse', by contrast, starts gaining currency from 1917 and crests in popularity in the post-war years. In her 1917 essay 'Contemporary British War Poetry, Music and Patriotism', Marion Scott – friend and music teacher of Ivor Gurney – noted an 'enormous increase in poetic output' related to the war, ranging 'from genius to doggerel'.[9] This was partly the result of a conjunction of particular historical factors: a late Victorian culture of heroism and patriotism, a dominant public school ethos among the officer classes as well as the more general spread of education. Above all, the processes of recruitment – first voluntary and then the Conscription Act of 1916 – meant that the British army had an enormous number of highly educated young men.[10] Some 2,225 poets from Britain and Ireland alone, according to Catherine Reilly's exhaustive bibliography, wrote war poetry; only a handful among them are remembered today.[11] In his letters of 1917, Owen refers to 'war impressions', 'war poem' and 'War Poetry', but in the celebrated Preface (1918) to his intended collection of poems, he eschewed the term 'war poet': 'That is why the true ~~War~~ Poets must be truthful'.[12] This makes Gurney perhaps the first soldier-poet to consciously lay claim to the title; from 1923, he referred to himself as 'First War Poet' [sic], signing it on the back of the envelope in the place of the seal.[13]

The conflation of First World War poetry with the trench lyric was encouraged by the soldier-poets and anthologists, and consolidated with the publication of memoirs such as Graves's *Good-Bye to All That* (1929) and Sassoon's *Memoirs of an Infantry Officer* (1930). Rapidly, the trench poets claimed centre-stage; civilian poets such as Hardy and Kipling moved to the margins. In the politicized climate of the 1930s, Owen and Sassoon became cultural icons. Both figure prominently along with other combatant poets in Frederick Brereton's *Anthology of War Poems* (1930) and Robert Nichols's *Anthology of War Poetry, 1914–18* (1943). However it was with the renewed swell of interest in the group in the 1960s, with the musical *Oh What A Lovely War* (1963) and anthologies such as Brian Gardner's *Up the Line to Death* (1964) and I.M. Parsons's *Men Who March Away* (1965), that the canon began to take shape more firmly. The process was completed by, among others, two literary critics: Paul Fussell, with his enormously influential *The Great War and Modern Memory* (1975), and Jon Silkin with the *Penguin Book of First World War Poetry* (1979). And the circle of knowledge that Vera Brittain lamented shut her off from her beloved Roland in the trenches seemed to tighten forever.

Over the last thirty years, the First World War and its literature have been powerfully reconfigured. Works such as Jay Winter's *Sites of Memory, Sites of Mourning: The Great War in European Cultural History* (1995) have broadened our understanding of the war and its plural legacies, while feminist scholars have drawn attention to the experience of women and children, fundamentally changing the way we 'reconceptualise war – and therefore the vocabulary of war'.[14] First World War poetry has not remained untouched. The recovery in recent years of poetry by women, civilians, dissenters, working-class and non-English (particularly Irish, Scottish, Welsh and American) writers in anthologies by critics such as Simon Featherstone, Dominic Hibberd, Margaret Higonnet, Tim Kendall, Vivien Noakes, Catherine Reilly and Mark W. Van Wienen has led both to a powerful expansion and rethinking of the canon.[15] Moreover, developments in the general critical field – cultural studies, queer theory, work on testimony and trauma – have left their mark. The frameworks and critical idiom used to understand the popular soldier-poets have accordingly shifted: we have moved from a moral register of the 'truth of war' to an exploration of textual complexity and wider socio-cultural contexts; there is closer interrogation of the relationship between poetic form and historical, political and psychic processes; and far greater attention is being paid to questions of difference (class, nationality, gender and sexuality, among others).[16] Many of the scholars contributing to this *Companion* have, through their editions, anthologies and monographs, played a seminal role in this transformation. Often, work on a specific area such as Anglo-American modernism or women's war literature or Irish war poetry has altered our idea of the whole corpus. W.B. Yeats's decision to leave out Owen from the *Oxford Book of Modern Verse* (1936) is well known, but to understand Yeats's own 'war poetry', as Fran Brearton does in *The Great War in Irish Poetry* (2000), is to 'extend the idea of war to the idea of conflict, of which actual warfare is, as it was for the soldier poets, only one manifestation'.[17] The same could be said for war poems by non-combatants and civilian writers further afield, such as the 'Canadian Kipling' Robert Service or the Indian Nobel Laureate Rabindranath Tagore whose wartime writings alert us to the global contexts of war poetry. However, colonial war poetry remains barely visible even in the recently expanded canon. On the other hand, to read Ezra Pound's *Homage to Sextus Propertius* (1919), H.D.'s *Choruses from the Iphigenia in Aulis and the Hippolytus of Euripides* (1919) or T.S. Eliot's *The Waste Land* (1922) through the lens of the First World War (see chapters by Sherry, Howarth and Froula in this volume) is to recognise a form of war poetry in which the war may not be the only or even the dominant story, or may get mixed up with other wars, or with peace. First World War poetry is often perceived as a bend in the course of twentieth-century verse, gathering only the detritus of the trenches, but this *Companion* shows instead how the war fed into and funneled the main poetic currents of the day, including different traditions of nineteenth-century lyricism and early-twentieth-century modernism.

Canons are retrospective constructions, and few more so than what we consider today as First World War poetry. Between 1914 and 1918, the most famous war poem was Brooke's 'The Soldier', followed by Julian Grenfell's 'Into Battle'. Angry responses such as Arthur Graeme West's 'War Poets' (1916) – directed at 'a University Undergraduate moved to verse by the war' and beginning with 'God! How I Hate you, you young cheerful men' – hint at the dominant contemporary culture of commemorative or patriotic war verse West rails at and which has not survived.[18] The battle lines we erect today between soldier-poets and civilians were not that sharply drawn then. Anthologies published in 1914 – *Poems of the Great War* and *Songs and Sonnets for England in War Time* – included poems by both combatants and civilians, as did the first 'anti-war' collection, *Poems Written during the Great War* (1918).[19] George Herbert

Clarke's compendious *A Treasury of War Poetry: British and American Poems of World War, 1914–1919* (1919) cuts across both soldier/civilian and pro-/anti-war divides and gives us an idea of the popular war poets of the day: Brooke and Grenfell appear alongside not just Sassoon, Graves, Robert Nichols, Francis Ledwidge, Gilbert Frankau and Frederic Manning but also writers such as Walter de la Mare, John Drinkwater, Thomas Hardy and Rudyard Kipling. Prominent by their absence are Owen and Isaac Rosenberg. War poetry could also be more international, if of an imperial cast. In the Christmas of 1918, the periodical *The Bookman* included a supplement devoted to the war poets: it featured poems by Sassoon, Graves, Gurney, Grenfell, Madox Ford, alongside American Alan Seeger, Canadians Robert W. Service and John McCrae, Australian Leon Gellert and the lone woman-poet, Vera Brittain.[20] Definitions are seldom static, and the label 'war poetry' has journeyed somewhat like Owen's 'long-strung creatures' which 'curve, loop and straighten' as they move.[21]

So we may have to reframe the question: what is First World War poetry in English as we understand it now? At its expansive best, it is a diffuse category cutting across different genres and nationalities: it includes works by the familiar soldier-poets and the anonymous contributors to the famous trench journal *Wipers Times*; non-combatants and civilians; men and women; jingo-imperialists and conscientious objectors; Georgians and modernists; poets from England, Ireland, Scotland, Wales and the United States as well as from the former dominions and colonies (see the 'Chronology of Poets' for an extended list). In formal terms, it ranges from epic and satire through the sonnet, villanelle, ode, pastoral, elegy and ballad to the limerick and the trench song. Our contemporary understanding of the First World War as 'different wars', the cultural turn in literary studies and, at a more experiential level, our heavily mediated relationship as witnesses to violent events around the world have widened our perspectives. Does this expansion blur the distinction between cultural history and literary criticism, especially when the works by the majority of the poets listed in Reilly's bibliography veer towards 'doggerel' than 'genius'? The anthologist today has to tread a delicate line between questions of literary value and the representation of different voices. Moreover, does this seemingly catch-all definition put 'First World War poetry' as a special category at risk? In the concluding 'Conversation,' Jon Stallworthy notes that the term has 'become so elastic now' that one has to use it 'in a sort of quotation marks.' Indeed, 'Lest we forget' seems to have become 'Lest we exclude'. Yet, given the history of marginalization and for a fuller understanding of First World War poetry, it is important to retain an expansive definition and a flexible critical framework alert to different political, cultural and historical trajectories. All First World War poetry was not written by 'war poets', just as all poetry written by the war poets is not war poetry. *The Waste Land*

and 'After Troy' can be read as war poems but they do not make Eliot or H.D. 'war poets'; on the other hand, it is debatable whether Owen's 'Maundy Thursday', even if revised at Craiglockhart in 1917, is a 'war poem'.

Where do we draw the line? Are all poems written between 1914 and 1918 war poems? Not necessarily – all wartime poems, like all poems by war poets, cannot be called war poetry. To qualify as a First World War poem, the war does not have to be directly present or mentioned, but at the same time some context of the war has to be registered and evoked, however obliquely. In the 'Conversation', Michael Longley observes: 'if the cosmos of a poem is the Great War, then that's it'. Longley's father fought in the First World War and his celebrated poem 'Wounds', written in 1972, shows how private memories of his father's service on the Western Front resurfaced during the Irish Troubles and got fused with images of contemporary violence. In her discussion of the poem in this volume, Fran Brearton uses the resonant phrase 'post-war Great War poems' to refer to such later but intimate engagements with the conflict (Chapter 15).

Combatant Poetry: Testimony, Lyric and the Body

In her 1918 review, 'Two Soldier Poets', Virginia Woolf raises a point that continues to fuel debates about combatant poetry. 'It is difficult to judge him dispassionately as a poet', Woolf writes of Sassoon, 'because it is impossible to overlook the fact that he writes as a soldier'.[22] Given the perilous intimacy of life and art, writings on trench poetry remain one of the last citadels of humanist criticism. After all, Owen's poetic credo – 'My Subject is War, and the pity of War; the Poetry is in the pity' – provides one of the most powerful refashioning of poetry as testimony in the twentieth century.[23] Some critics might say: after such experience, what theory?

This privileging of the overtly testimonial, the experiential and the affective in writings on First World War poetry, often resulting in the marginalization of other voices, has been critiqued in recent years. James Campbell has called it the 'ideology of combat gnosticism': the idea that 'the experience of fighting provides a connection to Reality, an unmediated Truth' to which only combatants with direct exposure have access.[24] As he rightly notes, combat experience is by no means the 'only' voice of the war and even less an index of a poem's literary value; moreover, it cannot be used either to define or 'authenticate' a war poem. However, it will be almost equally unwise to go to the other extreme and ignore the particular contexts of trench poetry: recognition of difference does not necessarily mean fetishization, or a politics of hierarchy and exclusion. The poetry of the trenches cannot be wholly dissociated from its material conditions: to overlook their specificity would empty the genre of its intimate bodily and emotional history. Our knowledge of such extreme circumstances *does* affect our reading of even such formally superb poems as 'Futility' or 'Break of Day in the Trenches'. The epistemological relation of these real-life experiences to artistic form, affect and cultural memory is historically more complex, delicate and deep-rooted than a neat, gendered ideology of 'combat gnosticism'. Indeed, the question of why and how a group of soldier-poets came to represent the voice of a nation in Britain forms the basis of the cultural historian Jay Winter's essay in this volume (Chapter 16).

The trench experience was one of the most sustained shatterings of the human sensorium: it thrust the soldier's fragile body between the ravages of industrial modernity on one hand and the formlessness of matter on the other. Trench artefacts and documents – letters, diaries, notebooks, sketchbooks – regularly fuse meaning and materiality, pointing to the 'contactzone', the daily conditions which inspired much of the poetry.[25] The idea of chance, so prominent in trench writing, finds its poignant material trace in the diary of A. Reid. Here, on the last page, the date 'Sunday 29th July, 1917' is inscribed in anticipation of the day's record, but only a blank space exists: Reid was killed before the day ended (Figure 2). As one opens the diary of J. Bennett (Figure 3a), one sees on the first page a sketch ('Old Bill') followed by a piece of witty doggerel about 'Mud', showing how humour, drawing and verse existed together as a coping mechanism, while his obsessive repetition of 'Dull cold day' (Figure 3b) echoes the commonest theme of trench verse. Rosenberg's poem 'In the Trenches' is contained within a grimy and fragile letter (Figure 4), and Vivien Noakes recalls how, while editing his poems, dustings of mud fell off from many of the manuscript pages. After three weeks at the Front, Owen writes to his mother, 'I have not seen any dead. I have done worse. In the dank air, I have perceived it, and in the darkness, *felt*'.[26] For Owen, touch becomes the ground of both testimony and trauma. As I have argued elsewhere, the visual topography of everyday life was replaced by the tactile geography of the trenches: in the dark, subterranean world of the Western Front, men navigated space not through reassuring distance of the gaze but through the tactile immediacy of their bodies.[27] 'Creep', 'crawl', 'burrow' and 'worm' are regular verbs in trench lyrics, suggesting the shift from the vertical axis of the human body to the horizontality of the beast. In the foreword to Rosenberg's *Collected Works*, Sassoon notes: 'Sensuous frontline existence is there, hateful and repellent, unforgettable and inescapable'.[28]

However, this does not make combatant poetry the unmediated receptacle of experience. If the surrounding material world was important, so was

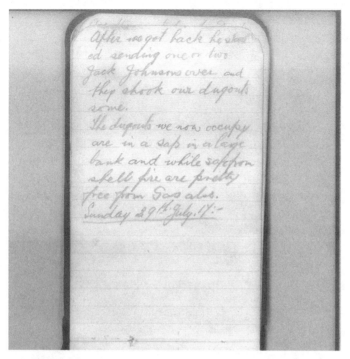

Figure 2 The final entry from the diary of A. Reid. Imperial War Museum 87/8/1.

a sense of poetic convention. Contrary to popular perception, not all soldier-poets belonged to the officer class or went to public schools, but his education and largely middle-class background (Rosenberg was an exception) set him apart from the average 'Tommy'. And he had a solid sense of literary tradition. Investigation into the literary culture of the trenches – from Paul Fussell's chapter 'Oh! What a Literary War' in *The Great War and Modern Memory* (1972) to Jon Stallworthy's *Survivors' Songs: From Maldon to the Somme* (2008) – shows 'the instinctive and unapologetic' engagement of this group of soldier-poets with a vast range of literature, from the *Iliad* through Shakespeare, Milton and the Romantics to Hardy and Housman.[29] If trench poetry was one of the most profound ways of body-witnessing history, it was the body at war brought into the most intimate dialogue with the body of form through intricate negotiations with literary tradition. Words such as 'sploshed', 'muck', 'sludge', and 'funk' were not just new words or ways of introducing the body but processes of aligning some of the deeper impulses of 'Georgianism' (examined by Sherry in Chapter 1) to the newfound world of the senses. The finest trench poetry revels in the meeting of tradition and

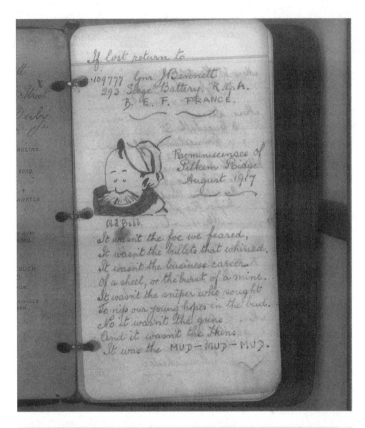

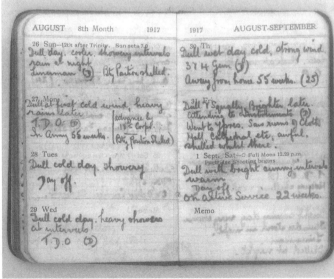

Figure 3 (a and b). Two pages from the diary of J. Bennett. Imperial War Museum 83/14/1.

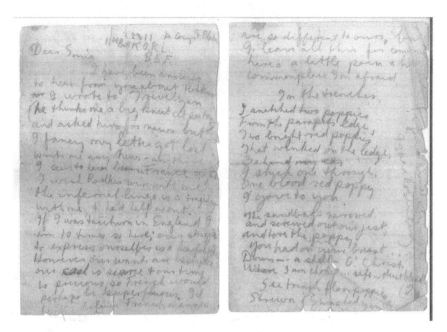

Figure 4   Letter of Rosenberg containing the poem 'In the Trenches'.
Imperial War Museum, Special Misc R5.

innovation: in Gurney's exquisite handling of trochee, caesura and sibilance in the terrifying, haptic image of 'Darkness, shot at: I smiled, as politely replied –' ('The Silent One'); in Sassoon's powerful rhymes which compact visceral horror and religious blasphemy while conjuring up the commonest trench expletive – 'And someone flung his burden in the muck/Mumbling: 'O Christ Almighty, now I'm stuck!' ('Redeemer'); or in Rosenberg's alignment of his modernist eye with that of the private soldier in 'Marching – As Seen From the Left File' which Neil Corcoran (in Chapter 6) compares to a 'Wyndham Lewis drawing or an early David Bomberg painting':

> All a red brick moving glint.
> Like flaming pendulums, hands
> Swing across the khaki –
> Mustard-coloured khaki –
> To the automatic feet.[30]

Trench lyric stubbornly inhabits the formal, in spite of or perhaps because of the all-surrounding threat of the formless.

A constant tension in First World War poetry criticism is whether the accent should fall on war or on poetry, on cultural history or on aesthetic value. In her illuminating essay 'The Great War, history, and the English lyric', Edna Longley has argued that the war lyric may be the 'quintessential case' of the encounter between 'form and history'. She further observes: 'War infiltrates and tests all poetry's mechanisms of tradition. Great War poetry can resemble a computer checking itself for viruses. And if poetry improvises, it also trawls.'[31] Familiar war poems, often considered as trench transcripts, emerge after close reading as intricate palimpsests. Consider the following stanzas from Owen's 'Dulce Et Decorum Est':

> Gas! GAS! Quick, boys! – An ecstasy of fumbling,
> Fitting the clumsy helmets just in time;
> But someone still was yelling out and stumbling,
> And flound'ring like a man in fire or lime …
> Dim, through the misty panes and thick green light,
> As under a green sea, I saw him drowning.
>
> In all my dreams, before my helpless sight,
> He plunges at me, guttering, choking, drowning.
> [...]
> If you could hear, at every jolt, the blood
> Come gargling from the froth-corrupted lungs,
> Obscene as cancer, bitter as the cud
> Of vile, incurable sores on innocent tongues, –
> My friend, you would not tell with such high zest
> To children ardent for some desperate glory,
> The old Lie: Dulce et decorum est
> Pro patria mori.[32]

This is considered as the classic example of 'war realism' in its full-frontal shock value. Indeed, there is terrible, brilliant symmetry in the way the testimony of the gas attack – which often corrodes the body from within – moves from visual impressions to visceral processes: from sounds produced between the body and the world (fumbling, stumbling, flound'ring, drowning) to sounds within the body (guttering, choking, writhing, gargling). Sound plays a central role in a poem that climaxes on a macabre contrast between tongues: the lacerated tongue of the soldier and the grand polysyllabic sound of the Latin phrase as Owen plays on the two meanings of 'tongue' (language and bodily organ, as in Latin 'lingua'). Such linguistic wordplay when the real-life soldier has lost his powers of speech raises disturbing questions.

Sassoon, while reading the manuscript, underlined the word 'ecstasy' and put a question mark beside it (Figure 5): how can a gas attack produce 'ecstasy'? Is 'ecstasy', whose religious connotations would not have been lost on Owen, used to suggest the nervous energy of the moment of bodily crisis, a 'limit-experience' where terror and exhilaration meet in the frenzy

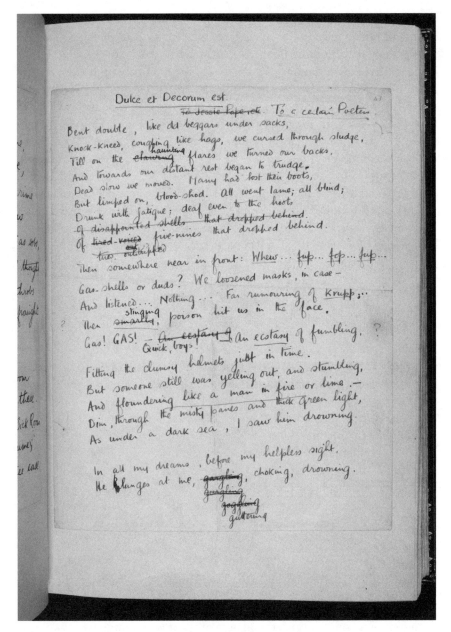

Figure 5   First page of a manuscript version of Wilfred Owen, 'Dulce Et Decorum Est'.
Courtesy of the Wilfred Owen Estate and the British Library, London (Add. 43721.41).

of 'fumbling/Fitting the clumsy helmets just in time'? Or does it also suggest a sense of bodily release – terrified yet exhilarating – after being cooped up in dugouts where 'nothing happens'? In a letter to his brother Colin, Owen observes that the 'sensations of going over the top are about as exhilarating as those dreams of falling over a precipice' and of feeling 'no horror at all but only immense exultation at having got through the Barrage'.[33] Coming from the Greek word *ekstasis* literally meaning 'a standing outside of one-self' (*ek* – out of, *stasis* – a position, a standing), the word bears testimony to this primal moment, but perhaps also draws from the retrospective exul-tation of survival as he remembers and relives it at Craiglockhart in October 1917. Yet, the word remains singularly odd, posing a challenge to the trans-parency and realism of the poem. In fact, sound bears out the sense even as interpretations prove inadequate. In a poem that explores the complicity of language in violence – the dangers of Horace's 'sweet' phrase[34] – there is a perverse linguistic 'ecstasy' as poetic language, asked to describe violence, starts singing through alliteration ('s', 'l', 'f'), echo (ecstasy/clumsy/misty) and the rhyming extra foot ('fumbling', 'stumbling', 'drowning'), replacing real-life horror with semiotic pleasure, with *jouissance*. Owen, while criticis-ing the 'sweetness' of a particular poetic tradition, seems to be trapped in the 'sweetness' of the lyric form himself. Asked to describe a moment of high risk, the vocabulary ends up risk-taking itself, setting the sensuous swell of language against the horror of the sense experience it recounts. Moreover, the poem cannot be limited to the world of the trenches. Words such as 'guttering' (or the crossed-out alternatives – 'gargling', 'gurgling', 'goggling') or 'froth-corrupted lungs' are grimly realistic in the context of war, but they also tunnel underneath to his pre-war medical history, a morbid absorption with his health, particularly throat and lung infections. As Jon Stallworthy notes in his biography, even in the pre-war years, Owen had begun to see himself as a 'Chattertonian figure, consumptive and impecunious'.[35] At the same time, 'vile incurable sores on innocent tongues' is a masterly rewriting of Keats's 'palate fine' as Owen at once inherits and subverts the aesthetic of his beloved mentor; it shows war poetry's complex negotiation with Romanticism even when recording such extreme moments. The ultimate testimony of the gas attack is placed not in the act of perception, but in the unconscious testimony of 'all my dreams': the compulsive repetition of the gerundive '-ing' suggests the eternal now of the trauma victim who, as Freud noted in *Beyond the Pleasure Principle* (1920), is doomed to a compulsion to repeat past experience as perpetual present. Thus, in 'Dulce' – a poem fre-quently equated with the 'truth of war' – we see instead that realism is edged with linguistic fantasy, the pity of war jousts with creative pleasure and pre-war medical history gets connected to shell-shocked visions. In this volume,

Sherry and Gilbert briefly refer to the poem in other contexts, showing how it continues to yield different meanings.

Owen is regarded as the patron saint of pity, and with abundant reason. But of all the trench poets, he is also the one who draws us, Caravaggio-like, into moments of extreme sense experience, weaving linguistic-tactile fantasies around processes we would otherwise flinch from: moments when limbs are 'knife-skewed', the flesh 'ripped … in scarlet shreds' or the mouth starts bleeding ('I saw his round mouth's crimson deepen as it fell'). A linguistic-visceral thrill as well as an acute bodily empathy constitute the body in pain in Owen's poems. Repressed homoeroticism and a strong Protestant ethic, combined with the loathing and the pity of war, contribute to such tortured images: the male body that cannot be touched, either legally or morally, is mutilated in the poems. His poetry is a powerful example of war literature going beyond neat moral agendas. Works such as Adrian Caesar's *Taking It Like a Man: Suffering, Sexuality and the War Poets* (1993) show how much of war poetry more generally resists simple ethical or political equations: their inner histories are often more fraught, compelling and disturbing. Are poems such as Sorley's 'All the hills and vales along' with its enigmatic refrain 'So be merry, so be dead' or Gurney's 'First Time In' with its Welsh songs 'never more beautiful than here under the guns' noise' or Owen's altogether more terrifying 'Apologia' where 'power was on us as we slashed bones bare' pro-war or anti-war – or do they reveal the inadequacy of these categories and point to something entirely different?[36] Moreover, for us, there is an additional problem: while the soldier-poets own the experience they describe, such intimate and sensuous descriptions raise for their readers questions about ethical responsibility and the vexed issue of 'how moral is taste'.[37]

Many of our ideas of First World War poetry have developed around the figure of Owen, but he is by no means the only kind of war poet. The soldier-poets were a far more diverse group than what is usually acknowledged. The chapters in Part II ('Soldier-Poets') examine a number of figures, from the public-school educated 'early poets' such as Brooke, Grenfell and Sorley, to 'later poets' such as Blunden, Graves, Nichols, Sassoon and Read, to men who served as privates and often had very little money, such as Rosenberg, Gurney and Jones. They testify to the remarkable range of combatant poetry which can be compulsive, curative, testimonial, traumatic, funny, forlorn, ironic, elegiac, Georgian or modernist, and often take us beyond the war. Indeed, many of them cannot be detached from their wider socio-political contexts. The contributors challenge many of the prevailing myths, such as that of the absolute division between the home front and the war front or between a pro-war and anti-war stance or a straightforward poetic journey from 'innocence' to 'bitter experience': the Somme, as Rawlinson reminds

Figure 6   Men of the Duke of Wellington's Regiment after the capture of Marfaux on
23 July 1918 during the Battle of Marne. Imperial War Museum Q6867.

us in Chapter 4, was no turning point for the poetry. Trench poetry can also
be curiously celebratory: the nearness of death often gives ordinary sights
or sounds, blossoms and birdsong an intense beauty, a 'strange joy'.[38] This
is most exuberantly articulated in the sphere of comradeship (see Figure 6).
Male intimacy in the trenches, the lyrical core of Remarque's novel *All Quiet
on the Western Front* or Sherriff's play *Journey's End,* finds some of its most
tender physical testimony in the poetry which can be seen as a phantasmatic
space where these men continue to reach out to their friends: 'My comrade,
that you could rest/Your tired body on mine'.[39] Pity, affection, vulnerability as well as a diffuse eroticism are often fused and confused, defying the
established categories of gender and sexuality.

The work of the soldier-poets provides some of the most intimate literary
record of the (male) history of emotions. Traditionally cordoned off from
the rest of early twentieth-century poetry, where the category of 'modernism' has been dominant, this is a body of work whose influence on lyric
poetry across the twentieth century we are now beginning to understand
more fully.[40] While a previous generation of critics drew attention to the
richness of the corpus, if limiting it to the trenches, the chapters in Parts I
and II extend the intertextual map and connect it to a wider cultural and
literary milieu in the early twentieth century.

Beyond the Trenches: Civilians, Women and Forms of Witnessing

In December 1914, as Edward Thomas sat down to review the year's crop of 'war poetry', it was verse by civilians that he had on his desk and in his mind. Literary history provided precedents, from William Blake's 'War Song to Englishmen' to Alfred Tennyson's *Six Patriotic Poems*. 'One tiny volume would hold all the patriotic poems surviving in European languages', he observed. What he saw being written on the current war by the likes of Robert Bridges and Laurence Binyon inspired little hope: 'the demand is for the crude'. 'By becoming ripe for poetry', he instead noted, 'the poet's thoughts may recede far from their original resemblance to all the world's, and may seem to have little to do with daily events'.[41]

Civilian war poetry is largely written out of the Great War and modern memory. True, much of this poetry was patriotic or commemorative, and forgettable. It ranges from variations on Horace's 'Dulce Et Decorum Est' to Harold Begbie's popular recruiting number, 'What will you lack, sonny, what will you lack', to poems such as 'Christs All!' by John Oxenham, whose khaki-coloured paperbacks were sent to soldiers by their mothers, including Owen's.[42] But civilian war poetry, like combatant poetry, is a very diverse body of work, and there is much that is original and startling. In the introduction to *The Winter of the World* (2007), Hibberd and Onions observe how, contrary to popular perception, the first 'Sassoonish' poems were written by two poets who remained civilians until 1916–17 and never saw fighting: Harold Monro and Wilfrid Gibson.[43] Both were 'Georgians', the loose group of poets who, in different combinations, were published in the five volumes of *Georgian Poetry* (appearing between 1912 and 1922). If Gibson in 'Breakfast' showed how newspaper reportage (rather than experience), when coupled with Georgian directness, could produce '[trench] realism of the right, the poetic kind',[44] Monro in his poem incorporated song, horror, pastiche, dialogue and slang:

> Damn this jingle in my brain.
> I'm full of old songs – Have you ever heard this?
>
> *All the roads to victory*
> *Are flooded as we go.*
> *There's so much blood to paddle through,*
> *That's why we're marching slow.*
>
> Yes sir; I'm here. Are you an officer?
> I can't see. Are we running away?
> How long have we done it? One whole year,
> A month, a week, or since yesterday?
>
> Damn the jingle. My brain
> Is scragged and banged [...].[45]

Published in December 1914, this poem – whose questions, vocabulary and ventriloquism anticipate T.S. Eliot's 'Prufrock' (published in June 1915) – suggests complex connections between Georgian and modernist poetry. The poem also challenges the equation of 'war realism' with combat experience, or the idea of an absolute divide between combatants and non-combatants. When Owen met Monro on 15 November 1915 at the Poetry Bookshop, he quoted from the latter's 'Youth in Arms' after Monro had 'smiled sadly' at his uniform.[46] Owen's famous lines, 'Are limbs, so dear achieved, are sides/ Full-nerved, still warm, too hard to stir?' are prefigured by Monro ('And the lovely curve/Of your strong leg has wasted') while also resonating with Rose Macaulay's 'Shadow': 'Are the spilt brains so keen, so fine, crushed limbs so swift'?[47] Combatant, non-combatant and women's poetry operated within a larger poetic field and shared common ground.

However, some of the most distinguished civilian war verse does not mention the war directly, let alone the trenches. As the volume explores, the recession of the conflict into the intimate layers of the self and its oblique modes of address – like Thomas's fallen elm, Hardy's red fuchsia, Mew's invocation of spring, daily sights, dialogues, patterns of thought – provide some of the subtlest testimonies to the war's penetration of civilian spaces and consciousness. James Longenbach has argued how lyric poets in the early twentieth century – poets as different as Hardy, Marianne Moore and H.D. – resist 'twentieth-century's epic challenges' and instead embrace a 'diminished aesthetic', focussing on a circumscribed world of small objects. This art of the 'studied miniature', for Longenbach, is most evident within the Imagist movement, particularly in H.D's poems where the universe becomes so small 'that it threatened to seem precious'. But such preciousness is for H.D. 'a kind of weapon' against the militarism and masculinity of the war.[48] For many civilian poets, the art of the intimate, precise detail becomes a mode of registering the war's epic blasts. A range of familiar forms – ballad, elegy, sonnet, pastoral – are employed as civilian lyric poetry bears witness not just to the war, but to the act of witnessing itself – a crisis both epistemological and stylistic. For Walter de la Mare, the war has reduced civilians to 'Spectators', 'Aghast at its agony,/Yet absorbed in it'; in John Masefield's 'August 1914', the ancient countryside is 'Rutted this morning by the passing guns'; in Hardy's 'Before Marching and After', his elegy for his cousin killed in Gallipoli, the focus narrows down to 'the fuchsia-bells, hot in the sun,/[That] Hung red by the door' as the postman arrives with the news.[49] Attitudes and styles vary widely across the group. In Chapter 13 of this volume, Tim Kendall points out the significant differences through a sustained focus on the two most eminent writers of the time: Hardy and Kipling.

The art of indirection would, however, be perfected by Edward Thomas. A civilian until July 1915, Thomas wrote all his poems in England before leaving for France in late January 1917 and getting killed in April 1917 in the Arras offensive. He is a soldier-poet who did not write any trench poems and thus 'eludes or disturbs' the category 'war poet'.[50] Edna Longley here investigates his poems alongside Ivor Gurney's (Chapter 8 in this volume) and shows how, for Thomas, the war's profound effects on the rural landscape were connected with 'the end of pre-war worlds'. Intimate and oblique, these poems 'embrace a whole community', as in 'In Memoriam (Easter 1915)':

> The flowers left thick at nightfall in the wood
> This Eastertide call into mind the men,
> Now far from home, who, with their sweethearts, should
> Have gathered them and will do never again.[51]

If, according to Longenbach, 'a generation of studiously diminished lyric poets was confronted with an epic subject',[52] there are few finer examples in the English language of an epic subject being accommodated within miniature form, or suffusion of the pastoral with the elegiac or the evocation of loss through such a vivid imagining of touch. Not that epic ambition or achievement was absent. One of the last works to emerge out of the trench experience was David Jones's magisterial *In Parenthesis* (1937), examined by Adrian Poole in Chapter 9 of this volume (also see discussions by Howarth, Goldie and Froula in Chapters 2, 10 and 14 respectively). Jones is the main modernist among the soldier-poets, alongside Herbert Read and Rosenberg (in varying degrees).

War literature has an angular relationship to the categories of 'modernity' and 'modernism'. There have been two main lines of thought within cultural history. According to Paul Fussell in *The Great War and Modern Memory*, the war gave rise to modern consciousness that is 'essentially ironic'; this view, however, has been powerfully challenged by Jay Winter who, through attention to a variety of art forms, argues that the war signified a return to traditional forms of mourning.[53] Trench poetry, with its deep roots in nineteenth-century lyricism and evocation of twentieth-century trauma, puts pressure on the very definition of the term: is 'modernism' defined by a set of formal and linguistic features associated with the writings of Eliot and Pound or is it to be used as a historical category, marked by themes such as wartime trauma, technological modernity and changes in perceptual structures and subjectivity? For some time now, 'modernism' has been a rather fluid concept, with a gradual shift from a textual model of Anglo-American 'high' modernism to a more expansive one alert to different political, social and cultural trajectories; alternative maps of modernism have been proposed, both extending and reconceptualising the term. If in the past war literature and modernist writing were considered to have parallel if occasionally intersecting careers, scholars such as Sarah Cole, Peter Howarth, Vincent Sherry and Trudi Tate have highlighted in recent years the vexed relationship between the two.[54] With reference to modernist poetry, Sherry has shown how its verbal texture was shaped by the public culture of the war. Modernist war poetry and its connections with combatant poetry are addressed in Chapters 1, 2, 6 and 9 in this volume. It receives its fullest treatment in Froula's investigation of the poetry of the 'London Vortex' between 1914 and 1922 in Chapter 14. 'The Great War did not make modernist poetics but it did make modernist poems' she notes, as she shows how the wartime poems of Eliot and Pound 'register a crisis of poetic voice – and poetic silence' as they grapple with the war's moral contradictions.

One writer who moves between and collapses different categories – and it is a cause of regret that he does not figure in this volume because of pressures of space – is D.H. Lawrence. Embittered by his war experience, he wrote not only two of his greatest novels (*The Rainbow*, 1915 and *Women in Love*, written and revised during 1916 and 1917, but published in 1920) during the war years, but also a striking, if small, body of verse. The utter strangeness of such poetry is evident in 'Resurrection':

> And still against the dark and violent wind,
> Against the scarlet and against the red
> And blood-brown flux of lives that sweep their way
> In hosts towards the everlasting night,
> I lift my little pure and lambent flame,
> Unquenchable of wind or hosts of death
> Or storms of tears, I lift my tender flame
> Of pure and lambent hostage from the dead [...].[55]

This is unlike anything else in First World War poetry. Contemporary violence is accommodated into a private vision of death and resurrection, themes that occupy Lawrence in his fiction. Sorley's 'mouthless dead' are absorbed into an intensely personal drama. The evolution of a historical catastrophe into a private world of myth and allusion – one is reminded in this respect of H.D.'s 'After Troy' or Yeats's 'A Vision' – raises questions about the expectations and ethics surrounding First World War poetry. Yet, such poems bear the fullest testimony to Thomas's dictum: 'by becoming ripe for poetry the poet's thoughts may recede far from their original resemblance to all the world's'.[56]

Over the last couple of decades, feminist critics have powerfully recovered women's war experiences and writings. Women's prose – for example, Vera Brittain's *Testament of Youth*, Rebecca West's *Return of the Soldier* or Woolf's *Mrs Dalloway* – now figure prominently in the canon. But women's poetry, although showcased in such anthologies as Catherine Reilly's *Scars Upon My Heart: Women's Poetry and Verse of the First World War* (1981), remains marginal. Why this discrepancy? Is it because of the continuing conflation of war poetry with combat experience, or does the uneven nature of much of women's war verse trouble even sympathetic critics with questions about form? Dorothy Goldman has noted that 'it was not simply their lack of first-hand military experience that inhibited women's poetry, but the inheritance of worn-out and inappropriate modes and language without the catalyst which the experience of the War provided in forcing more shocking and brutal forms of expression'.[57] If discussions of such poetry are often more sociological and cultural than literary, Margaret Higonnet (Chapter 12 in this volume) examines a number of writers – Charlotte Mew, Rose Macaulay, Eleanor Farjeon and Margaret Cole – who both inherit and interrogate the traditions of nineteenth-century lyric verse with remarkable power. Such poetry is intricately crafted, intensely moving and often politically engaged. There are also modernist impulses. Mary Borden's memoir, *The Forbidden Zone* (1929), draws on a modernist aesthetic of fragmentation to provide testimony not just to what she saw in the military hospital she ran behind the lines, but to the terrifying dissolution of the category of gender itself:

> There are no men here, so why should I be a woman? There are heads and knees and mangled testicles. There are chests with holes as big as your fist, and pulpy thighs, shapeless; … There are these things, but no men; so how could I be a woman here and not die of it?[58]

Visual trauma is the ground of protest in her savagely aestheticised 'Unidentified', first published in *The English Review* in December 1917:

> But look.
> Look at the stillness of his face.
> It's made of little fragile bones and flesh, tissued of quivering muscles fine as silk;
> Exquisite nerves, soft membrane warm with blood,
> That travels smoothly through the tender veins.
> One blow, one minute more, and that man's face will be a mass of matter, horrid slime and little brittle splinters.[59]

This is one of the early powerful examples of what Susan Sontag in *Regarding the Pain of Others* (2003) has called the pacifist politics of visceral affect: 'Photographs of mutilated bodies certainly can be used the way Woolf does, to vivify the condemnation of war'.[60] Such poetry remains an important counterweight to Sassoon and Owen's images of the jingoistic woman, with Jessie Pope often used as the straw figure. By contrast, in Borden's poem, as in Owen's, a fin-de-siècle corporeal aesthetic ('quivering muscles', 'exquisite nerves') is brought into dialogue with the realism of 'horrid slime' which

Figure 7   *Die Eltern* by Käthe Kollwitz. Roggevelde German War Cemetery,
Vladslo, Belgium. Personal photograph.

cannot be contained within traditional meter. But there is a fundamental
difference: Borden, unlike Owen, cannot claim ownership over the experience she describes. Herein lies much of the pain of women's war writing:
how can one bear witness to the bodily pain of another when it is the one
condition that cannot be shared? If Borden exhorts us to 'look', it is in the
visual arts on the other side of no-man's-land that female elegy – and civilian
grief – finds one of their most poignant expressions: in the German artist
Käthe Kollwitz's monument at the Roggevelde German war cemetery to her
eighteen-year old son Peter, killed in Flanders. The focus, however, is not on
the dead son, but on the parents (Figure 7).

Beyond 'Englishness': Archipelago, Empire and the Colour of Memory

It is often forgotten that the First World War was a *world* war: the first shot
fired by a British soldier was in Togoland and even after all became quiet
on the Western Front on 11 November 1918, German *askaris* and Allied
forces continued fighting in East Africa. Sassoon and Blunden mention colonial troops in their memoirs, but they are absent in their verse, as if the

existing poetic vocabularies did not know how to accommodate them with-out lapsing into imperial-jingoistic rhetoric. Owen's adoration for Tagore never translated into an engagement with his Indian comrades-in-arms; it is only Kipling who commemorates the Hindu sepoy in 'Epitaphs of the War' (1919).

The colonies and dominions contributed huge number of troops and suf-fered traumatic losses; New Zealand had the highest casualty rates across the empire. Gallipoli and Vimy Ridge remain as central to Australian-New Zealand and Canadian national identity respectively as the Somme is to the British. Moreover, between 1914 and 1918, in a grotesque reversal of Conrad's vision, hundreds of thousands of South Asians and Africans were voyaging to the heart of whiteness and beyond – Mesopotamia, Gallipoli, Palestine, Egypt – to take part in the horror of Western warfare.[61] The war was also a catalyst for nationalist movements. Near the imperial centre, the Easter Rising erupted in 1916. Given the charged contexts, one may wonder: 'Where are the archipelagic and colonial war poets'? What were their responses to the conflict? Moreover, is the colour of First World War poetry – like Eurocentric assumptions about the war's cultural memory – exclusively white?

War poetry has remained stubbornly 'English'. However, most of the major soldier-poets had a conflicted relationship to 'Englishness': Sorley was Anglo-Scottish; Jones, Owen and Thomas were aware of their Welsh con-nections; Rosenberg, the son of Lithuanian immigrants, had a strong sense of his Jewish identity while Sassoon's *Memoirs of a Fox-Hunting Man* could be read as an extraordinary act of construction of the persona of an English country gentleman by someone who could trace his recent family history to Baghdad Jewry.[62] Moreover, a substantial body of poetry in English was written and read enthusiastically outside England: in Scotland, Ireland, Wales, the United States and across the British empire. Colonial war poetry, coming out of different political, social and cultural contexts, is a remark-ably copious and varied body of work: it ranges from volumes by individ-ual soldier-poets to anthologies such as *Soldier Songs from Anzac* (1915), *Indian Ink* (1915–16) and *Canada in Khaki* (1917) to poems by established figures such as Rabindranath Tagore in India, Robert Service in Canada and Clarence Dennis in Australia. For a variety of reasons, such poetry – with the exception of John McCrae's ubiquitous 'In Flanders Fields' – has proved resistant to assimilation within the war canon. Similarly, archipelagic dif-ferences are often flattened, with critics as sensitive otherwise as Catherine Reilly using the term 'English poets' to include 'poets of England, Ireland, Scotland and Wales'.[63] Yet such differences, as John Kerrigan has powerfully shown, were vital to the cultural and literary history of what he calls 'archi-pelagic English'.[64] Jones's *In Parenthesis* remains one of its finest expressions as he goes back to the idea of Britain (rather than of England) of the sixth-century Welsh epic poem *Y Gododdin,* linking Somme to the Welsh defeat at Catraeth. His identification with Celtic and Norse sources might signify, as Howarth notes in Chapter 2 of this volume, 'Jones's sense of his fight being *with* the English, and their industrialism, as much as for them'.

The near-invisibility of archipelagic and colonial poetry within the First World War canon points to a greater problem: the continuing absence of a critical and contextual framework to address and sometimes even being able to recognize poems that do not conform to the British constructions of war memory or the dominant model of the trench lyric (notwithstanding attendant questions of aesthetic value).[65] Of the different genres, war poetry is most closely bound up with the politics of cultural memory. The proximity of events such as the Easter Rising (1916) in Ireland, the anti-draft riots in Quebec (Easter 1918) or the Amritsar massacre (1919) in India often determined the place of the First World War and its literature in the cultural life of these nations. As these former dominions and colonies became nation-states, their war contribution was either marginalised or reconfigured. Ireland is a powerful example of how, until recently, memories of the First World War and its literature were suppressed in the national consciousness. Even in countries where the war's legacy is related to national identity, as in Australia and New Zealand, trench poetry does not have the same relation to cultural memory as in England: Charles Bean's *Official History*, rather than Leon Gellert's poetry, is foundational to the Anzac myth.[66] Moreover, the majority of the soldiers from South Asia and Africa were not wholly literate. A poignant picture from the Imperial War Museum archives shows an Indian sepoy, unable to write, giving his thumb impression as he accepts his pay (Figure 8). Under such circumstances, the corpus of war writing by non-white combatant writers is severely limited but it is not wholly absent: being non-literate does not mean being non-literary. There was often a robust oral literary culture in the places from where these colonial troops came, flourishing through practices of story-telling, narration of folklore, poetry reading and singing (as in the Punjab from where most of the South Asian troops were recruited). The censored letters of Indian troops sent home from France often include verses (translated by the colonial censors into English from various regional languages), and a number of South Asian and African songs sung by the soldiers have been recovered in recent years. Moreover, there is a substantial body of civilian war literature from across the empire. Part of our challenge lies in recovering not just colonial 'soldier-poets', but recognising the war more widely in colonial poetic cultures.

In this volume, Goldie and Featherstone recover the archipelagic and colonial dimensions of war poetry respectively. Both observe that while such poetry is not always different just by dint of being written by a colonial or

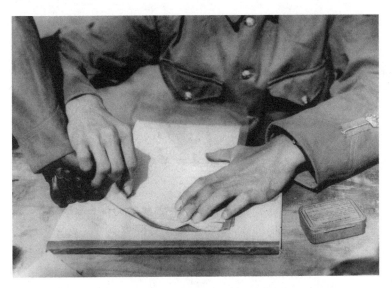

Figure 8   An Indian, unable to write, is making a thumb impression on the pay sheet instead of signing for his pay. Imperial War Museum.

archipelagic subject, many of the poems are distinctive, marked by specific anxieties, repressed histories or dissenting politics, while being 'in no simple sense anti-imperialistic' (Featherstone). Since the colour of First World War poetry remains largely white (with the exception of Tagore, examined in Chapter 11 by Featherstone), I will conclude by briefly examining two poems which challenge this conflation – the famous sonnet 'If We Must Die' by the Jamaican-American poet Claude McKay and the Bengali poem 'The Rebel' (here in translation) by the revolutionary Indian/Bangladeshi poet, Kazi Nazrul Islam. The poems were written in the aftermath of the war, but do not figure in the canon of war poetry.[67] In each, the war and its languages get mixed up with other histories – locally more charged than the war – and stretch our understanding of the term 'First World War poetry'.

McKay's 'If We Must Die' is often considered as the 'inaugural address' of the 'Harlem Renaissance', that extraordinary explosion of black literature and culture in New York from 1919 to the early 1930s.[68] Some of the most politically engaged war literature came from here. During the war, some 347,000 African Americans were inducted into the army, of whom some 47,000 saw active service. They fought, as Jessie Fauset notes, 'a double battle in France, one with Germany and one with white America'. In Walter E. Seward's 'Who Went Over the Top', no-man's-land is not the deathbed of European civilisation but, as he notes with bitter irony, a democratic space: 'Bullets have no special people,/No one especially they hate;/And the Germans' large artillery/Sure did

27

not discriminate'.[69] The civic rights leader W.E.B. Du Bois, who closed ranks with the whites for the war, noted that the black veteran returned 'to fight a sterner, more unbending battle against the forces of hell in our own land': 'We return./We return from fighting./We return fighting' ('Returning'). Such fighting was often literal, for race riots erupted across the United States in the 'red summer' of 1919.[70] Moreover, at least sixteen veterans were lynched between November 1918 and the end of 1920, some of whom were still serving.[71] In this context, Claude McKay's 'If We Must Die', published in the July 1919 issue of *Liberator*, accretes fresh intensities of meaning:

> If we must die – let it not be like hogs
> Hunted and penned in an inglorious spot,
> While round us bark the mad and hungry dogs,
> Making their mock at our accursed lot.
>
> …
>
> Oh, Kinsmen! We must meet the common foe;
> Though far outnumbered, let us still be brave,
> And for their thousand blows deal one death-blow!
> What though before us lies the open grave?
> Like men we'll face the murderous, cowardly pack,
> Pressed to the wall, dying, but – fighting back![72]

Writing about the poem's genesis, McKay noted: 'The World War had ended. But its end was a signal for the outbreak of little wars between labor and capital and, like a plague breaking out in sore places, between colored folk and white'.[73] McKay rewrites the war sonnet as protest poetry, starting with Brooke and ending with Du Bois. His conscious echo of Brooke and use of the sonnet form is at once an acknowledgement of British influence and a sign of dissent: the war's dominant vocabulary and values – courage, sacrifice and comradeship – are appropriated for a different war as Brooke's 'richer dust' is refashioned as 'precious blood' shed not in foreign fields, but in homeland against fellow countrymen. From there it is a short distance to Richard Wright's claim in 1941: 'Our black boys do not die for liberty in Flanders. They die in Texas and Georgia. Atlanta is our Marne, Brownsville, Texas is our Château-Thierry'.[74]

South Asian war literature has a different trajectory. Around one-and-a-half million South Asians, including combatants and non-combatants from present-day India, Pakistan, Nepal and Bangladesh, were recruited for the war and a substantial number of them served in the war, in places as diverse as France, Gallipoli, Mesopotamia, Egypt and East Africa (Figure 9). Tagore is the Indian poet best known to Europe and he wrote some war poetry. However, one of the few literary figures who underwent military training for the war (although he was not mobilised) and wrote some

Figure 9 Viceroy's Commissioned Officers (VCOS) and other ranks of 129th Baluchis take aim in the trenches on the outskirts of Wytschaete, Belgium in October 1914. Imperial War Museum Q56325.

startling war poetry was Kazi Nazrul Islam. Known in Bengal as the 'soldier poet' or 'rebel poet' for his revolutionary anti-colonial politics and lyric excess, Islam's popularity almost outstripped Tagore's in the interwar years.[75] At the outbreak of the war, for reasons not entirely clear, he joined the (British) Indian army. What is remarkable about his war writings – which include stories, poems and an epistolary novel – is the way the First World War gets fused with other events such as the October Revolution, the Turkish War of Independence, the Third Afghan War and the Indian nationalist struggle to form a vision of revolutionary violence, incandescent for him with a terrible beauty. Consider the Whitmanesque 'The Rebel', once the rallying cry for the Bengal revolutionaries and which remains even today one of the most popular poems in Bengali:

> I trample on bonds,
> obey no law,
> recognise no rule.
> I sport with loaded boats
> In my revels

And send them down to the sea's bottom
Without mercy.

I'm a torpedo
An explosive mine.
I am the Spirit of Shiva, the destroyer.
I am the summer's storms
Always seething with turbulence,
I am the wild wind:
I crush and sweep away all in my path.
…
I am the quenchless fire
In subterranean volcanoes,
dark with no glow.
I leap from region to region
Unhampered, reckless,
While the earth trembles in dismay underneath.[76]

Poetry in translation is outside the scope of this volume, but the above extract should serve as reminder of how First World War poetry was written across the British empire in non-European languages. In India during the war years, stories of the German submarine Emden torpedoing boats created widespread panic. The images of boats, torpedo, mine and 'subterranean volcanoes' come directly out of the First World War, but more importantly, the aesthetics of violence is made possible by the knowledge of the war and turned by this sepoy-turned-rebel into the service of Indian revolutionary nationalism. A far cry from the poetry of Owen and Sassoon, Nazrul's apocalyptic verse remains an example of how the war could be adapted, reworked and laid claim on within the colonial literary sphere.

In his poem 'The War Graves', Michael Longley writes, 'There will be no end to cleaning up after the war'.[77] The war's debris will be inspected afresh in 2014–2018. As we move fully from remembrance to history with the death of the last war veteran, will First World War poetry be called on even more to bear the weight of the past or will distance allow the poetry to speak more to us as poetry? The following chapters pay close attention to the linguistic texture of the poems and how they bear witness to history's 'blood-dimmed tide'. In the process, they also explore how the traumatic material of war inspires, energises and even excites poetic language. War poetry is sometimes aligned too neatly with a moral agenda. While it is crucial to recognise the political force of First World War poetry, individual poems, as examined, can be more complex and disturbing. Remember that 'ecstasy' occurs in the most grimly realistic of Owen's poems and 'strange' remains one of the most recurring words in First World War poetry. Powerful war poems, such as Hardy's

'I Looked Up from My Writing', often ask the most difficult ethical questions. As we approach the centennial commemoration of the war with pomp and ceremony and young men and women continue to get killed in military action, these poems bring us no immediate hope or assurance or comfort, but in their combination of pity, anger, moral complexity and linguistic pleasure, remind us as readers what it is to be idealistic, thoughtful, mortal, guilty – and make us question what it is to be human.

NOTES

A number of friends read the Introduction at – literally – a day's notice and provided acute criticism. I would like to thank Guy Cuthbertson, Kate McLoughlin, Jane Potter, Toby Smith, Hugh Stevens and Trudi Tate.

1 Charles Hamilton Sorley, *Marlborough and Other Poems* (Cambridge: Cambridge University Press, 1916), 69.

2 Letter to Mrs Sorley, 28 April 1915, in *The Letters of Charles Sorley* (Cambridge: Cambridge University Press, 1919), 263.

3 For a discussion of Keats's poem, see John Kerrigan, 'Touching and Being Touched', *London Review of Books*, Vol. 24 No. 18, September 2002, 19–22.

4 Jon Stallworthy, *Anthem for Doomed Youth: Twelve Soldier Poets of the First World War* (London: Constable, 2002), 37.

5 Robert Graves, 'The Poets of World War II' (1942) in *The Common Asphodel: Collected Essays on Poetry* (London: Hamish Hamilton, 1949), 307.

6 Matthew Bevis excavates these words in 'Fighting Talk: Victorian War Poetry' in Tim Kendall ed. *The Oxford Handbook of British and Irish War Poetry* (Oxford: Oxford University Press, 2007), 10 (7–33).

7 See Jon Stallworthy's illuminating introduction to *The Oxford Book of War Poetry* (Oxford: Oxford University Press, 1984), ix–xxxi; also see Malvern van Wyk Smith, *Drummer Hodge: The Poetry of the Anglo-Boer War* (Oxford: Oxford University Press, 1978).

8 Edmund Blunden, 'Introduction' to Frederick Brereton ed. *An Anthology of War Poems* (London, 1930). 13.

9 The title of Marion Scott's essay 'Contemporary British War Poetry, Music and Patriotism' (*The Musical Times*, 1 March 1917, 120–1) suggests the recognition of a genre. There were exceptions such as R.H. Thornton's *War Verses: August, 1914* (1914), but it was from 1918 that anthologies with titles such as *The Lyceum Book of War Verse* (1918) and *War Verse* began to mushroom. I am grateful to Jane Potter for the reference to Scott's article.

10 See, for example, Simon Featherstone ed. *War Poetry: An Introductory Reader* (London: Routledge, 1995), 15.

11 Catherine Reilly, *English Poetry of the First World War: A Bibliography* (London: George Prior, 1978), xix.

12 'Preface' in Jon Stallworthy ed. *The Poems of Wilfred Owen* (London: Chatto & Windus, 1990), 192.

13 I am indebted to the research of Philip Lancaster and Tim Kendall for this information about Gurney: hear Kendall on 'Gurney: First War Poet', http://podcasts. ox.ac.uk/tim-kendall-ivor-gurney-first-war-poet-audio.

14 Margaret Higonnet, 'Not So Quiet in No-Woman's Land', in Miriam Cooking and Angela Woollacott eds. *Gendering War Talk* (Princeton, NJ: Princeton University Press, 1993), 208. The work of a number of feminist critics – including Sandra Gilbert, Margaret Higonnet, Jane Marcus, Jane Potter, Angela Smith, Trudi Tate and Claire Tylee – has led to the powerful recovery of women's war writing.

15 See Featherstone ed. *War Poetry: An Introductory Reader*; Mark W. Van Wienen ed. *Rendezvous with Death: American Poems of the Great War* (Urbana: University of Illinois Press, 2002); Vivien Noakes ed. *Voices of Silence: The Alternative Book of First World War Poetry* (Stroud: Sutton, 2006); Dominic Hibberd and John Onions, eds. *The Winter of the World: Poems of the Great War* (London: Constable, 2007). Also see Catherine Reilly's pioneering anthology *Scars upon My Heart* (London: Virago, 1981) and Tim Kendall ed. *Poetry of the First World War: An Anthology* (Oxford: Oxford University Press, 2013, forthcoming)

16 See the long introduction to Featherstone, *War Poetry: An Introductory Reader*, 7–115, for an astute discussion of these shifts as registered within First World War poetry criticism. Also see the essays collected in Vincent Sherry ed. *The Cambridge Companion to the Literature of the First World War* (Cambridge: Cambridge University Press, 2005), Tim Kendall ed. *The Oxford Handbook of British and Irish Poetry* (Oxford: Oxford University Press, 2007) and Adam Piette and Mark Rawlinson eds. *The Edinburgh Companion to Twentieth-Century British and American War Literature* (Edinburgh: Edinburgh University Press, 2012) for a variety of critical approaches.

17 Fran Brearton, *The Great War in Irish Poetry* (Oxford: Oxford University Press, 2000) 78. Also see Tim Kendall, *Modern English War Poetry* (Oxford: Oxford University Press, 2006), particularly pages 3–4.

18 The Oxford undergraduate has been identified as Rex Freston. See Dominic Hibberd and John Onions eds. *The Winter of the World: Poems of the Great War*, 135–6 (Hereafter abbreviated as *Winter*).

19 See the introduction to *Winter*, xxviii, xxxiii (vi–xxxvi).

20 See Jane Potter, '"The Essentially Modern Attitude Toward War": English Poetry of the Great War', in *The Edinburgh Companion to Twentieth-Century British and American War Literature*, 20.

21 'The Show' in *Owen*, 132.

22 'Two Soldier-Poets', in Andrew McNeillie ed. *The Essays of Virginia Woolf*, Vol. III (London: Hogarth, 1988), 269.

23 Stallworthy, *Owen*, 192.

24 James Campbell, 'Combat Gnosticism: The Ideology of First World War Poetry Criticism', *New Literary History*, 30 (1999), 207. According to Campbell, 'combat gnosticism' has also become 'the ideology of First World War poetry criticism' (215). This has been a powerful and influential critique, though interestingly Campbell's essay was written at a time when feminist critics such as Nosheen Khan, Elizabeth Marsland and Claire Tylee, as he notes, had started challenging the equation of war with combat and reconceptualising the canon of war literature.

25 See, for example, Stephen Greenblatt's essay, 'Touch of the Real' where he speaks of material objects providing insights into 'the charmed space where *genius literarius* could be conjured into existence' (*Representations*, 59, Summer 1997, 29).

26 Harold Owen and John Bell eds. *The Collected Letters of Wilfred Owen*, (London: Oxford University Press, 1967), 429.

27 I have argued this at length in *Touch and Intimacy in First World War Literature* (Cambridge: Cambridge University Press, 2005).

28 Sassoon, 'Foreword', in Ian Parsons ed. *The Collected Works of Isaac Rosenberg*, (London: Chatto, 1979), ix.

29 Fussell, *The Great War and Modern Memory* (Oxford: Oxford University Press, 1975), 161; Stallworthy, *Survivors' Songs: From Maldon to the Somme* (Cambridge: Cambridge University Press, 2008).

30 *Winter*, 290, 69, 74.

31 Longley, 'The Great War, History and the English lyric', in Sherry ed. *Cambridge Companion*, 66.

32 Stallworthy, *Owen*, 117. For the manuscript versions of the poem, see Stallworthy, *Complete Poems and Fragments*, Vol. 2 (London: Chatto and Windus, Oxford University Press and Hogarth, 1983), 296.

33 Owen to Colin Owen, 14 May 1917, *Collected Letters*, 458.

34 *Collected Letters*, 500.

35 *Collected Letters*, 201, 205; Stallworthy, *Wilfred Owen: A Biography* (Oxford: Oxford University Press, 1974), 95.

36 Sorley, *Marlborough*, 71; P. J. Kavanagh ed. *Collected Poems of Ivor Gurney* (Oxford: Oxford University Press, 1983), 149; 'Apologia' in Stallworthy, *Owen*, 101.

37 See David Bromwich, 'How Moral is Taste', in *Skeptical Music: Essays in Modern Poetry* (Chicago: University of Chicago, 2001), 232–51. Bromwich does not engage with war poetry, but the premise is strikingly similar. Also see my chapter on Owen in *Touch and Intimacy*, 137–72.

38 'Returning, we hear the larks' in Parsons, *Rosenberg*, 109.

39 Robert Nichols, 'Casualty', in *Aurelia and Other Poems* (London: Chatto, 1920), 75.

40 Longley, 'The Great War, History and the English Lyric'; also see Tim Kendall, *Modern English War Poetry* (Oxford: Oxford University Press, 2006).

41 Edward Thomas, 'War Poetry', *Poetry and Drama*, II, No. 8 (December 1914), np.

42 See *Winter*, 79.

43 *Winter*, xiv.

44 Woolf, 'Mr Sassoon's Poems', *Essays*, 120.

45 Harold Monro, 'Youth in Arms' in *Winter*, 21.

46 Ibid., 22.

47 'Futility', *Owen*, 135; Monro, 'Youth in Arms', *Winter*, 21; Macaulay, 'The Shadow', in Catherine Reilly ed. *Scars Upon My Heart* (London: Virago, 1981), 68.

48 James Longenbach, 'Modern Poetry', in Michael Levenson ed. *The Cambridge Companion to Modernism* (Cambridge: Cambridge University Press, 2011), 101–5 (99–127).

49 *Winter*, 47, 16, 76. Also Kate McLoughlin's incisive chapter on 'Diversion' in *Authoring War: From the Iliad to Iraq* (Cambridge: Cambridge University Press, 2011), 135–63.

50 Edna Longley, 'Introduction', to Longley ed. *Edward Thomas: The Annotated Collected Poems* (Tarset: Bloodaxe Books, 2008), 11.

51 'In Memoriam (Easter 1915)' in *Thomas: Annotated Collected Poems*, 80.

52 Longenbach, 'Modern Poetry', 108.

53 Paul Fussell, *The Great War and Modern Memory*; Jay Winter, *Sites of Memory, Sites of Mourning: The Great War in European Cultural History* (Cambridge: Cambridge University Press, 1995).

54 See Trudi Tate, *Modernism, History and the First World War* (Manchester: Manchester University Press, 1998); Sarah Cole, *Modernism, Male Friendship and the First World War* (Cambridge: Cambridge University Press, 2003); Vincent Sherry, *The Great War and the Language of Modernism* (New York: Oxford University Press, 2003); Peter Howarth, *British Poetry in the Age of Modernism* (Cambridge: Cambridge University Press, 2006).

55 'Resurrection' in Vivian de Sola and F. Warren Roberts eds. *The Complete Poems of D.H. Lawrence* (Harmondsworth: Penguin, 1964), 745.

56 Thomas, 'War Poetry', np.

57 'Introduction' to Dorothy Goldman ed. *Women and World War I: The Written Response* (Basingstoke: Macmillan, 1993), 7.

58 Mary Borden, *The Forbidden Zone* (London: William Heinemann, 1929), 60.

59 Borden, 'Unidentified', in *Winter*, 203.

60 Susan Sontag, *Regarding the Pain of Others* (Harmondsworth: Hamish Hamilton, 2003), 10.

61 See Santanu Das, *Race, Empire and First World War Writing* (Cambridge: Cambridge University Press, 2011).

62 I am grateful to Amitav Ghosh for discussing Sassoon's *Memoirs* with me.

63 See Reilly, *English Poetry of the First World War*, xiii.

64 John Kerrigan, *Archipelagic English: Literature, History and Politics, 1603–1707* (Oxford: Oxford University Press, 2008).

65 Also see Brearton, *The Great War in Irish Poetry*, 43–50.

66 See Alistair Thompson, *Anzac Memories: Living with the Legend* (Melbourne: Melbourne University Press, 1994). Charles Bean edited the twelve-volume *Official History of Australia in the War of 1914–1918*.

67 While Nazrul is virtually unknown outside India, Bangladesh and Turkey, McKay's famous sonnet is included in Mark W. Van Wienen's anthology *Rendezvous with Death: American Poems of the Great War* (Urbana and Chicago: University of Illinois Press, 2002).

68 See Mark Whalan, *The Great War and the Culture of the New Negro* (Gainesville: Florida University Press, 2008).

69 Jessie Redmon Fauset, *There is Confusion* (1924; Boston: Northeastern University Press, 1989), 269; Walter E. Seward, 'Who Went Over the Top?', in *Negroes' Call to the Colours and Soldiers: Camp-Life Poems* (Athens, GA: Knox Institute Press, 1919), 46. Both are quoted in Whalan, 'The War and African American literature', in *Race, Empire and First World War Writing*, 283–300.

70 See *Rendezvous With Death*, 251–2.

71 See David Levering Lewis, *When Harlem Was in Vogue* (Oxford: Oxford University Press, 1981), 14–24.

72 'If We Must Die', *Rendezvous With Death*, 263.

73 Cited in http://www.english.illinois.edu/maps/poets/m_r/mckay/mustdie.htm

74 Quoted in Whalan, 284.

75 For India and WWI, see Das, 'Indians at Home, Mesopotamia and France, 1914–1918', in *Race, Empire and First World War Writing*, 70–89.

76 'The Rebel', in Rafiqul Islam ed. *Kazi Nazrul Islam: A New Anthology* (Dhaka: Bangla Academy, 1990), 20–3. Translated from Bengali.

77 Michael Longley, 'The War Graves', in *Collected Poems* (London: Jonathan Cape, 2006), 256.

I

VINCENT SHERRY

First World War Poetry:
A Cultural Landscape

The year 1914 was iconic already by 1915, when it provided the main title for a small volume of poems by (the now posthumous) Rupert Brooke. Inscribing the first year of the First World War in headline-like style, this title caught the sense of tremendous eventfulness in the moment. It also marked wartime against pre-war and, subsequently, post-war, drawing a line across time and defining a watershed in literary history that has grown more vivid in critical and poetic retrospect. Nearly a half-century later, in 1960, Philip Larkin revisited the year and reinscribed the date in his title as 'MCMXIV'. The Roman numerals lend the sense of a time immemorial to the last moments of existence in history before this war, when, in anticipation of the British declaration of hostilities at eleven o'clock on the evening of 4 August 1914, a photograph from a newspaper of that day shows:

> These long uneven lines
> Standing as patiently
> As if they were stretched outside
> The Oval or Villa Park,
> The crowns of hats, the sun
> On moustached archaic faces
> Grinning as if it were all
> An August bank holiday lark.

These 'archaic faces' depict the last pre-war moment as a kind of prehistory. This is the place in imaginative time which Larkin stakes later in the poem with a reference to 'Domesday lines', the first land survey of Britain, drawn up in 1085–6, which provides an image of a residual but ancient and now obviously foregone form of social order for the landscape of the last day of peace. 'Never such innocence', goes the poetic editorial, attributing a value he reiterates thus in the final line: 'Never such innocence again'.[1]

The magnitude of this Great War may account for some of the intensity with which Larkin registers the change it made in British history. But how does this war qualify as the watershed event in Larkin's archetypal story of lost 'innocence'? Allowing for the fact that the horrors of war draw a poetic imagination toward the explanatory and consolatory powers of primary myths, the fact remains that Larkin had not even been born at the time his poem is recording. His is a presumptive understanding of the history he is registering. He has received this story of a fall from the innocence of peace to the experience of war as a legend of history, and he has recycled it with a degree of imaginative confidence that bespeaks the cultural sanction it owns: the eloquence of his finale is as assured as it is terse. This is a story formed under the conditions that governed much of the poetic production early in the war. Revisiting these cultural circumstances in an analytical history may provide an explanation of the genesis of this myth, a story that exerted an extraordinary appeal in the understanding of the subsequent century.

Georgianism: A Politics, A Poetics

The primary factor in the generation of that legend was the contemporary convention of 'Georgian' poetics. Named after the reigning King George V, drawing on an incidental but relevant connection with the Georgic mode of classical literatures, Georgian poetry inhabited a pastoral circumstance primarily. In this venue, its poets found one of their rhetorical and affective mainstays in the imaginative value of natural innocence. Given the national-istic character 'Georgian' invokes, this innocence will be politicized as well as militarized when it goes to war, and these aspects of its poetic identity reveal their complexity in the context of the literary and political history of the pre-war period.

A detailed account of the circumstances of political history in pre-war Britain will indicate that those years resist assimilation to that myth of the 'Golden Summer of 1914', which Larkin recycles in 'MCMXIV'. In *The Strange Death of Liberal England: 1910–1914* (1935), for instance, George Dangerfield proposes that the war, far from shaking the foundations of English society, actually helped to preserve the status quo by diverting the energies of social revolution, which was being threatened contemporane-ously by the workers' and women's movements, not to speak of the steadily escalating menace in Ireland.[2] This is the era in cultural history that is nor-mally understood as the forcing ground of those disruptive energies that would crest into the productions of English modernism. Therefore, in the interests of dramatic literary history, and in the simplifying binaries of ret-rospect, Georgianism is often presented as a reactionary opposition to the convention-dismaying temperament of modernism. A more searching inter-rogation suggests that its poetic sensibility was seen by contemporaries to be in synergy with the sense of invention and experiment which, if rhyming distantly with the social turmoil of these years, participated nonetheless fundamentally with the artistic revisionism of modernism. The cleansing of the poetic dialect of a fustian, now-deceased Victorianism was a firm motive in the cleaner and sparer line and newly idiomatic accent. *Georgian Poetry 1911–1912* was thus praised in a *Times Literary Supplement* (*TLS*) review for its divergence from still current tradition, specifically, as a 'reaction from a mood which was characteristic in its latest Victorian years', although, as this anonymous reviewer is careful to point out, this poetic sensibility is 'not a revolt'.[3] 'There is no sense of revolt', A.C. Benson emphasizes again in his review of the same volume in *The Cambridge Magazine*, and went on to laud a poetic spirit that seemed 'adventurous without being disordered'.[4] A renovation that was well-behaved on the surface of the verse nonetheless suggested a challenge to existing norms sufficiently strong to prompt the negation of danger that both pieces of critical praise seemed to require.

The *TLS* review goes on to characterize the more extreme poetic temperament of those troublous times as a bravado of fragmentation, complaining of a sensibility which would feel 'that it is braver and more sensible to leave the broken fragments where they lie than fondly to set about piecing them together again'. This poetic temperament, the reviewer goes on to aver, may be 'justly called decadent',[5] and it is in relation to this judgmental category of 'decadence' that Georgianism develops its political poetics in the war years. 'Decadence' was indeed a fraught and charged term: it included associations of decay in the reign of empire, now falling to senescence in a bio-historical model of history, and a range of behaviors as scandalously bad as the representatives of the now fabled English Nineties. If this proclivity was sensed in the imaginative memory of the early Georgian years as a residual susceptibility, the war presented a challenge and an opportunity of renewal, that is, a cleansing and purgation of this 'decadence'. It is within these cultural circumstances that Georgianism may be read in its development during the war as a return to the cultural center of an English national imaginary, where decadence was disclaimed and innocence reclaimed.

'As swimmers into cleanness leaping': thus Brooke images the ceremony of cleansing through which, in a poetic music as exquisite as its notion is counterintuitive, he portrays the young men of the nation going to war. The phrase appears in the octave of a sonnet that presents a history in miniature of those cultural circumstances in which Georgian poetry will forge its special identity in the war:

> Now God be thanked Who has matched us with His hour,
>   And caught our youth, and wakened us from sleeping,
> With hand made sure, clear eye, and sharpened power,

> To turn, as swimmers into cleanness leaping,
>   Glad from a world grown old and cold and weary,
>   Leave the sick hearts, that honour could not move,
>   And half-men, and their dirty songs and dreary,
>   And all the little emptiness of love.[6]

The condition of England is presented as an inventory of the symptoms of decadence. Entropy, a scientific idea newly formed and anxiously elaborated in the later nineteenth century, shows a 'world grown old and cold and weary'. Equally run-down is the custom and manner of romantic love, whose 'little emptiness' can be sung only in 'dirty songs and dreary' by 'half-men', where the quantitative adverb, which recurs in the poetic lexicon of decadence always as a measure of loss (a half of a whole is always less), also encodes the homosexual identity so menacingly associated with the more notorious characters of the English Nineties. But the 'problem' adduced in this octave – the condition of decadent England from which the speaker seeks reprieve – has already found the solution which, in the conventional economy of sonnet form, it usually takes the concluding sestet to produce. War is the deliverance from a fallen and disorderly experience into an existence which, in being finer and cleaner, is capable of sustaining the resolving value of innocence. The otherwise unlikely title for a poem about going to war, 'Peace', suggests an obviously paradoxical quality to this imaginative reasoning, which, far from discrediting it, actually strengthens its effective power. The Georgian response to the war exhibits a quasi-religious significance. The innocence it reclaims will undergo a sort of baptism by fire, which, in turn, will authenticate and indeed consecrate the condition of innocence that this poetic temperament takes as its mainstay.

The importance of this condition of innocence in the imaginative episteme of Georgianism may be demonstrated in the lengths to which it is occasionally taken. 'Into Battle', a piece by Brooke's fellow traveler Julian Grenfell, pushes this poetic temperament into a dimension of actual combat which, if it is not realistically described, is at least intensely registered:

> And when the burning moment breaks
>   And all things else are out of mind,
> And only joy of battle takes
>   Him by the throat and makes him blind …

At this extremity, the usually pacific character of Georgian nature organizes support for the martial enterprise:

> The woodland trees that stand together,
>   They stand to him each one a friend;
> They gently speak in the windy weather;

> They guide to valley and ridge's end.
> The kestrel hovering by day,
>> And the little owls that call by night;
> Bid him be swift and keen as they,
>> As keen of ear, as swift of sight.[7]

The voice of Georgian innocence, recovering nursery-rhyme cadences and offering the fabulous companions of childhood's natural friends as fellows in arms, provides a striking, perhaps even ridiculous, dissonance to the actuality of war that Grenfell has already recorded. Involuntary comedy of this kind bespeaks the power of the forces suborning a poetic intelligence that is capable otherwise of very promising work (like Brooke, Grenfell would die in 1915). If the ceremonies of innocence would be drowned in the blood of actual combat, even as the sweet concords of sonnet form provided the music to perpetuate its value in sacrifice, the Georgian sensibility owes much of its enduring appeal to the forces of cultural nationalism into which it was also tapping.

This is a nationalism for which Brooke becomes the most representative spokesperson in his best-known poem, 'The Soldier', where the words 'England' or 'English' occur half-a-dozen times in the short span of fourteen lines. Specifically, in the place reserved for the tonic note in the musical score of the sonnet, the first line of the concluding sestet presents the national landscape as another scene of innocence recovered: 'And think, this heart, all evil shed away'.[8] Whether or not this Georgian ideal exists subsequently just as a gorgeously fossilized record of fated attitudes, the innocence it valorizes remains in the memory and poetic legacy as a touchstone that is also a milestone: it measures the distance traveled to the war as it actually happened, as it will be recorded more accurately by the poets experiencing it in later years.

One example stands out as a particularly vivid instance of the ongoing importance of the Georgian imaginary even – or especially – as it is ultimately foregone. Ivor Gurney's 'To His Love' may be read as a sort of Georgianism manqué. It is, more particularly, a riposte to the idealization of death for Brooke's 'Soldier' in 'a foreign field that is forever England'. Here a strategic use of rhetorical negatives indicates all in English pastoral that does *not* accommodate the untoward event of the subject's death in alien lands:

> He's gone, and all our plans
>> Are useless indeed.
> We'll walk no more on Cotswald
>> Where the sheep feed
>> Quietly and take no heed.
>
> His body that was so quick

> Is not as you
> Knew it, on Severn river
> Under the blue
> Driving our small boat through.
>
> You would not know him now ...[9]

While Gurney inserts his 'not's and 'no's into the Georgian idiom, its unavailable topographies still control the representation of poetic feeling. The voice of this once dominant convention holds its greatest potential for expression, then, when its tongue is tied. The military internment service of the final stanza begins thus with nervous words, exclamatory stammering:

> Cover him, cover him soon!
> And with thick-set
> Masses of memoried flowers—
> Hide that red wet
> Thing I must somehow forget.[10]

The enjambment across the final two lines brings the heavy stress of a building rhythm down hard on 'Thing', a word that offers its ultimate subject, the loved body of the fallen soldier, in its generic non-specificity. It is remarkably, shockingly, movingly inadequate. It powerfully expresses the pathos of the loss of those poetic conventions of Georgianism, its innocence most particularly. This is the literary history Larkin has recycled into his picture of the difference the war made in the national story.

Reportage: The Space of History

'There are strange hells within the minds war made':[11] Gurney's words (in the poem that takes its title from this first line) strike the note of a register sharply distinct to the idealizing diction of the early Georgian poetic report. Protest against the actual horror of war is most often cited in literary histories as the defining task and accomplishment of this verse. This standard critical narrative tells the story through its now canonized poetic legacy: it follows a general development from a poetics of national idealism, as featured in the poetry of Brooke and Grenfell, to the lyric realism and imaginative disenchantment with the national cause that we find in the last years of the war in the verse of Wilfred Owen and Siegfried Sassoon, whose 'views' are read again in an intensified version in the great surge of prose works – memoirs as well as novels – in the later 1920s and early 1930s. This poetry of protest is doubtless an essential dimension in the literary record of war, and it will be recognized in any critical work of fitting record. The very power of this poetry, however, gives it a place greater than the proportionate space it actually takes in the poetic record. There is a problem in such accounts which might be characterized as reading history backward; it simplifies the story by editing out of the account anything that does not conform to a preconception of its destined end, which is usually formulated in terms of a history of political opinion which is not often the most urgent concern of the poets writing *in* and *ex medias res*. Opening the frame of reference to a broader modality of report helps to recover a range of verse of exceptionally high quality. What begins to become clear in this enlarged compass is the meaning and value of experiential immediacy in the poetry of war, which may comprise but exceed the 'pro-war' and 'anti-war' binary that simplifies the account and misses the textured dimensionality of the represented experience. The aims and motives of this poetic witness direct us to centers of imaginative attention that make sense of the English experience of the war in the context of its deeper backgrounds in European history.

The extraordinary performance of national expansiveness in the capital cities on the continent as well as in London in the early days of August 1914 is a phenomenon that tends to be read, in historical retrospect, with the sense of irony that now attends much of the understanding of the war. Looking at these events from the perspective of antecedent history offers another view on those massive sensations of liberation and deliverance, which were shared across several national cultures in the early moments of the war. The special intensity and exceptional breadth of war-feeling go to motive interests and cultural sources stronger than the appeals of individual national mythologies, let alone national demagogueries. For these energies stem from cultural traditions that can genuinely be assessed as pan-European; they can be understood as a system of comprehensive value for the major national protagonists. This value is, in a word, liberalism.[12] This term, which refers not to a partisan interest but an attitudinal frame of mind, locates the point of defining reference in the cultural history of post-Enlightenment Europe. Its root meanings have to do with ideas and feelings of liberation, and this radical semantic shows in the experiences of deliverance into that zone of emancipated possibilities that is chronicled – ironically or not, and the irony is an important part of the longer story of this salient value of liberalism – across the major literatures of the opening moments of the war. Allowing for the fact that no one feeling is uniform in any one country, let alone in several, the dominance of this sensation of liberation in British and French as well as German (and Austrian) writers of the early war is not to be gainsaid.

Its intensity can be explained through an extended frame of historical reference and with an analytical understanding of liberal ideology, which may be considered both as a motive psychology and an evolved, political economy. For this understanding, the frame of historical reference needs to pull back further and take into account the revolutions in France in 1789 (and again in 1830 and 1848) and in proto-national Germany in 1848; in England, there was the residual but persistent and increasing pressure of an ever-deferred revolution, which the centralized war effort of 1914 helped again to deflect. The promise of emancipation through these revolutions (or near revolutions) gave the content and depth of intimately known expectation to the namesake value of liberation to the liberalism of post-Enlightenment Europe. By 1914, however, this imaginative value has engendered a system of mercantile capitalism whose failure to satisfy the expanded masses of a European population was more than manifest. Unrealized, the dream of freedom in those European revolutions (or near revolutions) led to the more profound 'restlessness' in the populations it purported to serve. The extraordinary release of war-feeling in summer 1914 expresses a climacteric, at once the failure and the apotheosis, of mainstream European liberalism.

The motive idea of liberation finds its proof by refutation in the experience of imprisonment in the trench system, where the dream of a freedom of movement finds its awful inversion in stalemate, stasis, and paralytic terror. Again and again, the physical prepossession and emotional intensity of being closed in may be read as the representation of the negative space of the positive concept and mythology of the liberal freedom that initially brought them there. It is in terms of this absconded promise of liberalism that the event discovers its import and consequence in the history, memory and consciousness of post-Enlightenment Europe. The experience is represented in English poetry of the war with a variety and particularity that provide one index of its major imaginative importance.

This expansive feeling of release into the nationalist cause was probably most pronounced in its German version, where crowds supported the cause in proportions whose enormity would be recalled throughout the war as 'the spirit of 1914'.[13] Thus, it is no surprise that the representation of the German psyche by the English poet Herbert Read, in his 'Meditation of a Dying German Officer', reveals this as the compelling motive in his opponent, who is recalling the first days of his war, when

> I crossed the Fatherland, to take my place
> in the swift-wing'd swoop that all but ended
> the assay in one swift and agile venture.

But the words of this German officer also bring the representation of the whole European war under the aegis of the force that has compelled him:

> I have seen
> The heart of Europe send its beating blood

> like a blush over the world's pallid sphere
> calling it to one life, one order and one living.[14]

'When first this fury caught us, then / I vowed devotion to the rights of men', goes the explanation for the English version of the spirit of 1914 in the second part of this diptych, 'Meditation of a Waking English Officer', where the assignably liberal idealization of the political motives being claimed is the burden of the case for Read's English speaker. In his words, he

> would fight for peace once it came again
> from this unwilled war pass gallantly
> to wars of will and justice.[15]

The apologias Read's speaker offers here echo the idiolect of the English political war, but the political idealism is not without compulsion. The release experienced in the deliverance into war could be expressed through the available analogy of the spatial extension of empire. A civilian on the British side presents this feeling of fanciful expansion, authorizing the impulse Read's German speaker has expressed but in the familiar images of imperial duty: 'you and I / Dreamed greatly of an Empire in those days', May Wedderburn Cannan writes, 'Setting our feet upon laborious ways'. 'We planned a great Empire together, you and I', she indicates more expansively, 'Bound only by the sea'.[16] Although the fate of death for her lover provides one measure of the cost of this expansion, this is not a subject of direct reproach in the poem.

Other contributors to this record move between pro- and anti-war sentiments, but are more meaningfully examined for the report they leave of those experiences of deliverance and imprisonment in an extraordinary mixture of eloquence and bitterness. A soaring sense of liberation turns down into a paralytic terror of confinement, which presents the record of the war as an experience in the deeper cultural memory of Europe. This is a history that finds its site of primary revelation in the trench, which, as the locus of stalled action, presents itself as the place of the arrested dream of liberalism. The representations of this signal image in the cultural landscape of war may be read with a commensurate depth of resonance.

The enclosed space of the trench restricts but intensifies the sensory prospect in ways Siegfried Sassoon typifies in the poem he titles with the epithetical image of 'The Death Bed': 'He drowsed and was aware of silence heaped / Round him, unshaken as the steadfast walls'.[17] Where Sassoon has shifted the spatial imaginary of the trench into that of a field hospital ward, the experience of time is altered and stalled in ways that Edmund Blunden captures in the depiction of the daily ennui in his sardonically titled 'Preparations for Victory': 'Days or eternities like swelling waves / Surge on, and still we drudge in this dark maze', where 'The bombs and coils and cans by strings of slaves / Are borne to serve the coming day of days'; the limitation of variation in this rhyme scheme, with a single syllable repeating over four lines, provides a subtler image of the mechanical inanity of containment within the small world of the trench.[18] Change appears to be the possibility foregone with the contraction of time to the constraint of space, where the rituals of the day reiterate in ways Sassoon captures in the narrative of 'A Working Party'. 'Three hours ago he blundered up the trench, / Sliding and poising, groping with his boots', this story begins, taking the personage who 'tripped and lurched against the walls / With hands that pawed the sodden bags of chalk' into the completion of the three-hour cycle with the tersely worded notice of the body's return: 'Three hours ago he stumbled up the trench; / Now he will never walk that road again', now that 'He must be carried back, a jolting lump / Beyond all need of tenderness and care'. This circular pattern in the verse narrative conveys the impression of temporal enclosure, reinforcing the impressionistic connection between the experience of arrested motion in the trench and the closing down of temporal possibilities: within these earthly 'mounds of glimmering sand-bags, bleached with rain', Sassoon records in the most startling image of this poem, 'the slow silver moment died in dark'.[19] As the experience of temporality is distorted or distended from one's customary understanding of movement, the possibility of change is also foreclosed. This loss of the potential for alternate eventualities reads as the bleakest consequence among the casualties of liberalism in this war.

The to-and-fro scheme in Sassoon's narrative reads as a synecdoche as well for the larger tactical (if that is the word) pattern of back-and-forth motions across the small portions of contested terrain in the western front. Here the frustration of being closed in within the battle trench expands into the greater dimensionality of the open air and a proportionately stronger presentiment of despair. The return to sites formerly won, subsequently lost, then contested again: this is the paradigmatic memory Blunden revisits in 'Third Ypres', where, in recalling one of the primary sites in that pattern of murderous return, he depicts the longing for some transformative change. 'The War would end', goes the record of hope in this simulation of the soldier's speech:

> the Line was on the move,
> And at a bound the impassable was passed.
> We lay and waited with extravagant joy.
>
> Now dulls the day and chills; comes there no word
> From those who swept through our new lines to flood
> The lines beyond? but little comes ...[20]

The vertical space on the page opens to allow a hope for 'the impossible' (turning as the unspoken but irresistible sound-alike of 'the impassable') to resonate with all the pathos of the question afterward unanswered. 'But nothing happens', Wilfred Owen reiterates in a four-times repeated refrain in 'Exposure',[21] where the poet appropriately known as the most eloquent voice of poetic protest shows the preponderance of this common feeling – this sense of motion arrested within the quotidian stasis of the trench experience.

'An ecstasy of fumbling':[22] this stunning image, which Owen provided to depict the confusion an infantryman undergoes in trying to fit his gasmask in the face of an attack, brings its etymological memory – literally, 'out of this place' – into the spatial imaginary of the war experience. The experience of falling forward – all in all, a strangely exalted sense of losing control – recalls that now long-ago instigation of release into the expansive space of war. It is what remains of the exultation Herbert Read remembers for his dying German officer's experience of the spirit during the early days of this war: 'I have lived in the ecstasy of battle'.[23] The dream of freedom in that 'ecstasy' has diminished into the vertigo of 'fumbling'. The promise of liberation in the longer story of the history of liberalism has contracted accordingly.

The Modernist Turn

A consensus understanding represents the Great War of 1914–1918 as the signal episode of artistic modernism. In this account, the war stands as a watershed event in cultural as well as political history. Dividing the nineteenth from the twentieth centuries, it provides the shaping occasion for artists who take novelty, invention and revolutionary energy as their establishing aim and motive. The experimental verve of literary modernism was of course well launched before 1914, and so a more refined understanding of the meaning of 'modernism' needs to be established if we are to understand the special connection between the cultural experience of war and the poetic work we bring under this special heading.

Modern*ism*: the suffix provides the sense of an intensified version of the root meaning of the Latin 'modo' – 'today', 'now' or, most accurately, 'just now'. Accordingly, 'modernism' suggests an awareness of a more than usually acute temporal present, all in all, a consciousness of living in a Now distinctly and even overwhelmingly different from a Then. It is the recognition of this difference in history that is the establishing awareness of a modernist representation of wartime. If the imaginative values of cultural liberalism have been stressed in ways that the poetry of experiential report has revealed, the political traditions of the English Liberal Party also undergo a crisis in wartime. The poets of English modernism take this crisis as a moment of critical historical difference; that is, as their own defining moment as modernists.

The crisis in English liberalism in wartime turned on the tension between longstanding principles of intellectual liberalism and recent exigencies of international politics. The longer tradition, which lived still in the memory of the great Victorian Prime Minister W.E. Gladstone, preserved the ethic and method of rationalism at moral liberty: the decision to go to war turned essentially on the freely reasoned choice of ethical principle. On the other side, a new spirit of realpolitik understood the need to operate in alliance with other European states: these alliances might require involvement in hostilities, but such engagements could hardly be appealed openly to Gladstonian codes. Since 1906, the most powerful positions within the Liberal government were held by representatives of the newer sensibility – Prime Minister H.H. Asquith and his Foreign Secretary Sir Edward Grey – but the logic of foreign policy was still controlled in its public discussions by Gladstonian protocols. In this situation, Asquith and Grey needed to keep private their alliance-building with France and Russia. Officially, they continued to deny the existence of these 'secret agreements' (so dubbed by an already suspicious public), at least until early August 1914, when the network of European connections was activated.[24] This war must suddenly be understood as an urgent moral necessity and, indeed, as the conclusion of an ethically informed process of free reasoning. The doubtfulness of this account opened as a watershed in the cultural history of political England and, in this particular and local manifestation, in post-Reformation Europe, whose values of public reason were enshrined in Gladstone's protocols. The editorials and reports on Parliament in Liberal journalism became the space of the most extraordinary exertions in political rhetoric and case making. The forced and contorted logic left a record of somber preposterousness, while the actual consequences of this reason-seemingness gives the performance an air of darkening farce.[25] It is to this particular tone of the times that the poetry of modernism responds with a sense of defining timeliness.

'Out-weariers of Apollo will, as we know, continue their Martian generalities'.[26] Thus, in *Homage to Sextus Propertius* (1919), a creative translation of the Roman poet that Ezra Pound worked on through the last two years of the war, the classical deity of logic as well as of music is invoked as the muse of these days, where the interlingual play orchestrates Pound's own report of current political culture. Military *generals* and political 'generalities' are not related etymologically, but contextually, circumstantially, in a Liberal government whose reasoning for war wears Apollo out by a logic as compromised as the gamey word play of this translation.

This overture provides a key to the tonal wit of the *Propertius* sequence. Its conceit involves a kind of reason-seeming nonsense, which features an interplay between an archly rationalist syntax and a wittily impenetrable vocabulary. The persona of the classics translator thus demonstrates a declarative knowingness about the *materia poetica*, moving easily through a progression of apparently factual statements as logical, commonsensical propositions of obvious knowledge, but these allusions to chronicle legend and literary fable leave most readers in the darker depths of the Mediterranean antiquity from which they are fetched:

> For Orpheus tamed the wild beasts—
> > and held up the Threician river;
> And Cithaeron shook up the rocks by Thebes
> > and danced them into a bulwark at his pleasure,
> And you, O Polyphemus? Did harsh Galatea almost
> Turn to your dripping horses, because of a tune, under Aetna?
> We must look into the matter.[27]

The words Pound interpolates into his Latin original reveal the pressure he is exerting in the service of this tone of antic rationality.[28] 'For', to begin with: the conjunction establishes the expectation of cause-and-effect sequence, some presentiment of commonsense meanings, which Pound complements with those reassuring words of common speech. He steadily undercuts this promise, however, by enforcing the awareness that we do not know these mythological personages very well, if at all. Who, most of us must ask, was Galatea? And how close did she get when she '*almost*' turned to the horses of Polyphemus? That specifying adverb is Pound's interpolation, whose blank space in the Latin original reveals the hollowness of his own (carefully) concocted knowledgeability.

Where Pound's conceit echoes to the background sound of these times and represents a new register in his developing idiom, the pressure this moment exerts on his verse produces an equally novel accomplishment in the work of his compatriot and modernist accomplice, T.S. Eliot. The signature measure of the poetry Eliot wrote in wartime and the early post-war period is the quatrain form, otherwise unprecedented in his earlier oeuvre. Within its tightly closed structures, his metrical progressions could shape to an impression of regimented thought. By the same token, and by virtue of a cadence verging on the mechanical and a rhyme scheme on the hypnotic and at times idiotic, the deliberation runs on its well-paced feet straight into the intense inane. This voice is witnessed in poems as well known as 'Mr. Eliot's Sunday Morning Service', 'A Cooking Egg', and 'Whispers of Immortality'. A clear sign of the connection between the novel prosody of these quatrain poems and the forced logic of the Liberal war comes in the earliest poem in this measure, which takes Liberal war journalism as its target and point of mimicry.

'Airs of Palestine, No. 2' addresses the figure of John Spender, editor of *Westminster Gazette*, which had helped to promulgate Liberal war reasoning:

> God from a Cloud to Spender spoke
> And breathed command: 'Take thou this Rod,
> And smite therewith the living Rock';
> And Spender hearkened unto God ...
>
> They are redeemed from heresies
> And all their frowardness forget;
> And scales are fallen from their eyes
> Thanks to the Westminster Gazette.[29]

The hurdy-gurdy rhymes and rigmarole rhythms speak a sort of doggerel logic, a prosody that caricatures the quality of thought in much of the political war journalism. This is a register charged with the historical content and depth of its particular moment in local political culture, and it provides a tuning fork for the whole range of quatrain verse that Eliot would author in wartime and post-war London.

The poem Eliot was writing at the official end of the war, when the Versailles Treaty was being signed, presents its own conclusive summary of the import of the story which the modernist poetry of this event has recorded. 'Gerontion': the 'little old man' of the title speaks an extended monologue, which presents a character-in-voice of contemporary liberalism in its senescence. This is a generation that has authored in words a war its old men have not fought in body, generating the opposition between old and young men that was written into the literature as an enduring memory of this event. Eliot's title personage speaks for that older generation in the opening lines, admitting his inactivity in the recent war and offering an apologia in the attitudes of a verbal ritual, at once well-rehearsed and ill-performed:

> I was neither at the hot gates
> Nor fought in the warm rain
> Nor knee deep in the salt marsh, heaving a cutlass,
> Bitten by flies, fought.[30]

The strenuous extremity of war reasoning in partisan Liberal discourse is the performance Eliot encores in this overture in the extraordinary pressure he places on the sense-making gestures of this sentence. Its clausal construction projects the progressive discriminations of verbal reason – 'neither /

Nor / Nor' – as its stipulating spirit, its motivating action. The ambitious program and plan of a thrice-suspended period turns into the wreckage its phrasal sequence actually makes of it in the end, however. The rhetorical fiction which an older Liberal ideologue had denominated as 'the grand syllogism of history' has devolved into the unlovely muddle of the final line. This is the same 'History' which, in the well-known meditation in the central section of this poem, presents a maze of 'cunning passages' as a trope not only of the confusions of experience in historical time, nor as an image alone of the map of trenches that had been etched into the spatial imaginary of every European.[31] This is also and most of all a figure for the many 'cunning passages' in which the political warrant of this Liberal war was writ, and which the modernist poetry of the war represents at once in a heckling echo and creative counter rhythm.

While these modernist poets obviously composed in circumstances radically different to those of the combatant poets, we must challenge the longstanding notion that first-hand military experience is the test and requirement of genuineness in the poetic record. From the political capital of London no less than from the closed space of the trenches, the crises of liberalism – pan-European in background and scale and English in its local inflections – provide a language of varied but shared imaginative understandings. Heard together, these poets provide a record of this experience in its larger coherence and broader import.

NOTES

1   Philip Larkin, 'MCMXIV', in Anthony Thwaite ed. *Collected Poems* (1988; rev. London: Faber, 1990), 127–8.
2   George Dangerfield, *The Strange Death of Liberal England: 1910–1914* (1935; rpt. New York: Putnam, 1980).
3   'Georgian Poetry', *Times Literary Supplement* [Hereafter *TLS*], 27 February 1913, 81.
4   A.C. Benson, 'Georgian Poetry', *Cambridge Magazine*, 18 January 1913, 209–10.
5   'Georgian Poetry', *TLS*, 81.
6   Rupert Brooke, 'Peace', in *1914 and Other Poems* (London: Sidgwick and Jackson, 1915), 11.
7   Julian Grenfell, 'Into Battle', in Jon Silkin ed. *The Penguin Book of First World War Poetry* (1979; 2nd ed., rev. London: Penguin, 1996), 83–4. Most of the war poems cited in this essay, except otherwise stated, appear in this anthology, which will be referenced subsequently as *PBFWWP*.
8   Brooke, 'The Soldier', *PBFWWP*, 81–2.
9   Ivor Gurney, 'To His Love', in P.J. Kavanagh ed. *Collected Poems* (Manchester: Carcanet, 2004), 21.
10   Ibid.

11 Gurney, 'Strange Hells', *Collected Poems*, 141.

12 In using a lower case designation for 'liberalism', I am referring to a broadly cultural attitude or frame of mind; an upper case designation will refer subsequently to the Liberal Party in England.

13 A good account of the German circumstance comes from Modris Eksteins, *Rites of Spring: The Great War and the Birth of the Modern Age* (Boston: Houghton Mifflin, 1989), 54–89.

14 Herbert Read, 'Meditation of a Dying German Officer' in his sequence 'The End of a War', *PBFWWP*, 163.

15 Read, 'Meditations of a Waking English Officer' in 'The End of a War', *PBFWWP*, 175.

16 May Wedderburn Cannan, 'Lamplight', *PBFWWP*, 151.

17 Siegfried Sassoon, 'The Death-Bed', in *The War Poems of Siegfried Sassoon* [Hereafter *War Poems*], introduced and arranged by Rupert Hart-Davis (London: Faber, 1983), 52.

18 Edmund Blunden, 'Preparations for Victory', *PBFWWP*, 103.

19 Sassoon, 'A Working Party', in *War Poems*, 26.

20 Blunden, 'Third Ypres', *PBFWWP*, 123. Emphasis added to the title in the text. The Ypres battles formed a recurring contest along a variegated front which, during the war, was called Passchendaele. 'Third Ypres' was the name given to a particular set of engagements later in 1921, when the British Battles Nomenclature Committee published its report, the year before Blunden's poem was published. I am grateful to Jonathan Sawday for the background information.

21 Owen, 'Exposure', in Jon Stallworthy ed. *The Poems of Wilfred Owen* [Hereafter *Poems*](London: Chatto, 1983), 162–3.

22 Owen, 'Dulce et Decorum Est', in *Poems*, 117.

23 Read, 'Meditations of a Dying German Officer', *PBFWWP*, 163.

24 The existence of these 'secret agreements' and the influence they exert on British policy constitute the subject of the major exposé by the director of the Union of Democratic Control (of foreign policy), E.D. Morel, *Truth and the War* (London: National Labour Press, 1916), esp. 35–41, 273–300.

25 I have reconstructed this crisis in the political and intellectual history of English liberalism in *The Great War and the Language of Modernism* (New York: Oxford University Press, 2003), esp. 23–47.

26 Ezra Pound, *Homage to Sextus Propertius,* in Lea Baechler and A. Walton Litz eds. *Personae: The Collected Shorter Poems of Ezra Pound* (New York: New Directions, 1990), 205.

27 *Personae*, 206.

28 The relevant texts of Propertius's Latin and a standard prose translation are provided by K.K. Ruthven, *A Guide to Ezra Pound's 'Personae' 1926* (Berkeley: University of California Press, 1969).

29 T.S. Eliot, 'Airs of Palestine, No. 2', in Christopher Ricks ed. *Inventions of the March Hare: Poems 1909–1917* (New York: Harcourt Brace, 1996), 84–5.

30 Eliot, 'Gerontion', in *Collected Poems 1909–1962* (New York: Harcourt Brace, 1968), 29.

31 Eliot, 'Gerontion', 30.

2

PETER HOWARTH

Poetic Form and the First World War

The story of the First World War poets is often told as a move from idealism to realism, without quite realising what those terms imply for a poet's form. When we speak of soldier poets' idealism in an everyday sense, we usually mean their deluded early hopes that this war was an honourable affair, whose trial by combat would reward those in the right. Although some death was likely, it would be classically heroic or somehow justified through a Christian moral economy of 'sacrifice' for national honour or the common good. In formal terms, this idealism is linked to bad poetry: a diction full of abstract moralising, or medieval-chivalric vocabulary, or the jauntiness of the end-of-the-pier show, all moulded into overly familiar rhythmic templates. By realism, we usually mean writing which was based on bitter experience, writing which took the wretched daily conditions of fighting soldiers as war's real truth, rather than trying to justify those conditions through appeals to higher ideals of personal valour or national honour. We mean also the recognition that an industrialised war was utterly indifferent to who and how it killed, and that it brutalised all who fought in it. We also imply that good poetry should *reflect* this ugliness and purposelessness in its form. Its vocabulary should convey direct observation rather than overlaying the real mess with figurative language, while its rhythms and silences should present those truths without giving an aesthetic order to events which could never be balanced or justified in moral terms.

Unfortunately, this version of poetic realism puts the attitudes of many of the most famous First World War poets badly out of kilter with their form. Rosenberg's 'Dead Man's Dump' is famous for its brutally inert registration of 'A man's brains splattered on / A stretcher-bearer's face', but the lines immediately preceding it (which he subsequently omitted) have the luxuriant gothic of much of his work:

> Maniac Earth! howling and flying, your bowel
> Seared by the jagged fire, the iron love,

> The impetuous storm of savage love.
> Dark Earth! Dark heavens! swinging in chemic smoke,
> What dead are born when you kiss each soundless soul
> With lightning and thunder from your mined heart,
> Which man's self dug, and his blind fingers loosed?[1]

While Sassoon's vocabulary is more consistently this-worldly, he wraps up his exposés of the devastating effects of war on soldier's psyches with perfect rhythmic neatness. Wilfred Owen experiments ceaselessly with conspicuously artificial rhyme. Meanwhile, the great bulk of war poetry by combatants and non-combatants alike is written in rhythms and genres whose patterns long preceded the war. If realism is taken to mean direct, unillusioned observation of the catastrophe of First World War combat, then the artificial forms of its poets can only be means to deflect or skirt around those observations.

Well, naturally, it might be said. The war involved such profound changes to our sense of national good and of aesthetic value that they could never be fully recognised by those in the middle of it. Like the frontline troops some of them were, poets were dealing with a new kind of war using yesterday's tactics and equipment. Many of them were the products of the new state education system, whose consistent advice – together with the manuals of instruction the poets bought to improve themselves afterwards – was that prosody replicated an ideal, disciplined, civilised order. 'If the technical art of poetry consists in making patterns out of language', one began, 'the substantial and vital function of poetry will be analogous; it will be to make patterns out of life'.[2] Brewer's *Orthometry*, which Owen prepped himself on, told him that real poetry 'chooses picturesque images and quaint words and epithets that would be out of place in prosaic description ... many words protected by poetic association from vulgar use'.[3] If poetry is supposed to use 'high' diction and its forms always to pattern experience, it will always struggle not to turn the physical and moral mess of the war into something more coherent than it was. Even if it conveys the awfulness of particular experiences, the way it orders them will inevitably provide aesthetic compensation for what should remain uncompensatable. This is the worry behind Edward Thomas's innocuous-sounding sonnet, 'February Afternoon':

> Men heard this roar of parleying starlings, saw,
> A thousand years ago even as now,
> Black rooks with white gulls following the plough
> So that the first are last until a caw
> Commands that last are first again, – a law

Which was of old when one, like me, dreamed how
A thousand years might dust lie on his brow
Yet thus would birds do between hedge and shaw.

Time swims before me, making as a day
A thousand years, while the broad ploughland oak
Roars mill-like and men strike and bear the stroke
Of war as ever, audacious or resigned,
And God still sits aloft in the array
That we have wrought him, stone-deaf and stone-blind.[4]

The opening eight lines appear to be about the unchanging countryside, quietly ironising the self-importance of human scales of time. Only when the word 'war' enters in line 12 do we realise that this is the word which has been haunting the innocent 'shaw' and 'caw' all along, and has been there, too, in the sound of 'broad' and 'roar', and their imagery of the wind's angry blast sweeping everything down to darkness, like a shell barrage. The war is ever-present in Thomas's countryside walks, both because the land is depopulated by military service, and because he is walking there in uniform himself, remembering the past and anticipating his own death by imagining the scene persisting after he is gone. But Thomas's process of wry self-resignation is itself rebuked by the final two lines. It is not merely blaming our version of God for being deaf and blind to human suffering, but articulating an anxiety that, by taking a God's-eye view ('making as a day / A thousand years' is God's prerogative in 2 Peter 3:8), Thomas has been somehow deafening and blinding himself to the war, too. Taking the long view to ironise present anxieties – seeing, for example, the Day of Judgment when the 'last shall be first' as somehow already here in the rooks and gulls – has been functioning as a kind of self-protection, and the hint is that the neatness and antiquity of the sonnet form can only be part of that deflection. The balances internal to the form itself can only render the war less violent than it really is. So what we see in much First World War verse is the struggle of older forms with a reality which cannot be 'contained' by them, and with which twentieth-century poetics spent much of its time trying to catch up. It follows that only modernist fragmentation can really convey the derangements of the war on the psyche, or the abandonment of any moral scheme of overall justification for war.

But the post-war success of more fragmented poems did not mean that they *stopped* having to do the work of moral justification previously associated with high-flown vocabulary and the forms sanctioned by custom and education. Take Robert Nichols's 'The Assault', the centre of a sequence of poems written in various metrical forms, from blank verse to ballad metre, changing with the mixed emotions of its protagonist: a soldier going up towards the front line, into attack, and then back to billets. At the moment of the assault, everything is forgotten but the present:

> Go on. Go.
> Deafness. Numbness. The loudening tornado.
> Bullets. Mud. Stumbling and skating.
> My voice's strangled shout:
> *'Steady pace, boys!'*
> The still light: gladness.
> *'Look, sir. Look out!'*
> Ha! ha! Bunched figures waiting.
> Revolver levelled quick!
> Flick! Flick!
> Red as blood.
> Germans. Germans.
> Good! O good!
> Cool madness.[5]

The free-verse lines and telegraphic syntax convey the white-hot urgency of the situation, without any attempt to steady the pace, reflect and so begin any kind of self-justification. Still, the soldier seems to be sensing himself as if from outside, hearing his own voice, noticing 'bullets' and 'deafness' as if they were nothing to do with him, and the self-conscious effect is magnified by the unpredictable but insistent rhyme. When one realises that 'madness' has long been prepared for by 'gladness', the immediacy itself looks as staged as any sonnet – indeed, Nichols actually begins the whole volume with lengthy quotations from another manual of verse construction to justify his own prosody. However, the fact that the events are being re-staged as if live from the battlefield does not so much take the reader to the scene as reveal the moral question we sense is missing: the gleeful ending has an unfortunate feel of the boys' action comic because it refuses to do any reflection. This messy assault *is* morally incoherent, a realist might reply: under extreme pressure, the soldier's bloodlust is up. But even the need to write a poem whose ending is so sudden and undirected reveals the moral pressure in the act of writing a poem about war at all. The demand for 'realism' is itself a moral demand, resting on principles of honesty and authenticity no less ideal than the ideals of loyalty and group sacrifice they displaced.

So while it is true that the experimental poetics of the 1920s and 1930s allowed profound aspects of the war experience to be recognised in ways quite impossible for more formally patterned verse, there is a much more deep-seated problem with making that opposition between real and ideal the test of a war poem's form. Insisting on realism as the poet's primary criterion implies that the experience comes as itself first of all, and must then be translated into the artificial frame of the poem. But the word 'experience' itself comes from the Latin *experiri*, 'to try, to put to the test' (OED), because the 'pure present' itself must always be altered by consciousness and memory, never mind by being put in a poem. No one experienced the war without a cultural framework of ideals already there, be that the public school ethos of Homeric valour, or the military drill of Empire day (in which primary school children chanted Kipling while marching in unison), or the Tolstoy-inspired repulsion towards armed conflict among the central-European Jewish immigrants to Whitechapel, including the parents of Isaac Rosenberg and John Rodker. One of the tasks of the poets' more obviously artificial forms was to make more evident those less-obvious frameworks already shaping people's perceptions. They do this through quotation and satire, of course, but also through the techniques which draw one's attention to details, experiences or emotions unassimilated by people's culturally-formed habits of attention. Everyone knows the official *Battle of the Somme* film was propaganda, but as Owen wrote to his mother, its problem was also being a film:

> I have not seen any dead. I have done worse. In the dank air I have *perceived* it, and in the darkness, *felt*. Those 'Somme Pictures' are the laughing stock of the army – like the trenches on exhibition in Kensington.[6]

Almost as a rebuttal to such safely distant 'Pictures', he later wrote to Sassoon, 'Catalogue? Photograph? Can you photograph the crimson-hot iron as it cools from smelting? That is what Jones's blood looked like, and felt like. My senses are charred'.[7] It was partly because the memories were so scorching that Owen found composed forms so necessary. The chances and collisions involved in composing to a pattern became a means to *explore* experience otherwise unavailable to consciousness because it was too frightening.

While modernist techniques may record war's devastation more vividly than a set form, then, the war was so overwhelming an experience that for many, the defensive artifice of regular prosody testifies just as clearly to its threatening presence. Writing from his dugout, Gurney thought that Sassoon 'cannot fully manage his material as yet', and then offered an excuse for the vital discrepancy between the urgency of Sassoon's protest and his artistic forms:

> But you must remember that a lot of this has been written to free himself from circumstance. They are charms to magic him out of the present. Cold feet, lice, sense of fear – all these are spurs to create Joy to such as he; since Beauty is the only comfort.[8]

The inappropriateness of the forms themselves speaks of the war from which they seek relief. Take Archibald Bowman's *Sonnets from a Prison-Camp,* written between April and August 1918 from the prisoner-of-war (POW) camps at Rastatt and Hesepe. Bowman's foreword remarks that '[i]t is no mere poetical exaggeration to say that in the first days of captivity at least, the writing of sonnets was a labour that "stood between my soul and madness"'.[9] Nevertheless, the sonnet forms Bowman used as a device for mental escape, each one dated and placed like a diary entry, become technical explorations of the freedoms available for the prisoner, updating Wordsworth's metaphor of the sonnet's 'plot of scanty ground' to the yard Bowman is walking:

> Within these cages day by day we pace
> The bitter shortness of the meted span.[10]

By insisting throughout on using the repeated rhymes of the Petrarchan sonnet, so difficult to attain in English, Bowman's volume describes captivity, but attempts an inner act of regaining freedom by choosing his own limitations, for as Wordsworth's sonnet 'Nuns Fret Not' says, 'the prison, unto which we doom / Ourselves, no prison is'.[11] It is partly because most people's experience of national mobilisation, either as combatants or non-combatants, was of compulsion, frustration, unexpected comradeship and unwanted results, that an unsuitable form could itself *become* right nonetheless, as in this anonymous elegy published in *The Wipers Times*:

> Just one more cross by a strafed road-side,
> With its G.R.C., and a name for guide,
> But it's only myself who has lost a friend,
> And though I may fight through to the end,
> No dug-out or billet will be the same,
> All pals can only be pals in name,
> But we'll carry on till the end of the game
> Because you lie there.[12]

The prosody and diction are clumsy, but clumsy because the writing itself is trying to 'carry on to the end of the game', too. In its mix of aspiration, team spirit and compulsion, one might say that this poem's awkwardness is utterly realistic.

It is also testimony to the different public work that poetry had to perform at the time. War poetry is written not only for the public record, but for the survivor's own psychic needs. The neatly arranged lines of epitaphs and elegies are part of the process of segregating the living from the dead – especially important in the trench zone where this often did not physically happen – and of inviting others to share your grief. Binding the community together around the loss, they can also defiantly draw the outsider's attention to the community's sense of social injustice.[13] Owen's 'Anthem For Doomed Youth' is a small sonnet, not a full-scale anthem, because the public rites for the dead are being performed by the shells rather than at home, where the drawn-down blinds of houses mimic the lowered eyes of mourners turning away from others' gazes. But Owen told his mother that Sassoon had 'supplied the title "Anthem", just what I meant it to be', which implies he deliberately gave this public, elegaic role to the sonnet to emphasise its littleness – and oddness – amid what should have been the huge cathedral ceremonies of national grief.[14] In a situation where everyone had lost somebody, where all public statements about the war mattered because they invoked something painful and private to each hearer, the forms of war poems are invitations to public recognition, and a means of flouting it. To disturb the form is not only to do justice to the violence of individual experiences, but to pick away at the shared faith combatants and non-combatants had in each other, and occasionally to suggest new kinds of public sympathy which rerouted official channels. Yet this, as much as a more honest recreation of trench experience, was an essential motivation for modernist formal innovations in war poetry, too.

Modernist Form and Public Dissent

The great majority of poems penned by serving soldiers were written in simple regular forms, and a surprisingly large number of these are comic or semi-comic. Their humour comes from being circulated between men needing to cheer each other up, and from the need to establish group loyalty by making jokes that outsiders could never make without being appallingly insensitive. Following the lead of Kipling's *Barrack-Room Ballads*, much of the poetry written for this soldier audience sounds like the basis for a mess-hall turn or camp entertainment, and its rhythms have Kipling's mixed quality of jollity and frogmarching which their content frequently complains about. Any attempt to write in the modern techniques of free verse would completely miss this sense of participation, as the topical satirist Hampden Gordon suggested in 'Concert':

> Then a Voice …
> Oh dear me, what a Voice!
> And the hoarse applause of scores of paws on paws;
> Because
> Of the sweet politeness of them,
> And the great good nature of them,
> And also because a man can only die once…
> Generally speaking.[15]

By suspending rhythmic expectations, Gordon implies, free verse misses any opportunity for real connection with the audience. When serious free-verse poems are written about the war, then, their form implies a deliberate affront to the norms of shared performance, mutual encouragement and entertainment which kept the troops engaged, as with the Imagist-affiliated Frederic Manning's contemptuous little 'Grotesque':

> And we,
> Sitting with streaming eyes in the acrid smoke,
> That murks our foul, damp billet,
> Chant bitterly, with raucous voices
> As a choir of frogs
> In hideous irony, our patriotic songs.[16]

Corporate song shores up the same culture that damns the platoon; only free verse allows the inwardly free to preserve themselves (and Manning's sly reference to Aristophanes's anti-war comedy *The Frogs* is precisely what the others in the billet would never get). Mary Borden's 'The Song of the Mud' ironically uses Whitman's expansive American free-verse line to suggest how the Flanders mud has become the war's all-embracing substance, uniting everyone and everything by sucking them into it. As her lines gather impetus and then trail off, so does any sense of independent motion:

It has drowned our men.
Its monstrous distended belly reeks with the undigested dead.
Our men have gone into it, sinking slowly, and struggling and slowly disappearing.
Our fine men, our brave, strong, young men;
... Into its darkness, its thickness, its silence.
Slowly, irresistably, it drew them down, sucked them down,
And they were drowned in thick, bitter, heaving mud.
Now it hides them, Oh, so many of them!
Under its smooth glistening surface it is hiding them blandly.
There is not a trace of them.
There is no mark where they went down.
The mute enormous mouth of the mud has closed over them.[17]

Whitman's embrace of America's diversity always has an erotic, sensual dimension to it, which here become the mud's kiss of death. But Borden's plain repetitions of 'them' and 'there' suggests that surrounded by this morass, the poet's mind, too, can go nowhere else but with the soldiers, sucked back down into the mud.

Indeed, a great many modernist innovations in poetic form can be seen as a perfect analogue for war experience. The blasts and sudden collisions in rhythm and imagery; the syntax which moves away from individual agency, or personal identity; the freezing of time and rational causation into the timelessness of apocalypse or the eternal haunting of the unburied dead; the inability to see ahead, living instead moment by moment, detail by detail; all these are essential structural features of *The Waste Land*, and of the First World War wastelands it draws on, psychic and geographical. In his introduction to David Jones's modernist war poem *In Parenthesis* (1936), Eliot put Jones in company with himself, Joyce and Pound because 'the lives of all of us were altered by that War, but David Jones is the only one to have fought in it' (viii), implying that Jones had belatedly provided a first-person correlative for the aesthetic effects that Eliot, Pound and Joyce's form had earlier intuited, or channelled.[18] As well as the shocks and alarms of violent bombardment, Jones's modernist use of prose extracts connects to the 'penetrating tedium' of the trench landscape, too:

> The untidied squalor of the loveless scene spread far horizontally, imaging unnamed discomfort, sordid and deprived as ill-kept hen-runs that back on sidings on wet weekdays where wasteland meets environs and punctured bins ooze canned-meats discarded, tyres to rot, derelict slow-weathered iron-ware disintegrates between factory-end and nettle-bed.[19]

It is not clear whether we are still in France or the industrial cities which lie behind the war, because they are so alike; those 'punctured bins', for instance, are both ex-urban decay and – within the poem – anticipations of dead soldier's bodies fed on terrible rations, or the smashed tanks spilling out their inhabitants. No wonder the degrading anonymity, aimlessness and filthy conditions could only be experienced by many officers as their own enforced proletarianisation.[20]

But modernism's interest in overlaying the war with other experiences, times and places in this manner means that First World War trench experience is not allowed to become the real point of historical grounding from which all its techniques stem. Jones overdubs his own forward march with semi-mythical Celtic warriors, Viking myth and medieval mystery plays to suggest that, psychically, he was playing his part in a soldier archetype which long predated him. To Paul Fussell, that meant Jones had 'romanticized the war', but the identification with Celtic and Norse sources might equally signify Jones's sense of his fight being *with* the English, and their industrialism, as much as for them.[21] Rather than address the war directly, Pound's *Cathay* (1915) translates/adapts Rihaku's poems about homesick soldiers from eighth-century China, while H.D. used the choruses from Euripides's *Iphigenia in Aulis* to explore the complex attraction of women to violence, and their own sacrifice, which was currently propping up the war effort. At the beginning, an unnamed voyeur comes across the massed Greek army:

> I crept through the woods
> Between the altars:
> Artemis haunts the place.
> Shame, scarlet, fresh-opened – a flower,
> Strikes across my face.
> And sudden – light upon shields,
> Low huts – the armed Greeks,
> Circles of horses.
> I have longed for this.[22]

Why she blushes is not at first apparent, nor why the flower 'strikes'. It is only when we have heard about the 'bright stain' of blood (13) that the Greeks will leave on the stones of Troy, and then the 'stain' (19) of the sacrifice of Iphigenia to Artemis for Agamemnon's war effort, that the unspoken sexual excitement underlying female sacrifice and male slaughter can be intuited. Like *Cathay*, H.D.'s short, fragmented lines leave their internal logics and their connections with the present war for their reader to pick up in the process of reading, because only by such indirect 'rhymes' – between Greek and Trojan, between then and now – can readers be distracted from the overwhelming emotional pressure to displace blame onto the enemy, and enabled to intuit their own aggression. If the worlds of China or Greece are far from the minds of most people in a war, the high-cultural alienation that these modernist works embody nevertheless contains a paradoxical identification with veterans like H.D.'s husband Richard Aldington, who, having been to the waste lands, are also unable to reintegrate back into the everyday.

Common Forms and Public Mourning

Modernist poets were not the only ones to reframe war experience, however. As James Winn remarks, the 'formal ordering of verse and the echoing of previous poems are ways for poets to close or contain the horror, to assert control over the uncontrollable'.[23] Daniel Hipp has argued that poems like 'The Sentry' or 'Mental Cases' emerged from Owen's own process of therapy, deliberately re-entering the past in order to free himself through the process of writing them into form.[24] But the war's uncontainable spread meant success was not at all inevitable, as the friction between set forms and the experience they deal with implies. After comforting himself the whole war through with the thought of being able to get back to composing music about his beloved Gloucestershire, Ivor Gurney found himself uncomfortable in civilian company, unable to settle or hold down a job, restlessly walking like the soldier he had been in 'rainy midnight', and still promising himself relief:

> Fields for a while longer, then, O soul
> A curtained room close shut against the rime –
> Where shall float music, voice or violin's
> Denial passionate of the frozen time.[25]

This stanza's ostensible contrast between musical warmth and frozen exile is undercut by the homophonic link between rime and rhyme, as if the making of rhymes like this one belonged to the frozen time of Gurney's war experiences now repeating themselves in his despair. The making of rhyme and half-rhyme became Gurney's means to make the past present again in much of the quirky poetry that followed. In 'Laventie', the insistent internal rhymes bring back profound and incongruous details one after the other, while the syntax holding self and situation or then and now in place begins to give way:

> The letters written there, and received there,
> Books, cakes, cigarettes in a parish of famine,
> And leaks in rainy times with general all-damning.
> The crater, and carrying of gas cylinders on two sticks
> (Pain past comparison and far past right agony gone)
> Strained hopelessly of heart and frame at first fix.
>
> Café-au-lait in dug-outs on Tommies' cookers,
> Cursed minniewerfs, thirst in eighteen-hour summer.
> The Australian miners clayed, and the being afraid
> Before strafes, sultry August dusk time than death dumber.[26]

The sound-chains of books / cakes / leaks / sticks / fix, cursed / minniewerfs / thirst, or Australian / clayed / afraid / strafes link disparate inner sensations, external events and remote details together, the form bringing back memories in the writing. Gurney's frequent use of unpredictably stretched half-rhyme – 'tavern' and 'recovering' in 'Robecq Again' – or the way he will break a line short to reveal a rhyme, like that between 'as' and 'space' in 'That Centre of Old', makes these memories feel like the mixture of effort and surprise they were. 'This is not a happy thought', as the second poem recalling 'Riez Bailleul' says, 'but a glimpse most strangely / Forced from the past, to hide this pain and work myself free / From present things'.[27] Writing by now from inside the asylum, Gurney's forced glimpses become a means to escape back into a time in which he was once slightly more whole – and yet the memories of longing to be free from the noise of the guns then instantly speak of his confined state now, without foreseeable release, and his continuing inward mental bombardment. The past is bringing back the present as the present is bringing back the past, and Gurney's war never stops.

Involving a formal 'frame' with the experiences like this also invites questions about the social purpose of that form. For as Wilfred Owen's doctor, Arthur Brock, encouraged him to see, a form's therapeutic significance emerges not only in the way it reframes its interior 'content', but the social surroundings it brings into that reframing. To Brock, 'shell-shock' symptoms were not merely private trauma, but 'were in essence extreme instances of the dissociation or separatism of … pre-war conditions', the dehumanised, atomised society of nineteenth-century industrial capitalism.[28] Brock's cure was re-association by resocialisation: the sufferer needed to do some work, to go out in public, to immerse himself in a common life, and so re-establish a dynamic relation between 'organism and his environment, the interplay between men's soul and the *genius loci*'.[29] He also saw a profound parallel between the influenza epidemic of 1918 and the hyperactive immune systems of defensive individuals, or nations:

> Just as ergophobia and refusal to face facts in the moral field lead to undigested complexes (foreign bodies) in the sub-conscious mind, so apparently with these bacteria; refused admittance as guests, they force themselves in as enemies.[30]

Owen's therapy, then, could never mean just reincorporating private memories into poems, but using poetry to move away from the them-and-us thinking of the entire war. The phrase 'strange friend' in 'Strange Meeting' is not only Owen's means to bridge German and English hostilities or homo/heterosexual ones, but a description of the consonantal rhyme technique he was developing, where rhyme words are recognisable in each other but remain assymetric, metamorphosing into each other rather than coincidentally positioned in a manner entirely appropriate to his mobile sympathies. And 'strange friend' also describes his own public position in writing back to the British public, because for all his bitter criticism of the home front, Owen does not position himself as its enemy. Like many disillusioned veterans, his poems criticise civilian indifference, like the warm citizen who never thinks of the soldiers who gave him his cozy peace in 'Miners', or the reference to soldiers as 'secret men who know their secret safe', of 'Smile, Smile, Smile'. But in each case, Owen's act in writing takes him out of their ranks, too. Syntactically, it is Owen's 'I' who is in the chair in 'Miners', and *he* is certainly not keeping much secret about the war. 'Why speak not they of comrades that went under?', asks the final line of 'Spring Offensive', but this is just what Owen's poem is doing. Owen knew he could not carry on a war with non-combatants in the name of seeking peace.

Indeed, opposing the war without sustaining it at another level was perhaps the challenge the First World War brought to poetic form. As the scale of the waste of human life became clearer, every writer or reader was brought up sharp against the difference between their loss and the public justifications for it. But however realistic one's account of the mess, just writing a poem at all would involve questions about making an art out of other people's suffering, involving the whole relationship of form to content in the problem of writing about war without formally harmonising or balancing it in some way. Vandiver's study of classically trained poets in the First World War quotes the sestet of a post-war sonnet by Anthony de Candole which is groping towards the issue:

> And yet, behind the strident howling blast,
> The blinding lightning and the deaf'ning storm
> Still moves, I know, the one eternal Form,
> The unity of all things, silent, vast,
> And That shall yet restore creation's norm,
> And clear all doubts, and heal all wounds, at last. ('Hope', q. Vandiver 214)

Only by moving away from the stormy chaos of present life can we perceive the ideal 'Form' in which all our painful contradictions are reconciled, de Candole suggests, and he probably chose the ideal form of the sonnet for this very purpose. But for poets who could not believe in Plato's ideal 'Form' working behind the scenes, or its Christianised equivalent, the material detail of the poem had to be seen to be *making up* the form of the poem, if the doubts and wounds are not to be easily wiped away. This could mean the expressiveness of free verse, or the untotalisable experience of the fragmentary poem. It could also mean familiar forms whose patterns now emphasise their own inadequacy, and so bring into play all they are resisting. Above all, the war makes satisfactory form more difficult, because refusing easy satisfactions also means refusing to be self-satisfied in one's tough-minded, 'realistic' refusal of compensation, a disillusionment which becomes a continuation of war heroism by other means.

Imprisoned for his pacifism during the war, knowing the fighting would be 'just a bloody mess', John Rodker hated the belated sanctification of the dead under the smooth stone of the Cenotaph. In 'War Museum', he finds himself in a chamber full of surgical specimens jars with instructively wounded kidneys, bowels and heads. Here, he implies, was the truth of the whole affair:

> Therefore for the unknown warrior
> let us make a Christ
> sweating blood but speechless.
> With the open chest
> the snapped heart

the gashed liver
and cutaway bowels,
the pale stomach that died of gas
and an obliterated face
that dribbles a tear from an eye corner.[31]

The jerky free verse of the middle lines emphasises Rodker's modernist logic, that we must only make the image of the whole through the assemblage of particulars, rather than by conscripting them into an arrangement already decided on. But the comparison to Christ threatens to put this poem back into the war's primary discourse of justification through sacrifice nonetheless, even if the tortured body is as much Frankenstein's monster as Christian suffering. His terse comment on the later boom in war memoirs perhaps stems from recognising the difficulty. Sassoon and Graves were for peace, he remarks, but now we have 'All Quiet, Good-bye to all that, and the rest to satisfy our hunger to destroy, and be destroyed, but this time in safety, in our homes, arm-chairs'.[32] Rodker also knew that when writing his own memoir, he would probably reinvigorate the war mentality he had wanted to stop; telling the story of his cat-and-mouse experiences as a conscientious objector could not help but belong to the escaped prisoner-of-war genre either. Whether they were writing poems in therapy or in protest, in fragments or in strict metre, the war poets' difficulty was finding a form which could recognise what happened without extending the war's own remorseless grip in the process of writing.

NOTES

1 'Dead Man's Dump', in Ian Parsons ed. *The Collected Works of Isaac Rosenberg* (London: Chatto and Windus, 1984), 111–12.

2 J.W. Mackail, quoted in J.B. Esenwein and M.E. Roberts, *The Art of Versification* (Springfield, MA: Home Correspondence School, 1913), 4. Meredith Martin discusses the influence of this and other manuals on war poetry in *The Rise and Fall of Meter: English Poetry and National Culture, 1860–1930* (Princeton, NJ: Princeton University Press, 2012), 136ff.

3 R.F. Brewer, *Orthometry: A Treatise on the Art of Versification and the Technicalities of Poetry* (London: Deacon, 1893; repr. Edinburgh: John Grant, 1918), 3.

4 Edward Thomas, in Edna Longley ed. *The Annotated Collected Poems* (Tarset: Bloodaxe, 2008), 109.

5 Robert Nichols, 'The Assault', *Ardours and Endurances* (New York: Frederick Stoker, 1917), 41.

6 Letter of 19 January, 1917, in Harold Owen and John Bell eds. *Collected Letters of Wilfred Owen* (London: Oxford University Press, 1967), 429.

7 Letter of 10 October 1918, *ibid.*, 581.

8 Ivor Gurney, *Collected Letters*, ed. R.K.R. Thornton (Manchester: Mid-Northumberland Arts Group / Carcanet, 1991), 308.

9 A.A. Bowman, *Sonnets from a Prison-Camp* (London: John Lane, 1919), v.

10 'Rastatt: III', *ibid.*, 37.

11 Wordsworth, 'Nuns Fret Not' in Jonathan Wordsworth and Jessica Wordsworth eds. *The Penguin Book of Romantic Poetry* (London: Penguin, 2006), 433.

12 'To My Chum', *The Wipers Times* 2.4, 16 March 1916 (repr. London: Macmillan, 1988), 40.

13 See Erik Mueggler, 'The Poetics of Grief and the Price of Hemp in Southwestern China', *Journal of Asian Studies* 57:4 (1998), 979–1008.

14 Owen, *Collected Letters*, 496.

15 Hampden Gordon, 'Concert', in Vivian Noakes ed. *Voices of Silence: The Alternative Book of First World War Poetry* (Stroud: Sutton, 2006), 107.

16 'Grotesque', *Eidola* (London: John Murray, 1917), 35.

17 Mary Borden, 'The Song of the Mud', *The Forbidden Zone* (London: Heinemann, 1929), 181–2.

18 David Jones, *In Parenthesis* [1937] (London: Faber and Faber, 1963), viii.

19 *Ibid.*, 75.

20 Eric Leed, *No Man's Land* (New York: Cambridge University Press, 1979), 94.

21 Paul Fussell, *The Great War and Modern Memory* [1975] (Oxford: Oxford University Press, 2000), 147.

22 H.D., *Choruses from the Iphigenia in Aulis and the Hippolytus of Euripides* (London: Egoist Press, 1919), 4.

23 James Anderson Winn, *The Poetry of War* (Cambridge: Cambridge University Press, 2008), 8.

24 Daniel Hipp, *The Poetry of Shell-Shock* (Jefferson, NC: McFarland, 2005), 81.

25 Ivor Gurney, 'The Change', in P.J. Kavanagh ed. *Collected Poems* (Manchester: Carcanet, 2004), 60.

26 *Ibid.*, 109.

27 *Ibid.*, 203.

28 Brock, *Health and Conduct* (London: Williams and Norgate, 1923), 139.

29 *Ibid.*, 155.

30 *Ibid.*, 183.

31 John Rodker, 'War Museum – Royal College of Surgeons', in Andrew Crozier ed. *Poems and Adolphe, 1920* (Manchester: Carcanet, 1996), 125.

32 [John Rodker], *Memoirs of Other Fronts: A Novel* (London: Putnam, 1932), 196.

PART II

Soldier-Poets

3

ELIZABETH VANDIVER

Early Poets of the First World War

The soldier-poets of 1914 and 1915 have suffered, in critical estimation, by comparison with soldier-poets writing from 1916 onward. By definition, the early soldier-poets were not describing a war of attrition that had dragged on for years. Also by definition, they were all volunteers, given that conscription was instituted in January 1916. Most early poems, even those written at the Front, strikingly lack the 'fury' that Stallworthy identifies as the hallmark of a 'battlefield poem'.[1] Indeed, two of the famous early poems, Rupert Brooke's 'Peace' and Julian Grenfell's 'Into Battle', openly glorify battle. All these factors have produced a 'myth' according to which the early poets rushed to enlist, motivated by fervent patriotic enthusiasm and in almost complete ignorance of what modern war would mean: 'At the start there were Rupert Brooke and Julian Grenfell, patriotic, naïve, deluded; later, mostly after the Somme, there were Sassoon, Owen and many more, writing in savage indignation from the bitterness of front-line experience. So runs the myth'.[2]

Hibberd and Onions are right to call this a myth. The vast amount of poetry written during the war precludes the possibility of a single unified 'early' viewpoint: scores of poems appeared every week in newspapers from the outbreak of the war and the first anthologies such as *Poems of the Great War* and *Songs and Sonnets for England in War Time* were in print by December 1914. Poets such as William Noel Hodgson, Nowell Oxland, R.E. Vernède, Joseph Lee and A.P. Herbert – as well as Kipling, Hardy, and Bridges among non-combatants – all remind us of the wide range of voices that constituted 'war poetry' from the very beginning. Indeed, the striking differences even among the best-known early poets demonstrate the insufficiency of purely chronological criteria for categorising either the tone or the themes of war poetry; Charles Hamilton Sorley's detached compassion and Patrick Shaw Stewart's resigned acceptance are very different from the exalted glorification of war that marks Brooke's and Grenfell's works. Romanticism does not always depend on civilian ignorance, nor does realism always reflect post-Somme disillusionment. Wilfrid Gibson's apparently experience-based 'Breakfast' and W.N. Ewer's satiric 'Five Souls' were both written by civilians and published in October 1914, while Brooke and Grenfell wrote their best-known works after actual front-line service.[3]

Any end point for the classification 'early' must be arbitrary. A less frequently acknowledged problem concerns undated poems by writers who survived into the 'late' period. Patrick Shaw Stewart's great poem, 'I Saw a Man This Morning', refers to a leave on Imbros, datable to July 1915, but Shaw Stewart died in France on 30 December 1917.[4] The poem is written on the flyleaf of his copy of A Shropshire Lad and is undated. Probably he wrote it immediately after the leave it mentions, but he could have written it much later, reflecting back on that experience. In this instance, we cannot know if we are reading an early poem or a late one. This chapter concentrates on three poets unequivocally established as early by their deaths in 1915: Rupert Brooke died on 23 April of blood poisoning; Julian Grenfell on 26 May of a head wound suffered thirteen days previously; and Charles Sorley on 13 October by sniper fire at Loos. They were in uniform by autumn 1914 and at the Front by (at the latest) summer 1915. Their poems include some of the earliest reactions to the war written by combatants.

The myth about the progression of war poetry makes two key assumptions: that the early poets were naively enthusiastic and that they were factually ignorant about the war. Neither assumption stands up under scrutiny. Certainly many of the public-school boys who enlisted as soon as they left school were naive. The 'public-school ethos' created a romanticised form of chivalry by a carefully tendentious reading of Greek and Roman literature suitably refracted through a Christian lens.[5] The examples of Christ on Calvary and Leonidas at Thermopylae worked in parallel to impress on the boys the essential value of self-sacrifice. The emphasis (in the classroom and on the playing field) on self-sacrifice and endurance inculcated 'a code of "manliness" ... which actively encouraged and rejoiced in pain', and this code undoubtedly had a powerful effect on many young volunteers who went almost directly from the schoolroom to the battlefield.[6] But Brooke and Grenfell, the two poets most often accused of naiveté, were twenty-seven and twenty-six, respectively, when war broke out. Grenfell was already in the Army as a professional soldier; Brooke had published his first book of poetry in 1911 and had been crucially involved in both the conception and the production of the first Georgian Poetry anthology (1912).[7] Nor were they entirely ignorant about what war would mean when they wrote their war poems. Grenfell wrote 'Into Battle' after he had been in France for more than five months and, contrary to common assumption, Brooke wrote his sonnets not immediately on England's declaration of war, but after he had witnessed the retreat from Antwerp in October 1914. Charles Hamilton Sorley was only nineteen in August 1914, but when war was declared, he was at the end of seven months' travel in Germany.[8] He planned to take up his scholarship for University College, Oxford, in autumn 1914 and had insisted on travel in Germany beforehand.

Grenfell was eager to see combat, but his enthusiasm was not based in fervent patriotism. Rather, he was drawn to the idea of war itself, as (like sport) a venue for individual accomplishment through violence. Brooke and Sorley both knew and loved Germany and neither enlisted out of unambiguous enthusiasm. When war was declared, Sorley returned to England immediately to enlist, but wrote in early August that he was 'full of mute and burning rage and annoyance and sulkiness'.[9] His sonnet 'To Germany', sent to his parents from camp in April 1915, addresses the 'enemy' in deeply compassionate terms: 'In each other's dearest ways we stand ... / And the blind fight the blind'. The sonnet looks forward to a time after the war, when 'we'll grasp firm hands and laugh at the old pain'.[10] Brooke wrote on 31 July 1914 that 'it will be Hell to be in it; and Hell to be out of it' and even after witnessing the retreat from Antwerp in October, he told a friend that 'it hurts me, this war. Because I was fond of Germany'.[11] Yet within a few months, Brooke was writing his five *1914* sonnets. They were first published in early spring 1915 (in the last issue of *New Numbers*, retrospectively dated December 1914) and became famous almost immediately. Brooke's glorification of willing self-sacrifice and redemptive death struck a resonant chord in the public's mind, especially after Dean Inge read the fifth sonnet, 'The Soldier', from the pulpit of St. Paul's on Easter Sunday in 1915.[12] The sonnets were reissued in book form in *1914 and Other Poems* in June 1915, just a few weeks after Brooke's death.

The first sonnet, 'Peace', presents the exultation of the idealised volunteer:

> Now, God be thanked Who has matched us with His hour,
>   And caught our youth, and wakened us from sleeping,
> With hand made sure, clear eye, and sharpened power,
>   To turn, as swimmers into cleanness leaping,
> Glad from a world grown old and cold and weary,
>   Leave the sick hearts that honour could not move,
> And half-men, and their dirty songs and dreary,
>   And all the little emptiness of love!

Brooke makes equally exalted claims for the dead in the third sonnet:

> Blow, bugles, blow! They brought us, for our dearth,
>   Holiness, lacked so long, and Love, and Pain.
> Honour has come back, as a king, to earth,

> And paid his subjects with a royal wage;
> And Nobleness walks in our ways again;
> And we have come into our heritage.[13]

Both sonnets claim that sacrifice eagerly undertaken is somehow mystically effective. The soldiers' enraptured embrace, in the first sonnet, of 'God['s] hour' as a kind of 'cleanness' is mirrored by the third sonnet's claim that young men's death has replaced 'dearth' with Honour and Nobleness. The disjunction between both the mood and the language of these sonnets and Brooke's earlier poetic style is striking; as one of the founders of Georgian poetry, Brooke was noted for his 'cool, witty, and irreverent style', terms that could scarcely be less apposite for describing the war sonnets.[14] Soon after Brooke's death, E.J. Dent wrote that the sonnets were atypical of Brooke's poetry: 'In the first shock of the moment that romanticism he so hated came uppermost'.[15] Much of Brooke's previous work had created a tension between intentionally shocking content and traditional form and metre, as in his carefully wrought sonnets on nausea or the horrors of senility. The Georgians (no less than the rival Imagists) prided themselves on discarding threadbare archaic rhetoric and on using direct, clear, immediate speech. Brooke's style in the war sonnets was thus a radical break from his earlier poetics. But far from reflecting civilian naiveté, the sonnets were written as a response to Brooke's sight of 'Antwerp, deserted, shelled, and burning ... ruined houses, dead men and horses' and to his grief over the wounding or death of school friends.[16] He embraced archaising and romanticised diction in the sonnets to claim that this war was causing a return from modern superficiality to older and 'truer' values. He reacted with an increased sense of purpose, but he did not fail to realise what was at stake; 'the eye grows clearer, and the heart', he wrote to a friend, in words that directly recall the first sonnet. 'But', the letter continues, 'it's a bloody thing, half the youth of Europe blown through pain to nothingness, in the incessant mechanical slaughter of these modern battles'.[17] In the autumn of 1914, this was a remarkably realistic assessment of what 'modern battles' implied; the 'shock of the moment' was one of facing, not denying, what modern war meant.

Much has been written about the impact of Rupert Brooke's complicated personal life on his reaction to war. Enlistment offered him a welcome escape from private entanglements that had become increasingly intolerable. He had suffered a nervous breakdown in 1912 and in summer 1914, his emotional difficulties were still unresolved.[18] There is little doubt that Brooke's psychological state and his ambivalent sexuality affected his use of the imagery of 'cleanness' and his embrace of war as a means to escape from 'all the little emptiness of love' and from the 'dirtiness' of 'half-men'.[19] His queasiness over sexuality and the body and his horror of senility seem, similarly, to have influenced his welcoming of death as an escape from the complications of adult life. The third sonnet, 'The Dead', and the fifth sonnet, 'The Soldier', both fetishise death as a source of 'richness' dependent on an eager renunciation of normal human life:

> Blow out, you bugles, over the rich Dead!
>   There's none of these so lonely and poor of old,
>   But, dying, has made us rarer gifts than gold.
>   These laid the world away; poured out the red
>   Sweet wine of youth; gave up the years to be
>   Of work and joy, and that unhoped serene,
>   That men call age; and those who would have been,
>   Their sons, they gave, their immortality.[20]

The list of things that the dead 'laid away' culminates in children, strikingly called 'their immortality'. The importance of this line for Brooke comes into clear focus when we read it beside one of his letters: 'When they told us at Dunkirk that we were all going to be killed in Antwerp, ... I didn't think much (as I'd expected) what a damned fool I was not to have written more and done various things better and been less selfish. I merely thought "What *Hell* it is that I shan't have any children – any sons." I thought it over and over, quite furious, for some hours'.[21] But Brooke's 'fury' over the thought that he would have no sons (the masculinist bias of the phrasing is typical of Brooke's anti-feminism) changes, in the sonnet, to an exultant triumphalism. The dead are rich precisely because what they gave up was so precious and mattered so much. Winston Churchill's celebrated obituary for Brooke epitomises the idea that voluntary self-sacrifice is ennobling, beautiful (with a hint of pathos) and in itself proof of the sacrificed life's value: 'Joyous, fearless, versatile, deeply instructed, with classic symmetry of mind and body, he was all that one would wish England's noblest sons to be in days when no sacrifice but the most precious is acceptable and the most precious is that which is most freely proffered'.[22] Brooke's final sonnet, 'The Soldier', echoes this same idea by turning it inward towards the individual soldier-poet rather than towards his society. 'There shall be / In that rich dust a richer dust concealed' depends on the assumption that 'the thoughts by England given' are gifts so precious that their acceptance, and later their renunciation, enrich the actual body of the dead soldier and hence the ground in which he is buried.[23]

Modern critics no longer rank Brooke very highly. But Churchill's obituary and Dean Inge's quotation of 'The Soldier' on Easter Day 1915 fixed Brooke in the public consciousness as not merely *a* war poet, but *the* war poet: 'There was never a moment of the war ... when, to the majority of Englishmen, including those in the trenches, his rhetoric did not seem the most appropriate way of speaking and writing about the ideals of war'.[24]

His unironic invocation of patriotism and courage resonated deeply with many readers. Throughout the war, men wrote home from the trenches 'to ask for copies of Brooke's poems, and quoted them to cheer their families, or to express their own feelings'.[25]

Few contemporary poems approached this level of popular acclaim; one that did was Julian Grenfell's 'Into Battle'. According to his diary, Grenfell wrote 'Into Battle' on 29 April 1915. He had written few other poems and had published none. He sent a copy of 'Into Battle' to his mother on 30 April with the comment, 'Here is a poem, if you can read it. I rather like it. Publish it if you like'. This letter ends 'How sad about R Brooke'.[26] Grenfell had read and admired Brooke's 1911 *Poems* and had apparently read at least one of Brooke's war sonnets because a letter of 7 March 1915 says, 'I got Brooke's poem, and liked it very much – *awfully*'.[27] The news of Brooke's death may have helped motivate him to write 'Into Battle'. Its opening stanza lays out Grenfell's view of war:

> The naked earth is warm with spring,
> And with green grass and bursting trees
> Leans to the sun's kiss glorying,
> And quivers in the loving breeze;
> And Life is Colour and Warmth and Light
> And a striving evermore for these;
> And he is dead who will not fight;
> And who dies fighting has increase.[28]

This presentation of violence as a mode of apprehending fuller life was deeply rooted in Grenfell's psychological makeup. Mosley's biography of Grenfell reveals a troubled young man striving to escape his mother's overwhelming control.[29] Enlistment in the Army in 1910 had offered him a way both to meet his mother's expectations and to flee from her presence, and in 1914, he took to war quickly and with enthusiasm. After his first experience of enemy fire on 24 October 1914, he wrote to his mother that it was 'bloody' and that he could not pretend he liked it, but he soon embraced the Front's violence.[30] 'Into Battle' mirrors emotions that Grenfell was reporting in letters home by November; he wrote that life at the Front 'just suits my stolid health and stolid nerves and barbaric disposition. The fighting excitement vitalises everything – every sight and word and action. One loves one's fellow man so much more when one is bent on killing him'.[31] Even allowing for the breezy tone that Grenfell often used to his mother, this probably reflects his genuine sentiments. Well before the war, Grenfell had found his fullest vitality in hunting and especially in such dangerous modes as the

pig-sticking he enjoyed while stationed in India, where he wrote the poem
'Hymn to the Fighting Boar'.[32]

'Into Battle' celebrates the hunter's view of Nature as source of both life
and death:

> The fighting man shall from the sun
> Take warmth, and life from the glowing earth;
> Speed with the light-foot winds to run,
> And with the trees a newer birth;
> And when his fighting shall be done,
> Great rest, and fulness after dearth ....
>
> The kestrel hovering by day,
> And the little owls that call by night,
> Bid him be swift and keen as they –
> As keen of sound, as swift of sight.
>
> The blackbird sings to him 'Brother, brother,
> If this be the last song you shall sing,
> Sing well, for you will not sing another;
> Brother, sing!'[33]

The fighting man allies himself with nature, represented especially by birds
of prey; the 'swiftness' and 'keenness' of the kestrel and the owl are, of
course, crucial to their success as hunters. The war allowed Grenfell to use
the skills he had honed in hunting animals, in a context that made killing human beings not just acceptable but praiseworthy. He wrote in detail
to his parents about solitary sniping expeditions in which he killed three
Germans. He recorded the dead in his game book after an entry listing 105
partridges.[34] Yet, describing the Germans' slow advance against the British
trenches after his second sniping expedition, Grenfell wrote 'we simply
mowed them down; it was rather horrible'.[35] Machine gun fire did not fit his
conception of war as 'sport', but shooting an individual did; firing at a man
was disturbing at first, 'but very soon it gets like shooting a crocodile, only
more amusing, because he shoots back at you'.[36]

Grenfell's letters openly transfer the hunter's field of operations from
animals to humans, but his poem presses this a step further; it contains
no human beings at all apart from the 'fighting man' and human culture
appears only through the domesticated horses. Whereas the hunting imagery is maintained by the kestrel and the owls, the combat that the fighting
man faces is a proving ground to measure himself against death, not against
an enemy. Death itself is lightly personified ('In the air Death moans and
sings'), but the enemy's role in causing that death is barely mentioned; the

penultimate stanza's 'lead' and 'steel' and the last stanza's 'thundering line of battle' seem to operate as independent agents.

Yet Grenfell also expressed other emotional reactions to the war. Although he insisted to his mother that it was all great fun, he was not unaware of war's horrors. His diary, written in extremely laconic style, gives some hints that the war's toll appalled him: 'dead bodies buried in parapet of trench, & washed out when rain came ... Foul state of decaying flesh in Zillebeke. All houses bashed in'.[37] Yet in the poem there is no hint that war brings anything other than 'increase' and, with death, a release from worries and troubles ('Day shall clasp him with strong hands / And Night shall fold him in soft wings'). Indeed, 'Into Battle' celebrates a burgeoning Nature whose fecundity war enhances; the contrast with the actual effect of war on the French and Flemish countryside could scarcely be more marked, but Grenfell's love of war had little to do with the specific present circumstances. It is no accident that 'Into Battle' contains no reference to any motivating 'cause'. For Grenfell, the point was the Homeric *aristeia* (an individual warrior's moment of outstanding glory) in its own right; the war merely provided a context in which the warrior could flourish.[38]

As Brooke does with the 'rich dust' of the English dead, Grenfell elides the physical realities of war into a form of romanticised nature worship that moves the warrior out of the context of this particular war. Both men's private writings testify that they were appalled by the realities of the Western Front, but both used their poetry as a vehicle for claiming a transformative value in the act of fighting, a value that does not deny the physical realities of death so much as transcend them. The later critical foregrounding of 'poetry of protest' has taught us to find such claims of transcendent value morally repugnant as well as aesthetically suspect. But even Charles Hamilton Sorley, who is often considered a 'transitional' figure on the way to protest poetry, wrote a poem that has sometimes been read as a glorification of the fighting spirit and that presents a Nature not unlike Grenfell's. It begins:

> All the hills and vales along
> Earth is bursting into song,
> And the singers are the chaps
> Who are going to die perhaps.
> > O sing, marching men,
> > Till the valleys ring again.
> > Give your gladness to earth's keeping,
> > So be glad, when you are sleeping.

'All the Hills and Vales Along' treats death's inevitability as a cause for (ironic?) rejoicing. Sorley may have begun the poem as early as August

1914; he sent it to his parents in April 1915. This disturbing poem has inspired radically differing interpretations. Some critics read it as a straightforward expression of joy in nature and in death, enhanced by the jaunty metre; others, 'as an oblique subversion of jocular stoicism'.[39] The poem's tone remains difficult to define throughout its four stanzas, from the opening lines through the concluding 'Strew your gladness on earth's bed, / So be merry, so be dead'. The deaths of famous individuals – Socrates, Jesus, Barabbas – illustrate the utter indifference of earth to individual merit. Christ died and Barabbas was released on the same day; furthermore:

> Earth that bore with joyful ease
> Hemlock for Socrates,
> Earth that blossomed and was glad
> 'Neath the cross that Christ had,
> Will rejoice and blossom too
> When the bullet reaches you.

The only consolation – if such it is – for this cosmic indifference to righteousness is that 'Teeming earth will surely store / All the gladness that you pour'.[40] Bergonzi says the poem treats death as 'an act of existential assertion of human values in the face of an alien universe'.[41] But the representation of Barabbas as morally equivalent to Jesus, and Earth's joy at Socrates' and Jesus' deaths, scarcely 'assert human values'. Rather, the poem seems to reject the idea that individual death has any 'existential' meaning.

Sorley died at age twenty after slightly more than four months at the Front. He did not consider his poems ready for publication and called his mother's suggestion that some of them be printed 'premature'.[42] His father edited a posthumous collection, *Marlborough and Other Poems* (1916). In his few war poems, Sorley frequently insists that death has no meaning. It is 'no triumph: no defeat: / Only an empty pail, a slate rubbed clean'.[43] The most powerful example is the famous sonnet 'When You See Millions of the Mouthless Dead' [quoted in full on p. 3].[44] The strongly spondaic rhythm and the preference for Anglo-Saxon rather than Latinate words give the poem both its solemnity and its bluntness, effects encapsulated in the final two lines where the heavy thud of monosyllables builds to the culminating (and devastating) 'evermore'. The poem's rejection of sentimentality pivots on the crucial words 'Yet many a better one has died before', a direct reference to *Iliad* 21.106–7. Just before killing the young Trojan Lycaon, who has pled for mercy, Achilles says: 'So, friend, die also. Why do you lament so about it? / Patroclus also has died, who was far better than you'. Sorley refigures Achilles' merciless words to highlight the utter anonymity of death and to reject any easy comfort; any glimpse of a beloved individual among the 'o'ercrowded mass' of dead is only an illusion. The proper response, Sorley says, is neither lamentation nor praise, but calm acceptance of inevitability.

'When You See Millions', written after Sorley's experience at the Front, presents death in a stark and somber fashion while 'All the Hills and Vales Along' treats it as a matter for joyous celebration, but neither poem admits that the individual's death has any worth. In this regard, Sorley stands in stark opposition to the idea that the soldiers' voluntary deaths are redemptive. Even poets of protest – such as Sassoon in 'The Redeemer' – drew on the idea of redemptive sacrifice when they figured soldiers' deaths as a source of rebuke to non-combatants or warning to the future. But Sorley neither rebukes, nor accuses, nor warns; he simply presents the fact that these men who were living are now dead. In this aspect, he is closer to classical models than almost any other war poet; the unadorned language and utterly unemotional tone of 'When You See Millions' recall Simonides' greatest poetic epitaphs.

Sorley's quotation of Homer of course brings to mind the famous wrath of Achilles, but the sonnet itself repudiates anger as it repudiates glory or pride. Its overall tone is strikingly reminiscent of Patrick Shaw Stewart's 'I Saw a Man This Morning', which marks the distance between epic and modern war through its evocation of Achilles' great and driven vengeance for Patroclus:

> Achilles came to Troyland
> And I to Chersonese:
> He turned from wrath to battle,
> And I from three days' peace.[45]

In contrast to Achilles' intensely personal motivation for battle, Shaw Stewart's poem offers no reason for the speaker's return to combat beyond the unadorned recognition of inevitability. The stark statement, 'I will go back this morning / From Imbros over the sea' suggests that the poem's central question 'Fatal second Helen, / Why must I follow thee?' cannot in fact be answered in any terms other than those of bleak necessity. Individual motivations such as the desire for glory, honour, or even vengeance have no place here. For Shaw Stewart as for Sorley, the Homeric model serves ultimately to signal its own distance from the modern war.[46] Hibberd and Onions remind us that '"realism" in First World War poetry is not always evidence of opposition to the war';[47] neither is 'high diction' always evidence of naiveté or ignorance, and evocations of tradition can both support and interrogate the war. Early poetry of the war, far from consisting only of simplistic glorifications of the 'nation's cause', included a variety of complicated and nuanced positions. In the early years, as later, there was nothing simple or monolithic about First World War poetry.

NOTES

1 Jon Stallworthy, *Survivors' Songs from Maldon to the Somme* (Cambridge: Cambridge University Press, 2008), 178. Hereafter abbreviated as *Songs*.

2 Dominic Hibberd and John Onions eds. *The Winter of the World: Poems of the First World War* (London: Constable, 2008), xiv. Hereafter abbreviated as *Winter*.

3 *Winter*, xv-xvii, 23–6.

4 See Elizabeth Vandiver, *Stand in the Trench, Achilles: Classical Receptions in British Poetry of the Great War* (Oxford: Oxford University Press, 2010), 272–3. Hereafter abbreviated as *Stand*.

5 On the 'public school ethos', see Peter Parker, *The Old Lie: The Great War and the Public-School Ethos* (London: Constable, 1987), 84–99 [Hereafter abbreviated as *Old Lie*]; Adrian Caesar, *Taking It Like a Man: Suffering, Sexuality and the War Poets. Brooke, Sassoon, Owen, Graves* (Manchester: Manchester University Press, 1993), 225–7 [Hereafter abbreviated as *Taking It*]; Stallworthy, *Songs*, 8, 11–14; Vandiver, *Stand*, Ch. 1.

6 Parker, *Old Lie*, 212–15; Vandiver, *Stand*, 36–7.

7 See Christopher Hassall, *Rupert Brooke: A Biography* (New York: Harcourt, Brace, World, 1964), 360–3, 365–6, 371–2. Hereafter abbreviated as *Brooke*.

8 Jean Moorcroft Wilson, *Charles Hamilton Sorley: A Biography* (London: Cecil Woolf, 1985), 89–92, 105–7.

9 William Ritchey Sorley ed. *The Letters of Charles Hamilton Sorley* (Cambridge: Cambridge University Press, 1919), 220–1.

10 *Winter*, 37.

11 Geoffrey Keynes ed. *The Letters of Rupert Brooke* (New York: Harcourt, Brace, World, 1968), 601, 632.

12 Hassall, *Brooke*, 502–3.

13 *Winter*, 38–9.

14 Dominic Hibberd and John Onions eds. *Poetry of the Great War: An Anthology* (Basingstoke: Macmillan, 1986), 10.

15 *The Cambridge Magazine*, 8 May 1915; quoted in Hassall, *Brooke*, 520.

16 Brooke, *Letters*, 632–3.

17 *Ibid.*

18 Caesar, *Taking It*, 37–50; Hassall, *Brooke*, 320–58, 396–447.

19 'Peace', Hibberd and Onions, *Winter*, 38.

20 *Winter*, 39.

21 Brooke, *Letters*, 633; 20 November 1914, to Rosalind Toynbee.

22 Quoted in Edward Marsh, *Rupert Brooke: A Memoir* (New York: John Lane, 1918), 186. Marsh probably wrote the draft of the eulogy.

23 *Winter*, 40.

24 Samuel Hynes, *A War Imagined: The First World War and English Culture* (New York: Collier, 1992), 109–10.

25 *War Imagined*, 109. On the sonnets' popularity, see Hassall, *Brooke*, 516–28.

26 Kate Thompson ed. *Julian Grenfell, Soldier & Poet: Letters and Diaries, 1910–1915* (Caxton Hill: Hertfordshire Record Society, 2004), 282 (letter); 295 (diary).

27 Nicholas Mosley, *Julian Grenfell: His Life and the Times of His Death* (New York: Holt, Rinehart, Winston, 1976), 208; Thompson, *Grenfell*, 267; emphasis original.

28 Mosley, *Grenfell*, 256.

29 See Mosley, *Grenfell*, especially 161–72.

30 Thomson, *Grenfell*, 229–30.

31 Thomson, *Grenfell*, 237.

32 Galloway Kyle ed. *Soldier Poets: Songs of the Fighting Men* (London: Erskine Macdonald, 1916), 32–4.

33 Mosley, *Grenfell*, 256–7.

34 Thompson, *Grenfell*, 242–3 (letter); 335–6 (game book).

35 Thompson, *Grenfell*, 243; emphasis original.

36 *Ibid.*, 225.

37 Thompson, *Grenfell*, 291; diary entry 13 Feb 1915.

38 On 'Into Battle' and Homer, see Vandiver, *Stand*, 186–93.

39 George Parfitt, *English Poetry of the First World War: Contexts and Themes* (London: Harvester Wheatsheaf, 1990), 135.

40 *Winter*, 36–7.

41 Bernard Bergonzi, *Heroes' Twilight: A Study of the Literature of the Great War* (Manchester: Carcanet, 1996), 52.

42 Sorley, *Letters*, 273, 13 June 1915.

43 Charles Hamilton Sorley, *The Collected Poems*, ed. Jean Moorcroft Wilson (London: Cecil Woolf, 1985), 88.

44 *Winter*, 68 [published as 'A Sonnet' in *Marlborough and Others Poems*, Cambridge University Press, 1922, 78].

45 *Winter*, 54.

46 On Sorley's refiguration of Homeric epic, see Vandiver, *Stand*, 293–7; on Shaw Stewart, 270–7.

47 *Winter*, xxiv.

4

MARK RAWLINSON

Later Poets of the First World War

> By 1917 war poems were being published by the thousand. A typical
> anthology was E.B. Osborn's *Muse in Arms*, with authors drawn from
> almost every regiment or corps in the Army – all very gallant and
> idealistic but with hardly a poet among them.[1]

Robert Graves rehearsed the particular history of poetry in the Great War
to explain why there could be no 'war poets' in 1942. He argued that before
1917, the 'war-poetry boom' had functioned to reproduce 'volunteer pride':
there would be no 'fashion' for 'self-dedicatory' poetry in the era of the
Conscription Act (1939). The poetry of the 'angry veteran' was just as 'peculiar' to the Great War, and equally irrelevant to the conditions of bored
safety in which soldiers were garrisoned during a home front war.[2] Robert
Nichols, whom Graves went on to abuse as a species of war-poetry profiteer
(as an internationally touring 'crippled warrior'), had himself, as early as
the beginning of 1940, laid out the literary relations between the Great War
and the Second World War. Whereas Graves had long disowned his own war
writing, Nichols offered an anthology of verse from 1914–18 – including his
own and Graves's work to a generation on the verge of surrendering their
own lives to military excitement and servitude.

Graves, whatever his later misgivings about the influence of the 'war-
poetry boom' on his poetry, would have disputed that he was a *later* poet of
the Great War, having joined up in 1914 from Charterhouse. The other poets
discussed here – Robert Nichols, Edmund Blunden and Herbert Read – all
spent time at Oxford University (Leeds in the case of Read) before enlisting,
but none of them were temporarily commissioned so late as to be Military
Service Act (1916) soldiers. Blunden would write that '[w]ar became part
of the author's experience at a date so early … as to mould and colour
the poetry almost throughout [*Poems 1914–1930*]'.[3] Nevertheless, it makes
sense to group them as later poets of the Great War to distinguish the temporality and reception of their writing from that of writers who did not
survive the conflict, as well as from that of the earliest of the exponents of
'recruiting' verse. In their different ways, all would become veteran war
poets.

Of the forty-six poets represented in *Muse in Arms* (1917), fourteen were *late* rather than later poets: the 'fallen' included Rupert Brooke (April 1915), Julian Grenfell (May 1915) and Charles Sorley (October 1915). Nichols and Graves were among the *Muse in Arms* authors who survived to put the war behind them, the former speaking to America for the Ministry of Information from 1917, the latter with his 'anti'-war memoir, *Goodbye to All That* (1929). Siegfried Sassoon and Ivor Gurney, who also appeared in Osborn's anthology, both remained captive of their war experience: Sassoon's serial re-composition of his war story was a life-long struggle with the legend that overcame the late poets of the war.

Larkin claimed that Owen was 'chained to an historical event': this is true of canonical First World War poets more generally, but especially in terms of their literary and historical reception and their continual refashioning as national heroes in an English memorial heritage.[4] The later poets of this chapter were not 'bodies [...] melted down to pay for political statues';[5] their subsequent careers as writers and/or academics have stood in the way of such legendary simplicity. The four discussed here – Graves, Nichols, Herbert Read and Edmund Blunden – are nevertheless commemorated on the stone in Poets' Corner, Westminster Abbey which was unveiled on Remembrance Day 1985 by Ted Hughes, and on which the names of sixteen war poets are encircled by Owen's famous words: 'My subject is War and the pity of War. The Poetry is in the pity'. An emblem of the difference in cultural status between different groups of war poets is Robert Graves's role, a role he was partially responsible for scripting, as Horatio to the Hamlets (Sassoon and Owen) of Craiglockhart Military Hospital, as recreated in Pat Barker's trilogy of historical novels, starting with *Regeneration* (1991). Such distinctions are salutary if they remind us to read against the ideal type of the war poet as an anticipatory spokesman who connects post-modern opposition to war with the authority of combatants' witness to mechanised slaughter. Samuel Hynes speaks for generations of critics (including Graves in the essay cited earlier) when he notes that '[T]he principal war poets allied themselves not with the new avant-garde of Eliot and Pound and Imagism, but with the Georgians'.[6] Although the poets discussed here do not compose an ideological grouping which programmatically negates this commonplace, their variance is a caution against too ready an assumption of the artistic consequences of bearing the label 'war poet'.

Graves's war certainly has a different kind of narrative to that of Sassoon and Owen. This is evident in the contrast between the Milliganesque form and satire of *Goodbye to All That* and the longer-range ironic structures of Sassoon's George Sherston trilogy. Moreover, Graves's poetry from 1915–18, notably the contents of *Over the Brazier* (1916) and *Fairies and*

Fusiliers (1917), does not compose a narrative of combatant *Bildung* or dis-illusionment. That this wartime war verse progressively disappeared from public view, to be substituted by *Goodbye*, as Graves reassembled his poetic career first in *Poems 1914–26* (which preserved about one-third of his war poems) and then *Collected Poems* of 1939 (which excised the remainder from 1914–18), is a further act of authorial dissociation from the idea of the war poet.[7]

The archetypal pattern of much canonical war poesis is revision. The war's modernity, its demographic and technological amplification, have come to be symbolised in cultural terms as the rejection of heroic motifs by 'a new real-istic school of soldier poets'.[8] The 'horror' of this war is widely held to have changed war poetry, and the way poetry envisaged the war's transformative powers. But Graves's own early writings on war had reproduced the rhetoric of heroic afflatus and self-transcendence. 'A Renascence' mobilises cosmolog-ical and sanitary motifs we associate respectively with the Boer War Hardy and with Rupert Brooke (whose 'The Soldier' appeared in January 1915):

> White flabbiness goes brown and lean,
> Dumpling arms are now brass bars,
> They've learned to suffer and live clean,
> And to think below the stars

but imbricates them with elements that are at once tougher (that metalization of flesh) and more idealistic,

> But of their travailings and groans
> Poetry is born again.[9]

In the post-war, second edition of *Over the Brazier*, Graves wrote that his decision in the field to 'suppress' this poem came 'too late' to prevent publication. 'Big Words', which appeared in *The Muse in Arms*, was more effectively revised – its self-dedication to death was re-punctuated into a dramatic monologue whose comparison of war and climbing in Snowdonia is undercut by the addition of what would become a hallmark of Sassoon's satirical reframing – the ironising couplet reversal:

> But on the firestep, waiting to attack,
> He cursed, prayed, sweated, wished the proud words back.[10]

'The postscript was added after Loos': Graves's scrutiny of his rhetoric after the campaign of September 1915 fits the pattern of the poet-witness's re-education by exposure, although it does not fit the way this cultural learning curve has been simplified to before and after the Somme offensive of later 1916. But the poem that has been presented as Graves's signal contribu-tion to war realism, 'A Dead Boche' (misdated in *Poems About War*), does fit – and it incarnates the new apperceptions of war later enumerated by Pound in *Hugh Selwyn Mauberley*:

> frankness as never before,
> disillusions as never told in the old days,
> hysterias, trench confessions
> laughter out of dead bellies.[11]

Encountering the same German corpse in *Good-bye to All That*, in an anecdote about looting greatcoats for his men to use as blankets – 'He had a green face, spectacles, close shaven hair; black blood was dripping from the nose and beard' – Graves moves without pause to the spectacle of soldiers who 'had succeeded in bayoneting each other simultaneously'.[12] This is more akin to Ted Hughes's vision of the violence of the natural order in 'Pike' ('one jammed past its gills down the other's gullet') rather than the allegory of poetic transmission in the embrace of enemies at the end of Owen's 'Strange Meeting'.[13] Whereas the German corpse gives local colour in the description of Mametz wood in the prose memoir, in the poem of 1916, it is an ostensive definition in a pedagogic mode of address. The idealism of 'war, the world's only hygiene' is countered with 'a certain cure for lust of blood':

> Big-bellied, spectacled, crop-haired
> Dribbling black blood from nose and beard.[14]

But the 'apparition' (to invoke Pound's Imagist template 'In a Station of the Metro') does not itself perform this remedial schooling, an early instance of 'modern' war poetry not quite conforming to the definitions which have arisen to explain its significance. Instead, the poem's outspokenness consists in its representation of its own authority, the way it plays on Judaeo-Christian taboos ('things unclean') and its deliberate confusion of the injunction to the reader – look! – with the gaze of the corpse ('scowled', 'spectacled').[15] But just as the poem negates bellicist discourse – it charts the evolution of war poetry from 'blood and fame' to 'black blood' – it also undercuts its own claim to first-hand witness, insisting that the reader has heard many times that 'War's Hell'. 'A Dead Boche' is undercut again, in Yeatsian fashion, in 'The Patchwork Quilt', written in the summer of 1918 (by which time Graves had been told he would never be fit again for active service):

> 'If you stare aghast perhaps
> At certain muddied khaki scraps
> …
> Blame my dazed head, blame bloody war'.[16]

Realism in war poetry (Sassoon, Owen, Blunden) is associated with a retooling of the topical poem – portraying a time and a place – to capture the haptic, traumatic, olfactory and auditory qualia of war; Graves's enduring poems do not compete on this ground. His poem 'The Legion' reconfigures the motifs of the civilian and militarised self (see 'A Renascence') in a 'Roman' dialogue – with echoes of Housman's *A Shropshire Lad* – about the citizen soldiers of Kitchener's army. The historical displacement has the effect of veiling war's 'great mess' ('A Dead Boche'), which is to be glimpsed obliquely in the distinction between the muscular poise of the lost legion and their 'slovenly', 'diseased' urban replacements.[17] The resonance of 'The Legion' is a consequence of a proto-modernist juxtaposition of perspectives embodied in utterances. Grachus's confidence that 'The Legion is the Legion while Rome stands' recalls the imperial ironies of Conrad's *Heart of Darkness* in its implied parallelism between Roman and British imperial destinies. The opposition between form (discipline, battle) and content (human beings) is both pathetic and ironic.

Graves shares this capacity for formal distancing with Herbert Read, who unlike him, was a pacifist and, unlike some pacifists, did not permit his creed to become what Orwell would later call 'objectively pro-Fascist', or in this case pro-Prussianist.[18] As a pacifist, he joined Leeds University Officer Training Corps and as a pacifist and veteran of the Great War, he wrote 'To a Conscript of 1940' to redeem soldiering from the inauthenticity imposed on the individual by the disciplines of military service and also from bellicist ideologies of heroism:

> To fight without hope is to fight with grace,
> The self reconstructed, the false heart repaired.[19]

Read's poems of 1914–18 employ a sparer, more exacting language to undertake a thoroughgoing examination of militarist myths and identities. In *Naked Warriors* (1919), his anarchism – a fundamental opposition to the usurpation of the individual by military authority to be contrasted with Robert Nichols's Wildean individualism – already has a modernist voice: his 'revolt of the individual' is enacted in imagistic economy, and dispenses with strophic organisation and rhyme.[20] 'Kneeshaw Goes to War', an Everyman narrative of the militarisation and mutilation of the very ordinary citizen, anticipates Henry Williamson's fabular novel on the same theme, *A Patriot's Progress* (1930), by more than a decade. Ernest Kneeshaw is an unlikely war poet, one who is content to 'contemplate/His [...] boots' and who hence appears already regimented in his dullness (the antithesis of Remarque's idealist Paul Bäumer, ripe for violation in *All Quiet on the Western Front*). In places, Read approaches the sprezzatura of Pound's Mauberley quatrains, an apparently nonchalant phrase-making which invites an attitude of historical transcendence:

> For a while chance was kind
> Save for an inevitable
> Searing of the mind.
> But later Kneeshaw's war
> Became intense.[21]

In 1918, Read concluded that 'the means of war had become more portentous than the aim'; how far his own verse extends these reservations to the emergent grandiloquence of protest poetry is debatable.[22] Read's vocabulary in the fourth section of the poem (Polygonveld) is recognisably that of the new war poetry – 'earth … scarr'd', 'torrents of plunging shells', 'a sucking, clutching death' – but his account of Ypres asserts a dispassion which is quite alien to Sassoon or Owen. The mercy killing of a man who cannot be rescued from drowning in earth would become an iconic scenario in diverse modern representations of war – for example, David Lean's *Lawrence of Arabia* (1962) and Pat Barker's *The Ghost Road* (1995):

> An officer shot him through the head:
> Not a neat job – the revolver
> Was too close.[23]

The overtones – the absurdity of the desires captured by 'neat', the multiple ironies of proximity, friend and foe – are more finely controlled than the dynamic but already commonplace metaphors for the battlefield already quoted. The modern language of war is, however, further contrasted – internally – by Kneeshaw's 'war-song', which resolves on the poem's epigraph from Chaucer's 'Balade de Bon Conseyl', a courtly lyric counselling self-discipline as a means to win deliverance by 'Truth'. Anticipating the trope of standing up which would structure Ford Madox Ford's *Parade's End* tetralogy (1924–8) – among other things, a reversal of the troglodyte instinct for keeping one's head out of harm's way in the space above the trenches – Read has Kneeshaw sing his recognition that 'I was a bloodier fool' than Judas, and acceptance of 'Chance that gave me a crutch and a view', that is survival as a *mutilé de guerre*.[24]

'The Scene of War' announces more explicitly its political and aesthetic inversions by adapting lines from Imagist poet H.D.'s 'The Gift' (from *The Sea Garden*, 1916):

> And perhaps some outer horror
> some hideousness to stamp beauty,
> a mark
> on our hearts.[25]

In pursuit of this Baudelairean project of discovering aesthetic form amidst modern carnage, the component poems exhibit a range of effects: the anti-nomian rhetoric of Wyndham Lewis's periodical *Blast* in 'The Crucifix' (ii), Vorticist diagrams of the dynamics of war in 'Fear' (iii), burlesque comedy in 'Liedholz' (v). The last section (viii) is a radically unstructured ballad about the deserter Cornelius Vane, whose rebellion is to target violence against himself rather than the enemy, shooting away his trigger finger so that he is taken out of battle. The emergency of a German offensive requires that he is put back in the line to 'stab' the enemy (a more primitive military drill which Vane has not been able to disown by self-mutilation), so he deserts, travel-ling West: '[T]he peace of the fields/Dissipated the terror that had been the strength of his will' in running away. The deserter's last words, spoken blind-fold to a firing squad, echo the naïve incisiveness of Kneeshaw's war song:

> 'What wrong have I done that I should leave these:
> The bright sun rising
> And the birds that sing?'[26]

The endemic sadness of his death at dawn contrasts with the state of the 'Happy Warrior' (iv) who is competent to 'stab/and stab again' but who 'cannot shriek'.[27] Vane's direct appeal to nature is explicitly antithetical to the ironic, distracted stances of the sequence which incorporates him, but in its candour it is the most iconoclastic statement in that sequence. Vane, as a literary character who first shoots himself, and is then shot by his own regiment, is a standing critique of the motifs of self-sacrifice and of cama-raderie. Read draws another, more cautious distinction between the virtues of a unit's camaraderie, 'a body and soul entire', and the viciousness of the circumstances, together with the disengagement required to depict them, in 'My Company' (vii):

> 3
> A man of mine
> lies on the wire.
> It is death to fetch his soulless corpse.
> ....
>
> 4
> I can assume
> a giant attitude and godlike mood
> and then detachedly regard
> all riots, conflicts and collisions.[28]

Vane and Kneeshaw emerge as mediating figures, neither the spoken for, nor the transcendently articulate, anticipating aspects of the point of view achieved by Frederic Manning in his creation of Private Bourne in the novel

The Middle Parts of Fortune (1929), one of the few significant works of British war fiction which is not predicated on the experience of a subaltern officer.

The End of a War (1933) disperses its perspectives in a different way, by ventriloquising the dead as well as giving voice to the survivor. War at the terminal pitch of its inhumane brutality – massacre in 'cold blood' by machine gun, gratuitous mutilation ('In excess of horror/War died') – is chosen as the vantage from which to examine life (and in particular, what Read later called the 'no- man's-years-between-the-wars').[29] The volume's title is both literal – its third part, 'Meditation of the Waking English Officer', is an Armistice Day reflection on the moment of winning through – and a revision of Wells's 1914 invocation of the grim consolatory fiction of a 'war that will end war'.[30] The poem's coda also reassesses the literary record of the war. It is alleged that daily cohabitation with death had transformed political hope ('from this unwilled war pass gallantly/to wars of will and justice') into 'a little pool of bitterness'; however, waking into peace is accompanied by a wager that human acts are 'obscure' traces of providence rather than a passive acceptance that the world is a blind, mechanical process.[31] This rejection of what Robert Nichols later labeled 'futilitarianism' is the clearest reason why this poem, and not the work of Owen, represented war poetry in Yeats's *Oxford Book of Modern Verse* (1936): 'passive suffering is not a theme for poetry'.[32]

Robert Nichols's work appears to belong to Graves's category of a poetry of self-dedication written 'imitatively' (either by civilians or by soldiers writing 'as though they had seen more of the war than they had').[33] Indeed, a perennial problem for students of war poetry is not calling into question what James Campbell has called 'combat gnosticism' (the Owenesque idea that soldiers have a secret knowledge denied to non-combatants).[34] 'Comrades: An Episode' is dated 1915, when Nichols was hospitalised during training. At the end of the narrative, Mr Gates – who drags his mortally wounded body across No Man's Land in the direction of his men's voices – does not 'die alone' but with those of his men who are killed hauling him over the parapet at the point of his last breath. Death in this poem, as Nichols put it later, is 'a flowering', registered intriguingly as a shuttling between consciousness:

> 'No good...
>
>   Lift me.' They lifted him
> He smiled and held his arms out to the dim,
> And in a moment passed beyond their ken
> Hearing him whisper, 'O my men, my men!'

as if at the point of death the man transmutes into a verbal trace of an affirmation of comradeship in collective memory ('their ken').[35] Much in this poem seems to prefigure the relationship between sentiment and violence in R.C. Sherriff's record-breaking, and now oft-revived, domestic (dug-out) drama, *Journey's End* (1928). This play reveals, perhaps more eloquently than any other work representing the war, the double bind of the militarist culture we still inhabit, in which the soldier is both killer and nurse, and military experience is both pedagogy and vandalism. But Nichols's story is a symptom rather than a diagnosis of this cultural dissociation.

Writing twenty years later, Nichols distinguished a pre-Somme 'valour of ardour', 'a valour of attack and of attack envisaged in comparative ignorance and romantically' from a 'valour of endurance' keyed to the 'continual gloomy, unrelenting drench which seemed so inevitably to characterise later month-long battles'.[36] This perhaps is not so much an analysis of the changing sentiment of soldiers as a projection of poetic fashions onto history, echoing the title of one of his wartime volumes. 'Battle', a sequence of eleven poems published in *Ardours and Endurances* (1917), illustrates Nichols's facility as a war poet, but also reveals the essential instability – another symptom of the contradictions in modern militarism – which is to be found in his long theoretical statement on war poetry at the beginning of the Second World War. In the first poem, men wait 'like cattle in a pen'. The imagery aims at verisimilitude, among its effects, but is deflected by a temptation to the emphatic and rhetorical. Nichols renders the heat and sensory irritation cogently – '[a] buss and blaze of flies' – but loses focus as the scene is confused with proverbial wisdom to unintentionally comic effect:

> Sometimes a soldier sighs and stirs
> As in hell's frying fire.[37]

This unevenness of tone is characteristic of Nichols's war verse: in 'Night Bombardment' (ii) syntax is again overridden by ellipsis (a tentative approach to the post-Imagist collage); additionally, a trochaic opening stumbles into iambic/anapaestic rhythms and typographical features (font size, italics) are used over-emphatically to dramatise the relations of self-conscious observation, traumatic empathy and rhetoric. Nichols's ideas can be striking, as in the way the wind searching for the 'forgotten dead' suggests the work of involuntary memory:

> Hidden in the hedges or trodden in the muck
> Under the trenches, or maybe limply stuck
> Somewhere in the branches of a high lonely tree –
> He was a sniper once. They never found his body.[38]

Tim O'Brien would fashion an iconic anti-narrative of the Vietnam War, *The Things They Carried* (1990), from the resonance of just such an uncanny transposition – a man blown into the canopy of a tree – but Nichols's is a restless poetry, constantly modulating onto perspectives and ideas that squander the force of his imagery. Whereas Read and Graves enforced significant formal constraints on their material, Nichols's poems are notable for their lack of architecture. 'The Assault' (ix) is exemplary:

> On, on. Leăd. Leăd. Hail
> Spatter. Whirr! Whirr!
> *'Towards that patch of brown;*
> *Direction left'.* Bullets a stream.
> Devouring thought crying in a dream.
> Men, crumpled, going down....
> Go on. Go.
> Deafness. Numbness. The loudening tornado.
> Bullets. Mud. Stumbling and skating.
> My voice's strangled shout:
> *'Steady pace, boys!'*[39]

When Graves suggested this was 'exciting' (simultaneously joshing at its author's 'brief and uneventful service in France'), he was reiterating his view of the basic cultural work of 'war poetry' – 'stimulus to recruiting'.[40]

Nils Claussen has argued that the claim for an experiential basis to the new war poetry is radically unhistorical: instead, it is the literary model which has priority in the articulation of poetic statements.[41] The commitment to 'combat Gnosticism' is an additional sense in which the study of war writing has until recently been largely anti-modernist. In Claussen's Eliotian view, however, the 'trench lyric' is to be seen not as the outcome of an unprecedented socio-technological conjunction in Flanders, but as a cultural formation in English literature – a generic adaptation of the Romantic nature lyric, exemplified in the verse of Rosenberg, but particularly by Edmund Blunden in his war pastorals. His 'Third Ypres' is a deictically complex, unrhymed poem of more than a hundred lines (manuscript date July/August 1917) which counterpoints military and psychological operations, resolving on the apparent remoteness of the possibility of relief. In structure, it presents successive phases in two nights of an offensive, opening strikingly in a mood of 'triumph' and 'extravagant joy'.[42] The strategic fantasy of movement replacing stasis and the human longing that 'The War would end' are each turned into 'mockery triumph' by the weather, and imaged as inversions of a bucolic order. The men have 'flood[ed]' forward to die 'on the entanglements':

> The wire stood up like an unplashed hedge and thorned
> With giant spikes – and there they've paid the bill.[43]

The pun on bill (the edged tool of the hedge layer) is not a pastoral consolation, but an index of the fracturing of consciousness in emergency: 'I liked
him, that young runner,/But there's no time for that'. The central passage
of the poem describes an advance to relieve a frenzied forward troop: their
laggard bodies Blunden describes as 'a strange whim' in contrast with the
mental 'armour' that could 'live out these poor limbs'. But that capacity for
endurance is self-defeating. The restored channel of the field telephone cre-
ates a double burden: impotence coupled with a consciousness of '[a] whole
sweet countryside amuck with murder'.[44]

That conjunction of sweetness and muck/murder, recalling to us Owen's
negation of the Horatian *dulce* in his celebrated gas poem, might stand for
Blunden's reputation as 'war poet', which is as askew from the vocation of
protest poetry as is Graves's verse. 'Surrounding pastoral urged them to forget' describes the effects of returning to the rear of the line ('The Guard's
Mistake'), but it anticipates a critical anxiety about an escapist tendency
in the ironic juxtaposition of military and bucolic landscapes, martial and
pastoral diction in Blunden's poetry.[45] In the poem 'Escape', 'A Mind' turns
away from having to 'view those ravished trunks/And hips and blackened
hunks'.[46] Even when, in the poem 'Illusions', trench 'loveliness' appears to
be negated by the 'nemesis of beauty' – an attack – the attackers turn out to
be another apparition:

> Death's malkins dangling in the wire
> For the moon's interpretation.[47]

These scarecrows inhabit the same realm of enchantment as military decoys,
the straw men and tree-stump observation posts of the early camoufleurs.
'Thiepval Wood', a geographical companion piece to Grave's 'Dead Boche',
might be definitive of this Blundenesque effect, in its blurring of the body
and the landscape, or ordnance and natural forces:

> The shell-fountains leap from the swamps, and with wildfire and fume,
> The shoulder of the chalkdown convulses.
> Then abbering echoes stampede in the slatting wood,
> Ember-black the gibbet trees like bones or thorns protrude ...[48]

Paul Fussell dubbed Blunden the 'gentle infantryman' in contrasting the
autobiographical narrative on which he worked after 1918 to Graves's
programmatically disloyal performance as military memoirist.[49] But the
two later Oxford Professors of Poetry are alike in being identified by posterity with those works of retrospection, books which exemplify another,

later fashion for war writing, the 'war book boom of 1928–1933': whereas Graves said goodbye to his war verse, Blunden's circulated as a supplement to the widely read *Undertones of War* (1928). It was Herbert Read's career as a spokesman for modernism (as curator, academic, broadcaster, editor and popular writer of *The Meaning of Art* [1931]) which eclipsed his output as poet and novelist, although his political views came closest to those often erroneously assumed to lie behind the poetry of Sassoon and Owen. Robert Nichols, after spells in Japan (Blunden would follow him to Imperial University Tokyo) and Hollywood, returned to England and an unsuccessful career as dramatist. He died in 1944.

NOTES

1 Robert Graves, 'The Poets of World War Two' (1942) in *The Common Asphodel: Collected Essays on Poetry, 1922–1949* (London: Hamish Hamilton, 1949), 308.
2 Ibid., 307–9.
3 Edmund Blunden, *The Poems of Edmund Blunden, 1914–1930* (London: Cobden-Sanderson, 1930), vii.
4 Philip Larkin, 'The War Poet', in *Required Writing* (London: Faber, 1983), 159. For a discussion of Great War pedagogy and heritage, see Dan Todman, *The Great War: Myth and Memory* (London: Hambledon Continuum, 2005).
5 Wilfred Owen, *Selected Letters*, ed. John Bell (Oxford: Oxford University Press, 1985), 119.
6 Samuel Hynes, *A War Imagined: The First World War and English Culture* (London: The Bodley Head, 1990), 202.
7 See Ronald Gaskell's review of Robert Graves, *Complete Poems*, in *Essays in Criticism*, 51.3 (2001): 378–84, 378–9 and Robert Graves, *Poems about War*, ed. William Graves (London: Cassell, 1988), 7.
8 Chris Baldick, *The Modern Movement 1910–1940* (Oxford: Oxford University Press, 2007), 336.
9 Graves, *Poems about War*, 15.
10 Ibid., 21.
11 Ezra Pound, *Selected Poems* (London: Faber, 1973), 175.
12 Robert Graves, *Good-bye to All That* (1929; London: Jonathan Cape, 1931), 264.
13 Ted Hughes, *Selected Poems 1957–1981* (London: Faber, 1982), 59.
14 F.T. Marinetti, 'The Founding and Manifesto of Futurism 1909', in Vasiliki Kolocotroni, Jane Goldman and Olga Taxidou eds. *Modernism: An Anthology of Sources and Documents* (Edinburgh: Edinburgh University Press, 1998), 251. Graves *Poems about War*, 30.
15 Ibid.
16 Graves, *Poems about War*, 53. See Dominic Hibberd, '"The Patchwork Flag" (1918) an Unrecorded Book by Robert Graves', *The Review of English Studies*, ns 41.164 (November 1990), 521–32.
17 Graves, *Poems about War*, 33.
18 George Orwell, 'Pacifism and the War', *Collected Essays, Journalism and Letters*, Vol. 2 (Harmondsworth: Penguin, 1970), 261.

19 Herbert Read, *Selected Poetry* (London: Faber, 1966), 153. Hereafter abbreviated as *Poetry*.

20 Quoted in Jon Silkin ed. *Herbert Read: A Memorial Symposium* (London: Methuen, 1970), 74. Hereafter abbreviated as *Read*.

21 Read, *Poetry*, 31.

22 Silkin, *Read*, 74.

23 Read, *Poetry*, 32.

24 Ibid., 33.

25 Ibid., 34.

26 Ibid., 44.

27 Ibid., 35.

28 Ibid., 37, 39.

29 Read, *Poetry,* 109; Silkin, 75.

30 H.G. Wells, *The War That Will End War* (London: Frank and Cecil Palmer, 1914).

31 Read, *Poetry*, 113.

32 Robert Nichols, *Anthology of War Poetry 1914–1918* (London: Nicholson and Watson, 1943), 71 [Hereafter abbreviated as *Anthology*]; W.B. Yeats ed. *The Oxford Book of Modern Poetry, 1892–1935* (Oxford: Oxford University Press, 1936), xxxiv.

33 Graves, 'The Poets of World War Two', 308.

34 James Campbell, 'Combat Gnosticism: The Ideology of First World War Poetry Criticism', *New Literary History*, 30.1 (Winter 1999), 203–215: 204.

35 Nichols, *Anthology*, 51; *Ardours and Endurances; also, A Faun's Holiday, and Poems and Fantasies* (London: Chatto and Windus, 1917), 26.

36 *Anthology*, 51.

37 Robert Nichols, *Ardours and Endurances*, 18.

38 Ibid., 20.

39 *Ardours and Endurances*, 41.

40 Graves, 'The Poets of the Second World War', 308, 310.

41 Nils Clausson, '"Perpetuating the Language": Romantic Tradition, the Genre Function, and the Origins of the Trench Lyric', *Journal of Modern Literature*, 30.1 (Autumn 2006), 105–6 (104–28).

42 *Undertones of War* (1928; London: Collins, 1965), 230.

43 Ibid., 231.

44 Ibid., 232.

45 Ibid., 214.

46 Ibid., 217.

47 Ibid., 216.

48 *The Poems of Edmund Blunden 1914–1930*, 11.

49 Paul Fussell, 'Modernism, Adversary Culture, and Edmund Blunden', *The Sewanee Review*, 94.4 (Fall 1986), 589 (583–601).

5

SARAH COLE

Siegfried Sassoon

On 31 July 1917, a proclamation was printed in *The Times* (having been read aloud and discussed in the House of Commons the day before) and signed by its author, S. Sassoon. 'I am making this statement as an act of wilful defiance of military authority, because I believe that the War is being deliberately prolonged by those who have the power to end it', the Soldier's Declaration began, and went on to portray its writer, first and foremost, as a representative of the fighting men. 'I am a soldier', it affirmed, 'convinced that I am acting on behalf of soldiers' and more, 'I have seen and endured the sufferings of the troops, and I can no longer be a party to prolong these sufferings for ends which I believe to be evil and unjust ... On behalf of those who are suffering now I make this protest....'[1] Siegfried Sassoon was in many ways an unlikely person to write such a statement. Having grown up in a gentrified country atmosphere he loved for its 'fox-hunting' and cricket, he had enlisted two days before war was declared, trained as an officer, taken part in the Somme offensive, and received the Military Cross. As Virginia Woolf describes her fictional First World War soldier Septimus Warren Smith, who owes more than his unusual name to Sassoon, 'he had gone through the whole show, friendship, European War, death, had won promotion, was still under thirty and was bound to survive'.[2] Unlike the stifled and suicidal Septimus, Sassoon had found a voice early in the war, and several of his war poems were published in the prestigious coterie volume, 'Georgian Poetry' of 1916–17.[3] His poems testified to his having 'seen and endured the sufferings of the troops', as the protest put it, especially in works written after the brutal Somme fighting of 1916, a critical period in sharpening his attitude of bitterness toward the war. Sassoon's claim to speak 'on behalf of' the serving men was forged in poems that often take as their subject the single, unnamed soldier, and are frequently addressed at a target standing just in front of the reader. The Soldier's Declaration – a dangerous gambit that might have led to court martial and imprisonment had it not been for the assiduous work of his well-connected friends – can be taken as a political, public documentation of Sassoon's broad commitment to developing a language of protest from within the war's compass.[4]

The Soldier's Declaration offers a prism for reading Sassoon's poetry, a body of verse that installs dissent against the war at its center – at the level of word, line, image and voice. His lyrics operate in polemical fashion, constructing strong antagonisms, as well as implying affiliation across the ranks of serving men, and in so doing, are on common ground with others in this volume, many of whom aim to speak for the 'patient men who fight' ('Banishment').[5] Yet Sassoon has his own distinct idiom, exemplified by the regularly used verb 'loathe', his creation of a self-portrait as an 'angry' poet, and his use of satire as a primary genre. His defiant, tonally acerbic poems carry less pity than those of his friend Wilfred Owen and, by the same token, fewer of the attributes that cluster around pity, such as intimacy, gentleness and the blending of identities in the spaces of combat.[6] Nevertheless, if the primary motivation of Sassoon's lyrics is to denounce war and indict its promoters, other quieter currents pull against these imperatives in a corpus that has, too, its meditations and its metaphysics.

But it begins with outrage. 'You've heard me, scornful, harsh, and discontented,/ Mocking and loathing War', opens 'The Poet as Hero', written in late 1916 and offering a rationale for the poet's brazen new tone: 'you've asked me why/Of my old, silly sweetness I've repented – /My ecstasies changed to an ugly cry' (WP, 61). It is a poem of address, with a literal 'you' in the position of interlocutor, and it makes the claim of righteousness, declaring that 'there is absolution' in the poet's 'ugly' songs. The poem is structured along an axis of transition, the poet justifying his abandonment of 'the Grail' and 'Galahad', along with the language that accompanies these Christian quests. Instead, shockingly, he is motivated by an almost primal violence, by the thirst for revenge, propelled by his friends' deaths: 'For lust and senseless hatred make me glad,/ And my killed friends are with me where I go./Wound for red wound I burn to smite their wrongs' (WP, 61). These killed friends are not solely fellow soldiers lost along the way or the generalized dead of war; Sassoon was particularly devastated by the death on 18 March 1916 of his friend David Thomas, whom Sassoon loved intensely, and whose killing haunted him for the rest of the war. Sassoon was homosexual (although Thomas was not), and the searing nature of his pain in losing Thomas, a combination of deep loss that cannot be mourned under wartime conditions and a wrathful desire for revenge, infuses his poetry from this time onward. It also helps to account for his desire, as he put it, 'of getting a bit of my own back', and for a particularly dramatic episode in his war service when he single-handedly occupied a German trench, contributing to his earning the nickname, 'Mad Jack'.[7] In 'The Poet as Hero', despite the use of archaic words like 'smite', Sassoon generates a vocabulary and style attuned to this rawness of war – its wounds, its blood, its frustrations. As in any style ordered by reprisal, the parallelism within the line ('wound for red wound') performs the deadening repetitiveness of reprisal violence in the real world, and contains its own irrefutable logic of eye for eye, violence for violence. There is something internal and circular in the poem's account of its own heroics, its 'scornful, harsh, and discontented' voice constitutive of the war world as imagined across Sassoon's works.

There is much to make this poet angry: military incompetence at the highest level; hypocrisies and absurdities emanating from the press, the church, and the government; and perhaps above all, a continued adherence, among too many at home, to a pre-1914 adulation of the heroic ideal of war – what Owen tags 'the old Lie'. Sassoon's signature tactic in exposing old (and new) lies, along with his viral tone, is to incorporate into his poetry the voices of those he holds culpable, in the form of dialogue, adopting the mode of satire. Thus, 'The General' begins genially enough ('"Good-morning, good-morning!" the General said/ When we met him last week on our way to the line'), but then turns quickly, via the men's 'cursing' and jolting colloquialism ('"He's a cheery old card," grunted Harry to Jack'), into an almost ghoulish irony as the general gets the last laugh: 'But he did for them both by his plan of attack' (*WP*, 78). '"They"', similarly constructed, has a bishop inaugurate the poem's dialogue: '"When the boys come back/ They will not be the same; for they'll have fought/ In a just cause: they lead the last attack/ On Anti-Christ"'. '[T]he boys' indeed concur that all are transformed, '"For George lost both his legs; and Bill's stone blind;/ Poor Jim's shot through the lungs and like to die;/ And Bert's gone syphilitic ..."' (*WP*, 57). But before the poem – or the reader – can recover from this grotesque bodily litany, entirely appropriate to this war's technologies, there is further satire, as the final words are given back to the bishop: '"The ways of God are strange!"' Overall, both 'The General' and '"They"' establish the men's salty language as an ironizing and irreconcilable contrast to the official rhetoric of state and church.

In 'Editorial Impressions', Sassoon again incorporates a conventional language meant to infuriate – this time in the voice of the press, whose cheery correspondent is full of enthusiasm for '"the amazing spirit of the troops"', the fineness of '"those flying-chaps"'; 'through it all', he rhapsodizes, '"I felt that splendour shine/Which makes us win"' (*WP*, 89). Commenting laconically on the ironies inherent in such froth is an injured soldier, more amused than outraged at the journalist. 'Editorial Impressions' has a light touch, and yet the indictment is serious, as suggested by the term 'witnessing'. Witnessing here is overtly linked to the journalist's 'big impressions' – his '"notes made while witnessing the fighting"' – only to be pitted against a genuine witness existing almost as a shadow: the 'grin[ning]... lad' sipping his wine, speaking little but testifying in his silent, injured body to the falsity of the journalist's report. The place of the witness in documenting the crimes of the modern world, a central tenet in the moral life of the second half of the twentieth century, emerged distinctly from the trenches of the First World War, with poets like Sassoon demonstrating that artistry and direct reporting need not be seen as divergent endeavors; on the contrary, they are firmly allied in the work of the soldier-poet.

More complex than these poems that turn on a relatively simple undermining of voice by voice, yet in the same family, are those that take the shell-shocked soldier as their focus. Following his protest, and spared court martial, Sassoon was sent instead to the Craiglockhart War Hospital to be treated for shell shock (or what he and his doctor joked was his 'anti-war complex'), where he spent four months (July–late November 1917). This was a period of intense poetic fruitfulness for Sassoon, as it was for his co-inmate Owen, in part as they responded to the exceptional medical faculty at the hospital. Not himself shell shocked (although certainly in a state of strain), Sassoon found himself a visitor in a world where men were suffering from a range of profound and little-understood psychic ailments. It was an 'underworld of dreams', as he described it in his memoir, where nights, in particular, were alive with terrors, the traumatized soldiers confronting war horrors that forced the 'disintegration' of their very manhood, their humanity.[8] By this point in the war, shell shock had become a subject of tremendous interest among civilians and combatants alike, and an inescapable scourge for medical authorities, who were deeply divided about its meaning, legitimacy, causes and treatment. For Sassoon, there was no such uncertainty: 'In the name of civilization', he wrote, 'these soldiers had been martyred'.[9] At Craiglockhart, Sassoon was treated by W.H.R. Rivers, a brilliant Cambridge psychologist and anthropologist, representative of the progressive arm of the medical establishment. Admiring and liking Rivers, although also somewhat competitive with him, Sassoon responded in his own medium, naming a poem 'Repression of War Experience' as a mime of Rivers' lecture of (almost) that name, in which Rivers argued that the ubiquitous recommendation for men suffering from war trauma to 'forget' the war is precisely the wrong advice.[10] For Sassoon, the question is not only about the control of memory, but about the invidious power of language to penetrate and distort the already fragile, wounded mind.

The soldier in 'Repression' has been thoroughly interpolated, his interior monologue permeated by the medical authorities whose advice and admonishments continually enter his stream of consciousness – such that he becomes 'you' or 'them', even to himself. The poem begins:

> Now light the candles; one; two; there's a moth;
> What silly beggars they are to blunder in
> And scorch their wings with glory, liquid flame –
> No, no, not that, – it's bad to think of war,
> When thoughts you've gagged all day come back to scare you;
> And it's been proved that soldiers don't go mad
> Unless they lose control of ugly thoughts
> That drive them out to jabber among the trees.
>
> Now light your pipe; look, what a steady hand.
> Draw a deep breath; stop thinking; count fifteen,
> And you're as right as rain ... (*WP*, 84, ellipsis in original)

The poem is in free verse, somewhat atypically for Sassoon, and its meter is irregular and bumpy, shifting tracks along with its protagonist, buffeted by the directives of doctors, with their studies and assurances, and by his own casual derision toward those who 'jabber among the trees'. The soldier, in a monomaniacal state, projects his own experiences onto the universe, seeing the war's danger and meaninglessness coloring the natural world, and yet we know that there is a singular consciousness at the base of such distortions. There is a gorgeous richness in his words, and something real and satisfying in his observational style. All of this is muted and derailed by the expertise around him, by the pull of conventionality ('right as rain'), and by the man's own disgust at the 'old men with ugly souls' of the civilian world (there is a good deal of Sassoon in this portrait). It is only at the end of the poem that the soldier's 'I' voice emerges, in a full break from all the poem's many efforts to soothe, silence or rescript, and a break, too, from even the most minimal vestige of poetic meter: 'O Christ, I want to go out/And screech at them to stop – I'm going crazy;/ I'm going stark, staring mad because of the guns' (*WP*, 85). In suggesting that the soldier's terrible paralysis answers not only to the rampaging violence of war, but also to the human establishment arrayed around and about its margins, 'Repression' upholds the protest banner. Other poems produce a similar configuration of voices and madness, especially 'Survivors', which recuperates the 'mocking and loathing' tone somewhat muted in 'Repression': 'Their dreams ... drip with murder', the poet hisses, as the struggling, suffering men stare at the reader, 'Children, with eyes that hate you, broken and mad' (*WP*, 97). In his landscape of defiance, Sassoon's shell-shocked relics present an especially outraging spectacle: a community whose frustration can only be expressed outwardly in angry looks, or, more tragically, in the inwardly directed violence of nightmare, even suicide.

Of all the culprits Sassoon constructs, one group stands alone: women. In the ironically titled poem 'The Hero', Sassoon offers up women, and particularly mothers, as the war's dupes: 'We mothers are so proud/ Of our dead soldiers' (WP, 49). Tired and bowed, the poem's mother figure nevertheless upholds the pose of pride – 'her weak eyes/Had shone with gentle triumph, brimmed with joy' – to be punctured in the poem by the true story of her son, a 'cold-footed, useless swine'. More elaborately, 'Glory of Women', one of Sassoon's most controversial poems, launches the full force of its animus against its decidedly unglorified addressees:

> You love us when we're heroes, home on leave,
> Or wounded in a mentionable place.
> You worship decorations; you believe
> That chivalry redeems the world's disgrace.
> You make us shells. You listen with delight,
> By tales of dirt and danger fondly thrilled.
> You crown our distant ardours while we fight,
> And mourn our laurelled memories when we're killed.
> You can't believe that British troops 'retire'
> When hell's last horror breaks them, and they run,
> Trampling the terrible corpses – blind with blood.
>   O German mother dreaming by the fire,
> While you are knitting socks to send your son
> His face is trodden deeper in the mud. (WP, 100)

You, you, you, you, you, you: more than any of his other poems, 'Glory of Women' ferociously confronts its projected interlocutors, constructing in its bubbling anger a portrait of women as bewitched by lore and lies. In an alliance of ignorance with their German counterparts, English women are very busy with their verbs: they love, worship, believe, listen, crown; above all, they 'make us shells' – in two overlapping senses (make artillery shells; hollow men out). If women's work in munitions factories was entreated by the government and remembered by many women as a fulfilling experience of independence, here it is imagined, alongside the more domestic contribution of home-knit socks, as a form of quiet violence. The poem is in high-defiance gear, thrusting an image of the dead and defiled body of the German boy before his mother's dreamy eyes. Its misogynistic energy seems to constellate much of Sassoon's general attitude of outraged loathing, forging a universalized image of regressive female war adulation and blind militarism. In the phrase 'blind with blood', moreover, Sassoon evokes a broader protest tradition, echoing Shelley's phrase 'blind in blood' from his poem 'England in 1819', a sonnet that evoked the Peterloo massacre of that year, in which British troops attacked a group of peaceful protesters who were demanding parliamentary reform.[11] In recruiting Shelley, Sassoon gestures toward a wider language of protest within the English literary canon, a move also made in Owen's 'Miners' which imagines an affinity between the war's soldiers and workers killed in a terrible mining accident in 1918. Nevertheless, 'Glory of Women', unlike the aching and sorrowful 'Miners', can spare no sympathy; its targeting of the poor old German mother in the final lines seems relentless, even gratuitous.

For all its potency in Sassoon's corpus, the choice to align women with the rest of the war's supporters in the manner of 'The Hero' or 'Glory of Women', runs up against a fundamental feature of soldiers' lives during war: their longing, concern and love for women. Sassoon's combatants think of their English homes, warm fires, rum, sports, trees, friends and horses, but almost never of women (although one soldier in 'A Night Attack' does have an open letter from a sweetheart resting on his knee, the fuel for his pleasant daydreaming). Sassoon, whose own, often troubled, emotional life was entirely bound up with men, cannot quite bring himself to incorporate into his war world this one band of deep and rich feeling. In 'A Subaltern', one of the poems to feature his beloved Thomas, the poet allows Thomas to articulate the rationale of such excision: 'But as he stamped and shivered in the rain,/ My stale philosophies had served him well;/Dreaming about his girl had sent his brain/Blanker than ever – she'd no place in Hell' (WP, 25). Women have no place in a man's world of suffering and struggle; nor are they welcome to its comradeship, a prejudice Sassoon inherited in part from the masculine Oxbridge culture to which he had been attached before the war and that he shares with Owen. Even the poem 'The Road', which begins 'The road is thronged with women', immediately erases them: 'soldiers pass/ And halt, but never see them' (WP, 51). As it turns out, the 'them' in this second line refers not or not solely to the just-named women, but to an even more invisible, liminal group: the dead. In the pronominal confusions that mark the poem's first stanza, Sassoon manages a double erasure of women, who are not only not seen by the passing troops but, as it happens, are not even the certain subject of that overlooking.

The effort to construct a world definitive of war and limited to soldiers takes many forms in Sassoon's works. If the creation, ironizing and hierarchizing of war voices represent the most visible strategy, a quieter motif is also at work in the form of vocabulary. Like all poets, Sassoon has his favorite words. 'Loathe', 'gloom', 'darkness', 'ruined', 'dull', 'sodden', 'sunken', 'grope', 'thudding', and 'the guns' are some of the most notable in creating aura, sound and mood across his works. Many are particular to the war, with its capacious terminology ('redoubt', 'crump'). Others are strange to modern ears ('sluice', 'frowst') or unusually redolent of English pastoral ('weald'). These last five are notable for their nearness to other more ordinary words – 'doubt', 'cramp/crimp', 'slice', 'frost', 'world' – and it is characteristic of Sassoon's method that he borrows from the meanings and associations of these more common terms while tilting his language into strange, new territory. The world of rain sluicing down belongs to Sassoon's war, but not in quite the same way as the wry, colloquial language of the men. Instead, one encounters here the English literary history that permeated Sassoon's imaginary – attesting, for instance, to the large presence of Hardy, with his ruddy heath settings (as well as his particular ironies[12]), of Shakespeare, and especially of Romanticism, which gave rich figure to the mutuality of outdoor environment and interior tumult.

Words like 'frowst' are atmospheric, and the atmosphere in Sassoon's poetry is itself a material reality. The air is thick with presences. At times his poetry faces the aggressive ubiquity of death with the attitude of a shrug, in other cases with poignancy and mournfulness (as in the lovely, terribly sad poem, 'The Death Bed'), often with his signature outrage, and then, too, in a mystical spirit. Powerfully influenced by Shelley's great elegy 'Adonais', in which the lamenting poet figures his dead male friend as 'one with Nature ... a presence to be felt and known/ In darkness and in light', Sassoon depicts his own killed friend Thomas as a kind of immanence.[13] If in the poem 'Enemies', Thomas appears as a bodily shadow, joining hands with a dead German, more emphatically he lives in the broad natural world. In 'The Last Meeting', the poet describes his effort to reconnoiter with his dead friend, 'And speak with him before his ghost has flown' (WP, 31). And meet they do. After an initial failure to find him in a ruined house, the poet has his epiphany:

> Ah! but there was no need to call his name.
> He was beside me now, as swift as light.
> I knew him crushed to earth in scentless flowers,
> And lifted in the rapture of dark pines.
> 'For now', he said, 'my spirit has more eyes
> Than heaven has stars; and they are lit by love.
> My body is the magic of the world,
> And dawn and sunset flame with my spilt blood.
> My breath is the great wind, and I am filled
> With molten power and surge of the bright waves
> That chant my doom along the ocean's edge'. (WP, 33)

Thomas's incarnation in the natural landscape infuses his own beauty into the wider world, and also fills it with the violence of war. This impregnating of the world with war (with its victims and its violence, a kind of force in the universe), contrasts with the more overt portrayal of soldiers as

Christ figures, a frequent usage throughout Sassoon's poetry. When Sassoon declares (twice) of the swearing soldier in his early poem 'The Redeemer' 'I say that He was Christ', or of his own writing in 'The Poet as Hero', 'there is absolution in my songs', or when he implies that the doubting combatant in 'Christ and the Soldier' has inherited the mantle of the forsaking savior, he is very much in the defiance mode, appropriating Christ's authority and dynamism, while dismissing religion (*WP*, 16–17, 61, 45–6). These poems dare the reader to dispute their rebellious claims to salvific power. Lyrics like 'The Last Meeting', by contrast, are inclusive in spirit, in their meditative incitements calling up alternate histories of thought, such as those elaborated by Romanticism. 'My spirit longs for prayer', the poet grieves in 'In the Church of St Ouen', 'lost to God, I seek him everywhere' (*WP*, 72).

'The Last Meeting' envisions Thomas's spirit being chanted by waves '"along the ocean's edge"', and this representation of the land as a snaking length along the water calls up one of Sassoon's recurrent tropes, the road. It would seem that the road is an inescapable image in war writing, which inevitably partakes of (and also deconstructs) several progress-oriented genres, such as the quest narrative and the *bildungsroman*. Roads are everywhere in Sassoon's poems. Sometimes these are the roads of the French countryside through which the poems move, via living and dead soldiers passing, marching, trudging; the trenches too are portrayed as roadways – hellish, dark and inverted; and memories of home have a tendency to locate themselves in country lanes, evocative of the neighborhoods of Sassoon's past. The persistence of roads as a primary site in Sassoon's poetry carries many connotations – of progress and thwarted progress, of movement across spheres, of older literary traditions, where the road is a privileged location, and also of the liminality that Eric Leed has characterized as definitive of this war.[14] But one thing they do *not* suggest is protest. Indeed, the road is an ultimate signifier of the individual – his life, his psyche, his journey – and hence counters the primary mode of outrage, which depends fundamentally on the poet stepping out of his own psychic territory to portray the 'sufferings of the troops'.

Sassoon's poetry might be figured, then, according to two divergent tendencies: protest, which keeps its focus on the men and its voice in the mode of satire and declamation, and an attention to the more soluble, private self, raveling and unraveling, as boundaries separating world from person dissolve.[15] Indeed, these two styles, unequal in the poet's reputation, extend into the post-war period, when Sassoon, now established as an important war writer, continued to produce poetry, attuned to the tense, swirling issues surrounding the war's remembrance. Thus, the muscular 'On Passing the New Menin Gate' resurrects Sassoon's old animus in striking new terms, while 'To One Who was With Me in the War' takes to the 'sunken ruinous roads' of that alternate space and style, where borders of mind and body are precarious and permeable. 'Menin Gate' replays the indignation of Sassoon's earlier poetry, expressing outrage at the reemergence of pre-war ideals in the form of a huge memorial, erected in 1927 to commemorate the missing of the Ypres area (some 55,000 men whose bodies were never recovered), built on the spot. Pitting himself against what he presents as a benighted message of retrospective uplift, Sassoon shouts back at the 'pile of peace-complacent stone' (WP, 153). 'Here', he declares, 'was the world's worst wound', – a wound that will not be healed, just as 'these intolerably nameless names' can never be reattached to the bodies buried around the Ypres region, the site of particularly grim and wasteful battles. Above all, it is the memorial's Christian language of redemption that infuriates the poet, who envisions a unity of defiance among his fellow soldiers, especially those being memorialized. They will have none of this narrative: 'Well might the Dead who struggled in the slime/ Rise and deride this sepulchre of crime' (WP, 153).

If 'Menin Gate' reignites Sassoon's protest, 'To One' dips downward and forward, in an idiom that comes as close to modernism as any of Sassoon's poems, as the speaker moves, side by side with an old war-mate, into uncharted territory. Rife with mixed metered lines, enjambments, structural and semantic ambiguities, and a style of 'visual fragments' that mirrors the two old soldiers 'who seem, ourselves, like relics casually preserved', it is a poem of its time – 1926 (WP, 151). The poem takes a tour into the unconscious mind, not in an effort to channel or confront medical authorities, as with the earlier shell-shock poems, but as the site and source of its action. The war dominates in ways as complex as the mind itself, and with language to match:

> We forget our fear ...
> And, while the uncouth Event begins to lour less near,
> Discern the mad magnificence whose storm-light throws
> Wild shadows on these after-thoughts that send your brain
> Back beyond Peace, exploring sunken ruinous roads.
> (WP, 151, ellipsis in original)

It is a poem about memory and forgetting, operations that here are less oppositional than inextricable, and its boundary slippage across a host of seemingly differentiated spheres surpasses even lyrics of immanence like 'The Last Meeting'. Indeed, in the 'Wild shadows' thrown by 'storm-light', the poem offers a figure for its own style, and more generally for a poetry that must answer for complexities greater than what the politics of protest can attest: the haunting shapes and patterns projected – wildly and forcefully – by a still-living war onto the minds of men who can never really leave it behind.

NOTES

1 Siegfried Sassoon, *The Complete Memoirs of George Sherston* (London: Faber, 1952), 496. Hereafter abbreviated as *Sherston*. For biography of Sassoon, see the two–volume *Siegfried Sassoon* by Jean Moorcroft Wilson (New York: Routledge, 1999, 2003) and Max Egrement, *Siegfried Sassoon: A Life* (New York: Farrar, Straus and Giroux, 2005).

2 Virginia Woolf, *Mrs. Dalloway* (San Diego: Harvest, 1925), 93.

3 Three volumes of Sassoon's war poetry were published during and just after the war: *The Old Huntsman* (1917), *Counter-Attack* (1918), *War Poems* (1919).

4 As part of his protest, he also is said to have thrown his medal into the Mersey River, although he may only have thrown the ribbon. Years after the war, the medal was found in an attic in the home of Sassoon's relatives, and was auctioned at Christie's in London in 2007. For coverage, see *The Telegraph*, 11 May 2007.

5 Siegfried Sassoon, *The War Poems* (London: Faber, 1983), 108. Hereafter abbreviated as *WP* in the text.

6 Sassoon met Owen at Craiglockhart War Hospital in July 1917 and became something of a mentor to the younger poet. It is a famous collaboration, fictionalized in Pat Barker's novels *Regeneration* and *The Eye in the Door* (New York: Penguin, 1993, 1995). For discussion of the poetic scene at Craiglockhart, see Meredith Martin, *The Rise and Fall of Meter: Poetry and English National Culture, 1860–1930* (Princeton, NJ: Princeton University Press, 2012), chapter five.

7 *Sherston*, 275; 343–7.

8 Ibid., 556–7.

9 Ibid., 557.

10 Rivers's essay, 'Repression of the War Experience', can be found in W.H.R. Rivers, *Instinct and the Unconscious: A Contribution to a Biological Theory of the Psycho-Neuroses* (Cambridge: Cambridge University Press, 1922). Sassoon had initially composed the poem before he had met Rivers.

11 *Shelley's Poetry and Prose* (New York: Norton, 2002), 326.

12 For the classic account of Hardy's irony and the war, see Paul Fussell, *The Great War and Modern Memory* (New York: Oxford, 1975), chapter one.

13 Shelley, 423.

14 Eric Leed, *No Man's Land: Combat and Identity in World War One* (Cambridge: Cambridge University Press, 1979).

15 As with any crisp dichotomy, this one is only partial, and the two modes at times intermingle in a single poem (a good example being 'Repression of War Experience').

6

NEIL CORCORAN

Isaac Rosenberg

'Break of Day in the Trenches' is Isaac Rosenberg's most celebrated poem and one of the best of the poems he wrote at the Front; and as such, it is one of the best poems of the First World War itself. For anyone who knows what preceded it in Rosenberg's short career but substantial poetic output, it also seems almost a miracle of emotional sensitivity, ironic self-awareness and technical subtlety. W.B. Yeats, although he had recommended Rosenberg to Ezra Pound, refused an invitation to introduce a collection by the poet in 1922, saying that he found it 'all windy rhetoric'.[1] This misjudgment is as crass as that with which Yeats dismisses all the war poets in his notorious introduction to the *Oxford Book of Modern Verse* in 1936: that 'passive suffering is not a theme for poetry'.[2] However, while Yeats's judgment of even the pre-war work would be indiscriminately harsh, it would probably not be altogether too harsh. The fact is that 'Break of Day in the Trenches' and Rosenberg's other outstanding war poems follow on a body of work in which large ambition often almost poignantly outruns technical capacity and sureness of allusive touch.

The intensely difficult circumstances of Rosenberg's youth – his origins, that is, in a penurious Jewish East-End family, which had made his formal education nugatory – also provoked in him a high degree of partly defensive but seemingly arrogant self-assurance. Under the circumstances, this may seem admirable; but Jean Moorcroft Wilson's biography catalogues the ways in which it often hardened into an almost impenetrable self-absorption.[3] This made Rosenberg sometimes a very difficult companion, tutee and even object of well-meaning if occasionally condescending patronage; and it can also be felt to diminish poetic force.

The human sympathies and ironies of 'Break of Day in the Trenches' and their unpredictable line-by-line flux, therefore, seem one of the most breathtaking instances of the truism about the poetry of the First World War: that the war itself rapidly, urgently and originally charged the work of its young poets in a way that it is almost impossible to believe anything else ever would. In fact, the poem opening with Rosenberg's first truly unforgettable line – 'Snow is a strange white word' – demonstrates this with almost diagrammatic neatness: it is the poem entitled 'On Receiving News of the War: Cape Town'. 'Break of Day in the Trenches' therefore manifests achievement as the sudden precipitate of strength from hitherto inchoate ambition. It is a poem in which rhetorical strain is purified into lyric necessity; in which formal and even, on occasion, grammatical incoherence is electrified into sheer steadiness of articulation; and in which unbendingly self-assertive will, which can be poetically inhibiting, melts into the true power of imagination. It is therefore an exemplary poem of Rosenberg's speedy maturation, and we may read his contribution through it.

When Rosenberg sent 'Break of Day in the Trenches' in a letter to Edward Marsh in 1916, he recommended it as 'surely as simple as ordinary talk'.[4] As it opens, we do seem to overhear a mode of introspective rumination or meditation. This tone is a function of Rosenberg's insidious rhythm and cadence. 'Regular rhythms I do not like much', he wrote, again to Marsh, saying he would have preferred it if Andrew Marvell 'had broken up his rhythms more'.[5] 'Break of Day in the Trenches' constantly breaks up an iambic pulse with trochaic, spondaic and anapaestic measures, making for an intense liveliness of felt vocal presence and pressure. The opening trochee and the following four strong stresses, distributed among only eight syllables, of the line which introduces the poet's addressee, the rat, for instance – 'Only a live thing leaps my hand'[6] – are mimetic of the surprise and urgency of the event, as the poem's voice is startled out of meditation into perturbed apprehension and recognition. We therefore need to modify what Rosenberg says to Marsh: the poem is only as simple as ordinary talk *in poetry*; and that is not simple, but the fixing into memorable cadence on the page of what a finely tuned ear has apprehended as the music of human speech. The poem's ensuing cadences and rhythms, which include rhetorical elements (and rhetorical questions) not at all like 'ordinary talk', could be described to reveal similar subtleties of response and effect.

Donne's 'The Flea' has been adduced in relation to Rosenberg's rat. However, in Donne, the addressee of the poet is the woman, not the flea itself. By addressing the rat, and more specifically by addressing it with the ambiguous compliment of 'droll', Rosenberg is himself drolly inheriting and revising – downwards – a romantic tradition of apostrophe to the non-human, which reaches its apogee in Shelley's 'To a Skylark' and Keats's 'Ode to a Nightingale':

> Droll rat, they would shoot you if they knew
> Your cosmopolitan sympathies.
> Now you have touched this English hand
> You will do the same to a German

> Soon, no doubt, if it be your pleasure
> To cross the sleeping green between.[7]

Skylark and nightingale undergo an implicit metamorphosis in Rosenberg, of the kind David Jones makes explicit in Part 3 of *In Parenthesis*, where, remembering the Anglo-Saxon poem *The Battle of Maldon* and alluding to Darwin, he says that 'the speckled kite of Maldon / and the crow / have naturally selected to be un-winged'; to exchange their nature as birds, that is, for that of trench rats.[8] Both Keats and Shelley are influential but largely unassimilated presences in pre-war Rosenberg; and it is an irony of more than just literary history that his proper absorption of them should be so revisionist.

If drollness is an attribute shared by rat and poet, the rat's other epithets may seem applicable, too. This poem also has its 'sardonic' aspect, and other war poems of Rosenberg's have that more strongly. 'Queer', in its sense of 'odd' or 'peculiar', has relevance to a poet who often, even before the war and absolutely during it, as a private soldier, felt at odds and incapable, or – worse – was made to feel so by others. Additionally, 'cosmopolitan' is a word prominently associated with Jews, notably in the derogatory phrase in which it is accompanied by the adjective 'rootless' (the rat also has signifi-cance in anti-Semitic discourse). This rat, travelling indiscriminately between English and German soldiers, has no national attachments; and in wartime, that may be thought to give the potential for disloyalty. In a letter to Marsh, Rosenberg makes it plain that he 'never joined the army from patriotic rea-sons. Nothing can justify war'.[9] In fact, his motives were predominantly financial, as he sought a way to avoid poverty and dependency on his family, whose pacifism he appears fundamentally to have shared. The apparently ironic, witty use of the word 'cosmopolitan', therefore, has extensive ethical and political ramifications. Furthermore, the evocation of the potential conse-quences of cosmopolitan behaviour ('they would shoot you if they knew ...') is underwritten dreadfully by a letter to his fellow-Jew Sydney Schiff in 1916 in which, referring to a mutiny of private soldiers, Rosenberg says that 'some men got bayoneted'.[10]

These implications are all subtly muted in the poem, which maintains under extraordinary circumstances an extraordinary decorum. Just as the epithets applied to the rat appear sophisticatedly self-referential or poeti-cally self-reflexive, too, the poem's decorum is almost itself advertised by the slightly parodic element of its address: 'if it be your pleasure / To cross the sleeping green between'. This weird fastidiousness is a little like Alice's unnerving composure as she addresses the anthropomorphised creatures down the rabbit hole. Such courtliness is sardonically discrepant, of course, given that the pastoral 'green' is actually the desolation of no-man's-land where human corpses lie rotting beyond retrieval; and the rat's elective affinities are in reality dependent on nothing more fastidious than an opportunistic hunt for food.

In the phrase 'sleeping green', the epithet may be transferred. It may be the bodies of both English and German soldiers that lie 'sleeping', that common euphemism for death. And as this poet contemplates these bodies, one of which may well soon be his own, the sardonic element of his poem sharpens into something more angrily political. That soldiers slain in war are 'bonds to the whims of murder' undermines a great deal of the powerful political rhetoric, or cant, of the First World War. 'Bonds' makes the soldiers slaves (and in a letter to Lascelles Abercrombie in 1916, Rosenberg says that 'nobody but a private in the army knows what it is to be a slave');[11] 'whims' implies a negative judgment on the potential efficacy of any military strategy under these conditions; and 'murder' makes all military killing morally reprehensible.[12] But calling these deaths murder now provokes a rhetoric of Rosenberg's own; provokes rhetorical questions, in fact, in which the rat is asked what he reads in the eyes of those still living. The second of these questions suggests abject terror: 'What quaver – what heart aghast?' which introduces a further faint allusion to Romantic apostrophe: to Blake's 'The Tyger' ('What immortal hand or eye…?').[13] Blake ascribes 'fearful symmetry' to his tiger. 'Break of Day in the Trenches' is a poem about fearful asymmetry, the disproportion between the frail bodies of men and 'the shrieking iron and flame' of mechanised warfare. The much less successful poem 'In the Trenches', which immediately precedes it in Vivien Noakes's edition, casts a shadow over it. There the poem's speaker picks two poppies, sticking one behind his ear and giving the other to a companion. At the poem's end, a shell bursts, killing the companion and smashing his poppy.

In his use of such rhetoric, Rosenberg is as warm or as heated as Wilfred Owen in the perturbed erotic tenderness of 'I saw his round mouth's crimson' or as Ivor Gurney in the anguished, obsessive recoil of 'To His Love'; but 'Break of Day in the Trenches' is exceptional in the way it finally disciplines the heat of agitation, composing itself – in both senses – to a kind of cool. 'Cool' as in a lowering of the temperature, certainly, as the poem returns to the poppy of its opening lines. Then, the poet stuck it behind his ear. Now, the flower is first generalised, in the common fantasy or myth that poppies are stained red by human blood, and then personalised:

> Poppies whose roots are in man's veins
> Drop, and are ever dropping,
> But mine in my ear is safe –
> Just a little white with the dust.[14]

'Man's veins' – not 'men's veins' – serves as a reminder that mortality is the general condition; but then 'man's' cedes to 'mine' – the transient individual resistance to the common fate. Rosenberg manages this transition with a studied but tactful grace: casual, off-hand, throwaway, with a combative whimsy of his own. Behaving like this, 'Break of Day in the Trenches' also becomes cool in the idiomatic contemporary sense. The poet sticking the poppy behind his ear and then adverting to it again after everything his poem has confronted is playing the dandy, maintaining an elegant gesture and a pose.

In a curious pre-war prose fragment called 'On Noses', Rosenberg considers how what he calls 'noise projectivity and ostentation' – he means, I think, simply a lot of it – may seem useless and superficial, but can still act as 'echoes and heralds of the great, the useful and substantial'. His examples form an odd threesome: 'If we take religion as an instance, or a great cause like dandyism or women's suffrage, is not the spouting, the shouting, the foppishness but the effervescence, the first dribblings of a solid and profound idea, of an earnest soul-enthralling basis?'[15] It is hard to know what irony, if any, inheres in Rosenberg's making the politics of dandyism equivalent to those of women's suffrage, but the passage does reveal his clear understanding that Wildean provocation forms an oppositional position. A photograph of Rosenberg with a group of fellow art students at the Slade in 1912 shows him kneeling apart from the others, dressed quite soberly, almost certainly in what his biographer tells us was 'the one family suit'. Others of the students, however – notably, Rosenberg's friend David Bomberg and his acquaintance Mark Gertler – are distinctly dandyish, even foppish, with flowing neckties and huge, soft, bucket-shaped hats (Bomberg painted himself several times wearing one). In 'Break of Day in the Trenches', Isaac Rosenberg, who did not wish, or could not manage, to cut such a figure in life, does figure himself as a dandyish exquisite. This is now truly the dandyism of a great cause, the solid and profound idea that permits this private soldier to revise a fin-de-siècle style into an ability to withstand the ostentation of shrieking iron and flame. The poem, learning a style from despair, offers us the figure of the private soldier as dandy and the figure of the dandy as hero: defiantly, even jauntily resilient as he makes his cool refusal, and framing his gesture as a grimly off-hand, ironic joke – for how 'safe' is a poppy in a front-line trench?

The coolness of this poem is powerfully aided also by its quasi-Imagist poetic, which had affinities with the aesthetics of the plastic arts in the opening decade of the century. Rosenberg's letters reveal a distrust of imagism, just as he showed a suspicion of Vorticism in the plastic arts, although Bomberg had embraced it. Even so, Rosenberg admired some of the work of the imagist F.S. Flint, and had contact with Ezra Pound, who recommended him to Harriet Monroe, the editor of *Poetry* (Chicago), in which imagist poems appeared, and in which 'Break of Day in the Trenches' was first published in 1916. We could even consider the poem a kind of exploded imagist poem, with its opening two and its closing four quiet, quasi-imagist lines of mise-en-scène disrupted by the intervention of the unmannerly wartime rat. Despite Rosenberg's reserve about the avant-garde, it is clear that his war poetry gains from knowledge of it. Geoffrey Hill, in fact, makes an arresting case for considering Rosenberg's experimental way of 'thinking through the phrase or image', which is signalled by his propensity to repeat phrases and images across different poems, an equivalent of what Bomberg later called the 'sense of mass' in painting. The shared ideas and ideals of their many conversations, Hill thinks, may have contributed to the production of both.[16]

'Break of Day in the Trenches', then, concentrates three elements essential to an understanding of this poet's significance: his mythologising, his voicing the experience of the private soldier and his Jewishness. The poem's second line, 'It is the same old Druid Time as ever', personifies time as a prehistoric priest for whom dawn had high religious import but who also, ominously, engaged in human sacrifice. The figure registers both the poet's surprise that time continues as it always has, even in the apparently unique circumstances of the trenches, and also an undeceived acceptance of such continuity. The quasi-mythologising personification is consistent with a great deal in Rosenberg's pre-war poetry, in which he moves among the vast shadows of classical, biblical and Hebraic mythology, aiming at a synthesis whose primary avatar is probably Blake in his prophetic books. These poems are almost wholly unsuccessful, but they do make it clear that something deep in Rosenberg's imagination is compelled by the scope and economy of myth, its apparent capacity to resolve human complexity into symbolic opposition and resolution. Such compulsions are more successfully actualised in some of the war poetry, notably 'Daughters of War' and 'A Worm Fed On the Heart of Corinth'.

The former makes something compellingly strange out of a rather incoherent element in the pre-war poetry: a powerful, terrifying female deity; a savage god, synthesised from such sources as the Amazons, the Valkyries and the Babylonian-Talmudic figure of the demonic Lilith (who appears as a character in Rosenberg's play *The Unicorn*). Rosenberg admired Whitman, particularly his poems of the American Civil War. 'Daughters of War' therefore appropriately employs a quasi-Whitmanian free verse, apparently improvisatory in its rhythms, reiterations and intermittent rhymes, and a quasi-Whitmanian visionary ego ('I saw in prophetic gleams ...'),[17] to convey the image of a hideous afterlife in which soldiers' corpses are violated – both the sexual and sacrilegious connotations of the word are apt – by the rampaging figures of the poem's title. The rhythms of 'Daughters of War' imitate, in their careering momentum, the naked dances of the eponymous 'maidens' in their perverse 'blood-heat'. These 'daughters' corrode the corpses until 'the soul can leap out / Into their huge embraces' (144). Doing so, they bear a family resemblance to the mythological figure of 'sweet sister death' in Part 7 of *In Parenthesis*, who 'has gone debauched today and stalks on this high ground with strumpet confidence'.[18] Jones and Rosenberg are at these moments extravagantly disruptive and confrontational, melding the world of trench warfare with that turn-of-the-century iconology and iconography, instinct with both misogyny and the male fear of castration, such as we find in Picasso's *Les Demoiselles d'Avignon* (1907) and Baudelaire's *femme damnée*; and we know that Rosenberg had read Baudelaire. In this way, 'Daughters of War' brings fin-de-siècle decadence to an altogether unpredictable location, figuring a perverse apocalypse in which, as the representative sister who voices the poem's final lines says, 'My sisters have their males / Clean of the dust of old days'(145).

Although he hesitated about the contemporary avant-garde, Rosenberg still had a defiant sense of what he wished his own work to advance forward from. Rupert Brooke was one of his names for that, although he in fact admired several of his poems. Rosenberg castigates Brooke's 'begloried sonnets', believing, in one of the theoretical formulations that constantly enliven his letters, that the war 'should be approached in a colder way, more abstract, with less of the million feelings everybody feels; or all these should be concentrated in one distinguished emotion'.[19] When the savage goddesses of the battlefield strip the heroes 'clean' of their souls and of the dust of the old days in 'Daughters of War', therefore, we may regard this as a desacralising or 'deglorying' revision, won from catastrophic experience, of the trope Brooke adapted on the outbreak of war in his sonnet 'Peace', which imagines the young entering war 'like swimmers into cleanness leaping'.[20]

The rhythmic and syntactical energies of 'Daughters of War' are only insecurely, sometimes even crudely, disciplined to satisfactory poetic form, even if this has its mimetic point. 'A Worm Fed on the Heart of Corinth' has altogether greater command and compaction:

> A worm fed on the heart of Corinth,
> Babylon and Rome.
> Not Paris raped tall Helen,
> But this incestuous worm
> Who lured her vivid beauty
> To his amorphous sleep.
> England! famous as Helen

Is thy betrothal sung.
To him the shadowless,
More amorous than Solomon.[21]

Cut this worm in half and one half would writhe back, instinct with origin, to Blake's 'The Sick Rose' where, 'invisible', its 'dark secret love' is a negative agent of disintegration. Perhaps the poem's exclamatory apostrophe to 'England' draws on the word's appearances in Blake, too ('And did those feet in ancient time / Walk upon England's mountains green?' in 'Jerusalem', most famously) and the phrase 'amorphous sleep' on Blake's famous castigation of anti-imaginative 'single vision and Newton's sleep'. The poem is also haunted by Marvell's 'To His Coy Mistress', where what is surely the most chilling motive for sexual submission ever offered in poetry is phrased as the threat of a submission eventually to be made inevitable by the very fact of mortality ('Then worms shall try / That long-preserved virginity').[22]

Rosenberg's amalgamation of his sources is also richly transformative. The story of Paris and Helen that supplies the origin of Homer's *Iliad* is revised with an astonishing declarative boldness, making this worm the agent of the destruction of four ancient civilisations and not only of Troy. The figuring of the rape of a woman by a worm perceived as male is stark in its horror; and the worm is 'incestuous', I think, where Blake's is 'secret' because Germans and English are members of the same racial 'family'. The invocation of England as at least potentially the fifth in the poem's corrupted series – because a 'betrothal' is not yet, quite, a marriage – is an unnervingly devastating condemnation, even as it is also a brilliantly subtle revision of the ancient and enduring trope of war as amatory embrace. The poem's verbal compaction, its 'sense of mass', is clearest here in the way the worm's 'amorphous sleep' almost luridly tightens into his 'amorous' outranking even of Solomon with Sheba, and in the way 'amorous' itself rhymes in its dactylic rhythm and its assonance with the mysterious epithet 'shadowless'. The worm is 'shadowless' presumably because he works underground, out of the light, in the way secret incest may need to operate, too; and the epithet may also carry implications of the demonic. It retains an air of mystery and irresolvability wholly fitting to the strange mythological shape Rosenberg has constructed in this poem. Brief, clenched, bitten off and battened down, 'A Worm Fed on the Heart of Corinth' moves in the mind as a node of trapped energy, a permanent invitation to explication.

Both 'Daughters of War' and 'A Worm Fed on the Heart of Corinth' should be read as the myths of a poet who has seen too much, but has been stunned into speech rather than silence. If the mythical is one essential pole of Rosenberg's hectic wartime imagination, the harrowingly experiential is the other. His letters make the grimmest reading, with their accounts of the ordinary privations and terrors of the private soldier. These included disgustingly inadequate food (and the galling knowledge that officers fared far better), the constant threat of theft, boots that ruined men's feet and draconian punishments for minor misdemeanors. Rosenberg seems to have suffered these more often than most, referring frequently in his letters to his chronic absent-mindedness. The poetry itself was probably in large part responsible for this. Rosenberg was able to write only in the trenches themselves, permitted just ten days' leave in the whole period of twenty-two months which he served before his death; and Vivien Noakes piercingly tells us that 'dustings of mud' fell from the creases of some of his manuscripts when they were being rehoused.[23] Geoffrey Hill large-mindedly thinks that such forgetfulness 'is not actually a sign of weakness but of strength – the immense strength of other priorities, such as working on massive and complex poems in your head amid the manifold terrors and routine hard labour of life in the trenches'.[24] Poetry, therefore, may have made Rosenberg a bad soldier, even as being a soldier made him a poet.

Many of the experiences common to private soldiers feed Rosenberg's work, making it an exceptional anthology of deprivation and endurance. The private soldier's perspective is explicit in the very title 'Marching – As Seen From the Left File', but the poem concerns itself with another kind of perspective, too, as the poet's viewpoint has an almost expressionist or Vorticist dimension, in which this routine march seems like a Wyndham Lewis drawing or an early David Bomberg painting. The file is 'All a red brick moving glint', and human agency is read as disciplined to mechanical measure: the soldiers' hands are 'Like flaming pendulums' and their feet are 'automatic'. The epithet expresses the industrialised modernisation of human will just as T.S. Eliot's use of it in *The Waste Land* does, where the lovely woman who stoops to folly 'smoothes her hair with automatic hand'.[25]

Many of Rosenberg's poems depend on the dual perspectives of lived experience and a coolly, if not coldly, abstracted art; the poems are never mere reportage. But within these privileged perspectives of the soldier-poet – perhaps the only privileges permitted him – we gain access to such things as the distressed insomnia of being conveyed to war 'Grotesque and queerly huddled' in 'The Troop Ship'; the unendurable irritation of being lousy and flea-riddled, outstandingly defined in 'Louse Hunting' (Rosenberg at least once slept naked in the rain rather than endure his lousy clothing any longer); and the queasy repugnance and self-disgust of being a stretcher-bearer or a member of a burying party in 'Dead Man's Dump'. That poem makes its raw report ('A man's brain's splattered on / A stretcher-bearer's face') even as it discovers an enduring conceit for being shot to death. 'Conceit' in the sense in which it is used of seventeenth-century English poetry, which is often also the poetry of the charnel house, as Rosenberg brings a Donnean metaphysical wit into no-man's-land, yoking together the mortally wounding bullet and the busily questing insect: 'When the swift iron burning bee / Drained the wild honey of their youth'.[26]

Beyond these usual perturbations of the private soldier at the Front, Rosenberg had to endure a further exceptional one: anti-Semitism. Some of his letters, especially to Jewish correspondents, are explicit about what he had to put up with. In 'The Jew', he is articulate about it in the poetry itself, writing in wounded affront and baffled outrage:

> The blonde, the bronze, the ruddy,
> With the same heaving blood,
> Keep tide to the moon of Moses,
> Then why do they sneer at me?[27]

Insisting that Christians and Jews share so much of a common heritage, Rosenberg is here nevertheless making it plain, with the opposed pronouns 'they' and 'me', that no possessive pronoun of his could ever wholly include him along with the majority of those with whom he fought.

Early in 1918, Rosenberg wrote to John Rodker that he would 'like to read Elliott's work'.[28] Rosenberg is here misspelling the name of the poet who, the previous year, had published his first volume, *Prufrock and Other Observations*. Rosenberg never got the chance to read Eliot; but Eliot read and admired Rosenberg, calling him in 1953 'the most remarkable of the British poets killed in that war'.[29] Some years earlier, in 1935, he made a judgment which has since been the source of controversy: 'The poetry of Isaac Rosenberg does not only owe its distinction to being Hebraic: but because it is Hebraic it is a contribution to English literature. For a Jewish poet to be able to write like a Jew, in western Europe and in a western European language, is almost a miracle'.[30] Anthony Julius in *T.S. Eliot, Anti-Semitism and Literary Form* reads this as an anti-Semitic 'libel', asking 'What is it to write like a Jew?'[31] In a spirited defence of Eliot, however, James Wood thinks that it 'quite clearly means that Rosenberg was a distinguished English poet, but his particular addition to English literature was that he retained a Jewishness that was not assimilated; and that this retention, within the pressure that the English poetic tradition exerts to surrender one's literary Jewishness, was almost miraculous'.[32]

Although he has never been as well known as some of the other poets of the First World War, and his 'particular addition' to English literature has been very little regarded, the debate at least suggests that Rosenberg's work continues to carry insinuations and provocations a long way beyond the immediate, dreadful context of its origin. Eliot and anti-Semitism will persist as a topic of investigation. In this case, however, it seems to me that Rosenberg would have appreciated Eliot's observation as the insightful recognition of realised ambition: because, with genuinely admiring discrimination, Eliot regards Jewishness as an outstanding attribute of this poet's distinction, but does not limit his distinction to his Jewishness. That makes all the difference.

Nevertheless, the question remains: what is it for Isaac Rosenberg to write like a Jew? It is to write a poem like 'The Jew' about the experience of wartime anti-Semitism and to notice, with pained wit, the 'cosmopolitan sympathies' of a trench rat; it is to write – *in the trenches* – poetic drama like 'Moses' and 'The Unicorn' based on biblical and Talmudic material; and it is to refer in a letter to a fellow Jew, Sydney Schiff, to the nineteenth-century German poet as 'Heine, our own Heine', making the intensified possessive now simply, pleasurably inclusive: 'I admire him more for always being a Jew at heart than anything else'.[33] This suggests that, had he lived, Rosenberg may well have written with more obvious recourse to a wide European tradition, and not only to literature in English; in fact, his first language was not English, but Yiddish.

The dual exceptionality recognised by Eliot, however, sharpens the pain of loss; and sharpens, too, the perspective in which Rosenberg himself perceives loss. In 'August 1914', with slow gravity, he uses a plural possessive to suggest that what his generation may actually in the end have shared in common is only that they were so cruelly and pointlessly wasted:

> Iron are our lives
> Molten right through our youth.
> A burnt space through ripe fields,
> A fair mouth's broken tooth.[34]

NOTES

1 *The Poems and Plays of Isaac Rosenberg*, ed. Vivien Noakes (Oxford: Oxford University Press, 2004), 356. All quotations from the poems are taken from this edition. Hereafter abbreviated as *Poems and Plays*.
2 W.B. Yeats ed. *Oxford Book of Modern Verse* (Oxford: Oxford University Press, 1936), xxxiv.
3 See Jean Moorcroft Wilson, *Isaac Rosenberg: The Making of a Great War Poet: A New Life* (2008; London: Phoenix, 2009), passim.
4 Letter of 4 August [1916], *The Collected Works of Isaac Rosenberg*, ed. Ian Parsons (London: Chatto and Windus, 1979), 239. Hereafter abbreviated as *Collected Works*.
5 Letter postmarked 27 May 1917, *Collected Works*, 255.
6 *Poems and Plays*, 128.
7 'Break of Day in the Trenches', *Poems and Plays*, 128.

8 David Jones, *In Parenthesis* (1937; London: Faber and Faber, 1963), 54.

9 Letter written in late December 1915 [?], *Collected Works*, 227.

10 Letter written in March 1916 [?], *Collected Works*, 230.

11 Letter of 11 March 1916, *Collected Works*, 230.

12 *Collected Works*, 230.

13 William Blake, *Complete Poems* ed. Alicia Ostriker (Harmondsworth: Penguin, 1977), 125.

14 'Break of Day', 128.

15 'On Noses', *Collected Works*, 303.

16 Geoffrey Hill, *Collected Critical Writings* (Oxford: Oxford University Press, 2008), 456.

17 *Poems and Plays*, 142.

18 *In Parenthesis*, 162.

19 *Collected Works*, 237.

20 Rupert Brooke, 'Peace', in Brian Gardner ed. *Up the Line to Death: The War Poets 1914–1918* (1986; London: Metheun, 1976), 10.

21 *Poems and Plays,* 126.

22 Blake, *Complete Poems*, 149; Andrew Marvell, *Complete Poetry* ed. George deF. Lord (London: Dent, 1968), 24.

23 *Poems and Plays*, xviii.

24 Hill, *Collected Critical Writings*, 454.

25 *Poems and Plays*, 124; T.S. Eliot, *Complete Poems and Plays* (London: Faber, 1969), 69.

26 *Poems and Plays*, 127, 140–1.

27 *Poems and Plays,* 126.

28 Letter of 23 February 1918 [?], *Collected Works*, 268.

29 Cited by James Wood, *The Broken Estate: Essays on Literature and Belief* (1999; new ed., New York: Picador, 2010), 146. Hereafter abbreviated as *The Broken Estate*.

30 Eliot in the *Criterion*, cited by Anthony Julius, *T.S. Eliot, Anti-Semitism, and Literary Form* (1995; new ed., London: Thames and Hudson, 2003), 101–2.

31 Julius, *T.S. Eliot*, 102.

32 Wood, *The Broken Estate*, 146.

33 Letter of August 1916 [?], *Collected Works*, 242.

34 *Poems and Plays*, 130.

7

SANDRA M. GILBERT

Wilfred Owen

I thought of the very strange look on all the faces in that camp; an incomprehensible look ... without expression, like a dead rabbit's. It will never be painted, and no actor will ever seize it. And to describe it, I think I must go back and be with them.

    – Letter to Susan Owen, 31 December 1917 (*Collected Letters*, 521)

To think of Wilfred Owen at the Front is in a way to imagine an avatar of John Keats marching up the Line to a war that would have been unimaginable at the beginning of the nineteenth century. Consider the similarities – and then the differences. Keats and Owen were small impassioned young men from the lower-middle class. Each died young – in his middle twenties. Each, before death, had an *annus mirabilis* in which, as if touched by fever or fire, he wrote a series of powerful poems. Each became a sacrificial symbol of his generation because each died a resonantly representative death. And the twentieth-century poet quite consciously identified with his Romantic precursor.

Wilfred Owen had been haunted by John Keats from adolescence onward. Over and over again, as he constructed his own aesthetic, he conjured up images of this forerunner, whose similarity to himself he did and did not grasp. Viewing the poet's manuscripts on a visit to the British Museum in 1911, he observed with satisfaction that 'his writing is rather large and slopes like mine ... He also has my trick of not joining letters in a word'. In an early sonnet, 'On Seeing a Lock of Keats's Hair', he exclaimed, 'It is a lock of Adonais' hair!' and in another verse he declared 'Yet shall I see fair Keats, and hear his lyre!' Indeed, as he bemusedly confessed to his mother, after revisiting Keats's lodging at Teignmouth he was 'melancholy-happy' because 'to be in love with a youth and a dead-un is perhaps sillier than with a real, live maid'. By his own admission, his identification with his Romantic tutor in the arts of poesy was perhaps as homoerotic as it was fraternal and narcissistic.[1]

Owen was both a self-made literary man and a sophisticated one. Although he failed to achieve the university scholarships he sought, he educated himself in poetry with the ferocity that he brought to the innovations in rhyme and form shaped by such obsessive readings. Like his adored Keats, who was obliged to engage in professional studies of surgery instead of prosody, the young Owen had to supplement his forays into literary history with official studies of military tactics. Yet, like Keats, too, he compiled a kind of anthology of exemplary metrics with which he ceaselessly experimented. Early on, he worked in the 'old-fashioned' modes adopted by his poet cousin Leslie Gunston, but eventually he turned to formal techniques that were strikingly new, even avant-garde. Like Keats, whose brief, astonishing evolution led from the uncertainties of early verses to the development of the sonnet-based stanzas of the great odes of 1819, Owen rapidly moved from the conventional sonnets of his youth to the revisionary sonnets embedded in 'Dulce et Decorum Est' and the powerful half-rhymes of 'Strange Meeting'. And like Keats, he died before his literary career could develop further, and his untimely demise, marking the incompleteness as well as the achievement of that career, brought him posthumously the fame for which he had yearned. 'I think I shall be among the English poets after my death', Keats wrote to his brother on his birthday in 1818. Similarly, Owen wrote his mother on New Year's Eve 1917 that 'I go out of this year a Poet, my dear Mother, as which I did not enter it … I am a poet's poet'.[2]

At first, however, both poets were as renowned for the circumstances of their deaths as for their lives. To be sure, Owen could hardly have imagined that his fate would become as historically significant as his precursor's. A century before Owen was killed by German bullets on the banks of a French canal, Keats expired in Rome, consumed by tuberculosis, *the* fever that legendarily devoured 'pale and spectre-thin' nineteenth-century youth. Nearly one hundred years later, Owen became a poignant image of the boys sent to slaughter in the trenches, annihilated by a random bullet just a few days before the Armistice was declared in November 1918. Like Keats, who had confronted the omens of his death ('I know the color of that blood; – it is arterial blood – that drop of blood is my death-warrant'), Owen repeatedly claimed comparable forebodings. 'I know I shall be killed', he told his brother Harold. But the differences in the now legendary deaths of the two young men underline what became Owen's radical departure from the Keatsian mode of poetry.[3]

For to consider the disjunctions between these figures is to focus on the hole torn in history by the First World War, a yawning gap both cultural and literary. Keats, the sweetheart of Romanticism, was a theological skeptic, yet a *pastoral* poet. 'Now more than ever seems it rich to die', he wrote in his masterful celebration of the nightingale's song – for 'to cease upon the midnight with no pain' would be to merge voluptuously with the mysteries of a natural world enduring apart from human 'fever and fret'. After a century of industrial and philosophical transformation had persuaded

European intellectuals that not only was God dead, as Nietzsche proclaimed, but Blake's 'dark Satanic mills' had blighted landscapes even while
they churned out deadly new technologies, it was harder to imagine merging
with nature. The 'Great War' definitively marked what Malcolm Bradbury
has called a 'turn' into a modernity that was depersonalizing, defamiliariz-
ing and destructive. It was also a modernity that, as I have argued elsewhere,
put in question all the assumptions of both traditional pastoral, traditional
elegy and consolatory Christianity.[4] For a poet as self-consciously literary
as Owen, in fact, the military crisis came to embody not only a personal
and political crisis, but a poetic one. If he had gone to the Front as a contemporary avatar of Keats, he soon metamorphosed into an anti-Keats, or
at least an anti-Romantic. His lingering fondness for Keats would shape his
inventive prosody; his rage against a literary tradition in which he found
no precedent for the horrors of industrialized warfare would inform the
shock of his subject matter. 'What does Keats have to teach me of rifle and
machine-gun drill', his brother Harold reports him having said ironically,
after his first tour at the Front. 'How will Shelley show me how to hate or
any poet teach me the trajectory of the bullet?'[5]

The very word 'pastoral' takes on a bizarre cast in relation to the cities
of death that marked the waste land of no-man's-land, as does the genre's
focus on redemption and resurrection. As, in the words of the combatant-
poet Richard Aldington, 'an infernal cemetery' filled with 'smashed bodies
and human remains', the landscape of the war was really a gigantic charnel
house. Wrote the English memoirist Vera Brittain when the clothes of her
dead fiancé were returned from the Front, 'the mud of France' that stained
them seemed 'saturated with dead bodies': what once might have been fer-
tile earth was now a horrifying pollutant. The trenches themselves, many
sarcastically named after London landmarks (Waterloo Bridge, Elephant &
Castle), were six- to eight-feet deep, like graves, and seething with bloated
rats who fed on unburied corpses. (Surely T.S. Eliot's 'rat's alley', where the
dead men lost their bones', is a reference to such trenches.) Thus, to the
extent that life could be discerned in what Santanu Das has evocatively
termed the 'slimescape' of no-man's-land, it was a deadly life – a life that
was paradoxically *anti*-life.[6] Testified the British novelist Ford Madox Ford
of the fields along the Somme, 'in the territory beneath the eye, or hidden by
folds in the ground, there must have been – on the two sides – a million men,
moving one against the other [in] a Hell of fear that surely cannot have had
a parallel in this world'.[7]

Perhaps the most ferocious summary of this transformation of land to
limbo – or, worse, earth to hell – appears in one of Owen's bitterest letters
home. No-man's-land, he declared:

is like the eternal place of gnashing of teeth: the Slough of Despond could be contained in one of its crater-holes …

I have not seen any dead. I have done worse. In the dank air I have *perceived* it, and in the darkness, *felt*. Those 'Somme Pictures [by the establishment 'War Artist' Muirhead Bone] are the laughing stock of the army …[8]

Owen's comment on 'those Somme Pictures' probably refers to Bone's ludicrously bucolic landscapes called 'Battle of the Somme' – renditions of the battlefield on which 60,000 British soldiers were killed or wounded in a single day. What outraged Owen was that Bone (whose name is morbidly comic here) made only one concession to the reality of modern warfare: a string of barbed wire in the foreground – backed up by lines of healthy looking trees in a field where no trees could have survived.[9]

Musing on the vision of redemption Tennyson had confidently expressed in 'Crossing the Bar' ('I hope to see my Pilot face to face/When I have crossed the bar'), Owen set his own daily wartime confrontations with the haunting physicality of the dead against what seemed to him the nineteenth-century laureate's all-too-easy metaphor of a divine sandbar between the harbor of earth and the sea of heaven's bliss. Was Tennyson, he wondered:

ever frozen alive, with dead men for comforters? Did he hear the moaning at the bar, not at twilight and the evening bell only, but at dawn, noon, and night, eating and sleeping, walking and working, always the close moaning of the Bar; the thunder, the hissing, and the whining of the Bar?[10]

Solid and sinister, Owens's 'Bar' was the war itself – the thunder of its guns, the hissing of its gas, the whining of its descending shells – and its gruesome reality, as he argued in poem after poem, could be neither justified nor sentimentalized. Nor was Tennysonian sentimentality his only target; Shelleyan Platonism also earned his ire. In the brilliant dramatic monologue 'A Terre', his dying speaker sourly quotes 'Adonais' as he muses that soon

'I shall be one with nature, herb, and stone',
Shelley would tell me. Shelley would be stunned:
The dullest Tommy hugs that fancy now.
'Pushing up daises' is their creed, you know.[11]

Given this revulsion against Victorian and Romantic theological hopes, the personal literary manifesto Owen composed not long before his death defined his poems as elegiac but roundly repudiated traditional conventions of elegiac closure or consolation. 'These elegies are to this generation in no sense consolatory', he wrote, after explaining that 'The Poetry is in the pity'. Eerily, the word 'poetry', in this context, seems almost to have dissolved into the word 'pity', just as in the solemn para-rhymes of 'Strange Meeting' 'hall' became 'Hell' and 'moan' became 'mourn'. Nor is Owen's concept of 'pity', as has occasionally been alleged, analogous to sentimental concepts of pity. Rather, it has the gravity of the Aristotelian notion that tragedy should elicit 'pity and terror'.[12]

However, if the Keatsian natural world, the stellar Shelleyan cosmos and the Tennysonian imagining of redemption had failed, what other poetic ceremonies were available to an aspiring poet embedded in the mud of no-man's-land? Because such mud was both infertile and deadly – soldiers were sometimes buried alive in its depths or sucked into its heaving surface – Das and others astutely discuss the ways in which combatants recorded the sensory horror evoked by its stench, its *feel*. At the same time, however, despite their experience of living burial (or because of that), the angriest of the war poets were driven to testify to what *could* be seen, even in a territory where both friendly and hostile life were 'hidden beneath the ground'. Particularly, as a Keatsian metamorphosed into an anti-Keatsian, Owen seems to have felt an obligation to record the visions that, as it were, emerged out of muck and blood and blindness. His poetic eye became a sort of camera eye as, with increasing intensity, he sought to re-*present* the horrifying sights he had seen, even in semi-darkness.

Jon Stallworthy, Owen's first biographer, describes an encounter between Owen and his sometime German tutor, Frank Nicholson, that underscores this point:

> Owen spoke as he rarely did of the horrors of the Front. He told Nicholson of photographs of the dead and mutilated that he carried in his wallet and his hand moved towards his breast-pocket, only to stop short as he realized, with characteristic delicacy, that his friend had no need of that particular lesson in reality.[13]

More recent scholars have noted that 'there is no external evidence that those photographs existed', with Dominic Hibberd observing that a subaltern possessing such images would fall 'foul of the military censor' and arguing that the poet's wallet probably contained 'nothing more than a new war poem with which [he] hoped to "assault the civilian conscience"'. Yet as Hibberd also concedes, Owen himself described 'A Terre' as a 'photographic representation', and other sources note that the young writer had long been fascinated by photography and by cinema. To be sure, one of Owen's most impassioned references to photography suggests his awareness of the inadequacy of the photo as testimony. Late in his military career, he wrote to Siegfried Sassoon about the death of a comrade whose blood soaked his shoulder. 'Catalogue? Photograph? Can you photograph the hot iron as it cools from the smelting? That is what Jones's blood looked like, and felt like'. Yet even the reference to photography's inadequacy is telling here. If not photographs, what *could* convey the terrible 'pity of War'? Whether buried alive in the 'slimescapes' or feeling his way through the perilous shadows of no-man's-land, Owen was obsessed with the need to testify not just to what he learned through touch and sound but also to what he saw: 'what Jones's blood *looked like*' and how 'No Man's Land under snow is *like* the face of the moon, chaotic, crater-ridden, uninhabitable, awful'.[14]

Over and over again, therefore, in poems and letters he described scenes of horror that were, for his time, shocking in their brutal detail. If Keats had determined to 'load every rift with ore', Owen, as one critic has quipped, was driven to 'load every rift with gore'. The carnage he witnessed as he proclaimed that 'Red lips are not so red/As the stained stones kissed by the English dead' eventually led to the ghastly, ghostly spectacle of the English dead lingering on the battle field, as the young poet railed in a letter to his mother against

> the distortion of the dead, whose unburiable bodies sit outside the dug-outs all day, all night, the most execrable sights on earth. In poetry we call them the most glorious. But to sit with them all day, all night … and a week later to come back and find them still sitting there, in motionless groups, THAT is what saps the 'soldierly spirit'.[15]

As he turned to tales of his own visions of the living and the wounded, he also dwelt on their absence of vision, the literal blindness that the war had inflicted on them. Eyes – his own and the eyes of others – became increasingly crucial in his poems.

In the octave of one of Owen's earliest war sonnets, 'Anthem for Doomed Youth', his initial focus was on sound ('passing-bells', the 'rapid rattle' of machine gun fire, 'choirs of wailing shells'), but the sestet conclusively turns to sight: 'not in the hands of boys but in their *eyes*,/Shall shine the holy glimmers of goodbyes', while, to dramatize the centrality of vision, 'each slow dusk [shall be] a drawing-down of *blinds*' (emphasis added).[16] Ceremonially sorrowful, the funereal drawn blinds also suggest the blinders that so many at the Front associated with the home front's denial of the suffering in the trenches. More intensely, 'Greater Love' begins with spectacles of death as it enters into angry debate with the Romantic and Victorian traditions that had earlier energised the poet. Engaging with Swinburne's 'Before the Mirror/Verses Written under a Picture' – an ekphrastic work inspired by Whistler's 'Symphony in White', an image of the artist's mistress looking in a mirror – this is a text about looking based on another text about looking based on a portrait of looking.

Interestingly, Whistler's painting is relatively muted: the young woman glances sidelong into the mirror with a meditative gaze. But Swinburne's poem represents her as heatedly narcissistic in a way that must have fueled Owen's rage. Beginning 'White rose in red rose-garden/Is not so white … as this face grows from pale to bright', Swinburne dramatizes the subject's virtually masturbatory delight in her own self-image:

> I watch my face, and wonder
> At my bright hair;
> Nought else exalts or grieves
> The rose at heart, that heaves
> With love of her own leaves and lips that pair.[17]

The shocking first two stanzas of 'Greater Love' – and they must have been shocking to their initial readers – almost scandalously subvert such Romantic and narcissistic joys of looking, substituting instead a voyeurism that has necrophiliac overtones:

> Red lips are not so red
> As the stained stones kissed by the English dead …
> O Love, your eyes lose lure
> When I behold eyes blinded in my stead!
>
> Your slender attitude
> Trembles not exquisite like limbs knife-skewed,
> Rolling and rolling there
> Where God seems not to care;
> Till the fierce love they bear
> Cramps them in death's extreme decrepitude.[18]

True, the poet's horrified yet lingering gaze at 'eyes blinded in my stead' and the weirdly Keatsian 'attitude' ('O Attic shape! Fair attitude!') of 'limbs knife-skewed' is bracketed by relatively soothing Biblical references: 'Greater love hath no man than this, that a man lay down his life – for his friends' (John 15:13), and 'you may touch them not' (e.g., John 20:17 – 'Touch me not'). But the poem's ghastly interior, its rifts lined with the ore of other dreadful observations ('piteous mouths that coughed', 'hearts made great with shot') effectively subverts Biblical precepts and comforts.

Beholding eyes like those 'blinded in my stead' preoccupies the poet in various other ways, as he struggles to find figurative language to construct 'photographic representations' of the sights he has seen. The fragment beginning, 'I saw his round mouth's crimson deepen as it fell' ends with a look into the dead man's opened eyes in which 'cold stars [were] lighting, very old and bleak,/In different skies'. Later, the majestically visionary 'Strange Meeting' records the underworld moment in which the combatant speaker recognizes the enemy he killed when the 'other' stares at him 'With piteous recognition in fixed eyes'. Of course, the speaker of 'A Terre' immediately discloses that he is blind, explaining poignantly that 'This bandage feels like pennies on my eyes', a simile resonant in its evocation of the pennies placed on the eyes of the dead to close them forever and in its suggestion that 'pennies' were all that was given to the soldiers at the Front as recompense for their sacrifices. Just as movingly, the eponymous 'Mental Cases' in that poem suffer as 'their eyeballs shrink tormented/Back into their brains', while the wounded in 'Smile, Smile, Smile' are 'sunk-eyed' in their secret misery.[19]

But perhaps the two poems in which eyes, eyesight and the sights of eyes figure most prominently are 'The Sentry' and 'Dulce et Decorum Est'. The first of these dramatically expands an almost cursory observation Owen made in a 1917 letter to his mother: 'I kept my own sentries half way down the stairs ... In spite of this one lad was blown down and, I am afraid, blinded'.[20] A year-and-a-half later, the poet was still brooding on this event, which was clearly more traumatic than his comment suggested. In 'an old Boche dug-out', he and his men had 'herded from the blast/Of whizz-bangs; but one found our door at last':

> Buffeting eyes and breath, snuffing the candles,
> And thud! flump! thud! Down the steep steps came thumping
> And sploshing in the flood, deluging muck,
> The sentry's body ...
> We dredged it up, for dead, until he whined,
> 'O sir – my eyes, – I'm blind, – I'm blind, – I'm blind'.
> Coaxing, I held a flame against his lids
> And said if he could see the least blurred light
> He was not blind; in time they'd get all right.
> 'I can't', he sobbed. Eyeballs, huge-bulged like squids',
> Watch my dreams still....[21]

The poem ends with poignant confirmation of the sentry's claim. Later, the poet tells us, 'through the dense din ... we heard him shout/"I see your lights"– But ours had long gone out'. Hallucinating – perhaps dying – the wounded man is definitively condemned to darkness. But in the meantime, the poet, whose energetic onomatopoeia ('thud', 'flump', 'thud', 'thumping', 'sploshing') has captured the awful sound of a falling body, is himself condemned to haunting visions of a sight more grotesque than those sounds: the sentry's 'Eyeballs, huge-bulged like squids' ' staring at him in nightmares.

The look of one combatant at another can be especially dreadful to Owen, as in 'Strange Meeting', where the 'other' soldier and the speaker exchange a 'fixed stare', or here, where the poet is condemned to gaze at blindness. Several readers have suggested that such images of weirdly fixed or vision-less eyes derive from Keats's representations of Moneta's 'visionless' gaze in 'The Fall of Hyperion'. But awesome as the goddess's gaze may be, it is also comforting, and the eyes at which Owen stares are 'in no way consolatory'. If he is alluding to Keats, then he is still engaged in his struggle with Keatsian Romantic tradition. In 'Dulce et Decorum Est', perhaps his most power-ful poem of looking, he extends his quarrel with tradition to an assault on Horace and on 'a certain poetess', Jessie Pope, the author of patronizingly jingoistic verses ('Who's for the trench–/Are you, my laddie?') and even on his earlier self. For the poet who – perhaps ambivalently – declared that there is no 'greater love' than laying down one's life for a friend, now savagely sub-verts the notion that it is 'sweet and meet to die for one's country'.

Central to the memory of the sudden gas attack that triggers the poem is, of course, Owen's scrupulously intense description of the dying man who failed to put on his protective helmet in the 'ecstasy of fumbling' that saved his mates. Like the blinded sentry's, his image haunts the poet's dreams, as he plunges forward 'guttering, choking, drowning'. But here, in his rage of compassion, Owen attacks not only Jessie Pope but all who would glamor-ize warfare, and in his fury, his first thought is of the soldier's eyes, those antique windows of the soul:

> If in some smothering dreams you too could pace
> Behind the wagon that we flung him in,
> And watch the white eyes writhing in his face ...
> My friend, you would not tell with such high zest
> To children ardent for some desperate glory,
> The old Lie: Dulce et decorum est
> Pro patria mori.[22]

Yet even while Owen testifies so fervently to the scenes that put in question some of the highest themes of literary tradition, his skillful versification (this poem links together two Petrarchan sonnets with Keatsian invention) aligns him with the techniques of that tradition. In particular, the prosody of the last three lines, with the resonant rhymes of 'glory' and 'mori', emphasizes the writer's fury. 'Pro patria mori', the only trimeter line in a poem that is com-posed mostly in resolute pentameter, ends the piece with a strangled snarl.

Whether or not the photographs Owen supposedly carried in his wallet were real, the eye of his figurative camera often focused tightly on human eyes, especially dying, dead or blinded eyes. However, the poet's conscious-ness of photography and cinematography turned him towards other sights as well. 'The Show', perhaps a revisionary riff on a passage in Henri Barbusse's *Under Fire*, a book Owen deeply admired, offers a long-shot, overhead vision of the lines of combatants crawling like surreal 'thin caterpillars' over the waste land to which they had been condemned. 'My soul looked down from a vague height, with Death', the poet notes. Even the title of this piece obviously emphasizes vision: although 'Show' was soldiers' slang for battle, as Stallworthy reminds us, it also alludes to spectacles (plays, 'picture shows'), to showing, as in revealing evidence, and even to showings, as in mystical manifestations.

But if seeing was the camera eye's bitter gift, being seen (and captured in a photograph or the eyes of the enemy) was equally horrifying. When combatants left the muck-pits of their trenches to go 'over the top', they were sighted, targeted, out in the open, *exposed* to the enemy's 'whizz-bangs'. The shudder of dread induced by such vulnerability to the deadly territory 'hidden beneath the eye' infuses both the poem aptly titled 'Exposure' and Owen's last known poem, 'Spring Offensive'. In the first of these works, whose title puns on 'exposure' as both exposure to the weather and the exposure of film, the speaker and his men are helpless before the gun sights of the enemy and 'the merciless iced east winds that knive us'. At the end of the poem, the 'burying-party' appears, 'picks and shovels in shaking grasp' and its members 'pause over half-known faces'. Ambiguously, 'All their *eyes are ice*,/But nothing happens'.[23] Whose eyes are ice – those of the burying party or those of the dead? And does it matter? 'Exposure' itself 'mercilessly' exposes the death-in-life of the living and the nothingness of the dead.

If 'nothing happens' in 'Exposure', however, precisely the destruction that exposure threatens occurs in 'Spring Offensive', the last poem Owen completed in France, a few weeks before he himself was exposed to the enemy bullet that killed him. Again, the very title of this poem is ambiguous, referring literally to an attack in spring but figuratively to the offensiveness of a season that should be one of growth but has instead become one of death. Its beauty detains the soldiers for 'hour after hour' as they pause near 'a last hill' to rest before battle, pondering the 'warm field ... where buttercups/ Had blessed with gold their slow boots coming up'. But all too soon, they are ordered to attack:

> So, soon they topped the hill, and raced together
> Over an open stretch of herb and heather
> Exposed. And instantly the whole sky burned
> With fury against them; earth set sudden cups
> In thousands for their blood; and the green slope
> Chasmed and deepened sheer to infinite space.[24]

As the soldiers are seen by the enemy, the pastoral becomes anti-pastoral, buttercups metamorphose into crater cups, what had been a kindly sky burns with fury, the green slope becomes an abyss. And who will testify to this, the poet wonders. Of the 'few who rushed in the body to enter hell' and crawled 'slowly back', he asks, 'Why speak not they of comrades that went under?'

To bear witness to such events with the skill of a tradition whose verities he sought to repudiate and the verismo of a camera, was the imperative that energized all 'Wilfred Owen's photographs', whether they were real pictures or literary ones. As he wrote to his mother in the passage I have used as an epigraph here, the 'incomprehensible look' of the combatants – whether destined for death or survival – 'will never be painted, and no actor will ever seize it. And to describe it, I think I must go back and be with them'.

NOTES

1 Wilfred Owen, *Collected Letters*, ed. Harold Owen and John Bell (Oxford and New York: Oxford University Press, 1967), 82, 186 (Hereafter abbreviated as *CL*); Wilfred Owen, *The Complete Poems and Fragments*, 2 Volumes, ed. Jon Stallworthy (Oxford and New York: Oxford University Press, 1983), 447 (Hereafter abbreviated as *CP*). Also see Dominic Hibberd, *Owen the Poet* (Basingstoke: Macmillan, 1986) and Santanu Das, *Touch and Intimacy in First World War Literature* (Cambridge: Cambridge University Press, 2005), 137–72. For a particularly interesting discussion of Keats and Owen, see James Najarian, 'Greater Love', *20th Century Literature*, 47.1 (Spring 2001).

2 John Keats, *Selected Letters*, ed. Robert Gittings (Oxford: Oxford University Press, 2002), 151; Owen, *CL*, 521. For Leslie Gunston, see *The Nymph* (New York: Stockwell, 1916).

3 For Keats' 'arterial blood', see Charles Armitage Brown, 'Life of John Keats', in *The Keats Circle: Letters and Papers 1816–78*, ed. Hyder E. Rollins (Cambridge, MA: Harvard University Press, 1965), 73–4; Owen, *CL*, 310.

4 See Sandra Gilbert, 'Rat's Alley,' *New Literary History*, 30.1 (Winter 1999): 179–201; and (expanded) in *Death's Door* (New York and London: W.W. Norton and Company, 2006), 366–97.

5 Quoted in Harold Owen, *Journey from Obscurity* (Oxford: Oxford University Press, 1965), 144.

6 Richard Aldington, *Death of a Hero* (London: Chatto and Windus, 1929), 429; Vera Brittain, *Testament of Youth* (1933; London: Fontana/Virago, 1979), 252–3; and Santanu Das, 'Slimescapes', *Touch and Intimacy in First World War Literature*, 35–72. For a treatment of these issues from a somewhat different perspective, see my 'Soldier's Heart: Literary Men, Literary Women, and the Great War', in Gilbert and Gubar, *Sexchanges,* Volume 2 of *No Man's Land: The Place of the Woman Writer in the Twentieth Century* (New Haven, CT: Yale University Press, 1989), 258–323.

7 Ford Maddox Ford, 'Arms and the mind', as cited in Samuel Hynes, *A War Imagined: The First World War and English Culture* (London: Bodley Head, 1991), 106. For the war's 'cities of death' as compared to the civilized city idealized by nineteenth-century Europeans, see 'The Great War and the City of Death' in chapter 7 ('Technologies of Death') in *Death's Door*, 147–52.

8 Owen, *CL*, 429.

9 For further discussion of Bone's paintings, see Hynes, 160–1. More recently, David Williams has argued in *Media, Memory, and the First World War* (Montreal and Kingston: McGill-Queen's University Press, 2009), 115–17, that the phrase 'Somme pictures' refers to the widely-viewed propaganda documentary *The Battle of the Somme*. In any case, whether writing of landscapes or movies, Owen was denouncing what he experienced as visual fakery.

10 *CL*, 482.

11 *CP*, 179.

12 Distinguishing between Owen's concept of 'pity' and what he considers the more dispassionate stance of Keith Douglas, Tim Kendall identifies 'pity' with 'feeling' and claims that Douglas 'denies the consolatory gesture of inserting a human sensibility between the reader and the horror'. But in Owen's most powerful poems, Aristotelian 'pity' shapes visions for which there can be no consolation. See Kendall, *Modern English War Poetry* (Oxford: Oxford University Press, 2006), 157.

13 Jon Stallworthy, *Wilfred Owen* (Oxford and New York: Oxford University Press, 1977), 222.

14 Dominic Hibberd, *Wilfred Owen* (London: Ivan R. Dee, 2002), 273; Owen, *CL*, 581. See also Ted Hughes, 'Wilfred Owen's Photographs,' *Collected Poems* (New York: Farrar, Straus and Giroux, 2003), 78. *CL*, 428–9.

15 Peter Howarth, *British Poetry in the Age of Modernism* (Cambridge: Cambridge University Press, 2005), 188; Owen, *CP*, 166; Owen, *CL*, 431.

16 *CP*, 99.

17 Algernon Charles Swinburne, *Major Poems* ed. Jerome McGann (New Haven, CT: Yale University Press, 2004), 117.

18 *CP*, 166.

19 *CP*, 123, 148, 178, 169, 190.

20 *CL*, 428.

21 *CP*, 188.

22 *CP*, 140.

23 *CP*, 155, 185 (emphasis added).

24 *CP*, 192.

8

EDNA LONGLEY

Edward Thomas and Ivor Gurney

There is good reason to link Edward Thomas (1878–1917) with Ivor Gurney (1890–1937) – and to link any Great War poets with other modern poets. 'War poetry', as a category, can be too weighted towards war. In all its permutations and combinations, poetry of the Great War belongs to a larger poetic field. Thomas and Gurney – for both of whom memory is a crucial shaping force – set the war itself in long perspectives. Discussing the first spate of 'war poetry', Thomas says: 'by becoming ripe for poetry the poet's thoughts may recede far from their original resemblance to all the world's, and may seem to have little to do with daily events'. For Gurney, ideally: 'immediate events ... must sink in to the very foundations and be absorbed'.[1]

The poets' own creative timelines make them almost mirror images. Thomas supported his family (with difficulty) by working as a reviewer, by writing critical books and books about the countryside. An influential poetry critic, he began to write poetry himself in December 1914. The war, friendship with Robert Frost, and an improvement in his mental health (as will be discussed) mysteriously combined to release the poet inside this self-styled 'hurried & harried prose man'.[2] Thomas enlisted in July 1915 after 'a long series of moods & thoughts',[3] which also took shape as poems. He spent some months as a map-reading instructor; then, after more moods, thoughts and poems, joined the Royal Artillery. He embarked for France as 2nd/Lieutenant in January 1917, and was killed by shell-blast at Arras on 9 April. *Poems* appeared six months later, *Last Poems* in 1918. All written before he went to France, Thomas's poems might be called 'literature of preparation' – as they explore the present or past, they remember the future. Gurney was less prepared. A student at the Royal College of Music, he impulsively volunteered in August 1914, but was turned down. In February 1915, he again volunteered and was accepted by the 2nd/5th Gloucester Regiment as a private soldier. He was gassed at Passchendaele in September 1917. Gurney published two collections of (mainly) war poems: *Severn &*

Somme (1917) and *War's Embers* (1919). Most of Gurney's strongest poems are indeed retrospective, although their chronology is complicated because he wrote and rewrote obsessively. This behaviour, like his memory of war, was conditioned by bipolar illness, which troubled him for years, and which got worse after the war. To call Gurney 'shell-shocked', as the army did when he broke down in 1918, is a half-truth or metaphorical truth (as will be discussed). From December 1922 until his death, Gurney was confined in the City of London Mental Hospital, Dartford, Kent. By the mid-1920s, his poems and musical compositions were becoming less and less coherent.

Thomas as Gurney's Muse

In 1932, Thomas's widow Helen was asked by Marion Scott, Gurney's long-time confidante, to visit Gurney in the asylum because he 'passionately loved my husband's work'. On her first visit, Helen learned that Gurney was not allowed to visit his native Gloucestershire. On her second, she brought with her 'Edward's own well-used ordnance maps of Gloucestershire where he had often walked':

> Ivor Gurney at once spread them out on his bed and he and I spent the whole time ... tracing with our fingers the lanes and byways and villages of which Ivor Gurney knew every step and over which Edward had also walked. He spent that hour in revisiting his home, in spotting a village or a track, a hill or a wood and seeing it all in his mind's eye ... a mental vision sharper and more actual for his heightened intensity ... [H]e had Edward as companion in this strange perambulation ...[4]

This poignant memoir maps more than one kind of common ground, as do the poems in which Gurney invokes Thomas. The 'Edward Thomas poem' would become a (still-vital) subgenre that marks Thomas's significance for later poetic generations,[5] but Gurney had the most immediate use for his work. In *War's Embers*, 'The Lock-keeper' is dedicated 'To the Memory of Edward Thomas':

> A tall lean man he was, proud of his gun,
> Of his garden, and small fruit trees every one
> Knowing all weather signs, the flight of birds,
> Farther than I could hear the falling thirds
> Of the first cuckoo. Able at digging, he
> Smoked his pipe ever, furiously, contentedly.
> Full of old country tales his memory was;
> Yarns of both sea and land, full of wise saws
> In rough fine speech ...[6]

These lines echo several poems by Thomas, but principally 'Lob': a 150-line poem in pentameter couplets, which symbolises a spirit 'English as this gate, these flowers, this mire', and which Gurney learned by heart. In different incarnations, Lob has a 'land face, sea-blue-eyed'; 'love[s] wild bird and beast and dog and gun/ For killing them'; makes up 'weather rhymes/ Which others spoilt'; and 'can talk quite as well as anyone/ After his thinking is forgot and done'. 'Lob' begins with the speaker travelling through Wiltshire villages 'In search of something chance would never bring'; 'The Lock-keeper' ends with the speaker saying that he will find nobody 'more wise in ways of Severn river,/ Though her villages I search for ever and ever'.[7] Thomas showed Gurney how war might give a countryside, and a figure like the lock-keeper, larger cultural meaning.

In 'The Poets of My County', Gurney associates Thomas with his own poetic claims, his recall of Severn in France: 'The love of Edward Thomas is night-walkers' promise/ But I praised Gloucester city as never before ...'. Another post-war poem, 'The Mangel-Bury', begins:

> It was after war; Edward Thomas had fallen at Arras –
> I was walking by Gloucester musing on such things
> As fill his verse with goodness; it was February; the long house
> Straw-thatched of the mangels stretched out two wide wings;
> And looked as part of the earth heaped up by dead soldiers
> In the most fitting place – along the hedge's yet-bare lines.

'The Mangel-Bury' rewrites Thomas's 'Swedes', which concerns the opening-up of a 'long swede pile/ ... the white and gold and purple of curled fronds'. Calling the Swedes 'a dream of Winter, sweet as Spring', Thomas contrasts their organic survival with a spookier phenomenon: the artefacts in 'a Pharaoh's tomb'. Gurney works Thomas's death and the trenches into this scenario. By introducing an encounter between the ex-soldier poet-speaker and a 'thick-set' farmer, he also rewrites Thomas's 'As the team's head-brass'. In Thomas's poem, a ploughman talks to a soldier (poet) who has yet to see action:

> 'Have you been out?' 'No.' 'And don't want to, perhaps?'
> 'If I could only come back again, I should.
> I could spare an arm. I shouldn't want to lose
> A leg. If I should lose my head, why, so,
> I should want nothing more ... Have many gone
> From here?' 'Yes.' 'Many lost?' 'Yes, a good few.
> Only two teams work on the farm this year ...'

In 'As the team's head-brass', war and the plough's rotation disrupt the talk. In 'The Mangel-Bury', the speaker cannot properly converse with the

(Lob-like) farmer because 'my pain to more moving called/ And him to some barn business far in the fifteen acre field'.[8] War and rural landscape still interpenetrate in a way that marks larger socio-cultural upheaval. For Thomas, young countrymen going to war represent a further stage in the 'death of rural England', along with the end of pre-war worlds. He also wrote an elegy for an individual 'ploughman, dead in battle', and 'In Memoriam (Easter, 1915)', which embraces a whole community:

> The flowers left thick at nightfall in the wood
> This Eastertide call into mind the men,
> Now far from home, who, with their sweethearts, should
> Have gathered them and will do never again.[9]

Gurney's retrospective mirror images extend this aspect of Thomas's vision. Two names for their common ground might be 'cultural elegy' and 'poetry of cultural defence'.

Defending 'England'

Rupert Brooke kick-started (English) Great War poetry, however many kicks he may get himself. Like other poets, Thomas and Gurney attack Brooke's premises and language. Thomas calls Brooke 'a rhetorician', and in 'No one cares less than I', he subverts phrases from Brooke's sonnet sequence *1914* ('some corner of a foreign field', 'Blow out, you bugles, over the rich Dead!'):

> 'No one cares less than I,
> Nobody knows but God,
> Whether I am destined to lie
> Under a foreign clod,'
> Were the words I made to the bugle call in the morning ...

Gurney conceived his 'Sonnets 1917' as a 'counterblast' against Brooke's ignorance of 'the grind of war', as 'the protest of the physical against the exalted spiritual'.[10]

Yet Gurney wrote pastiche Brooke before he wrote pastiche Thomas. His sonnet 'To the Poet before Battle' begins: 'Now, youth, the hour of thy dread passion comes:/ Thy lovely things must all be laid away'. The sonnet's final appeal, to 'make/ The name of poet terrible in just war', takes from Brooke the (Europe-wide) belief that war can redeem nations, with poets having a special redemptive role. Dedicated to Brooke's memory, 'Sonnets 1917' retains some Brooke-like elements: 'What better passing than to go out like men/ For England ...?' But two sonnets invoke 'England' more ambiguously: 'If it were not for England, who would bear/ This heavy servitude?'

and 'England terrible/ And dear taskmistress'. 'Pain' makes pain 'physical': 'An army of grey bedrenched scarecrows', horses '[d]ying in shell-holes'. In 1917, Gurney called England 'only a hard and fast system which has sent so much of the flower of England's artists to risk death, and a wrong material-istic system'.[11] 'Home-Sickness' prefigures the disappearance of an abstract 'England' from Gurney's poems. This sonnet celebrates 'Earth's familiar lovely places'; names 'Blackbird, bluebell, hedge-sparrow, tiny daisies'; and exclaims 'O tiny things, but very stuff of soul'. The effect parallels Thomas's lists of particulars: 'copses, ponds, roads and ruts,/ Fields where plough-horses steam and plovers/ Fling and whimper ...'. That list, in a testamen-tary poem for his son, symbolises what Thomas is 'leaving' as opposed to what Gurney has left. An object of *Severn & Somme* is 'To say out what Gloucester is; and is to me'.[12]

Severn and Somme interpenetrate most powerfully when they come sharp up against one another. The speaker of 'Crickley Hill' is thinking of Gloucestershire as he walks with another soldier in Buire-au-Bois: 'When on a sudden, "Crickley" he said. How I started/ At that old darling name of home!' In 'The Battalion Is Now On Rest', the speaker wanders out of a French village 'Towards England – Westward – and the last glow of day'. Village voices make him briefly 'feel/ As I were on Cotswold, with noth-ing else to do/ Than stare at the old houses, to taste the night-dew'. Here England gives way to 'Cotswold', which signifies less the nation at war than all that is not war. No Great War poet takes 'homesickness' as far as Gurney: partly because his rhythms make 'the old hot desire' (the poem's last phrase) so insistent, the sickness so real. In his asylum poems, Cotswold becomes doubly distant.[13]

Thomas's 'The Owl', which reverses the direction of Gurney's gaze, might be called a poem of 'war-sickness'. Enjoying 'food, fire, and rest' at an inn, the speaker cannot forget 'what I escaped/ And others could not'. This suggests why, as Thomas told Frost, he dared not say that Brooke's 'sonnets about him enlisting are probably not very personal, but a nervous attempt to connect with himself the very widespread idea that self sacri-fice is the highest self indulgence'. He added: 'I daren't say so, not having enlisted'.[14] Brooke clearly entered the 'moods & thoughts' that had already led Thomas to think: 'either I had never loved England, or I had loved it foolishly, aesthetically, like a slave, not having realised that it was not mine unless I were willing and prepared to die rather than leave it'. Given his own literary track record, perhaps he was provoked, perhaps creatively, by Brooke's appropriation of 'England'. The quotation is from one of sev-eral essays that Thomas wrote on war and Englishness in autumn 1914. He also edited *This England* (1915), an anthology which, in opposition to 'professedly patriotic' anthologies, he aimed to make 'as full of English character and country as an egg is of meat'. 'Lob', the anthology's quintessence, is Thomas's main poetic statement of cultural defence. The poem interweaves places, place names, flower names, folklore, folk idioms and poetry in a way that, half playfully, offers the matrix of English literature as a contribution to *Kulturkampf*: Lob 'never will admit he is dead/ Till millers cease to grind men's bones for bread'. 'This is no case of petty right or wrong', which directly reacts to other takes on the war, is more upfront. The speaker doubts whether 'politicians and philosophers' (like the pacifist Bertrand Russell) 'can judge' so complex a case, and also seeks to wrest patriotism from jingoism: 'I hate not Germans, nor grow hot/ With love of Englishmen, to please newspapers'. (Gurney's poem 'To the Prussians of England' deplores their 'blither'.) 'This is no case' ends by calling England 'all we know and live by'.[15] If unusually rhapsodic for Thomas, this is at least an empiricist definition. His poetry, which often reworks passages from his prose, seems partly driven by a need to distil all he 'knows' of England.

Thomas complicates a neat antithesis between patriotism and protest. Both before and after enlisting, he approaches the war dialectically. 'The Manor Farm', a sunny epiphany of timeless Englishness, is countered by 'The Combe', which situates the war in a history of cultural self-mutilation: 'But far more ancient and dark/ The Combe looks since they killed the badger there,/ Dug him out and gave him to the hounds,/ That most ancient Briton of English beasts'. Derelict rural buildings, too, become ominous symbols. Additionally, whether evoking war-haunted landscapes or mounting forms of cultural defence (also against native ideologues), Thomas builds in long views. The speaker of 'Digging' finds a clay pipe, which connects him with 'a soldier/ Of Blenheim, Ramillies, and Malplaquet/ Perhaps', and with prehistoric 'bones of ancients who, amazed to see/ Almighty God erect the mastodon,/ Once laughed, or wept, in this same light of day'. A line in 'Roads', 'Now all roads lead to France', proposes that the war pervades all consciousness, including consciousness of the past. The war-dead, 'Crowding the solitude/ Of the loops over the downs', join other ghosts. 'The sun used to shine', which recalls walks with Frost in August 1914, refers to itself as 'memory's sand'. This poem's time frame spans 'rumours of the war remote', 'the Crusades/ Or Caesar's battles', 'sunless Hades fields', and the speaker's past self when he was neither soldier nor poet.[16] For Thomas, who sees himself as an 'inhabitant of earth',[17] history is not anthropocentric. Badger, combe, downs and mastodon share in his eco-historical vista. Human beings, as they laugh, weep or make war, are not the whole story of England, and may be a passing story.

Gurney's historical sense is more specific to 'Cotswold my two thousand years' home'. 'While I Write' claims: 'War told me … I was born fit/ To praise the three hundred feet depth of every acre/ Between Tewkesbury and Stroudway, Side and Wales Gate'. As war poet, Gurney identifies with the Romans who farmed and protected Severnside. In 'Felling a Tree', a poem that dramatises and manifests kinetic energies rare in Gurney, the speaker hears 'Hit, crack, and false aim echoed from the amphitheatre', and senses 'the hidden farm, and Rome's hidden mild yoke/ Still on the Gloucester heart'. He prides himself on having learned 'Roman fortitude at Laventie or Ypres'.[18] Rome's imprint on France helped Gurney to feel at home amidst war: 'Roman the road as of Birdlip we were on the verge,/ And this west country thing so from chaos to emerge' ('First March').[19] In Gurney's poetry, cultural defence merges into shorter-term memory, more immediate elegy. His elegies are less protest elegies, with public conscience their implied reader, than poems of familial mourning, which might touch that conscience more obliquely. 'Butchers and Tombs' rebukes shoddy war burials by supplying its own apt ceremony:

> And so the disregarders of blister on heel,
> Pack on shoulder, barrage and work at the wires,
> One wooden cross had for ensign of honour and life gone –
> Save when the Gloucesters turning sudden to tell to one
> Some joke, would remember and say – 'That joke is done,'
> Since he who would understand was so cold he could not feel,
> And clay binds hard, and sandbags get rotten and crumble.[20]

Gurney's 'Cotswold' need be neither a metonym for England nor an English microcosm. Defined by domesticities as well as miseries, at once distinctively regional and a self-enclosed war world, it is as if Gloucestershire has gone to France with the Gloucesters. No war poet so intimately dwells on the pleasurable oases of banter, bacon frying, Woodbine breakfasts, card playing, estaminets (small cafés) and farmhouse billets. 'Behind the Line' sensually remembers Robecq:

> In the estaminets I suppose the air as cool, and the floor
> Grateful dark red; the beer and the different store
> Of citron, grenadine, red wine as surely delectable
> As in Nineteen Sixteen; with the round stains on the dark table.

Robecq, Tilleloy and Laventie resonate in Gurney's poetry alongside Birdlip, Maisemore, Framilode and Crickley. His French home-from-home also accommodates soldiers from further afield. In 'First Time In', admittedly, a contingent who 'Sang us Welsh things' evokes Cotswold's Welsh horizons: 'we looked out as from the edge of home'. But his poetry also embraces

'The Silent One', whose '[i]nfinite lovely chatter of Bucks accent' appallingly ends in death 'on the wires', and Scottish soldiers singing at New Year: 'The North, and all Scott called me – Ballads and Burns again!' ('New Year's Eve'). Gurney, with his song-composer's ear, commemorates voices of war. He calls the Welsh songs – '"David of the White Rock", the "Slumber Song" so soft' – 'never more beautiful than here under the guns' noise' ('First Time In').[21] Gurney set some poems by Thomas to music, and Thomas adapted folksong structures to wartime themes.[22]

Thomas's spatial as well as historical relation to England differs from Gurney's in ways that condition his poetry's greater complexity, its symbolic reach. Thomas began with a triple sense of being an outsider: 'mainly Welsh', a Londoner in the countryside, 'one of those modern people who belong nowhere'.[23] Family roots in Wales and Wiltshire give his landscapes as westward a tilt as Gurney's, but their Anglo-Celtic horizons are both more precise and less tangible. In actuality, memory and poetry, Gurney walks 'Cotswold'. Thomas's roads of consciousness, which refract the criss-crossings of England and Wales in his prose works, are harder to map; even when poems pivot on Steep (Hampshire) where he lived. 'Adlestrop' is about not knowing a place: 'only the name' and the cosmos it conjures. While Thomas praises Hardy's way of 'using local names with no special significance for the stranger, and no special private value of sound or significance for the poet', this (which partly covers Gurney) implies that poetry can do more with place and names. 'Lob' is a (the) namer. 'If I were to own', the poem for Thomas's son, orchestrates Essex place names to symbolise cultural inheritance: 'Shellow, Rochetts, Bandish, and Pickerells,/ Martins, Lambkins, and Lillyputs'. Yet names may fail to encode or generate 'significance'. Thomas implicates them in dialectics (bound up with the war) between known and unknown, memory and oblivion. 'Old Man' begins by doubting the transfer of 'knowledge' between thing and name: 'Old Man, or Lad's-love, – in the name there's nothing/ To one that knows not Lad's-love, or Old Man ...'. It ends by contemplating 'an avenue, dark, nameless, without end'.[24]

Structurally, Thomas's poems often parallel his sense of England as 'a system of vast circumferences circling round the minute neighbouring points of home'.[25] But to give 'home' such local or cognitive coordinates potentially deconstructs nation, the *casus belli*: 'Home Front' is an oxymoron. For Thomas as for Gurney, war destabilises 'home', which destabilises 'England'. In 'Home' Thomas attaches 'nationality' and 'memory', not to the public world, but to earthly habitation, a tiny ecosystem, the poem's own compass: 'one nationality/ We had, I and the birds that sang,/ One memory'. In '"Home"', where home acquires inverted commas, a walk with fellow soldiers ends less happily than in 'Crickley Hill'. Mention of 'home' shows that the word means different things: 'Between three counties far apart that lay/ We were divided and looked strangely each/ At the other …'. The instability of 'home', as word and concept, epitomises an existential 'strangeness' which war has created, heightened or exposed. In 'Words', written just before Thomas enlisted, words themselves become 'lost homes':

Strange and sweet
Equally,
And familiar,
To the eye,
As the dearest faces
That a man knows,
And as lost homes are:
But though older far
Than oldest yew, –
As our hills are, old, –
Worn new
Again and again …

What Thomas and Gurney 'defend' does not coincide with England at war. When the speaker asks 'English words' to 'Choose me', he invokes England as language, language as England, English poetry (Thomas's poetry) as cultural defence. By pitting language against oblivion, by wearing it new, poetry may reconstitute 'lost homes'.[26]

'Strange Hells'

For Thomas and Gurney, 'home' is also an elusive psychological locus: hence their capacity to internalise war. Thomas's third poem called 'Home' contains the quatrain:

This is my grief. That land,
My home, I have never seen;
No traveller tells of it,
However far he has been.[27]

On reading Thomas's *Poems*, Gurney noted: 'he had the same sickness of mind I have – the impossibility of serenity for any but the shortest space'.[28] Strictly speaking, they did not have 'the same sickness of mind': 'paranoid schizophrenia is another name for Gurney's mental trouble; 'depression' (including anxiety) seems the best broad term for Thomas's. In the asylum, Gurney thought that electricity was persecuting him: 'And there is dreadful hell within me./ And nothing helps. Forced meals there have been and electricity'. This poem, 'To God', includes the line: 'And I am praying for death, death, death'.

Thomas, too, wrote death-wish poems. 'Rain' ends with his self-projection as one who has 'no love ... except the love of death,/ If love it be towards what is perfect and/ Cannot, the tempest tells me, disappoint'.[29] At least twice, Thomas almost committed suicide, and he suffered several breakdowns to which overwork and (it would seem) repressed poetic vocation contributed. He told a friend: 'the central evil is self-consciousness carried as far beyond selfishness as selfishness is beyond self denial'.[30] In 1912, Thomas received treatment from Godwin Baynes, who became Jung's leading British disciple. Psychoanalysis made him more productively 'self-conscious', prompting auto-biographical prose that helped poetry to emerge. From perspectives enabled by its existence, Thomas's poetry revisits still-latent neuroses. Two poems that explore a split psyche are 'The Other' and 'Wind and Mist'. The former is a quest parable in which the speaker pursues an alter ego: 'No release/ Until he ceases'. In the latter, mainly a dramatic monologue, Thomas betrays his own acquaintance with paranoia: 'I had forgot the wind./ Pray do not let me get on to the wind./ You would not understand about the wind ...'.[31]

There is a gulf between Thomas's structured psychodrama and Gurney's inability to detach his darker poems from his illness. Thomas's speaker switches roles between self and other, patient and analyst; whereas Gurney's remains trapped in unresolved distress. Gurney's 'To God' ends: 'Not often such evil guessed as between Man and Man'. Yet when he aligns himself with Thomas as lacking 'serenity for any but the shortest space', he points to a shared poetic trope: epiphany. The chemistry between mental turmoil and poetry sometimes maps onto the tension between war and peace. Gurney's 'sweet unexpected/ Balm' in 'First March' also seems to ease inner 'chaos'. 'La Gorgue' celebrates an estaminet as 'A mark in Time, a Peace, a Making-delay'. Before embarking for France, Thomas compressed all his delight in the senses and the seasons into a valedictory epiphany: 'While the glint/ Of hollies dark in the swollen hedges lasts –/ One mile – and those bells ring, little I know/ Or heed if time be still the same' ('The Lane').[32]

War appears on both sides of the epiphanic or psychiatric equation: witness 'The Owl' where *distance* from war causes unease. 'The Glory', which dramatises a frustrated desire for self-realisation, illuminates Thomas's enlistment from a different angle. Critics have long contested the view that this decision was all he needed to snap out of depression. Yet war focused his 'moods & thoughts', his poetry. And, aged thirty-seven, he need neither have switched to the artillery nor gone to France. 'There was a time' ponders the paradox that a real crisis may solve a (partly) self-created one:'

> I sought yet hated pity till at length
> I earned it. Oh, too heavy was the cost.

> But now that there is something I could use
> My youth and strength for, I deny the age,
> The care and weakness that I know – refuse
> To admit I am unworthy of the wage
> Paid to a man who gives up eyes and breath
> For what would neither ask nor heed his death.[33]

This poem, a Shakespearean sonnet with an extra quatrain, repeats words from Brooke's sonnets ('wage', 'gives up', 'breath'/'death'), while redirecting them towards a psychology, rather than rhetoric, of motives for going to war. The last line, which echoes 'No one cares less than I', renders war itself not a glorious cause, but an impervious fate. In Michael Hurd's view, Gurney 'felt that the physical effort of army life would somehow cure his "neurasthenia" and that he would come to feel as other men: mind and body at peace with one another'. Hurd also suggests that Gurney 'had found the family he had always been looking for'.[34] Thomas writes from the trenches: 'I have suffered more from January to March in other years than in this'; Gurney, who believed he had become 'saner', writes: 'It was a great time; full of fear of course, but not so bad as neurasthenia'; and again: 'my chief thought is that I have found myself unfitted for Life and Battle, and am gradually by hard necessity being strengthened'.[35] Although Thomas had practical skills that Gurney lacked, 'feeling as other men' and confronting life mattered to him, too. Yet in '"Home"', the speaker's self-image is split between seeing himself as 'another man' and the possibility that army life may be 'only an evil dream'.[36] Thomas's poetic dialectics about war continue to the end.

Both poets admit war into the most troubled recesses of the psyche. Thomas's 'Rain', set in a 'bleak [army] hut', associates the war dead with the speaker's nihilistic and suicidal mood: 'Myriads of broken reeds all still and stiff'. 'Gone, gone again', where the speaker likens himself to 'empty quays' and a ruined house, stresses the date 'when the war began/ To turn young men to dung'. 'Gone, gone again' belongs to a group of poems linked by an accelerating symbolic journey to France, the unknown, the 'dark'. This journey has metaphysical as well as psychological horizons, given that Thomas's ecocentric vision includes the perception that humanity may be surplus to earth's purposes: a perception sharpened by war. In 'The long small room', a fated and fatalistic speaker identifies with 'moon, sparrow and mouse/ That witnessed what they could never understand/ Or alter or prevent in the dark house'.[37] Yet 'Lights Out' represents the journey, on all its symbolic levels, as chosen:

> There is not any book
> Or face of dearest look

> That I would not turn from now
> To go into the unknown
> I must enter and leave alone,
> I know not how.[38]

Gurney's 'Strange Hells' also locates war in the mind:

> There are strange Hells within the minds War made
> Not so often, not so humiliatingly afraid
> As one would have expected – the racket and fear guns made.
> One Hell the Gloucester soldiers they quite put out:
> Their first bombardment, when in combined black shout
> Of fury, guns aligned, they ducked lower their heads –
> And sang with diaphragms fixed beyond all dreads …

The poem then asks: 'Where are they now, on State-doles, or showing shop-patterns', and ends: 'The heart burns – but has to keep out of face how heart burns'. Here war's 'dreads' appear less hellish than post-war ingratitude. Gurney's poetry might appear shell shocked, but the relation between war and his illness is not clear-cut. He was, rather, peace-shocked by society's disregard for him as soldier and 'war poet'. The speaker of 'Riez Baillieul' recalls being 'sick of body and heart' in France in order 'to hide this pain and work myself free/ From present things'.[39] Thomas and Gurney disconcertingly internalise the enormity of the Great War as something recognisable. If their 'hell', like their 'home', is not always '[as] one would have expected', it is because they configure war with the extent to which all life is 'strange' or *unheimlich*.

Heart and Art

Gurney's 'War Books' is a manifesto:

> What did they expect of our toil and extreme
> Hunger – the perfect drawing of a heart's dream?
> Did they look for a book of wrought art's perfection,
> Who promised no reading, nor praise, nor publication?
> Out of the heart's sickness the spirit wrote.
> For delight, or to escape hunger, or of war's worst anger …[40]

War poetry has license to be improvisatory, unfinished, at a loss for words. Yet, even as Gurney establishes that principle, odd syntax persists into this post-war poem: the four condensed genitives, for instance. Some poems previously quoted contain inversions that seem wholly dictated by rhyme: 'as of Birdlip we were on the verge'/ 'emerge'. We may attribute Gurney's syntactical elisions and contortions, as Hurd says, either 'to a genuine "style", or merely to a mind innately inclined to make sudden inconsequential leaps – a kind of stutter in the thought process, due perhaps to incipient mental disturbance'.[41] Certainly, when disturbance escalates, his syntax unravels further along the same lines. Yet 'stutter' seems integral to Gurney's most powerful poems. At the end of 'The Mangel-Bury', ellipsis, which befits the aborted talk, makes the speaker's 'pain' what calls the farmer to 'some barn business'. Gurney's illness merges with war more as problems of communication than as 'war's worst anger'. His poetic signals gain strength from being, somehow, jammed. To apply a dark trench image from 'The Not-Returning': we sense him 'stumbling blind through the difficult door'.[42]

Because Gurney remains, at some level, a naïve poet, few of his forms are indeed 'wrought' to a pitch that makes them more than vehicles for a voice that itself lacks tonal and dramatic modulation. This is very different from Thomas's relation to lyric form. On the one hand, Frost's theory and practice of the 'sentence-sound' influenced his 'fidelity to the postures which the voice assumes in the most expressive, intimate speech' – and hence his ability to 'express' war.[43] That applies to his soliloquies ('Lights Out' begins: 'I have come to the borders of sleep'), as much as to the disruptive dialogue of 'As the team's head-brass'. On the other hand, Thomas's deep reading of English poetry appears in a formal variety that backs up 'English words' as cultural defence. It includes the neo-Chaucerian couplets of 'Lob', the new concentration he gives blank verse ('As the team's head-brass', 'Old Man'), sonnet form's role as a (usually disguised) point of reference, his masterly short poems ('In Memoriam') and his range of stanzas, often one-off ('Words', 'Lights Out'). The 'sentence-sound' meets the English lyric in a complex syntax that maximises poetry's freedom to reorder prose sequence. 'Old Man' begins with a meaningful inversion. Thomas is the 'war poet' who most fully joined in the arguments that underpinned the making of modern poetry: arguments in which, like Frost and Yeats, he favoured the 'wearing new' of traditional form. Like these poets, too, he stayed in touch with the legacy of symbolism. His poems draw on nature, but are not naturalistic. Here, as with other aspects of Thomas's aesthetic, the Great War played a part that we may never entirely fathom.

NOTES

1 See Thomas, 'War Poetry' in Edna Longley ed. *A Language not to be Betrayed: Selected Prose of Edward Thomas* (Manchester: Carcanet, 1981), 132; R.K.R. Thornton ed. *Ivor Gurney: Collected Letters* (Ashington and Manchester: MIDNAG and Carcanet, 1991), 29 (Hereafter abbreviated as *Gurney: Letters*).
2 R. George Thomas ed. *Edward Thomas: Letters to Gordon Bottomley* (Oxford: Oxford University Press, 1968), 203.

3   Ibid., 253.

4   See Helen Thomas with Myfanwy Thomas, *Under Storm's Wing* (Manchester: Carcanet, 1988), 239–41.

5   See Anne Harvey ed. *Elected Friends: Poems for and about Edward Thomas* (London: Enitharmon, 1991); Guy Cuthbertson and Lucy Newlyn eds. *Branch-Lines: Edward Thomas and Contemporary Poetry* (London: Enitharmon, 2007).

6   Ivor Gurney, *Severn and Somme & War's Embers* (repr. Ashington and Manchester: MIDNAG and Carcanet, 1987), 99.

7   *Gurney: Letters*, 441; Edna Longley ed. *Edward Thomas: The Annotated Collected Poems* (Tarset: Bloodaxe, 2008), 76–9 [Hereafter abbreviated as *Thomas: Annotated Collected Poems*].

8   P.J. Kavanagh ed. *Ivor Gurney: Collected Poems* (Manchester: Carcanet, 2004), 257, 263 [Hereafter abbreviated as *Gurney: Collected Poems*]; *Thomas: Annotated Collected Poems*, 54, 123–4.

9   See Alun Howkins, *The Death of Rural England: A Social History of the Countryside since 1900* (London and New York: Routledge, 2003); *Thomas: Annotated Collected Poems*, 50, 80.

10   R. George Thomas ed. *Edward Thomas: Selected Letters* (Oxford: Oxford University Press, 1995), 132 [Hereafter abbreviated as *Selected Letters*]; Rupert Brooke, *Complete Poems* (London: Sidgwick and Jackson, 1932), 150, 148; *Thomas: Annotated Collected Poems*, 123; *Gurney: Letters*, 210.

11   Gurney, *Severn and Somme etc.*, 23, 49–51; *Gurney: Letters*, 288.

12   Gurney, *Severn & Somme etc.*, 51; *Thomas: Annotated Collected Poems*, 115; *Gurney: Letters*, 216.

13   *Gurney: Collected Poems*, 39, 25.

14   *Thomas: Annotated Collected Poems*, 65; Thomas, *Selected Letters*, 111–12.

15   Guy Cuthbertson and Lucy Newlyn eds. *Edward Thomas: Prose Writings, Vol. 2: England and Wales* (Oxford: Oxford University Press, 2011), 576; Thomas ed. *This England: An Anthology from her Writers* (Oxford: Oxford University Press, 1915), preface; *Thomas: Annotated Collected Poems*, 79, 104–5.

16   *Thomas: Annotated Collected Poems*, 48, 99, 107–8.

17   Ibid., 42, and see note, 161.

18   *Gurney: Collected Poems*, 251, 262, 252.

19   *Gurney: Collected Poems*, 144.

20   Ibid., 241.

21   Ibid., 153, 149, 250, 131, 149.

22   For example, in 'The Gallows', 'Early one morning'.

23   See Thomas, *The South Country* (London: Dent, 1909), 7.

24   *Thomas: Annotated Collected Poems*, 51, 116, 36–7; see Longley ed. *A Language not to be Betrayed*, 75.

25   Cuthbertson and Newlyn eds. *Thomas: Prose Writings, Vol. 2*, 538.

26   *Thomas: Annotated Collected Poems*, 81, 114, 92.

27   Ibid., 64.

28   *Gurney: Letters*, 375.

29   *Gurney: Collected Poems*, 197; *Thomas: Annotated Collected Poems*, 105.

30   Eleanor Farjeon, *Edward Thomas: The Last Four Years* (1958; Stroud: Sutton, 1997), 13.

31 *Thomas: Annotated Collected Poems*, 42, 74–5.
32 *Gurney: Collected Poems*, 197, 144, 140; *Thomas: Annotated Collected Poems*, 138.
33 *Thomas: Annotated Collected Poems*, 128.
34 Michael Hurd, *The Ordeal of Ivor Gurney* (Oxford: Oxford University Press, 1978), 53, 70.
35 Thomas, *Selected Letters*, 156; *Gurney: Letters*, 87, 103, 168.
36 *Thomas: Annotated Collected Poems*, 114.
37 *Thomas: Annotated Collected Poems*, 105, 131, 137.
38 Ibid., 136.
39 *Gurney: Collected Poems*, 141, 203.
40 Ibid., 258.
41 Hurd, *Ordeal*, 200–1.
42 *Gurney: Collected Poems*, 263, 168.
43 *Thomas: Letters to Bottomley*, 251.

9

ADRIAN POOLE

David Jones

Shortly before his death in 1974, David Jones expressed admiration for Wilfred Owen's best poetry, but also astonishment 'that anything at all could have been written in such extreme circumstances'.[1] As we shall see, the search for formal and stylistic ways of representing 'extreme circumstances' distinguishes Jones's masterpiece, *In Parenthesis*. It was composed slowly and with difficulty from 1928 onwards, and despite the manifest differences, it has as much if not more in common with longer memoirs of the Great War written in prose – such as Edmund Blunden's *Undertones of War* (1928), Robert Graves's *Goodbye to All That* (1929) and Siegfried Sassoon's *Memoirs of an Infantry Officer* (1930) – as with the short poems normally associated with First World War poets. After completing a draft in 1932, Jones suffered a serious breakdown, but he returned to complete and publish it in 1937 as another war loomed. *In Parenthesis* is drawn from and speaks to a particular moment in history, if also beyond it. Of the several connotations of its title, one appears now to declare its composition in a temporary space of relief *entre deux guerres*, yet one marked at the time by a sense of returning doom, of apocalypse now.

Jones enlisted in the 15th Battalion of Royal Welch Fusiliers (the same regiment as Graves and Sassoon). *In Parenthesis* draws on the seven months of his first term of service on the Western Front from December 1915 until the assault on Mametz Wood in the battle of the Somme in July 1916, in which Jones was wounded and many of his comrades died. He returned to the Front a few months later and served until the end of the war, and beyond, for a few uncomfortable months in Ireland. In his Preface, he emphasises that the Somme was a watershed, after which everything became 'a more relentless, mechanical affair' (ix), a truly modern war.

It is worth summarising some of the affiliations and commitments that mark Jones's work, beginning with matters of class and rank. Born in 1895 in Brockley, Kent, he was the son of a printer's overseer; his mother's father was a mast-and-block maker of Rotherhithe. Like Isaac Rosenberg and Ivor

Gurney, Jones served as a private soldier – not an officer like Owen, Graves and Sassoon. Although the voices of *In Parenthesis* range far beyond those of the common soldiers, the vantage point from which the war is immediately experienced is that of 'the essential foot-mob, [...] who endure all things' (126). At the most realistic level, it is the perspective of the London members of the Royal Welsh platoon, not 'the genuine Taffies', but the 'rash levied / from Islington and Hackney / and the purlieus of Walworth', and other districts of Greater London (160).

This points to a second distinguishing feature. Jones studied the historical origins of his divided ethnicity with extraordinary, near obsessional zeal. Hyphens play a significant role in the verbal texture of his writing, and 'Anglo-Welsh' is only one way of describing its author (painter-poet would be another). This split and conjoined inheritance is reflected on the title page, where beneath *In Parenthesis* we read '*seinnyessit e gledyf ym penn mameu*'. Most Anglophone readers must wait for the explanation in Jones's endnote of his debt to the sixth-century epical poem attributed to Aneirin, *Y Gododdin*, that commemorates the calamitous battle of Catraeth; then we learn that the Welsh means 'His sword rang in mothers' heads'. This pattern is partly repeated in the double headings to the poem's seven sections, where a title is provided by phrases from the English literary tradition (Coleridge, Shakespeare, Hopkins, Malory, Carroll), underpinned by a quotation from the Welsh epic – translated into English. There is a striking contrast between the variety, confidence and playfulness of the former and the steady, unvarying, plainness of the latter. The heading to Part 5, for example, 'Squat Garlands for White Knights', alludes, Jones's note alerts us, to the real shrapnel helmets issued for the first time early in 1916, and to lines from Hopkins's 'Tom's Garland' and Carroll's *Alice through the Looking Glass*; the subheading simply reads, 'He has brought us to a bright fire and to a white fresh floor-hide' (101). This suggests a certain ruefulness at the way one tradition has 'superseded' and now literally, on the page, 'sits over' the other.

Jones worked as a visual artist as well as with words, as did Rosenberg. (Gurney, too, had more than one art, although for him it was music.) A comparison is often drawn between Jones and William Blake, and the tradition that runs through Ruskin and the pre-Raphaelites, especially William Morris, supplies a useful perspective. There is a good case for seeing Jones the painter, engraver and book illustrator as no less important than the writer, an artist of a calibre and importance equivalent to contemporaries such as Ben Nicholson, Barbara Hepworth and Henry Moore, with whom he was associated between 1928–1932. But words and images were for him always closely related. Before he fully embarked on his writing, Jones illustrated *The Chester Play of the Deluge* (1927) and *The Rime of the Ancient Mariner* (1929), and his verbal art is deeply influenced by his formation as a maker of visual images. He invests a huge amount in the idea of 'shape', for example, with a feeling for the Old English roots of the word in the act of creation. In his later years he gives explicit expression to the theological convictions underlying his belief in the human need for 'signs', most notably in the essay on 'Art and Sacrament' (1955), that Rowan Williams has called 'one of the most important pieces of writing in the twentieth century on art and the sacred'.[2]

In Parenthesis is different in form, style and ambition from other British 'war poetry', in so far as it is a single long piece of work, suggesting that the traditional genre to which it owes allegiance is epic rather than lyric. But it is also distinguished by its indeterminate commitment to usual definitions and expectations of what constitutes 'poetry', given that far more of it looks like prose rather than verse. Jones himself speaks of it simply as 'writing' (i). The 'look' of it is indeed very largely the point. Some blocks are laid out according to the conventions of prose whereas others follow the conventions of verse, as this for example:

> And the severed head of '72 Morgan,
> its vision grins like the Cheshire cat
> and full grimly. (180)

In the absence of inverted commas signalling direct speech, the layout often assists the illusion of voices, as in the opening lines:

> '49 Wyatt, 01549 Wyatt.
> Coming sergeant. (1)

Or on occasion, of song:

> Never die never die
> Never die never die
> Old soljers never die (84)

But the cunning fluctuation of these verbal 'shapes' on the page thwarts any attempt to categorise its medium as either prose or verse.

Jones was sensitive to allegations of influence, but he readily acknowledged the inspiration he drew from Eliot and Joyce, or to be more exact, from Eliot's *The Waste Land*, and Joyce's *Anna Livia Plurabelle* (1930). He revered the latter as 'the most creative literary genius of this century' (although, amazingly, he appears not to have read *Ulysses*).[3] Jones was encouraged by these modernist peers to take the liberties that the exorbitant memories of life and death in the trenches might seem to require. The verbal medium he created is consonant with the treacherous, water-logged terrain of the Western Front, in which the totem creature is the rat, making himself at home in 'his amphibious paradise' (54). The very form of this environment and the shapes it contains is indeterminate: 'Substantial matter guttered and dissolved, sprawled to glaucous insecurity. All sureness metamorphosed, […] ' (76). William Blissett describes the sense of peril induced in the reader by this verbal 'no-man's land, […] a danger zone fraught with sudden breaks in syntax, prickly hyphenations, explosive verbal nouns, deceptive underpunctuation, and other risky devices'.[4]

Jones was impatient with two common responses to the position of war in his work. *In Parenthesis* was not intended as a 'War Book', he insisted; 'it happens to be concerned with war' (xii), but its subject is larger than the term implies. He was also prompt to reject the claim that it was somehow 'anti-war'. Although it is risky to extract single statements from a work with so many voices and perspectives, there is a telling moment when we hear this, of the two armies confronting each other: 'They're worthy of an intelligent song for all the stupidity of their contest. A boast for the dyke keepers, for the march wardens' (88–9).

This declaration raises questions about the ethics and politics that the work supports and promotes. There are readers who want to hear more about the stupidity of the contest, and why exactly the dyke keepers and march wardens are blowing each other to bits, desecrating the amphibious landscape they would be better off attending to. Should there not be more sardonic humour like this? 'They bright-whiten all this sepulchre with powdered chloride of lime. It's a perfectly sanitary war' (43). Should there not be more protest at the thought of war veterans being supplied with 'synthetic parts to walk in the Triumphs, without anyone feeling awkward and O, O, O, it's a lovely war' (176)? More indignation about the prospective 'Cook's tourist to the Devastated Areas' (186)? One may well wonder, if not agonise, about the place of Christian charity in war (any war, including the one looming at the time of publication in 1937), such as the dedication clearly extends to:

THE ENEMY FRONT-FIGHTERS WHO SHARED OUR PAINS AGAINST
WHOM WE FOUND OURSELVES BY MISADVENTURE

A little hatred for the enemy is allowed into the poem – Joe Donkin vows to avenge his five brothers on 'these miscreant bastard square-heads' (145) – but more enmity is reserved for the soldiers' own Olympian officers. Outside the poem, Jones declares his commitment to the intelligent song as a primary kind of human 'making', for which 'war' provides the most brutal challenge, yet not one different in kind from life's other conditions. War provides one of the shaping metaphors by which we understand our being in the world, he proposes: 'We find ourselves privates in foot regiments. We search how we may see formal goodness in a life singularly inimical, hateful, to us' (xiii).

In an essay appended to 'Art and Sacrament', he affirmed that 'Ars is ada-
mant about one thing: she compels you to do an infantryman's job'.[5]

The poem gives rich expression to the goodness of life and the sad calamity of its unmaking: to the beauty of the natural world, 'the grassy bank with
million daisies spangled' (110), the 'blue-winged butterflies' (131) and the
horror of its violent destruction. Trees, 'signs' of huge importance to Jones
(as, for example, in one of his greatest paintings, 'Vexilla Regis' [1947]), are
thus 'stripped stumps for flowering limbs – this discontent makes winter's
rasure creaturely and kind' (30) – that is, 'kind' by comparison with what
man can do to it. He also asks us to admire the validity of man-made cre-
ations such as the old barn in which the soldiers listen to lectures, 'with its
great roof, sprung, upreaching, humane, and redolent of a vanished order'
(13); the enduring everyday love, such as three friends share on a grassy
slope before the final assault in Part 6; and all forms of 'created-dear' things
that are violently unmade by war, like the dead Corporal Aneirin Lewis –
'unwholer, limb from limb, than any of them fallen at Catraeth' (155).
Meanwhile, he demonstrates the entanglement of created goodness and the
weapons of man-made destruction: 'iron warp with bramble weft' (165).
As for the poet himself, it is the search for 'formal goodness' on which he
lays his prime stress: 'I have only tried to make a shape in words'(x). Hence
the importance to the poem of words such as 'order' (especially the 'star-
light order' borrowed from Hopkins as the heading for Part 3, from 'The
Bugler's First Communion'), 'liturgy', 'ritual', 'patterning' and 'discipline'.
And of wonder at the creaturely capacity to make a habitation for oneself
and others, however adverse the circumstances: 'They would make order,
for however brief a time, and in whatever wilderness' (22).

Related to this, it should come as no surprise to find Jones's work nour-
ished by religious beliefs inseparable from his artistic ones. He converted
to Roman Catholicism in 1921, and as Rowan Williams and others have
shown, his art and thought owe a debt to Catholic theology, especially to the
contemporary French thinker, Jacques Maritain. No less important, especially for those who cannot share such beliefs, is Jones's appealingly catholic
tenderness for all forms of the 'creaturely', and his invitation to us to 'look
more intimately'. Just before the final assault on the dark wood we are
asked to look around: 'and if you look more intimately all manner of small
creatures, created-dear things creep about quite comfortably' (157).

In Parenthesis invokes a classic kind of narrative from initiation through
to climactic ordeal. There are allusions to the idea of the voyage (especially
Coleridge's 'Rime of the Ancient Mariner') and of the hunt ('The Hunt' is
the title of one of Jones's best-known shorter poems). Although the 'par-
enthetical' framings that enclose and mark off each of the seven Parts are

of great importance, there is a clear and traditional sense of progression, of young soldiers, initiates or novitiates, participating in some ritual process. The action moves from winter to high summer, and concludes with an assault on a 'dark wood'. In fact, it is the second such wood, an engulfing version of the 'twisted wood across no-man's land' in Part 4 when its mythic, romantic and folkloric associations could still be contemplated at leisure: 'To groves always men come both to their joys and their undoing' (66). But in Part 7, the undoing becomes all too real.

There is no single central character(s), no consistent 'I', no 'protagonist'. However, Jones makes a couple of cameo appearance as '79 Jones, when we see him 'in his far corner, rearrange and arrange again a pattern of match-ends' (108), and again, as Private W. Map (127). *In Parenthesis* meets head-on the challenge always entailed by the representation of war as a massive collective experience, by the too-muchness of it all, the excess of characters, sensations, fortunes and fates. But it is given shape by the relative prominence of certain named figures, whose destinies we can follow if we keep our wits about us. Most notably Private John Ball, and the young officer who commands his respect, Lieutenant Piers Dorian Isambard Jenkins, both Englishmen; and on the Welsh side, Lance-Corporal Aneirin Lewis, Private Watcyn and Dai Great-Coat. This last is particularly significant in that he declaims an extraordinary 'boast' at the centre of the poem in Part 4, that bursts all realistic frames of reference. In the most extended first-person passage of the whole poem, he declares that 'I was with Abel when his brother found him, [...] I am '62 Socrates, [...] I heard Him cry: [...] I saw Him die [...] I was in Michael's trench when bright Lucifer [...]' (79–84). Dai reappears at the end of the poem when the Queen of the Woods, in a justly famous passage that complements his boast at the poem's centre, hands out her 'bright boughs of various flowering' to the dead soldiers under her trees. Or rather, he mysteriously does not, for 'she can't find him anywhere – she calls both high and low' (186). But no less important than these salient figures is the general unpredictability to all the comings and goings; there is no knowing who is going to turn up next, to lurch or leap into view. The randomness of death is reflected in the identities of 'the secret princes' honoured by the Queen of the Woods, some of whom we have met before, like Mr Jenkins, Billy Crower and Fatty Weavel, and others whom we have not, like Ulrich and Sîon, or Hansel with Gronwy lying 'in serious embrace'. Or most surprisingly, 'That swine Lillywhite', only slightly less scornful an epithet than the one on his first appearance as 'that shit Lillywhite' (15); he receives 'daisies to his chain – you'd hardly credit it' (185).

At one level the poem provides a realistic representation of the here and now, of specific times, places, persons, events and deaths, although all these are relatively lightly inscribed. There are names and numbers who have voices of their own, voices rendered with particular care for the dense, idio-syncratic humour of military slang. It is unsurprising to be told by one friend that Jones was a 'lifelong Dickensian'. To another, he confessed the difficulty he had with the Cockney speech essential to the life of the trenches, his aim for '*a real enduring shape without being embarrassing*' (his own emphasis).[6] Nevertheless, readers need to get attuned to this tribal dialect, with some help from Jones's notes, before they can make sense of 'he'd clicked a cushy get away' (181), for example. This is, of course, a moderated realism: Jones does not reproduce the obscenities natural to men's speech in such circum-stances, although his reasons have less to do with propriety than with a wish to honour the liturgical quality, so he describes it, of 'Bugger! Bugger!' (xii), and 'the efficacious word' (53 and n.45, 201).

There is also a daunting array of references to other battles, war-riors and legends, both literary and popular, including *Y Gododdin*, *The Mabinogion*, *The Song of Roland*, Arthurian romance (especially Malory) and Shakespeare's *Henry V*. There is also a commemorative intent, a pur-posive anamnesis, in recalling the words in which these precedents have been memorialised; language more or less foreign to most modern-day read-ers. 'Rownsepykèd', for example, meaning 'stripped of their leaves', comes straight from Malory: 'leper-trees … rownsepykèd out of nature' (39). We can sense in the poet an extravagant desire that *nothing* should be lost or forgotten. If the poet is the rememberer of the tribe, as Jones conceived it, the weight of this responsibility weighs almost intolerably on his mod-ern avatar. Jones is often described as a poet's poet, but at least one other, Charles Tomlinson, has complained of the 'imaginative overcrowding' in his writing, and of the 'relentless typological parallels'. This latter is the burden of a well-known critique by Paul Fussell, who concludes *In Parenthesis* to be 'a deeply conservative work', one that seeks 'to rationalize and even to vali-date the war by implying that it somehow recovers many of the motifs and values of medieval chivalric romance'. Defenders of Jones have countered with arguments for the complex, reciprocal interplay between the contem-porary realities and the precedents he invokes: mythic, legendary, literary, scriptural. Jonathan Miles, for example, finds a good word for the physical-ising of such memories in Jones's writing: 'By intercutting Malory's wounds with shells splintering, Jones, rather than ennobling war, *re-carnalizes* the chivalric tradition lest heroism and battle should be misconstrued as glori-ous and desirable' (emphasis added).[7]

'In parenthesis': between the extremes of the here and now and there and then, a voice and perspective hang suspended. The reader is challenged by the absence of a single controlling authoritative centre – a familiar, defining feature of 'modernism'. But in 1956, Gwyn Williams found parallels in Jones (and Dylan Thomas) to a quality integral to the old Welsh poetry collected in his anthology, *The Burning Tree*. Jones was gratified, and particularly delighted by Williams's reference to '"the inter-woven inventions present in early Celtic MSS and on stone crosses where *what happens in a corner is as important as what happens at the centre because there often is no centre*"' [Jones's emphasis].[8] In *In Parenthesis*, every moment is a new centre; on their arrival in France, the young new soldiers clamber down from a bus, 'and at all their sense-centres a perceiving of strange new things' (18). They – and we – are faced with perpetual, often violent shifts of perspective, a want of connections, where 'want' connotes both lack and desire. Here, indeed, extremes meet: the unmaking force of war against the making powers of art.

Consider this image of men 'standing illusive in the dark light about some systemed task, transilient, regularly spaced, at kept intervals [...]' (28). In this vision of order, 'transilient' leaps out at us,[9] half-recognisable in its proximity to 'transient', 'resilient' and 'salient', yet slightly elusive, requiring an effort to discover its sense of 'leaping or passing from one thing or condition to another', with a further technical reference to mineralogy, 'of one rock substance passing abruptly into another'. (These and other definitions are taken from the *OED*). It is a word well-suited to Jones's own literary form and style as it passes abruptly from one angle, perspective or voice to another.

Here are some more words and phrases that are likely to ambush readers and send them scurrying for assistance: 'nainsook', 'loricated', 'purlin', 'glacis', 'huckaback', 'kelson', 'pavissed', 'predella', 'arbalestier', 'corposant', 'their catechumen feet', 'whose toe porrects the ritual instrument', 'by fascined track', 'the desolated cantrefs'. We may wonder at the motive and function of these technical terms. Do they oppress us with our ignorance of the *technê* to which they belong? Or invite us to share the satisfaction of craftsmen and initiates for whom they answer an exact need? Like the latch-key that falls out of Private Ball's pocket, 'so far from its complying lock' (23).

What of this, when we are told that the enemy's shrapnel bursts 'were gauffered at their spreading edges with reflected gold' (146)? 'Gauffered' (or goffered') indicates a kind of ornamentation, in dressmaking or bookbinding, especially in the phrase, 'goffered edges'. Still a term of craft, it has a distinctly aestheticising effect here, which puts it in touch with references to painters, to Hobbema, Fragonard and Boucher, and – more darkly – to a famous painting of Brueghel's, of the blind leading the blind (31). Also with moments when the scenery is beautified by sunlight or ordinary daylight, but especially by the silvering moon: 'grace this mauled earth – / transfigure our infirmity – / shine on us' (35). These are moments of solace, sparingly entertained, of beauty and goodness amidst horror and desolation, at its edges and interstices and junctions. But it is striking to find 'gauffer' recur in a passage from a later work in which, Neil Corcoran argues, Jones is reflecting with some savagery on his own procedures in the earlier poem, on the magical glamour it throws over the realities it reports. There is room for debate over how conscious *In Parenthesis* is of the questionability of its own 'techniques'.[10]

The generous view would be that the jagged transitions between its bits and pieces consistently draw attention to the evidence of human 'making', including its own. Sometimes these leaps are more violent than usual. At the end of Part 2, a celebrated passage reproduces the effect of a shell bursting near Private John Ball: 'Out of the vortex, rifling the air it came – bright, brass-shod, Pandoran; [...]'. The last two words precipitate a sense of catastrophic revelation – the horses of the apocalypse and the opening of Pandora's box; this cosmic nightmare continues in successive verbal coinages – 'up-rendings and rivings-through' – to be clinched in the finality of 'all unmaking' (24). Yet the nature of Jones's 'transiliences' is wonderfully varied. Here, for example, there is a relatively mild transition from a demotic opening to a resting place in Malory: 'how it was going to be a first clarst bollocks [...] for now [...] is this noble fellowship wholly mischiefed' (138). Or consider the high calm formality with which the last conversation between three friends is reported, on the eve of the assault that will be fatal for one of them: 'They talked of ordinary things. Of each one's friends at home. [...] Of how [...] Of if [...] Of whether [...]', and so on, of real public figures such as H.G. Wells, Rupert Brooke, Lloyd George and Eleftherios Venizelos (139–40).

Other means by which Jones works to preserve a sense of irresolution include the uncertainty of pronouns, where 'he' can mean both one of us or them, the enemy; even when it is the former, it is hard to know who is who: 'He found him all gone to pieces' (153). Hence the recourse to the nameless but intimate pronoun that floats appealingly between grammatical persons, first, second and third – 'you'. As, for example: 'You feel exposed and apprehensive in this new world' (9). The derangements of syntax also create the sense of suspended meaning, of a world half made and awaiting the connections that would give it coherence, yet equally ready to be blown apart into meaningless chaos. This helps to reproduce the experience of the foot soldier as a kind of passive agent, trying to follow orders, such as 'don't lose connection' (34), to find a way through the 'thought-maze' (37) and the all too literal 'mazy charnel-ways' (179), to avoid the enemy's 'meshed intricacies of wire and cunning nest' (148) and try not to 'stumble in a place of tentacle' (166).

Other characteristic word forms promote the general condition of suspend-
edness and imminent metamorphosis. There is a high number of hyphenated
compounds, such as 'fleet-passing sound-wraith' (33), 'world-edge' (38), 'a
bundle-thing' (43, presumably a corpse), 'damned-corpse-gossiping' (63),
'created-dear things' (157) and 'prince-pedigreed' (161). There are two
forms of noun to which Jones is attracted. One is the most 'verbal' form of
a noun, the gerund, that names a continuing activity (such that the adjecti-
val 'continuing' itself becomes a noun, 'a continuing'). The other is a noun
made with the suffix '–ess'. Some of these are so familiar we barely notice
them, such as 'darkness' – not the same as 'the dark', but the formalisation
of a quality belonging to it. Significant examples include 'brokenness', 'now-
ness', 'nearness', 'madeness', 'shapelessness', 'moistnesses', 'maze-likeness',
'immediateness'. Consider the choice of 'wiseness' rather than 'wisdom' in
this admiring description of a French priest pronouncing the Divine Office
amidst his vegetable beds: 'a canonical wiseness conserved in an old man's
mumblings, the validity of material things, and the resurrection of this flesh'
(118). It is the essential quality, the virtue or 'validity' in things, that this
word form is designed to abstract and preserve.

Finally, what of the title? *In Parenthesis* is not as memorable as *The Waste
Land* or *Ulysses*, although it is not quite as rebarbative as *The Anathemata*,
title of Jones's other long poem (1952). In his Preface, Jones tried to
explain:

> I have written it in a kind of space between – I don't know between quite
> what – but as you turn aside to do something; and because for us amateur
> soldiers ... the war itself was a parenthesis ... – and also because our curious
> type of existence here is altogether in parenthesis. (xv)

Jones was drawn to enclosing frames. We may think of all the dispersed literary allusions and references already mentioned, but also, in more formal
and authoritative positions, of the dedication, the epigraphs, the headings
and subheadings to the parts, the notes, the illustrations. All may be thought
to harbour and protect the matter within, as parentheses do. Or as Noah's
Ark does – the vital, central image of the ten wood engravings with which
Jones illustrated *The Chester Play of the Deluge* (Figure 10).

Yet we can detect a certain pathos to the idea of a parenthesis that tries to
enclose or envelope all this volatile, ferocious material in fragile protective
membranes as it were – a kind of body. Jones was profoundly attracted to all
such containing images, as the beautiful chalices of his paintings bear witness. Yet what could possibly hold the sheer inundating force of the experiences recalled in this writing? Furthermore, there is danger in the very act
of opening up what might seem to be closed. The image summoned by the

Figure 10   David Jones, 'Building the Ark' from *The Chester Play of the Deluge*. Estate of David Jones.

'Prologue' that stands between the Dedication and Part 1 is a dark riddle from *The Mabinogion*. 'Evil betide me if I do not open the door [...]', someone says. And yet opening the door reveals 'all the evils they had ever sustained [...] and because of their perturbation they could not rest'.

This is why, if we reflect on the significance of all the water that afflicts and bathes and seeps into the human body from earth and sky in this poem, the words 'saturate' and 'saturated' may linger in our memory, as they did in the writer's. They are words that honour the capacity to absorb and endure and retain all the fluid and flood that threaten but fail to overwhelm the spirit. Such is the achievement of *In Parenthesis*.

NOTES

1 William Blissett, *The Long Conversation: A Memoir of David Jones* (Oxford: Oxford University Press, 1981), 90. References to *In Parenthesis* are to the 1978 impression of the edition first published by Faber and Faber in 1937.

2 Jones's essay can be found in Harman Grisewood ed. *Epoch and Artist* (first published 1959; London: Faber and Faber, 2008), 143–79; Rowan Williams, *Grace and Necessity: Reflections on Art and Love* (London: Continuum, 2005), 88.

3 Harman Grisewood ed. *The Dying Gaul and Other Writings* (London and Boston: Faber and Faber, 1978), 58.

4 'The Syntax of Violence' in John Matthias ed. *David Jones: Man and Poet* (Orono, ME: National Poetry Foundation, 1989), 198.

5 'The Utile', in *Epoch and Artist*, 183.

6 Blissett, *Long Conversation*, 68; René Hague ed. *Dai Great-Coat: a Self-Portrait of David Jones in His Letters* (London and Boston: Faber and Faber, 1980), 80.

7 Charles Tomlinson, *The Sense of the Past: Three Twentieth-Century Poets* (Liverpool: Liverpool University Press, 1983), 14; Paul Fussell, *The Great War and Modern Memory* (New York and London: Oxford University Press, 1975), 144–5; Jonathan Miles, *Backgrounds to David Jones: A Study on Sources and Drafts* (Cardiff: University of Wales Press, 1990), 87.

8 Letter to Blissett, *Long Conversation*, 46.

9 The first edition of 1937 reads 'tran-silient' (28).

10 The passage is from 'The Book of Balaam's Ass' in *The Sleeping Lord and Other Fragments* (London: Faber and Faber, 1974), 99–100; Neil Corcoran, 'Spilled Bitterness: *In Parenthesis* in History' in Matthias ed. *Man and Poet*, 209–10.

PART III

Archipelagic, Colonial and Civilian War Poetry

10

DAVID GOLDIE

Archipelagic Poetry
of the First World War

For more than a century before the First World War, the British Army had played a significant role in cementing the Union of Great Britain and Ireland, offering escape, a way out of poverty, or the opportunity of adventure for young men from the impoverished regions and smaller nations of the United Kingdom. Scots and Irish soldiers in particular were mainstays of the Victorian army, at times almost outnumbering English soldiers in the ranks. In the twenty years leading up to the war, many of the military's decision-makers had significant Irish or Scottish connections. Several commanders-in-chief of the army in this period, including Viscount Wolseley and Earl Roberts, were Irish and another, Lord Kitchener, had been born in Ireland. The man responsible for building the modern army as the Secretary of State for War in the decade before the war, Viscount Haldane, was a Scot. The first commander of the British Expeditionary Force, Field Marshal Sir John French came from an old Anglo-Irish family and its second, Field Marshal Sir Douglas Haig, was a Scot. A smattering of key generals, such as General Sir Ian Hamilton, who commanded the Dardanelles campaign, were Scots or Irish: of the five wartime Chiefs of the Imperial General Staff, two – General Sir Charles Douglas and Lieutenant General Sir James Wolfe-Murray – were Anglo-Scots and another, General Sir Henry Wilson, was an Ulsterman.

The army before and during the war was, then, perhaps one of the most fully integrated structures of the British state, and one in which the dominant ruling-class English voice was strongly inflected by the diverse accents of its Celtic fringes. At the higher levels, the idea of an army drawn from different parts of the British archipelago was expressed through the hegemony of an intermingled English, Anglo-Scottish and Anglo-Irish military caste. At lower levels, it was cemented culturally by popular writers such as Rudyard Kipling, who in the poems of *Barrack-Room Ballads* (1892) and in martial stories in collections such as *Soldiers Three* (1888) portrayed an imperial army in which a standard English intonation jostles with demotic cockney, Irish and occasional Scottish voices.

However, the First World War also occurs at a point of fracture in the Union. It was during the war that the movement for Irish independence took a decisive step forward, driven largely by the British authorities' disproportionate response to the 1916 Easter Rising. The post-war period would also see the first sustained nationalist movements in Scotland and Wales with the formation in 1925 of Plaid Cymru and the National Party of Scotland in 1928: with each movement having as its driving force, in Saunders Lewis and Hugh MacDiarmid respectively, a writer who had fought in the British cause in war, but who came increasingly to resent what they saw as England's domination of the post-war British state.

The poetry produced during the war by Irish, Welsh and Scots writers was, then, subject to a slightly different set of tensions than those that operated on English writers. All United Kingdom writers, whether soldiers or civilians, were subject to similar kinds of threat, whether that was to their own existences or those of their friends and families, and almost all shared a sense that this was – at least in its early stages – a just war which required a united national response, fought by a unified army with which they largely identified. But those from the state's smaller nations were subject to the countervailing anxieties common to minority partners in any enterprise – in particular, the concern that their distinctive national identity and rights to self-determination might be stifled rather than enabled by the vast machinery of a war effort driven from the English metropolitan centre. They might, in other words, share some concerns that in spite of their commitment and service, this war was not their war, that there may, after all, be no place for them under the 'English heaven' evoked by Rupert Brooke's 'The Soldier'.

For most wartime archipelagic writing, however, such tensions barely registered.[1] This was especially true of the war's public poetry, especially that which appeared in national and provincial newspapers in its early phases. This was uniformly supportive of the Allied cause, its content and form often following closely the rhetoric and rhythms of the Edwardian imperial poetry of William Watson and Henry Newbolt. Within two weeks of the war's outbreak, the *Scotsman* newspaper printed on its leader page a poem 'British Bugles', which is typical of those appearing at the same time in the *Western Mail*, the *Irish Times* (and papers like the *Birmingham Post*) in pledging the support of the Kingdom's regions and smaller nations:

> Every island, every last stretch,
> Where the ancient banner flies,
> Hears the braying of the bugles,
> And with one accord replies –

> Answers straightaway, 'we are ready,
> We are with you, Motherland,
> Though the strife be long and deadly,
> Armageddon be at hand'.
>
> Which from Erin, late divided,
> Racked by discord, sore dismayed,
> Thunders forth the glad assurance,
> 'We are one; be not afraid!'²

These civilian sentiments could be found, too, in the verses of serving soldiers that appeared in the United Kingdom's newspapers. Those of an 'Irish Fusilier', in the *Armagh Guardian* in January 1915, similarly celebrated – albeit with rather more enthusiasm than skill – the contribution of the archipelagic nations:

> Now here's to good old Ireland and bonnie Scotland too,
> The boys of merry England and the Welsh taffies so true.
> The Yankees are all watching us and the Irish people too,
>
> To see how we fight for the cause of our right
> And the fame of the red, white, and blue.³

In Wales, where there was a relatively strong cultural nationalism and where a little less than half of the population were still speakers of the native language, Cymraeg, there was similarly vocal popular support for the war, largely encouraged by their countryman David Lloyd George in his wartime roles as chancellor, secretary of state for war, and then prime minister. A number of the war's greatest poets, including Edward Thomas and Wilfred Owen, could trace their recent family history to Wales but they, like most people of more defined Welsh identity, supported the war's aims and did not demur from its prosecution.

Another soldier-writer, the Irish-born Patrick MacGill, might be said to typify the British hybrid identity of the time and to reflect the popular response to the war. Born in Donegal, MacGill emigrated to Scotland at the age of fifteen in 1905 where he found casual work as an agricultural and industrial worker, before moving to Windsor in 1912 to follow a career in literature and journalism. He had first come to notice as a poet in Scotland with his self-published *Gleanings from a Navvy's Scrap Book* (1911) and as a prose writer through contributions to the *Daily Express* and a lightly fictionalised autobiography, *Children of the Dead End* (1914). His war poetry, collected in *Soldier Songs* (1916), is based on his experiences as a rifleman and stretcher-bearer in the London Irish Rifles.

Although MacGill is often dismissed as something of a poetic naïf, his poem 'After Loos' written shortly after the traumatic experience of going over the top, and a month or so before he was wounded, is not untypical of his work in presenting a rich blend of simple, direct statement and symbolic suggestion. By choosing, uncharacteristically, to give the poem a subtitled date '*Michaelmas Eve, 1915*', MacGill subtly leads our attention to the Archangel Michael, who in Catholic orthodoxy is both the pre-eminent warrior angel – victor over Satan in the war in heaven – and the angel of death who transports the souls of the dead to rest with God. In evoking this ambiguous archangel – who symbolises both a revelatory war of faith and triumphant judgement – MacGill hints at a comprehending spiritual dimension to warfare that is, however, quickly undercut by the poem's plain language and refusal to invoke further religious imagery. The poem's register is deliberately, flatly secular, denying the possibility of transcendent feeling by insistently dragging the reader's eyes down from heaven to earth:

> Was it only yesterday
> Lusty comrades marched away?
> Now they're covered up with clay.
>
> Seven glasses used to be
> Called for six good mates and me –
> Now we only call for three.[4]

At its most interesting, MacGill's poetry trades in these kinds of juxtaposition, undercutting elevated ideas with prosaic reminders of the commonplace horror and desolation of the war. While this is far from being an exclusive trait of the literature of the archipelagic nations, it perhaps hints at that literature's predisposition to exploring states of duality and its interest in shifting perspective and destabilising convention. This heterodox instinct can be used, too, to challenge assumptions closer to home, such as the easy nostalgia for an idealised Celtic homeland. In 'A Lament', MacGill's speaker's self-indulgence is curbed by a common-sense reminder from his non-commissioned officer (NCO):

> I wish that I were back again
> In the glens of Donegal,
> They'll call me coward if I return,
> But a hero if I fall.
>
> 'Is it better to be a living coward,
> Or thrice a hero dead?'
> 'It's better to go to sleep, my lad',
> The Colour Sergeant said.[5]

In 'Death and the Fairies', MacGill employs juxtaposition again to make a sardonic comment on Irish credulousness, contrasting his formative years in

Donegal ('Where every night the Fairies / Would hold their carnival') with his undeceived present life in Flanders where 'men like wheat-ears fall, / And it's Death and not the Fairies / Who is holding carnival'.[6] Where his poetry exposes such fault lines, or where one poem contradicts the ideas of another, MacGill gets close to exposing not only the confusion of values felt by most early war writers, but the particular confusions of being a soldier in the army of a nation to which he does not wholly belong and to which his own nation has long been culturally and politically antipathetic. MacGill can write longingly about Donegal in a poem such as 'I Will Go Back', which begins in Yeatsian reverie, 'I'll go back again to my father's house and live on my father's land – / For my father's house is by Rosses' shore that slopes to Dooran strand', but his poetry also recognises the hard fact (in 'After the War') that 'I'm a British soldier / With a British soldier's pay' and that it is England to which he and his like will return rather than an idealised Ireland.[7]

MacGill's poetry, however, does not always make enough of these opportunities to explore his dichotomous situation. It is, instead, generally content to express the sentiments held in common with many of the robust, sensitive young men who faced the war: of admiration for the doughty resolve of 'the ole sweats' of the Regular Army, the mocking, levelling humour of the homosocial military world, the quiet moments of nostalgic longing for home, the melancholic remembrance of lost friends. The conventions that dominate MacGill's poetry are those of Edwardianism, and the rhythms often those of what F.S. Flint would later characterise as 'the tumpty-tum of hurdy-gurdy verses'.[8] His failure to create consistently a poetry adequate to the war's emotional and moral complexity and of his own position in it can be traced, as with much of the war's poetry, to his inability to slip off the genteel handcuffs of prevailing convention. That convention might chafe at him, but he cannot escape it. What makes this inadequacy especially noticeable in MacGill's poetry is the contrast it offers to his wartime prose. His unjustly neglected memoir *The Great Push* (1916) is one of the most mordant, disillusioned and graphically brutal books of the mid-war period. *The Great Push* centres on the Battle of Loos, which is also the subject of 'In the Morning'. The poem features many of the familiar landmarks portrayed in *The Great Push*, especially two towers that loom over the town and provide a dangerous vantage point for the enemy:

> The turret towers that stood in the air,
> Sheltered a foeman sniper there –
> They found, who fell to the sniper's aim,
> A field of death on the field of fame.[9]

Compare this description, with its archaisms and glib martial euphemisms, to the directness and simplicity of his account, in *The Great Push*, of a corpse over which he has sprawled in the dark: 'Worms feasted on its entrails, slugs trailed silverly over its face, and lean rats gnawed at its flesh. The air was full of the thing, the night stank with its decay'.[10] Not much 'foeman sniper' or 'field of fame' here, and even though MacGill allows himself the poeticism 'silverly', its use seems measured and appropriate to the context, standing out in its richness against the stark situating prose.

MacGill is far from being the only wartime poet from the British archipelago who found himself challenged less by national affiliation than by formal conventional constraint in attempting to construct a complex response to the war in verse. Joseph Lee, the so-called People's Poet of Dundee, sprung from a similar mould to that which produced MacGill. Having spent time adventuring around the world in labouring jobs, Lee had, like MacGill, settled down to a career in journalism in the years before the war, supplementing that work with occasional forays into demotic verse such as those collected in his *Poems: Tales o' Our Town* (1910). Like MacGill, Lee enlisted as a private soldier and, also like MacGill, his poetry veers from a demotic cockney modelled on Kipling's *Barrack-Room Ballads* (for example, compare MacGill's 'Matey' and Lee's 'Piou-Piou: The British Tommy Atkins to the French') to lyrics on the loss of comrades and remembrance of the landscapes of home. However, like MacGill, Lee rarely escapes the formal straitjacket of Edwardian popular verse. Where he does manage to break free and create something like poetry, it is through simplifying his language and creating a terseness close to that of Imagism or Kipling's wartime epigrams, as in his short poem 'The Bullet':

> Every bullet has its billet;
> Many bullets more than one:
> God! Perhaps I killed a mother
> When I killed a mother's son.[11]

The shackles of convention also constrained the poetic efforts of Scottish and Irish soldier-poets from higher up the social scale. Lieutenants Willoughby Weaving of the Royal Irish Rifles and Robert Sterling of the Royal Scots Fusiliers had both been students at Pembroke College Oxford, Sterling winning the prestigious Newdigate Prize in 1914. Weaving survived and produced two volumes of wartime poetry – *The Star Fields and Other Poems* (1916) and *The Bubble and Other Poems* (1917) – which won him the praise of Robert Bridges; Sterling was killed and his *Poems* appeared posthumously in 1916. In both poets, as in the work of other Anglo-Scottish and Anglo-Irish officers such as Hamish Mann, Alexander Robertson and

John Stewart, the attempts to convey the experience of war are derailed by the decorum and circumlocution of the traditions to which their education made them heirs. For these young officers, the temptations of classical allusion, Arnoldian melancholy and Romantic nature writing overpowered what desire they might have to write directly about the conditions of modern war; their war books are thick with poems such as 'The Stringless Lyre' (Weaving), 'Weep Not for Me' (Mann), 'If I Should Fall upon the Field' (Stewart), 'Rupert Brooke' (both Mann and Stewart) and 'Two Sonnets to Rupert Brooke' (Weaving). Each is capable of writing poetry of considerable technical ability and aesthetic quality, but none seems able to write a poem fully adequate to the experience of a twentieth-century attritional war. A poem like Weaving's 'Between the Trenches', for example, offers an interesting, at times moving, meditation on what it is to see a friend die and to consider how suddenly his spiritless corpse seems alien and uncanny:

> What stranger did the bearers lift
> In their soiled stretcher lightly laid
> Where I had seen you fall adrift
> From life – had time to be afraid ? –
> That, all of you that had breathed and moved.
> That, none of you that lived and loved,
> A shell that so I seemed to hate
> For claiming still its lost inmate,
> A false pretence, a solid shade.[12]

Arguably, however, the poem's intellectual and affective power is dissipated by its form and diction. This is a poem about the sudden shock of confronting a friend's death, yet its tetrameters are unruffled while its simple rhymes chime with glib felicity; it risks the realism of a 'soiled stretcher' but euphemistically describes violent death in the trenches as a falling 'adrift / From life'. It seems that Anglo-Scottish and Anglo-Irish officer-poets, like the overwhelming majority of their English equivalents, were on the receiving end of a sophisticated poetic education that left them ill-equipped to deal with even the simplest of war's arbitrary brutalities – like so many dashing, highly trained cavalrymen in a time of machine guns, barbed wire and high-explosive ordnance.

If both popular culture, as expressed by MacGill and Lee, and the elite culture of the officer class tended to homogenise the British poetic response to war, there remained an alternative in the Celtic literary ideal which had been encouraged in the nineteenth century by the cultural theories of Matthew Arnold and Ernest Renan and had flourished in the Irish literary revival and the Celtic and Doric revivals in Scotland, and in the persisting

Cymraeg bardic tradition in Wales. Alan Mackintosh was a young poet with a similar background to the aforementioned officer-writers. Scottish through ancestry, but English by birth and formation, Mackintosh threw himself into the Celtic idea at Oxford and restyled himself as a Highland poet, going so far as to learn Gaelic and the bagpipes. The persona that emerges in his poetry is that of a fatalist, drawing on a long tradition of Scottish defeat and lamentation to prepare himself for the sublime trial and inescapable suffering of war. This is seen most nakedly in 'The German and the Gael', which offers a kind of grim consolation by contrasting an enemy army sure in its purpose and confident of victory with Gaelic troops who advance, 'Hopeless as went our fathers' to what appears an inevitable, if fearlessly faced, annihilation: the Germans 'dream the fight is theirs, / Therefore they will not flee, / But we go darkly out to meet / The fate we cannot see'.[13]

In the case of Mackintosh, such fatalism may seem an acquisition rather than an imposition: the choice of a poetic mode and persona adopted primarily because it suits his own predisposition and premonitory fears of what the war will bring. But it is not at all dissimilar to the writing that comes in a rather less forced way from Celtic tradition. The Welsh soldier-poet Ellis Evans, known by his bardic name Hedd Wyn, is an example. Although he is now perhaps better known as the subject of a 1992 film which features him as an anti-war poet exposing the fracture between Cymraeg Welsh culture and British militarism, his poems are not so much protests against the atrocities of war as mournful expressions of resignation at its effects. They are similar in manner to those of Mackintosh and to Scottish Gaelic poems of the war such as the beautiful and stark 'An Eala Bhàn' ('The White Swan') by Donald MacDonald (Dòmhnall Ruadh Chorùna), and the poems of John Munro (Iain Rothach). Hedd Wyn's 'Y Blotyn Du' ('The Black Blot'), for example, asserts that sense of futility blankly, 'Nid oes gennym hawl ar ddim byd / Ond ar yr hen ddaear wyw' ('We can lay claim to nothing / But the tired earth's story), and his 'Rhyfel' ('War') goes further in emphasising the impotence of bardic poetry in the face of the war's suffering:

> Mae'r hen delynau genid gynt
> Ynghrog ar gangau'r helyg draw,
> A gwaedd y bechgyn lond y gwynt,
> A'u gwaed yn gymysg efo'r glaw.

> (Like the old songs they left behind,
> We have hanged our harps on the trees again.
> The blood of the boys is on the wind,
> Their blood is mingled with the rain.)[14]

Such resignation and lamentation similarly dominate the wartime Scots dialect poetry produced as part of the Doric revival in north-eastern Scotland. John Buchan was, like Mackintosh, an ambiguous Anglo-Scot who, although born and bred in Lowland Scotland, converted to a more overt Scottish cultural nationalism at Oxford. Alongside his punishing work as a novelist, historian of the war, and wartime director of information, Buchan published dialect poems. A poem such as Buchan's 'The Fishers' offers a convincing adaptation of Theocritan idyll to a Scottish context, while his 'Fisher Jamie' uses the simplicity of the Scots dialect to powerful effect – arguably a much stronger and more direct impact than Buchan was able to achieve in the stilted diction of his poems in English. 'Fisher Jamie' begins,

> Puir Jamie's killed. A better lad
> Ye wadna find to busk a flee
> Or burn a püle or wield a gad
> Frae Berwick to the Clints o' Dee.
>
> And noo he's in a happier land. –
> It's Gospel truith and Gospel law
> That heaven's yett maun open stand
> To folk that for their country fa'.
>
> But Jamie will be ill to mate;
> He lo'ed nae music, kenned nae tünes
> Except the sang o' Tweed in spate,
> Or Talla loupin' ower its linns.[15]

There is, arguably, enough that is strange in the Scots dialect here to persuade the English reader of an intriguing and distinctive Scottish response to the war: a quality deployed to great effect in the elegiac wartime poetry of Doric poets such as Violet Jacob and Charles Murray, and that Hugh MacDiarmid would use in the short post-war Scots lyrics that kick-started the Scottish Literary Revival. However, much Doric wartime writing remained stuck in the promotion of Scottish rustic stereotypes of canniness and stoical patriotism, as seen in the popular poems of George Abel's *Wylins fae my Wallet* (1915) or in the boasts in Murray's 'A Sough o' War' that the 'buirdly men, fae strath an' glen /An' shepherds fae the bucht an' hill, / Will show them a', whate'er befa', / Auld Scotland counts for something still'.[16]

There was similarly little in Welsh poetry, whether in English or Cymraeg (and excepting Owen), that protested against the war in emphatic terms or which dissented on grounds of nationalism from the Allied effort. The focus of much of this poetry, whether written at home or on active service, was on what Owen would characterise as 'the pity of war', which, while it might have a distinctive local impact, was generally seen as a suffering that transcended politics and the disputation of nations. Arguably the greatest modernist poet to emerge from the war, David Jones, was an Englishman of Welsh extraction and affiliation, who would much later detail both the war's mundanity and its grim horrors in *In Parenthesis* (1937) and relate those experiences to a narrative of the decline of the Brythonic-speaking ancestors of the modern Welsh in battles such as those of Catraeth and Camlann. Even here, however, Jones's modernist collage of war episodes and British regional voices has a centripetal rather than a centrifugal effect in emphasising the commonality of a shared British rather than a distinctive Welsh war experience.

For the reasons mentioned near the beginning of this chapter, it might be expected that the Irish response would be quite different: that in a nation that had some justification for thinking itself a colony of, rather than a partner in, the United Kingdom, there would be more outright opposition to the war and more anguished exploration of its tensions. But while the work of most Irish poets bore some trace of an Irish, or at least Celtic, distinctiveness that set them apart from English writers, it was for the most part as ambiguous or evasive as the war writing of Scotland and Wales. The most celebrated contemporary Irish poet, W.B. Yeats, was largely oblivious to the war but wrote, in 'An Irish Airman Foresees his Death' and 'Easter 1916', a pair of poems that in their different ways encapsulate a sense of Irish dislocation in regard to the war's events. In the first, Yeats celebrates the valour of Major Robert Gregory, a scion of the Irish Ascendancy killed in the service of the British, and in the second, he commemorates the Irish martyrs of the 1916 revolt against the British state and its occupying forces. Both poems, however, are deeply ambiguous. His Irish airman sacrifices himself in part for 'country', conceived as the nation's poor rather than the nation state, but mainly out of a sense of heroic excess, a 'lonely impulse of delight', that makes ordinary life seem undesirable and untenable. Desiring to celebrate the heroic act, but deploring its ultimate cause – service in the British military – the poem is transfixed and can say nothing meaningful about the war or the Irish experience of it. Yeats's revolutionary martyrs, on the other hand, are driven to their sacrifice by a national idea and a conception of a distinctive national history. But again, the poem is marked by a deep ambivalence, characterised by its recurring idea of a 'terrible beauty': a pervasive sense that for all its magnificence, there is something deeply troubling in the inhuman and unnatural action of sacrificing one's life in the cause of an abstract, and perhaps ultimately unrealisable, national ideal. In Yeats's poetic world of war, then, it almost seems that there is little to choose between sacrificing oneself, however ambivalently, in the cause of the British nation and giving one's life up to an idea of Ireland: the response in both cases is one of numbness and equivocation.[17]

Yeats's Protestant background and his hesitations over vulgar forms of democratic nationalism perhaps partly explain this ambivalence. But nationalist writers from the Catholic tradition display many of the same signs of divided loyalty. This derives partly from the apparently paradoxical support given to the Allied war effort by John Redmond, the leader of the Irish Parliamentary Party, who led a suspension of nationalist political opposition to British rule for the duration. Two of the best known Irish soldier-poets to die in the war, Tom Kettle and Francis Ledwidge, were Catholics and active members of the nationalist Irish Volunteers who embodied this paradox by enlisting in the British army. Kettle was an academic and politician who exercised his sharp wit in writing political poetry in response to William Watson in 'Reason in Rhyme' and, in 'Ulster', delivering a biting riposte to Kipling's 'Ulster 1912'. Kipling's poem had described Ireland as 'England's oldest foe', to which Kettle's memorably derisive response was that 'Kipling's banjo strings / Blaspheme a sacred text'.[18] This undermining continued in 'Paddy', an acute parody of Kipling's 'Tommy', in which Kipling's assertions about British neglect towards, and routine devaluing of, the ordinary soldier warp, in Kettle's hands, into nationalist accusations of British hypocrisy:

> For it's Paddy this, and Paddy that, and
> 'Don't annoy us, please!'
> But it's 'Irish Rifles forward – Fast!'
> when the bullets talk like bees,
> When the bullets yawn like bees, my
> boys, when the bullets yawn like bees,
> It's 'Connaught blood is good enough'
> when they're chanting R.I.P's.[19]

But with the advent of war, Kettle followed Redmond faithfully in asserting his hopes that what he described as 'this tragedy of Europe' would ultimately be conciliatory, that it 'may be and must be the prologue to the two reconciliations of which all statesmen have dreamed, the reconciliation of Protestant Ulster with Ireland, and the reconciliation of Ireland with Great Britain'.[20]

Similar thoughts prompted Ledwidge to volunteer for the British army and dominated his early wartime poems. Many of these are Celtic-inflected nature idylls: poems that are typical of much of the nostalgic pastoralism of the war's soldier-poets but which evoke a distinctive, romantic Irish landscape saturated in the drowsy historical myths of the Celtic Twilight. They benefit, too, from the use of the distinctive Irish *aicill*-rhyme, in which a line ending is picked up by a rhyme in the middle of the following line. In poems such as 'Ceol Shee', the sense of a critical comparison between a memoried

Irish landscape and the desolate battlefields of France and Belgium is implicit only: the fairy music to which the title refers is a tune untroubled by war. In 'The Dead Kings', however, the contrast is more explicit and stark, with the war intruding to break enchantment's circle. The speaker of the poem dreams of Rosnaree and the dead kings of Ireland who have come to entertain him with their tales of 'ancient glory, sweetly told', but the reverie is curtailed and the poem ends abruptly: 'A bomb burst near me where I lay. / I woke, 'twas day in Picardy'.[21]

The tension between nostalgia for a remembered domestic countryside and the realities of the ruined, almost denatured landscapes of France and Flanders is a common one in the British poetry of the First World War. Although there was in this war, unlike other wars before and after, no real threat of invasion to the home countryside – in spite of a vigorous invasion-scare literature in the years before the war – there remained a strong sense in which the poets of England, Wales and Scotland considered themselves to be fighting, and writing, in defence of that landscape, if only as a token of the values which they considered it to embody.[22] What Ivor Gurney's Gloucestershire, Charles Murray's Aberdeenshire and Hedd Wynn's Meirionnydd share is a sense of the regional particularity that provides the strands of the rich national tapestry for which British soldiers fought: a Union in action through which local landscapes are woven into a national *patria*. But the Irish landscape, steeped in the folkloric myth of the Celtic Twilight, is inevitably other to this. Topographically, it does not form part of the same land mass, and imaginatively it is insulated by reason of its cultural and political history and by the strenuous and self-conscious attempts to de-Anglicize it by Douglas Hyde and Yeats. An Irish writer like Ledwidge, then, experiences an affective gap in his war pastoral – to what end does a nostalgic invocation of his homeland operate when that homeland is neither under physical or imaginative threat and when the history it embodies is alien to the larger cause for which he fights? He is not so much fighting in defence of that home landscape as fighting for a return to it – an Allied victory will not further the values manifest in it, will not even necessarily preserve them, but may simply allow him to get back and re-immerse himself in them; if, that is, he can survive the war, which Ledwidge did not.

Such confused, dark undercurrents in Ledwidge's work are often obscured by the remarkable polish of his poem's surfaces, but they become at times a shade more apparent in his poetry after the Easter Rising, the aftermath of which he encountered when home on leave. He had been a friend of one of the Rising's leaders, shot by the British, Thomas MacDonagh, and wrote a poem in his memory. 'Thomas McDonagh', however, is a pastoral elegy with only the slightest hint of political symbolism in its bucolic imagery: as in the work of MacGill, one has to dig deeper to uncover the ways a distinctive, complicating Celtic element is providing a critique of the assumptions of Union. In prose, Ledwidge was bolder, writing to an American academic of his hope 'that a new Ireland will arise from her ashes in the ruins of Dublin, like the Phoenix', but also of his corresponding discomfort at being 'called a British soldier while my own country has no place amongst the nations'.[23] This is a statement that Seamus Heaney incorporated into his poem 'In Memoriam Francis Ledwidge' in *Field Work* (1979) to illustrate what Heaney reads as Ledwidge's disabling in-betweenness or double-mindedness, which renders him, as Heaney puts it, 'our dead enigma' in whom 'all the strains / Criss-cross in useless equilibrium'.[24] Ledwidge in his poetry, however, remained typical of the great majority of his fellow writers from the British archipelago in suppressing that double-mindedness, and choosing to march with his English comrades. As Heaney suggests, however, this was to march to the beat of a 'sure confusing drum' and to risk becoming, like many archipelagic war writers, a stranger to one's own country.

NOTES

1 The concept of archipelagic writing, denoting the interactivity of the literatures of Ireland, Scotland, Wales and England, derives largely from John Kerrigan's *Archipelagic English* (2008), a work that demonstrates convincingly the pervasiveness of such interactions in seventeenth-century 'English' literature.

2 'A.B.', 'British Bugles', *The Scotsman*, 15 August 1914, 10.

3 Quoted in Jim Haughey, *The First World War in Irish Poetry* (Lewisburg, PA: Bucknell University Press, 2002), 67.

4 Patrick MacGill, 'At Loos', *Soldier Songs* (London: Herbert Jenkins, 1917), 23.

5 'A Lament', *Soldier Songs*, 31.

6 'Death and the Fairies', *Soldier Songs*, 89.

7 'I Will Go Back' and 'After the War', *Soldier Songs*, 99, 111.

8 F.S. Flint, 'The Appreciation of Poetry' (1940), 2, quoted in J.B. Harmer, *Victory in Limbo: Imagism 1908–1917* (London: Secker and Warburg, 1975), 17.

9 'In the Morning', *Soldier Songs*, 86.

10 Patrick MacGill, *The Great Push: An Episode of the Great War* (Edinburgh: Birlinn, 2000), 114.

11 Joseph Lee, 'The Bullet', *Ballads of Battle* (London: John Murray, 1916), 21.

12 Willoughby Weaving, 'Between the Trenches', *The Star Fields and Other Poems* (Oxford: B.H. Blackwell, 1916), 13.

13 E.A. Mackintosh, 'The German and the Gael', *War, the Liberator* (London: John Lane, 1918), 18–19.

14 Hedd Wyn, 'The Black Blot' and 'War' in Menna Elfyn and John Rowlands eds. *The Bloodaxe Book of Modern Welsh Poetry* (Tarset: Bloodaxe Books, 2003), 67. Translations by Gillian Clarke.

15 John Buchan, 'Fisher Jamie', *Poems Scots and English* (London: Thomas Nelson, 1917), 69.

16 Charles Murray, 'A Sough o' War', *Hamewith: The Complete Poems of Charles Murray* (Aberdeen: Aberdeen University Press, 1979), 70.

17 W.B. Yeats, 'An Irish Airman Foresees his Death' and 'Easter 1916', *The Collected Poems of W.B. Yeats* (London: Macmillan, 1950), 152, 202–5.

18 T.M. Kettle, 'Ulster', *Poems and Parodies* (London: Duckworth, 1916), 69.

19 'Paddy', *Poems and Parodies*, 76.

20 T.M. Kettle, *The Ways of War* (New York: Charles Scribner's Sons, 1917), 72.

21 Francis Ledwidge, 'The Dead Kings', *The Complete Poems of Francis Ledwidge* (New York: Brentano's, 1919), 258, 264.

22 See I.F. Clarke, *Voices Prophesying War 1763–1984* (1966) for the classic account of pre-war invasion literature.

23 Quoted in Alice Curtayne, *Francis Ledwidge: A Life of the Poet (1887–1917)* (London: Martin Brian and O'Keefe, 1972), 180.

24 Seamus Heaney, 'In Memoriam Francis Ledwidge', *Opened Ground: Poems 1966–1996* (London: Faber and Faber, 1998), 186.

11

SIMON FEATHERSTONE

Colonial Poetry of the First World War

'The Great War transformed the British Empire and transfigured it in the eyes of the British people', wrote William Murphy in perhaps the first critical monograph to apply the generic term 'war poetry' to the verse of 1914–18. 'The vague abstraction had become a living, warm, pulsing thing of flesh and blood ... the most strangely mingled host that the world had ever seen'.[1] Such interest in the war's imperial consequences was also expressed in a sizeable body of poetry that has generally been excluded from subsequent formations of the war poetry canon. Individual poems maintained some prominence in popular anthologies, most notably John McCrae's 'In Flanders Fields', and specialised literatures developed around Canadian and Australian war poetries, but there has been little enthusiasm for reconstituting Murphy's 'strangely mingled host' as an object for critical study. Reviving it here through the perspectives of postcolonial studies presents fresh opportunities for thinking about a poetic genre that has remained stubbornly English or at least British-centred. The chapter focuses on Canada, Australia and India at the expense of other national and regional poetries such as those of New Zealand and the West Indies. This, in part, reflects the lack of a sustained body of work by individual poets from the latter places, but also, and more crucially, the absence of developed indigenous publishing industries which promoted poetry that addressed distinctively local readerships.[2] Anthologies of soldiers' verse produced in Canada and Australia will be considered alongside the work of John McCrae and Leon Gellert, volunteers who articulated more individualised versions of pan-imperial discourses. The changing cultural and political relationships between the imperial centre and its colonies during the war will be traced in the work of Clarence Dennis and Robert Service, two non-combatant writers from the same countries who shared a broad popular style and worked in often critical dialogue with emergent traditions of English war poetry. Rabindranath Tagore, who wrote usually in Bengali and sometimes in English, offers another, radically different version of the genre. A Nobel Laureate who was published in *The Times* in 1914, Tagore went on to develop arguably the most sustained political critique of the war of any other of its poets. His work, allied as it was to anti-colonial movements in wartime India, also makes him the figure that links the criticism of war poetry most directly with the broader field of postcolonial studies.

The importance of poetry for cultural projects demonstrating imperial commitment to Allied war aims was first represented by an elaborately produced anthology nominally edited by the Australian soprano Nellie Melba and published in 1915. This 'Australian book', as Melba terms it in her foreword, is dedicated to the Belgian Relief Fund, and the singer makes explicit the contrast between the two distant nations: one the victim of imperialist expansionism, the other an autonomous member of an alternative model of colonial polity.[3] It provided a template for other quasi-official anthologies which, as colonial military involvement increased, emphasised contributions from combatants over established authors. *Oh, Canada!* (1916), for example, had comparably high production values but carefully stated in its subtitle that all its contributors were members of the Canadian Expeditionary Force (CEF).[4] By contrast, *The ANZAC Book* (1916), which sold more than 100,000 copies in Australia, and the three volumes of *Canada in Khaki* (1917–19) shed the more decorative elements of the earlier publications, with bindings replaced by staples and a coarsened paper quality reflecting military utility (the 'Editor's Note' to the former stressed that '[p]ractically every word in it was written ... beneath the shelter of a waterproof sheet or of a roof of sandbags – either in the trenches or, at most, well within the range of the oldest Turkish rifle').[5] Contributors, while offered some latitude for good-natured complaint and mild satire, were marshalled to reinforce the point that the dominions were integrally bound to the British cause, and that their forces' presence in Europe and Asia Minor signalled the revival of the imperial commitments that William Murphy was later to celebrate. 'If there is one thing which this war has made clear', Sir Gilbert Parker and Captain T.C. Roberts write in the first volume of *Canada in Khaki*, 'it is that the British race has not degenerated, and that there is, both within the United Kingdom and in the overseas dominions, a dynamic vitality which responds in splendid measure to opportunity'.[6]

Appeals to imperial unity also marked the collections of individual dominion war poets. The Australian Archibald Strong, for example, devoted a volume of sonnets to the theme of empire in wartime and in the title poem of his collection, *The Fighting Men of Canada* (1918), Douglas Leader Durkin reiterated a familiar colonial conceit in his evocation of the 'Lion Mother's welcome to her brood', as in the CEF is found 'worthy kinsmen, bred to serve a worthy cause, / Men of British nerve and born of British blood'.[7] Such celebrations of imperial matrimony also form the context of John McCrae's 'In Flanders Fields', which became one of the first notable war poems on publication in *Punch* in December 1915. Its later independent life as a popular elegy – his eulogist, Sir Andrew MacPhail, claimed that it 'circulates, as a song should circulate, by the living word of mouth'[8] – depended largely on the lyrical evocation of landscape in its opening lines. 'In Flanders fields the poppies blow / Between the crosses, row on row' succinctly presents what were to become defining images of the Western Front. However, they also distract from the poem's minatory call to arms and proffered threat in the final section:

> Take up our quarrel with the foe:
> To you from failing hands we throw
> The torch; be yours to hold it high.
> If ye break faith with us who die
> We shall not sleep, though poppies grow
> In Flanders fields.[9]

MacPhail's tribute stresses the determining imperial politics at work here. The early experiences of the CEF on the Western Front were ones of defeat, he argues, and 'to a sensitive and foreboding mind there were sounds and signs that it would be given to this generation to hear the pillars and fabric of Empire come crashing into the abysm of chaos'.[10] In that context, 'In Flanders Fields' and its companion piece, 'The Anxious Dead', act as rallying points for militarist-imperialist values rather than as elegies. The absence of any specifically Canadian aspect to the lyric is actually central to its politics, despite, as Nancy Holmes has shown, its later significance for Canadian nationalism.[11] McCrae's dead do not address national armies but the soldiers of empire.

A fuller exposition of a comparable imperial-military poetic to that which informed McCrae's slight body of work is evident in the Australian Leon Gellert's *Songs of a Campaign*. First published in 1917, with five expanded editions issued by 1918, Gellert's collection articulates a personal and cultural transformation shaped by military processes of enlistment, training, action and repatriation – components, as Paul Fussell has argued, of the ritualised quest narratives of First World War literature more generally.[12] Gellert's collection traces the journey taken by many Australian and New Zealand soldiers to South Asia, followed by training in Egypt and combat at Gallipoli, with the poems assigned to each stage charting the consequences of the war for its protagonist as both an individual and an imperial agent. Beginning with an evocation of decadent pre-war complacency ('Old Mars is corpsed beneath great Bacchus' seat'[13]), they describe the recovery of martial spirit through an encounter with the mythical past of Egypt and the purgation of battle before the poet, transformed by these experiences, returns home. Gellert's heightened rhetoric emphasises the poetry's links to European literary and mythological sources, and his disappointed desire to be at the site of Britain's primary conflict is openly expressed in 'Dreams of France'. This lamented distance from the European centre ('But, lo, I sail the blue Aegean sea!'[14]) is rhetorically managed in the 'Songs of the Expedition' section. The modes of evoking the war in the Dardanelles highlight correspondences between the experiences of dominion and British soldiers, at least as they were mediated by their poetry in the early years of the war. 'The Soldier', 'A Night Attack', 'In the Trench', 'These Men' and 'Poppies', as the titles suggest, could all be poems written by an English poet on the Western Front. While this to some extent reflects the shared characteristics of trench warfare in the two theatres, it also confirms Gellert's commitment to an undifferentiated imperial poetic tradition, something made explicit in 'The Australian Muse' – the concluding sonnet of the collection and the only poem that engages explicitly with the writer's national identity. '[P]lay the soft tunes of thy infancy', he instructs his national muse, 'Then thou, whilst ageing in the pass of time, / Add fame to fame, and rhyme to gloried rhyme / Till fit thy lyre is for the song of Truth'.[15] In poetry, as in cultural and political identity generally, Gellert's Australia remains loyal to English tradition and only vaguely aspirational in its sense of independent nationhood.

If Gellert abrogated Australian identity in *Songs of a Campaign* and McCrae located 'In Flanders Fields' materially as well as ideologically within an imperial discursive project, their fellow countrymen Clarence Dennis and Robert Service developed what might be termed non-imperial colonial war poetries. The publication of their work in the Sydney-based *Bulletin* and Toronto's *MacLean's Magazine* respectively emphasised their differently localised perspectives. With its unambiguous banner 'The National Australian Newspaper / Australia for the White Man', *The Bulletin* had pursued an aggressively racialised cultural policy since its foundation in 1880. Although generally supportive of the war effort, it was interested in establishing a literary discourse for interpreting Australia's conduct in the war as one part of a wider nationalist project. *MacLean's Magazine* was also emphatic about its wartime credentials, advertising itself as a 'Canadian publication conducted on … broadly national lines', with content reflecting its editor's assertion that 'we are becoming more and more Canadian all the time'.[16] In Service and Dennis, the journals promoted poets willing to articulate in popular poetic idioms distinctive cultural perspectives on the conduct and implications of the war. In Service's case, this was represented by the independent and critical voices of his infantrymen personae whereas

Dennis developed an explicitly nationalist narrative in his wartime ballads written in the persona of the 'Sentimental Bloke'.

The Bulletin's representative Australian poet had long been Henry Lawson, a balladeer whose work had equated an idealised version of the rough and ready masculine values of bush culture with those of an emergent nation. Lawson's First World War poetry, however, reflected both the poet's personal decline and the inadequacy of his populist rhetoric for the new circumstances. The title poem of his collection *Song of the Dardanelles* (1916), for example, veers between racialised imperialism (Australian forces as the 'youngest of England's brood') and crude militarist doggerel ('they stormed the heights as Australians should, / And they fought and they died as we knew they would').[17] Clarence Dennis, by contrast, adapted Lawson's earlier vernacular idiom to the changing urban environments of wartime Australia in *The Songs of a Sentimental Bloke* (1915), a collection of monologues set not in the outback, but in the slums of Melbourne.[18] *The Bulletin*, in which several of the poems had appeared, was quick to link the book to the experience of the Anzac soldier. 'There must be many a Sentimental Bloke ... at Gallipoli', its reviewer wrote, 'to whom this volume ... will come smelling of eucalyptus, or maybe of Spadger's Lane. It is the most welcome bit of Australia that can be exported to the homesick heroes at the Dardanelles'.[19] Dennis's sequel to *The Sentimental Bloke* made explicit these suggestions of his poetry's relevance to the 'homesick heroes' and, more broadly, to the war's effect on discourses of national identity. *The Moods of Ginger Mick* (1916) traces the unlikely military career of one of the minor (and more socially recalcitrant) characters of the earlier collection. Mick 'wus no patriot / That sits and brays advice in days uv strife', the Sentimental Bloke remarks, ''E never flapped no flags nor sich like rot; / 'E never sung "Gawsave" in all 'is life'.[20] But it was such larrikin disparagement of the symbols of empire, along with the unexpected social advancement provided by war, which made Mick representative of a new version of Australian citizenship.

The Moods of Ginger Mick, like *Songs of a Campaign*, is organised through the classic Anzac journey narrative of transformation which sees the indigent volunteer become a hero. As his previously criminalised violence comes to be recognised as military utility in 'this 'ere orl-in fight', he is shown to emerge out of localised, subcultural allegiances into Australianness, feeling a 'noo, glad pride that ain't the pride o' class'.[21] Instead of Gellert's tentative sense of a nation coming to consciousness within imperial commitments, Dennis uses the same emergent narrative conventions of war poetry – ritual journeys, training, pledge of male companionship, test of battle – to explore the creation of new national-popular identities. Ginger Mick's is an implicitly anti-colonial education apparently pursued in the guise of imperial service as he heads towards the ultimate irony of his death as a 'Gallant Gentleman' at the end of the sequence. Even though he does not learn to sing 'Gawsave', he does learn to value previously despised fellow countrymen who do ("is lingo smells uv Oxford – but e's good Australian too',[22] Mick notes of an educated volunteer) as his own previously denigrated skills and attributes – reckless street fighting, for example – are in turn celebrated by official Australia. Henry Lawson had long before made the point that the 'creed of the outlawed push is chivalry – upside down',[23] but *The Moods of Ginger Mick* develops Lawson's bush anarchism into a coherent narrative of national reformation. *The Bulletin*, the cultural organ of such populist politics, had celebrated *The ANZAC Book* as 'a brilliant record of Australianism', but its reviewer found the expression of a more radical change in Dennis's collection. 'In the trenches', he writes, 'Australia, which is made up, more or less, of mere blokes, is finding her soul'.[24]

If Ginger Mick embodied the cultural politics of emergent nationalism, the volunteer personae of Robert Service's war poetry exploit the leeways of dominion journal publication to provide vivid descriptions of the Western Front and to speak their minds. His publisher described him as 'The Canadian Kipling', a reputation earned by the Yukon ballads of *Songs of a Sourdough* (1907) and its successors. However, it is migrancy rather than settlement that underpins a war poetry that draws on experience as a volunteer in an American ambulance unit rather than membership of a national military force. This 'ambivalent position of being in but not of the war', as Edwina Burness puts it,[25] shapes *The Rhymes of a Red-Cross Man* (1916). Eleven of the poems were first published in *MacLean's Magazine* which billed the author as 'Canada's great young poet',[26] despite only one of them making specific reference to Canada. Service's role as a national war poet was consequently less dependent on the linguistic and cultural references that characterised Dennis's work and more on the energetic style of his reportage, something that had been apparent in his earlier prose despatches for Toronto's *Daily Star*. *MacLean's* editor emphasised Service's combination of the 'humour and the horror, the pathos and the thrill of this titanic clash of nations – told for the most part in the words of the soldier himself',[27] an avowedly democratic outlook which, in its stark observation and political openness, defined an emergent cultural space that contrasted markedly with the threatened imperial ground of John McCrae.

Service's infantryman personae, speaking in stylised Cockney, Scots and Irish (although rarely Canadian) vernaculars, are, like Ginger Mick, routinely sceptical of imperial and patriotic rhetoric. The speaker of 'A Song of the Sandbags', for example, comments:

> They talks o' England's glory and a-'oldin' of our trade,
> Of Empire and 'igh destiny until we're fair film-flammed [sic];
> But if it's for the likes o' that bloody war is made,
> Then wot I say is: Empire and 'igh destiny be damned!

Unlike Mick's diatribes, however, such dissent does not contribute to national self-reconstruction, but to more general appraisals of the politics of European war. Domestic self-defence is identified as the only acceptable motive for participation, a reflection that leads to the acknowledgement that 'Fritz out there will tell you 'e's a doin' of the same'. The concluding vision of a day when ''Ans and Fritz and Bill and me / Will clink our mugs in fraternity /And the Brotherhood of Labour will be / The Brotherhood of Peace'[28] is one more readily associated with the then-imprisoned leader of Red Clydeside, John MacLean, than with a poet celebrated for the comedy of 'The Shooting of Dan McGrew'. 'A Song of the Sandbags' appeared only in the *Rhymes*, but *MacLean's Magazine* published comparably challenging material such as 'My Mate', with its bald observations of front-line death:

> 'E was killed so awful sudden that 'e 'adn't time to die.
> 'E sorter jumped, an' came down with a thud.
> Them corpsy-looking star-shells was a streamin' in the sky –
> And there 'e lay like nothin' in the mud.[29]

'Funk', which appeared in September, deals with the equally fraught subject of soldiers' fear ('For God's sake, kid, don't show it, / Don't let your mateys know it: / You're a-sufferin' from funk, funk, funk').[30] It is prefaced by an 'Editor's Note' describing Service's ballads as 'strong, virile, full of the hero-ism and daring and disregard of the soldier's life', an unlikely description of this poem but a recognition, perhaps, of the volatility of such material at a time when arguments over Canadian conscription and war aims were cur-rent (Service's earlier journalism in a similar vein had already been criticised by the dominion censor).[31] *MacLean's* championing of a writer who, as Edwina Burness suggests, emphasised a commonality of war experience that anticipates the later work of Wilfred Owen[32] represents a striking defence of such critical perspectives by media distant from London and intent on defining an independent cultural position.

Although both Service and Dennis, in different ways, explored discursive gaps between imperial centre and periphery, neither can finally be classed as 'anti-imperial'. Like the journals in which they were published, their poetry acknowledged the ways in which war altered colonial self-representations, but it advanced no coherent political analysis of those changes. India pro-vided a markedly different context for war poetry, however. As Robert Holland notes, British mistrust of indigenous troops, imperial philosophies that discriminated between 'martial' and 'non-martial' ethnic groups, and repressive emergency powers legislation made India's wartime politics particularly volatile.[33] In the Indian National Congress there was also a political organisation which, while overtly supportive of the war, was willing to protest and exploit its consequences. Indian war poetry, in both English and a range of Indian languages, inevitably reflected the complexity of these circumstances, and it was in the work of Rabindranath Tagore and in the *Modern Review* in which a good deal of his wartime work was published, that the political and cultural consequences of the war for India were most fully explored. From being readily co-opted for Anglo-imperial propaganda in its early stages, Tagore came to analyse the war's relationship to imperial rule in India and to articulate opposition to both.

In 1914, Tagore was one of the most celebrated poets of the empire. Translations of his Bengali lyrics had been championed by W.B. Yeats, who praised the 'innocence' and 'simplicity' of the verse;[34] his literary reputation had been consolidated by the award of the Nobel Prize for Literature in 1913; and his status within British letters was soon to be marked by a knighthood. This incorporation by the imperial centre was also confirmed by his being the only non-British contribution to the broadsheet supplement, 'War Poems from *The Times*', an anthology of patriotic verse published in August 1915. 'The Trumpet', illustrated by a picture of what is apparently a Sikh regiment's bayonet charge on the Western Front, is set beside poems by established English literary figures such as Rudyard Kipling's 'For All We Have and Are' and Laurence Binyon's 'For the Fallen'. Like 'The Oarsmen', also published in *The Times* in the following year, 'The Trumpet' appears to share some of the preoccupations of the work of Gellert and McCrae in its representation of war as a force that impels positive imperial action. 'The trumpet lies in the dust waiting for us', asserts its speaker who was once 'certain my wanderings were over and my debts all paid'. By the end of the poem, such complacency is transformed by the trumpet's discovery:

> Now I stand before thee – help me don my armour!
> Let hard blows of trouble strike fire into my life.
> Let my heart beat in pain – beating the drum of thy victory.
> My hands shall be utterly emptied to take up thy trumpet.[35]

It is easy to see how such discourse could be contained comfortably within *The Times*'s construction of war poetry. The trumpets, drums and armour and the exclamatory mode are of a kind with the verse of Henry Newbolt and William Watson who also contributed to the anthology and, as with 'The Oarsmen' and its 'Captain's call to steer the ship towards a shore yet unnamed',[36] notions of summoning and voyage suggest the much-repeated trope of the sons' response to their motherland's distress. Yet Tagore's assigned role as a pliant Indo-Anglian war poet during the years of the conflict ignores what Santanu Das has argued is the complexity of his poetic and political negotiation between cultures and languages.[37]

The orientalist framing of Tagore in Britain, Kalyan Sircar suggests, obscured the poet's long-standing involvement with Indian anti-colonial movements, a commitment that was re-intensified in his developing response to a war that, as his biographer notes, 'dazed and bewildered him'.[38] In a 1916 *Modern Review* essay, for example, growing conflict between colonial instructors and Bengali students becomes the ground for a meditation on worsening wartime conditions and a reconsideration of the relationship between coloniser and colonised. 'I had hoped that Bengali youths might have been taken as volunteers to serve in the present war', Tagore writes. 'If we could sacrifice our lives, – so I thought, – in the same cause with the English soldiers, we should at once become real to them, and claim fairness at their hands ever after'.[39] Such aspirations to equity through calculated military sacrifice suggest alternative interpretative possibilities for his early war poetry. Read in the context of its publication in *The Times*, 'The Trumpet' seems to share the pan-imperial enthusiasm for the European War expressed by other contributors; in wartime Bengal, by contrast, its central image might equally represent that strategy for addressing the iniquities of imperial rule through temporary military compact outlined in the *Modern Review*. In the latter reading, the discovery of the trumpet represents recognition of political opportunity rather than a hackneyed revival of military enthusiasm.

As the war went on and conditions in Bengal deteriorated, Tagore did not significantly change the style of his poetry; instead, he clarified its interpretative frames. In the lectures collected as *Nationalism* (1917) and in his *Modern Review* essays of the period, he developed a thoroughgoing critique of the relationship between the European war and empire, anticipating an imminent crisis in British imperialism. 'There is no nation so powerful that it can keep unnaturalness balanced on the point of its bayonet', he writes in 'The Small and the Great' (1918). 'The weight grows, the muscles relax, and the gravitation of the great world brings all bolstered up anomalies to the dust'.[40] In such changed contexts, Tagore's war poetry takes on new meanings. A *Modern Review* poem of January 1918, for example, contains the lines, 'Our voyage is begun, Captain, we bow to Thee! / The storm howls and the waves are wicked and wild, but we sail on'.[41] The imagery and urgent dialogue recall 'The Oarsmen' of three years earlier, but here the title of the poem, 'India's Prayer', establishes the cultural destination of the 'voyage', a political reference reinforced by Tagore's performance of it at the Calcutta meeting of the Indian National Congress a few weeks before its publication.[42] Without significant discursive change, the later war poetry is removed from the contextual ambiguities of *The Times* and relocated in broader currents of anti-imperialist activism that, as Edward Said has argued, link Tagore with Aimé Césaire, C.L.R. James, Frantz Fanon and W.E.B. Du Bois.[43] 'My boat is for crossing the deep water', he writes in April 1918, 'and perchance in the dead of night when the breeze springs up / the Captain will come to the helm'.[44] By this point in the war there is little doubt that the voyage is one away from what he terms in *Nationalism* the 'hydraulic press' of British imperialism.[45]

A reading of Rabindranath Tagore's war poetry returns us to William Murphy's sense of empire's 'strangely mingled host' with which the chapter began. Whereas Murphy, like the contemporary anthologists of *The ANZAC Book* and *Canada in Khaki*, projected a unification of purpose within that diversity, Tagore's poetry insists on the strains within imperialism itself. The very effort and anxiety that mark the strategic endeavours of poets such as John McCrae and Leon Gellert to establish an imperial mode indicate the tensions and dangers to which the close of 'In Flanders Fields' bears strident witness. As the war progressed, it was colonial difference rather than unity that preoccupied the most perceptive public poets, and while Clarence Dennis and Robert Service were in no simple sense anti-imperialist writers, their work marked the clear demarcations between the politics of empire and those of local, frequently dissenting experience. That *The Bulletin* and *MacLean's Magazine* were insistent on developing distinctive national rather than imperial identities, ones to which Dennis and Service prominently contributed, further suggests war poetry's involvement in a broader political shift towards strategically defined diversity. It is through Tagore's work, however, that a postcolonial trajectory for the study of war poetry can be fully realised. The incorporation of his poetry into the very centre of the production of imperial literature at the beginning of the war only emphasises the uncertainty of that centre's hold on the expressive differences that it attempted to co-opt. Tagore's subsequent revocation of his orientalised role and his reassertion of local and international anti-imperialist positions suggest the capacity of war poetry not only to express the experience of war, but also to anticipate and contribute to the political changes that it provoked.

NOTES

1 William S. Murphy, *The Genesis of British War Poetry* (London: Simpkin, Marshall, Hamilton, Kent, 1918), 166.

2 For New Zealand war poetry, see *New Zealand at the Front* (London: Cassell, 1918); W.M.W. Watt, *An Anzac's Moods* (London: Erskine Macdonald, 1919) and Jock Phillips, 'The Quiet Western Front: The First World War and New Zealand Memory' in Santanu Das ed. *Race, Empire and First World War Writing* (Cambridge: Cambridge University Press, 2011), 232–5. For a discussion of Caribbean war poetry, see Richard Smith, *Jamaican Volunteers in the First World War: Race, Masculinity and the Development of National Consciousness* (Manchester and New York: Manchester University Press, 2004), 42–3, 56, 94–5.

3 *Melba's Gift Book of Australian Art and Literature* (London & Melbourne: Hodder and Stoughton and George Robertson, [1915]), np.

4 *Oh, Canada! A Medley of Stories, Verse, Pictures and Music Contributed by Members of the Canadian Expeditionary Force* (London: Simpkin, Marshall, Hamilton, Kent, 1916).

5 *The ANZAC Book* (London: Cassell, 1916), xiii.

6 Sir Gilbert Parker and Captain T.C. Roberts, 'The Spirit of Heroism', *Canada in Khaki* (London: Canadian War Records Office and Pictorial Newspaper, 1917), 11.

7 Archibald T. Strong, *Sonnets of Empire* (London: Macmillan, 1915); Douglas Leader Durkin, 'The Fighting Men of Canada', *The Fighting Men of Canada* (London: Erskine Macdonald, 1918), 12.

8 Sir Andrew MacPhail, 'John McCrae: An Essay in Character' in John McCrae ed. *In Flanders Fields and Other Poems* (London: Hodder and Stoughton, 1919), 82.

9 *Punch*, 8 December 1915, 468.

10 MacPhail, 113.

11 Nancy Holmes, '"In Flanders Fields" – Canada's Official Poem: Breaking Faith', *Studies in Canadian Literature*, 30.1, 2005.

12 Paul Fussell, *The Great War and Modern Memory* (Oxford: Oxford University Press, 1975), 135–54.

13 Leon Gellert, 'The Invocation of Jealousy', *Songs of a Campaign* (Sydney: Angus and Robertson, 1918), 15. Hereafter abbreviated as *Songs*.

14 Gellert, 'Dreams of France', *Songs*, 35.

15 Gellert, 'The Australian Muse', *Songs*, 122.

16 'Editorial', *MacLean's Magazine*, January 1917, np; 'The Publisher's Page', *MacLean's Magazine*, March 1916, np.

17 Henry Lawson, *Song of the Dardanelles and Other Verses* (London: George G. Harrap, 1916), 13.

18 C.J. Dennis, *The Songs of a Sentimental Bloke* (Sydney: Angus and Robertson, 1916).

19 'The Sentimental Bloke', *The Bulletin* 14 October 1915, np.

20 C.J. Dennis, *The Moods of Ginger Mick* (Sydney: Angus and Robertson, 1916), 30. Hereafter abbreviated as *Moods*.

21 'Ginger's Cobber', *Moods*, 56.

22 'The Push', *Moods*, 40.

23 Henry Lawson, 'The Star of Australasia' (1895), in Colin Roderick ed. *Collected Verse Vol. 1 1885–1900* (Sydney: Angus and Robertson, 1967), 297.

24 'The Red Page', *The Bulletin* 29 June 1916, np; 'The Dirty Left of Ginger Mick', *The Bulletin* 19 October 1916, np.

25 Edwina Burness, 'The Influence of Burns and Fergusson on the War Poetry of Robert Service', *Studies in Scottish Literature*, 21, 1983, 144.

26 *MacLean's Magazine*, March 1916, 3.

27 'Editor's Note', *MacLean's Magazine*, January 1917, 36.

28 Robert W. Service, 'A Song of the Sandbags', *The Rhymes of a Red-Cross Man* (London: T. Fisher Unwin, 1916), 66, 67.

29 'My Mate', *MacLean's Magazine*, May 1916, 20–1.

30 'Funk', *MacLean's Magazine*, September 1916, 13.

31 See Peter J. Mitham, *Robert W. Service: A Bibliography* (New Castle, DE: Oak Knoll Press, 2000), 228.

32 Edwina Burness, 'Service's "Bonehead Bill" and Owen's "Strange Meeting"', *Explicator* 43.3, 1985, 24–6.

33 Robert Holland, 'The British Empire and the Great War, 1914–1918' in Judith M. Brown and William Roger Louis eds. *The Oxford History of the British Empire, Volume 4: The Twentieth Century* (Oxford and New York: Oxford University Press, 2001), 122–4.

34 W.B. Yeats, 'Gitanjali' (1912), *Essays and Introductions* (London: Macmillan, 1961), 394.

35 'War Poems from *The Times*', issued with *The Times* 9 August 1915, 10.

36 'The Oarsmen', *The Times*, 28 January 1916, 9.

37 Santanu Das, 'Sepoys, Sahibs and Babus: India, the Great War and Two Colonial Journals' in Mary Hammond and Shafquat Towheed eds. *Publishing in the First World War* (Basingstoke: Palgrave Macmillan, 2007), 68–9.

38 Kalyan Kundu, Sakti Bhattacharya and Kalyan Sircar eds. *Imagining Tagore: Rabindranath and the British Press (1912–1941)* (Calcutta: Shish Sahitya Samsad, 2000), p. xxxiv; Edward Thompson, *Rabindranath Tagore: His Life and Work* (Calcutta and London: Association Press and Oxford University Press, 1921), 54.

39 'Indian Students and Western Teachers', *Modern Review*, April 1916, 422.

40 'The Small and the Great', *Modern Review*, December 1917, 603.

41 'India's Prayer', *Modern Review*, January 1918, 98.

42 'Editorial', *Modern Review*, January 1918, 99.

43 Edward Said, 'Nationalism, Human Rights, and Interpretation', in *Reflections on Exile and Other Literary and Cultural Essays* (London: Granta, 2001), 425–6.

44 'The Captain Will Come to His Helm', *Modern Review*, April 1918, 353.

45 *Nationalism* (London: Macmillan, 1917), 17.

12

MARGARET R. HIGONNET

Women's Poetry of the First World War

Increasingly, critics have recognized the skill of women's poetic responses to the total warfare of 1914–18 that engulfed civilian as well as soldier-poets in the war economy. The question whether women could or should write about war if they did not carry a gun was laid to rest decades ago by Susan Schweik in an excellent essay on the meaning of 'war poetry' and women's writing in the context of modern warfare.[1] Like male poets, some women composed traditional forms whereas others played with modernist experiments. Some such as Rose Macaulay and Nancy Cunard recorded the experiences of war-work and bombardment at home; others on the continent such as Mary Borden composed close-to-battle lines amid the devastation of occupied territories. New roles shaped new attitudes and poetic personae; in Alice Meynell's phrasing, 'new duties ... have set women thinking of themselves not only as daughters of women, but as daughters of men'.[2] The war triggered women's powerful witness, social critique, anger and laments in the years following 1914.

For decades, the best known female British war poets were the melancholic Vera Brittain, Alice Meynell (said to be a 'Tory' in her poetic tastes) and the propagandist Jessie Pope. Several of the best, such as Mary Borden and Hilda Doolittle (H.D.) were cosmopolitan transnationals who did not fit tidily into national histories.[3] Today, following Catherine Reilly's bibliography of war poetry and her collection of seventy-nine women poets in *Scars Upon My Heart* (1981), critics have explored a much wider array of poets across lines of class, wartime occupation, artistic skills and audience. In the first major critical study, *Women's Poetry of the First World War* (1988), Nosheen Khan tied the 'comprehensive range of human emotions' to the varied vocations and new gender roles that women assumed in response to the war.[4] Many subsequent studies have also been primarily thematic and sociological. Given the situation of women as survivors whose own lives were rarely at risk, it is perhaps inevitable that mourning and melancholia as the consequences of war have garnered attention in a number of recent essays on women's poetry.[5] As Claire Buck has argued, 'women's elegy is a fundamental part of the history of British poetry'.[6]

The four poets I examine in this essay stretch across the generation that experienced the war: Charlotte Mew (1869–1928), Eleanor Farjeon (1881–1965), Rose Macaulay (1881–1958) and Margaret Postgate Cole (1893–1980). Well educated, some even trained in the classics, they moved in intellectual London circles, meeting other writers such as Thomas Hardy, Rupert Brooke, Siegfried Sassoon, Edward Thomas and Virginia Woolf. As we shall see, they draw on, yet modify, traditional forms such as the ballad stanza or the pastoral elegy to express the pain and loss attendant on war. Even though the war made clear that gender categories are not absolute, many women who remained in England, itself so often represented as a pastoral world, drew on the traditional lyric form that ironically contrasts death with rural springtime.[7] They also adapted the language and rhythms of canonical poems by S.T. Coleridge and Christina Rossetti to forge new anti-pastoral forms. Women's traditional role of lamentation endowed their elegiac poetry with social value and authorized their voice. Women's aesthetic choices, I suggest, are inseparable from their richly allusive conversations with poetic predecessors, as well as with contemporary official discourses about the war and with the poetry being published by men such as Brooke, Owen and Rosenberg. In female elegies responding to the social ruptures and violence of the Great War, we can trace subtle strategies of interrogation, startling images that defamiliarize traditional pastoral scenes and rhythms that wrench the tools found in canonical works. Here I propose to emphasize the ironic representation of peace, as a strategy particularly important for female mourners. While most lyric voices remain monologues, some of these poems verge on dialogues that reach out to the dead and interpellations that defiantly challenge those responsible for the war.

The fin-de-siècle poet Charlotte Mew was admired by Thomas Hardy, Virginia Woolf and H.D. for her original voice and forms that carry echoes of Coleridge, John Keats, Robert Browning and Christina Rossetti. For Woolf, she was 'unlike anyone else', and Siegfried Sassoon, who met her in 1919, wrote that she was 'the only poet who brought a lump to my throat'.[8] Critics have been attracted to her anguished spirituality with an undercurrent of lesbian sensuality, expressing passion through driving free-verse forms, where extended contemplative lines alternate with succinct spondees. Valerie Warner notes that she 'published nothing in magazines during the war years' beyond the 1916 *Farmer's Bride*; she cared for her family and volunteered at the War Pensions Committee. Most of her war poetry was published after the Versailles Treaty.[9]

Tim Kendall in a chapter sensitive to the force of her metrical innovations, connects Mew's descriptions of springtime rebirth to death in wartime; without comment, he closes on Satan's lament from *Paradise Lost* at the loss of vernal bloom.[10] In 'May 1915' wintry mutilated woods seem through pathetic fallacy to have suffered from artillery fire: 'scorched, blackened woods, where the wounded trees / wait'.[11] In these years, branchless trees had become an icon for men's wounded bodies, and the alliteration on 'w' suggests a moan. A traditional elegiac pattern at first points to natural cyclical renewal that is 'sure of the sky' and of the healing sea and sun. The promise of human rebirth, however, depends on eschatological time 'when God shall please'. If fulfilled, His promise will 'surprise' mourners who sit joined to the dead. Mew's incantatory repetitions – 'hands in their hands, eyes in their eyes' – foreground the grief that fuses mourners in this world with their 'great Dead', a loving union that resists fractures wrought by death. Blind to the change in 'scattered things', Mew's mourners may remind us of *Richard III*, in which Clarence dreams of shipwrecked jewels resting in empty eyesockets that 'mock'd the dead bones that lay scatt'red by' (I.iv.33). Union beyond death and Christian resolution elude us in 'Again', where the poet encounters in 'some heavenly street' a stranger 'scarred from head to feet' who speaks and reaches out a hand. In an image that slips between a scarred dead soldier and the symbolic body of Christ, the poet warns that 'you' will let go, not understanding who he might be 'nor yet who wounded him'.[12] The mutilated body bears witness and interpellates the reader who avoids the truth of war.

Mew's sensitivity to wartime mutilation and her reach for an apocalyptic resolution in these two poems frame her great ode 'Cenotaph' (1921), whose closing lines have puzzled readers.[13] The cenotaph erected by Lutyens in London in July 1919 was a hollow, temporary memorial to 'the glorious dead', whose empty tomb opened its symbolic value to investment by all mourners. The paradox of an absent presence catalyzes Mew's opening negatives and her repeated glance aside from the symbol she contemplates, which she ties to the shattered idealism of Rupert Brooke's 'sweet' red blood of youth. The re-greening of spring appropriate to pastoral elegies can 'not yet' be accomplished in the few months passed since the Armistice. The Victory Parade of Peace celebrated in July 1919 cannot remove the stain of a grave 'too long, too deep' that lies across the Channel.[14] Travellers to battlefields are compared to mourners who come to the Cenotaph. Internal rhymes pile up to connect the 'tread' of visitors who have gone on pilgrimage in the lands where blood was shed, to the parade through London, where lonely survivors who 'have more slowly bled' come to heap little purple and red country flowers on the empty bed of the dead. Humble as the rural flowers are, they resist the grand heroism of official verbal bouquets:

> Under the purple, the green, the red,
> It is all young life; it must break some women's hearts to see
> Such a brave, gay coverlet to such a bed!
> Only, when all is done and said,
> God is not mocked and neither are the dead.[15]

The cumulative rhyme gathers terms iconographically tied to death, lending an air of inevitability to 'the dead'. Even if empty, the foot of the Cenotaph is haunted by an invisible multitude, sheltering the ghosts of 'a thousand brothers', each of whom seems to lie there.

Can a memorial bear witness by mockery? Readers have paused at Mew's puzzling line, 'God is not mocked and neither are the dead', a reference to Galatians 6:7 – 'God is not mocked: for whatsoever a man soweth, that shall he also reap'. The poem foresees final justice in the eyes not only of God, but of the dead who will bear witness to the truths of the war. The subliminal metaphor of reaping, so often used to obscure the human agency in war, forces us here to ask the meaning of the human sacrifice. The final lines build on the symbolic location of the Cenotaph, at the heart of Whitehall, the administrative and financial center of government, where the Treasury stands opposite the Foreign Office. In this 'Market-place', cutting short her usual long meditative lines, Mew suddenly asks,

> Who'll sell, who'll buy
> (Will you or I
> Lie each to each with the better grace)?

She thereby taunts her readers with complicity in a political economy of war, where the coin paid out is the life of the soldier. Mew borrows from Christina Rossetti's 'Goblin Market' a variable metric that braids together long sequences of rhymes, piling up images in two-foot lines of savory fruits on sale for the token of a soul. The chime of 'buy', 'I' and 'lie' leads to a final repetition three times of 'face'. 'God is not mocked', we now understand, because he witnesses the face of the huckster, as does the young 'murdered face' of the mutilated soldier. Verbal compression conflates the huckster with a murderer whom 'we' must 'face' at the end of time.

Although a decade younger than Mew, Eleanor Farjeon used more traditional forms. Best known as an author for children, Farjeon also addressed a few intense poems to Edward Thomas; she completed his biography fifty years later. In her 1918 collection *Sonnets and Poems*, Farjeon's sonnet 'Now that you too' addresses Thomas, who enlisted in 1915, as a friend leaving to join 'vanishing armies', who probably 'will not come again'.[16] As in many other poetic letters or addresses to a soldier at the front, the anticipation of imminent death shadows a woman's struggle to find the right words, constrained by the emotional need for hope and for breathing space between the present moment and a threatening silence to come. How can you write to someone you love who is living under conditions that imply imminent death? The strain of writing across the divide in a way that holds out a breath of life and hope, while not denying the possibility of death, shapes complex layered messages that affirm and accept, delight and deny. Farjeon translates this impossibility of communication into self-conscious rhythms that reflect on the strain of projecting the future, clinging to a last touch, and contaminating the moments of pleasure before parting. Each sense – 'eyes, hands, and ears' – pulses with anticipation and undecidability. Anxiety breaks down the moments together into splinters of time that repeat insistently the fear of no future greeting: 'Is this the last of all? is this – or this?' Although directed to a succession of present moments, the question, which echoes Kent's 'Is this the promised end?' carries apocalyptic implications about the war ahead. The odd situation of a woman writing a letter to the Front produces elliptical deformations of the traditional love poem, where an illusion of continuity is tacitly agreed on, and pain is at once present and suspended.

Questions about suspended communication and deferred loss also mark her beautiful verse letter to Thomas, 'Easter Monday' ('In Memoriam E.T.'), which speaks to him across the barrier of his death on 9 April 1917. Drawing us into the narrative of the days that pass between their letters, Farjeon repeats words from their letters to suggest their mental intimacy – the 'lovely' morning, their thoughts of praise, the 'eve' with all that word implies. On the eve of battle and of Easter, he has received a basket of apples in which she has hidden a silver Easter egg. At home in England:

> That Easter Monday was a day for praise,
> It was such a lovely morning. In our garden
> We sowed our earliest seeds, and in the orchard
> The apple-bud was ripe. It was the eve.
> There are three letters that you will not get.[17]

The pastoral setting that characterizes so much war poetry, as Paul Fussell has pointed out, ironically underscores the presence of sacrificial death.[18]

At the turn of the sonnet, a caesura hides Thomas's death as a period in the middle of the poem, like the silver egg: 'Good-bye. And may I have a letter soon'. His letter crosses three of hers 'that you will not get'. If the apples suggest paradise and perhaps point to a transgressive love for her married friend, those last simple words and elision also remind us of the fall into mortality: 'It was the eve'. Ironically, the day linked to ritual rebirth closes off the possibility of communication and reunion, so that her voice speaks into a void.

Farjeon's darkest poem on the war in her 1918 volume is her double sonnet 'Peace'.[19] Peace himself speaks, claiming a power of knowledge that equals the power of war. His 'seamy scar' reveals the dark costs of war, stripped of frenzy and glamour. Cast in negatives of loss, costs and silence, Peace does not bracket or conclude war, but instead opens a 'pause' for recognition and horrified awe. Mirror-like, Peace will allow men to judge 'the thing' that is their own action, while its pause prepares a renewal of conflict.

Born the same year as Farjeon, Rose Macaulay was the daughter of a classicist. She worked during the war as an agricultural laborer in the Land Army, as a nurse, then also in the British Propaganda Department and the War Office, where she was concerned with conscientious objectors. Her propaganda work certainly made her alert to the saturation of daily life by what she called 'claptrap and catchwords' in a book by that title. On the margin of Bloomsbury, she wrote ironic fiction about the war (*Non-Combatants and Others*, 1916, and *What Not: A Prophetic Comedy*, 1918) that was sympathetic to conscientious objectors and challenged censorship. Less well known, her collection of poems, *Three Days* (1919), plays with the cadences of speech in poetic form and with complex structures of representation and allusion, like Farjeon's Miltonic echoes. Most of the poems in *Three Days* start from a binary structure that contrasts the speaker in a familiar civilian context to a distant world of war.

Her pastoral 'Picnic, July 1917', for example, evokes the three-year-old war, first distantly, then immediately. A summer wind from the south brings threatening sounds of war to Surrey, along with a promise of rain that prefigures the tears held back by those at home in England. Macaulay first invites the reader into an idyllic scene reminiscent of Thomas Hardy's *Return of the Native*, where two have lain in the bracken of 'Hurt Wood', named for the sweet, low-lying bilberries or 'hurt-berries' that they have eaten while lulled by the music of the trees, as if in an enchanted circle 'bound in a still ring' of apparently perfect harmony.[20] They might be lovers, or they might be coworkers in the Land Army (indeed the subject of other poems in the collection). Hints that the circle might be broken, however, come already in puns on the double meaning of 'hurt' and 'downs' that 'broke / To an unseen sea'. Hidden in that diction lies a cluster of allusions to Coleridge's celebrated fragment 'Kubla Khan', which opens on a 'pleasure dome' amid 'sunny spots of greenery', past which a river runs 'Down to a sunless sea'. As Kubla's dome is 'girdled round' by walls, so too in Macaulay's picnic idyll amid wild 'greenery', 'we' have been 'ringed all round by guarding walls' that shut off the view of war across the Channel. Yet despite psychological mechanisms of denial that muffle the sound of guns and inure us to the 'old tale' of 'the gates of hell', 'we' still hear the guns beating. That old tale and the dreams of blood running down to the 'wide waste sea' may remind us that in 'Kubla Khan' amid the tumult of waters falling through a chasm, 'Kubla heard from far / ancestral voices prophesying war'. In Xanadu, Coleridge celebrates the 'mingled measure' of sun and ice that endow him with visionary poetic powers. Macaulay's adaptation, by contrast, points not to empowerment, but to potential breakdown, borrowing the theme of loss of mental control from the representation of soldiers at the Front.

In Macaulay's adaptation of the Romantic fragment, the only way to maintain sanity is to keep the pain and 'hell' of the battlefields across the water separate from work in England. Macaulay's speaker interrupts the narrative five times with ellipses that betray the threat of psychological collapse. In the final section of the poem, the narrator addresses the guns and wind directly, begging them repeatedly to 'be still' – as we 'lie quite still' while the war shakes the earth's bounds. Death across the water mirrors the quiet that 'we' embrace. Even the metrical form breaks from a conventional ballad stanza when two short feet of spondees hammer like the great guns, their jerks conveying the narrator's fear that she 'should break ... should break ...'.[21]

Haunted by the fear of mental collapse, Macaulay returned to that theme and related archetypes several times in her volume *Three Days*. A vigorous, chthonic yet Christian poem entitled 'Lady Day, 1917' celebrates the 'wild' wind that breaks through the walls of the world, as 'the Sons of God' break through with a shivering lance, bringing not only a 'dark Friday' of passion and pain but the traditional equinoctial New Year, the possibility that 'God, the Lord God of anarchy, / Breaks through ...'. The darker song, 'New Year, 1918', foresees 'the ancient wheel of change' that brings 'nothing new', but instead a perpetual return of 'old worlds red with pain'. Macaulay most clearly harks back to 'Picnic' in 'Sanity' describing a fall

'When the world's rims crumbled', and maniacs and the mad were abroad, while 'reason shriveled up, like paper in flame'. Apocalyptic imagery charges the image of shriveled writing paper, as of poetic gifts burnt out. Her disenchantment about the healing power of time invites us to find sanctuary in a Wordsworthian miniature: 'Let me hold in my mind/ Things small, sweet and kind, ... and keep sane so'. But her repeated conditionals ('God, perhaps, cares') strip away the confidence of conventional comforts. This narrow world resembles the world that she describes in 'Revue', where a soldier gropes and chokes, alone in a world ringed by walls of fog. There Life is a 'a wild thing spinning', and Time is a 'monstrous wheel' whose rim flings man up momentarily to dance before slipping 'back into the quiet sea of silence'.[22] The wheel of repetition and the sea of silence clearly carry archetypal force for Macaulay.

One of Macaulay's best known poems, 'The Shadow', follows the familiar structure of symmetry between home front and battlefront (an analogy that originated during the war). Anti-pastoral, it starts with the threat of bombardment over a city, analogous to the starshells, searchlights and bombardment that illuminate a plain under attack at night on the continent. Machinery blots the sky. A single 'shadow' that falls on the moon pauses and tilts, sign of an exploratory enemy aircraft that will trigger the bright blaze of anti-aircraft explosions and shells. The smash-up that strikes civilians, described in long lines, is a mere '*Strayed shadow of the Fear that breaks/ The world's young men*'. Brief interludes abruptly challenge us: '*Fear wakes:/ What then?*'[23] The reader must weigh how meaningful such parallels are.

Like Farjeon, Macaulay interrogates the meaning of peace following such destruction. 'The Adventurers' starts on a conversational note with three stress lines about everyday occupations performed by estranged veterans, to convey a sinister image of the ostensible normalcy achieved at the end of war. Soldiers have returned as 'Strangers from foreign lands' with hard brown fighting hands and with distrustful eyes that have 'seen / Strange things under strange red skies' The contradictions that make these men dangerously different from their earlier selves well up into longer lines about 'grim and gay' laughter, or the 'surprise' of 'careless, watching' eyes. Tellers of tales about far-flung places: they plough, babble, write or steal 'just like other men', but 'There are tales they do not tell', as Walter Benjamin would recognize. 'They are sons of a desperate age' whose tales must be slipped in parenthetically by the observer.[24] Peace contains menace rather than calm.

As with the 'seamy scar' of Farjeon's 'Peace', Macaulay's poem 'June 28th 1919' ironically confuses peace with war, guns that have fallen silent with 'guns going' to celebrate peace.[25] Addressed to a dead soldier, the poem contrasts 'the peace you keep in France' with the 'frail and wordy pact' of Versailles. The distance of death that separates the soldier from the civilian keeps him from hearing the 'noisy' guns and prevents him from celebrating the peace. The concluding four lines mirror but invert the opening quartet. Not only the 'wordy' peace treaty of Versailles, but the profound 'peace' of the dead loses meaning and becomes 'nothing'. The poet startles us by comparing both to a 'dream': peace has become a cover story for the immobility of death.

A member of the same generation as the soldiers (with 'years and years' ahead of her to grieve), Margaret Postgate came from a conservative academic family; she studied classics at Girton in Cambridge, which she then taught at Saint Paul's Girls' School. Described by friends as 'shy untidy and wild' and as a 'tigress with blazing eyes' who smoked cigars when she was young, she realized at Girton that she was an atheist and socialist.[26] When her younger brother Raymond was tried and imprisoned as a conscientious objector in 1916, her mental world was transformed. She found herself thrust 'into a new world, a world of doubters and protestors, and into a new war'.[27] Both children were disinherited by their father. While she was working for the Fabian Research Department during the war, she met the magnetic G.D.H. Cole, a socialist economist whom she married in August 1918, and to whom she addressed some poems in her collection.

Postgate's slender chapbook of *Poems*, published in 1918 by her friend Francis Meynell, opened and closed with a declaration that she wished to write love poetry; darker snapshots of the war, however, cluster at the end of the volume, where they well out in a surge of angry wit. Postgate wrote that her friend Naomi Mitchison 'once explained to me why it wasn't poetry at all. So I suppose it isn't'.[28] Postgate's monologues speak of her dismay at the official abuse of language, using repetition to underscore the emptying out of meaning.[29] A pair of short lyrics entitled 'Rest' and 'Recruited – Poplar' (March 1917) expose the threadbare hypocrisy of repetitive official rhetoric. The free verse 'Rest, rest' refers to the language of religious consolation about 'eternal rest' as 'a pleasant joke' inappropriate for the 'restless' young men 'who sought / Nothing but life'. The fullness of a soldier's hunger for life unleashes a list of lost pleasures – the sensuous freshness of each new day, the challenge of mental 'play' or a daily 'fight' to remedy wrongs. Incomprehensibly, that lust has been rewarded by an exhausted euphemism: 'So they gave you eternal rest'. By contrast, the 'leading gods' who assign death and life kept life for 'us', which Postgate skewers as 'the peculiar pleasure of living on' alone. 'Recruited' picks up a phrase from 'Rest' – 'they say' – and repeats it in five different lines, to distance recruiters' boasts about the benefits of military service. Like 'Rest', which turns on the illogic of consolation, 'Recruited' turns on the ironic national pride in soldiering as a way of making a 'man': 'And so they went and killed you. That's their way'.[30]

Postgate's classical training attuned her to Greek models. Her group of 'Epitaphs', for example, combines classic succinctness with satiric address. More elegant than Sassoon's satire on the commanding classes, her second epitaph describes the 'great peace' in which a body lies beside 'the growing seed', then aims an apostrophe at 'you that sent him here' wishing good memory 'of this your deed'. Another calls on us without any closing punctuation: 'Here lies / A lover of sweet music, near the guns'. The epitaphic formula draws its force both from that open end and from the simple contrast, marked by a comma, denoting the burial of sensuous life. One of her most compact poems, 'Spring Song, 1917', carries an epigraph from Pericles on the young men who fell in the war: 'The Spring is gone out of the year'. That announcement of a natural order gone awry introduces a familiar visual trope for the barrenness wrought by the war: a thrush in a leafless, mutilated tree 'Singing his puzzled melodies'. The 'puzzle' of April winds and renewed light without green signs of return to life leads to an insistent question whether there was ever before a 'spring like this'. Anger erupts with the closing answer that 'captains in high places / Have stolen away the spring'. Despite that bitter indictment, the poem works by indirection: only the allusion to Pericles' funeral oration points to the death of young men in the spring of their lives. In 'The Veteran, May 1916', on a blind man who pities anxious recruits with nightmares as 'poor chaps', she similarly recounts their encounter in a colloquial exchange, reserving her revelation for the last line: 'And you're – how old?' 'Nineteen, the third of May'.[31]

Postgate's free-verse pastoral elegy 'Afterwards' has been praised as 'one of the best poems' in Catherine Reilly's anthology. The poet opens by remembering people 'resigned' to the war, who promised the young lovers a post-war idyll lying under the larches of Sheer, feasting on 'strawberries and cream and cakes', when they would plot 'new curves for the world'.[32] A return in peacetime, however, reveals the picnic spot is a burial site:

And peace came. And lying in Sheer
I look round at the corpses of the larches
Whom they slew to make pit-props
For mining the coal for the great armies.

Grotesque transpositions that wrench the conventions of pathetic fallacy underscore that spring cannot revive dead lumber. In an analogy between the mines and trenches, the lover too has been made into a 'pit-prop':

> And if these years have made you into a pit-prop,
> To carry the twisting galleries of the world's reconstruction
> (Where you may thank God, I suppose,
> That they set you the sole stay of a nasty corner)
> What use is it to you?[33]

Postgate wrenches the redemptive rhetoric of war propaganda (the soldier as 'sole stay of a nasty corner'). Her conversational voice combines images of the everyday with abrupt turns and flashes of wit, to undercut the twists of logic that present war as 'reconstruction'. Moreover, the slaughter of the larches for the war effort symbolizes the ugly impact of the war economy on England as well as the hypocritical rhetoric that justifies the slaughter of millions of men.

In the post-war reflections of Mew, Farjeon, Macaulay and Postgate, 'Peace itself becomes a doubtful quantity', as Judith Kazantzis reflects.[34] These writers interrogate common representations of peace and war as antitheses, confronting us with their tangled interrelationships. Noisy guns sound confusingly near a tennis court and war leaves the mutilated faces of blind men with empty sockets as well as loggers' marks on a 'wounded' countryside. In Mew, the hollow memorial in a marketplace defers recognition of responsibility until the end of time. The two-world structure so typical of war poetry leads not to the separation and security of the civilian speaker, but to disillusionment, despair and fear of the barely repressed violence figured by Farjeon's 'seamy scar' and Macaulay's estranged veterans who have no tales to tell. Language itself has been burnt up by the abuse of propagandistic rhetoric, leaving lines broken by ellipses, obsessive questions or even without concluding punctuation. Poetic arguments are set up not to trace the gradual achievement of consolation and renewal, but to challenge cyclical and exploitative social forms that perpetuate war in a 'monstrous wheel' of time.

NOTES

1 See Susan Schweik, 'Writing war poetry like a woman' (1987) in Elaine Showalter ed. *Speaking of Gender* (New York: Routledge, 1989), 310–11. The notion that 'war' (i.e., the battlefield) is men's domain, and that authentic writing about war must therefore come from men, has been repeated by critics of women's writings.

2 Anne Kimball Tuell, 'Mrs. Meynell in the "Lost" Columns', *Sewanee Review* 31.2 (1923) 161.

3 On Borden's poetry, see Higonnet's exploration of defiant blasphemy in 'The Great War and the Female Elegy: Female Lamentation and Silence in Global Contexts', *Global South* 1.2 (2007): 120–36.

4 Nosheen Khan, *Women's Poetry of the First World War* (Brighton: Harvester, 1988), 4.

5 See, in particular, Gill Plain, 'Great Expectations: Rehabilitating the Recalcitrant War Poets', *Feminist Review* 51 (1995) 41–65 and Jan Montefiore, '"Blind Mouths": Oral Metaphor, Literary Tradition and the Fantasy of the Mother in Some Women's Elegies of the Great War', *Paragraph: A Journal of Modern Critical Theory* 21.3 (1998): 376–90. In an overview of elegies by European women including Borden, I have followed Celeste Schenck, Sandra Gilbert and Jahan Ramazani in emphasizing an anti-elegiac turn toward blasphemy that refuses release from mourning.

6 Claire Buck, 'Reframing Women's War Poetry' in Jane Dowson ed. *The Cambridge Companion to Twentieth-Century British and Irish Women's Poetry* (Cambridge: Cambridge University Press, 2011), 34.

7 See Paul Fussell's chapter on 'Arcadian Recourses' in *The Great War War and Modern Memory* (Oxford: Oxford University Press, 1975), 231–69.

8 Val Warner, 'Introduction', *Charlotte Mew, Collected Poems and Selected Prose* ed. Warner (Manchester: Carcanet Press, 1997), xvi.

9 Published posthumously in the *Rambling Sailor* (1929), 'June 1915' and 'Here Lies a Prisoner' also propose reflections on war.

10 Tim Kendall, *Modern English War Poetry* (Oxford: Oxford University Press, 2006), 65–82.

11 Mew, *Collected Poems*, 48.

12 Ibid., 46.

13 Ibid., 40. I am indebted to Kendall's reading here.

14 'Cenotaph', Mew, *Collected Poems*, 40.

15 Ibid.

16 Eleanor Farjeon, *Sonnets and Poems* (Oxford: Blackwell, [1918]), 49.

17 'Easter Monday' in Catherine Reilly ed. *The Virago Book of Women's War Poetry and Verse* (London: Virago, 1997), 36.

18 Fussell, *The Great War and Modern Memory*, 235. Also see Montefiore, '"Shining Pins and Wailing Shells": Women Poets and the Great War' in Dorothy Goldman ed. *Women and World War I: The Written Response* (New York: Saint Martin's, 1993), 65–6.

19 Farjeon, 48.

20 Rose Macanlay, *Three Days* ([S.I.]: Constable, 1919), 11.

21 *Three Days*, 13.

22 *Three Days*, 20, 21, 22, 24, 25–7.

23 *Three Days*, 17.

24 *Three Days*, 39, 40.

25 William Kean Seymour ed. *A Miscellany of British Poetry, 1919* (New York: Harcourt Brace and Howe, 1919), 64.

26 Betty D. Vernon, *Margaret Cole, 1893–1980: A Political Biography* (Beckenham: Croom Helm, 1986), 23, 31.

27 Quoted in Khan, 26.
28 Vernon, *Cole*, 37.
29 Khan condemns Postgate's satiric poems as propaganda (Khan, 26–7).
30 *Margaret Postgate's Poems* (London: Allen and Unwin, 1918), 34, 35.
31 Ibid., 31, 30–1, 32–3.
32 *Margaret Postgate's Poems*, 35–6.
33 Catherine Reilly, *Scars Upon My Heart: Women's Poetry and Verse of the First World War* (London: Virago, 1981), xvi.
34 *Scars Upon My Heart*, xxi.

13

TIM KENDALL

Civilian War Poetry: Hardy and Kipling

Several days after the outbreak of war, Charles Sorley managed to identify the silver lining: 'I'm thankful to see that Kipling hasn't written a poem yet'.[1] His respite proved temporary, because '"For All We Have and Are"' was published in *The Times* three weeks later. Sorley's reaction to Kipling's loud alarum ('The Hun is at the gate!')[2] has not survived for posterity, but as a committed Germanophile who believed that this was 'a war between sisters',[3] he had been right to enjoy Kipling's silence while it lasted. Far from positing a familial relationship, '"For All We Have and Are"' was not even prepared to grant the Germans a shared humanity: their behaviour had 'knit[ted] mankind' against a 'crazed and driven foe'.

Thus began Kipling's outspoken campaign against an enemy which was at first merely brutish, but before long, insidiously bacterial: 'Our concern with [the Hun] is precisely the same as our concern with the germs of any malignant disease',[4] he explained in 1916. (The metaphor may have been prompted by the increasing currency of the term 'Germ-hun' among the more vitriolic sectors of the British press.) Impending triumph did nothing to soften Kipling's tone. His poem 'Justice', which he wrote in the month before the Armistice, demanded a heavily retributive punishment for 'Evil Incarnate', and expressed the hope that the Germans' sins would be remembered 'till the end of time'.[5] Working for the Commonwealth War Graves Commission, it was Kipling who chose a phrase from Ecclesiasticus – 'Their Name Liveth For Evermore' – as a suitable inscription on war memorials. This sacrifice made by the heroic dead was, in Kipling's mind, awarded eternal meaning and honour through simultaneous remembrance of the German wickedness which they had given their lives to defeat.

Sorley had reason to expect a more charitable attitude towards Germany from his favourite modern poet, Thomas Hardy, who had already made plain his hostility to war and war excitement in a sequence of Boer War poems at the turn of the century. Whereas Kipling took pride in having popularised the term 'Hun' (which he started applying to the Germans as early as 1902), Hardy saw such abuse as a dangerous provocation. He was appalled by Guy Louis Busson Du Maurier's play *An Englishman's Home* (1909), which described an invasion by an unnamed power clearly resembling Germany; Hardy believed that it 'ought to have been suppressed' because 'it gave Germany, even if pacific in intention beforehand, a reason, or excuse, for directing her mind on a war with England'.[6] This sensitivity was enhanced by Hardy's faith, shared with Sorley, that a blood relationship existed between England and Germany: in 'The Pity of It' (1915), he recorded the Germanic dialects still spoken in 'loamy Wessex lanes' and concluded that the two nations were 'kin folk kin tongued'.[7] After the war, Hardy remembered that 'Fussy Jingoes' had attacked the poem, but that the Germans had translated and approved of it, remarking in agreement that 'when relations did fall out they fought more bitterly than any'.[8]

Unlike Kipling, who had been predicting a major war with Germany for at least a decade (and who had written a story describing the Boer War as 'a first-class dress parade for Armageddon'),[9] Hardy was taken by surprise in 1914 when war was declared. He had confidently characterised the 'Battle-God' as sick and enervated at the end of the Boer War, and believed that 'zest for slaughter was dying out': war had grown too coldly scientific to stir 'ardent romance'.[10] Hardy was therefore an improbable recruit to the British Government's propaganda campaign. Yet on 2 September 1914, he attended a meeting of well-known writers at Wellington House in London, where the War Propaganda Bureau encouraged its guests to dedicate their work to the war effort. At seventy-four, Hardy was the grey eminence among such luminaries as Arnold Bennett, Robert Bridges, G.K. Chesterton, John Masefield, Henry Newbolt and H.G. Wells; Kipling, who preferred to avoid literary gatherings whenever possible, sent his apologies. One result of this summit was the publication of a letter a fortnight later in *The Times*: signed by fifty-two authors, including Hardy and Kipling, it asserted that no nation 'has the right by brute force to impose its culture upon other nations', and called for the 'iron military bureaucracy of Prussia' to be resisted.[11]

This intervention proved insufficient for Hardy, who had been stirred to make his own individual contribution to 'the various forms of manifesto' that had been discussed at the London conference. Chief among these had been the need to '[place] the strength of the British case and the principles for which the British troops and their allies are fighting before the populations of neutral countries'. Hardy fulfilled that obligation with 'An Appeal to America on Behalf of the Belgian Destitute', a poem which urged the United States to come to the aid of the 'Seven millions [who] stand / Emaciate, in that ancient Delta-land'.[12] Still more promptly, on 5 September he wrote

'Men Who March Away', a recruitment poem which presumed to imagine and endorse the motivations of enlisted British soldiers. Published in *The Times* four days later, the poem showed little sign of fraternal feeling in the portrayal of the enemy as 'braggarts' who 'must / Surely bite the dust'.[13] Hardy later claimed that the poem had 'won an enormous popularity',[14] but there was at least one dissenter: Charles Sorley, himself recently enlisted, was appalled that Hardy had fallen victim to the distorting pressures of war-time patriotism, condemning 'Men Who March Away' as 'arid' and 'untrue of the sentiments of the ranksman going to war'; the repeated line 'Victory crowns the just' was 'the worst... [Hardy] ever wrote', and sounded like it had been 'filched from a leading article in the *Morning Post*'.[15]

Sorley's objections to these public war poems demonstrated an acute and unusual sensitivity to bogus rhetoric. He proposed putting a fine on references to God, considered that 'talk of a just war' was self-deception, and admitted to being 'sick of the sound' of the word 'England'. ('Men Who March Away' and '"For All We Have and Are"' were each vulnerable to two of these three complaints.) As for those who 'say that war is an ennobling purge', Sorley insisted that they should be 'muzzled'.[16] Even in the early stages of the war, his objections were shared by a conspicuous minority of poets and critics. Harold Monro argued that patriotic poets were 'War Profiteers', adding laconically that 'the danger of writing verse to fulfil a demand is well known'; he was no keener than Sorley on poetry which sounded like 'rhymed leading articles'.[17] Along with Wilfrid Gibson, whose *Battle* (1915) provided unsentimental snapshots of trench life, Monro has been credited by Dominic Hibberd for being 'ahead of all other poets in making the imaginative effort needed to write about the actualities of the front line, even though neither man ever experienced fighting'.[18] It is one of the oddities of literary history that these civilian poets taught soldiers how to write about warfare; in doing so, they ensured their own demise. By 1917, E.B. Osborn could argue that the 'new phenomenon' of soldier poetry was 'far more valuable' than its civilian counterpart, and that '[t]he making of verse memorials is perhaps the only task to which the non-combatant poet may address himself without fear of losing his sincerity'.[19]

If implemented, Charles Sorley's list of financial disincentives would have reduced the storm surge of civilian poetry to a tiny trickle. Nevertheless, the nation's poets and poetasters continued their versifying inspired by the war and apparently unchecked and untroubled by any such concerns. Far more than 2,000 individuals saw their work published during the war years, of whom only a quarter were women and one-fifth soldiers; greater than half the poets suffered into print were male civilians. This group had no monopoly on the clichés of the age, and the best of them (such as Monro and Gibson, as well as Kipling and Hardy) made efforts to resist the popular discourse of divinely sanctioned patriotism which glorified the war. Even so, their work remained vulnerable to the sceptics' disdain, and increasingly they found themselves on the wrong side of literary debates. By the end of the war, their reputations were (with few exceptions) in serious decline. When in 1919 the anthologist Bertram Lloyd denounced 'silver-haired swashbucklers' and 'poetical armchair-warriors',[20] he offered a caricature of civilian poets – blustering, ignorant, pitiless, war-mongering – which dominated subsequent decades and led to their near exclusion from the canon of First World War poetry.

Patriotic establishment versifiers – William Watson, Owen Seaman, Robert Bridges, Henry Newbolt – dominated the wartime poetry scene, and could be forgiven for having failed to foresee their downfall. After all, history was in their favour. Soldier-poets may have attempted to commission 'Captain William Shakespeare' into the ranks,[21] but this wry appropriation could not camouflage the fact that, during previous conflicts, civilians rather than military men had given voice to war. Reviewing the first volume of Kipling's *Barrack-Room Ballads* in 1892, Lionel Johnson considered it 'a curious reflection that the British army at large, and the British soldier in particular, have received so little attention in literature of any excellence'.[22] The possibility that soldiers themselves might produce excellent literature seems not to have occurred to Johnson, but he was right to note that Kipling's literary devotion to the 'Army man' – 'Who does not spout hashed libraries / Or think the next man's thought' – marked a conspicuous departure from late-Victorian aesthetics.[23] *Barrack-Room Ballads*, together with parts of the Boer War volume *The Five Nations* (1903) and many of Kipling's short stories, ventriloquised Tommy Atkins during his imperial adventures in Asia and Africa, and became so influential that (as one retired Major General put it) Kipling 'made the modern soldier': 'I myself had served for many years with soldiers, but had never heard the words or expressions that Rudyard Kipling's soldiers used … But sure enough, a few years after, the soldiers thought, and talked, and expressed themselves exactly like Rudyard Kipling had taught them'.[24] This fashion for Cockney khaki was so prevalent that as late as 1917, E.B. Osborn still felt the need, in his introduction to the soldier-poet anthology *The Muse in Arms*, to mention his exclusion of all poems 'whereby the rank-and-file of our fighting men, by land and by sea, are made to speak a kind of Cockneyese of which no real Cockney is capable'.[25]

If the influence of Kipling and Hardy declined during the war, it was partly because of the rise of the soldier-poet. Osborn lavished praise only on those civilians who had shown enough decency to fall silent: Kipling and the Poet Laureate, Robert Bridges, were singled out as having 'earned the gratitude of their admirers, not so much for the few pieces they put forth, as for the many they left unwritten'.[26] Kipling, in fact, deserved no such thanks: he remained prolific as a writer of lyric poetry, short stories and journalistic essays. His literary output included *A Diversity of Creatures* (1917), a collection of short stories and poems including several about the war; *The Fringes of the Fleet* (1915) and *Sea Warfare* (1916), his wartime writings on naval matters; *The Eyes of Asia* (1918), compiled and embellished by Kipling using letters sent home by Indian soldiers fighting at the Front; and *The Years Between* (1919), which collected the wartime poems. *The Irish Guards in the Great War*, Kipling's record of his son's regiment, followed in 1923 and one of his greatest collections of stories, the war-traumatised *Debits and Credits*, in 1926.

Hardy's credentials as a war poet were almost as long-established as Kipling's. Despite deploring war in all its aspects, he freely admitted that there were few authors who 'like[d] better to write of war in prose & rhyme'.[27] Several of his Boer War poems ('The Colonel's Soliloquy', 'A Christmas Ghost-Story', 'The Souls of the Slain', 'The Man He Killed') attempted to record a soldier's speech and attitudes, and his three-volume epic of the Napoleonic campaigns, *The Dynasts* (1904, 1906, 1908), detailed with forensic fascination the psychology of combat. A generation of soldier-poets who came of age on the battlefields of France and Belgium learnt how to write about modern warfare from Hardy's example: Sorley loved *The Dynasts*, believing that it possessed 'a realism and true ring which ["Men Who March Away"] lacks';[28] Ivor Gurney admired it for its 'great power, quite Shakespearian [sic] in grasp and technique';[29] and Siegfried Sassoon showed his appreciation by dedicating to Hardy his first significant volume, *The Old Huntsman* (1917). Hardy was far less productive than Kipling, but his vast collection, *Moments of Vision* (1917), included seventeen 'Poems of War and Patriotism'. That subtitle raised the question of whether war and patriotism should be conjunctive, only for the poems themselves to answer with a clear denial. Most can be neatly categorised as either sombre private meditations (such as 'The Pity of It') or dutiful and gauche public performances ('Men Who March Away'). By his own admission, Hardy could not 'do patriotic poems very well – seeing the other side too much'[30]; he perfectly fitted Robert Frost's definition of a 'liberal' as someone who cannot take his own side in an argument. The poet who wrote so boastfully about braggarts biting the dust recorded more authentic feelings in the autumn of 1916 after he had visited a large prisoner-of-war (POW) camp at Dorchester and a nearby hospital filled with English casualties: 'Men lie helpless here [in the POW camp] from wounds: in the hospital a hundred yards off other men, English, lie helpless from wounds – each scene of suffering caused by the other!'³¹ The Germans were closer even than relatives; they were mirror images. This, and not his patriotic blustering, was Hardy's authentic credo, which he had already expressed in the aftermath of the Boer War: 'The Man He Killed' (1902) had described the 'quaint and curious' business of 'shoot[ing] a fellow down' whom '"You'd treat if met where any bar is, / Or help to half-a-crown"'.³²

Hardy, more than Kipling, hesitated over the appropriateness of transforming the war into art. Waterloo was nearly a century distant when he wrote *The Dynasts*, but the grief and suffering of the current war broached ethical questions which Hardy directly addressed in the last and most fraught of his 'Poems of War and Patriotism'. 'I Looked Up from my Writing' sets the solitary poet against a world of suffering with which he bothers to engage only in order to 'write a book':

> I looked up from my writing,
>   And gave a start to see,
> As if rapt in my inditing,
>   The moon's full gaze on me.
>
> Her meditative misty head
>   Was spectral in its air,
> And I involuntarily said,
>   'What are you doing there?'
>
> 'Oh, I've been scanning pond and hole
>   And waterway hereabout
> For the body of one with a sunken soul
>   Who has put his life-light out.
>
> 'Did you hear his frenzied tattle?
>   It was sorrow for his son
> Who is slain in brutish battle,
>   Though he has injured none.
>
> 'And now I am curious to look
>   Into the blinkered mind
> Of one who wants to write a book
>   In a world of such a kind'.
>
> Her temper overwrought me,
>   And I edged to shun her view,
> For I felt assured she thought me
>   One who should drown him too.³³

Hardy's speaker begins as an egotist: his first thought is that even the moon must be 'rapt in [his] inditing' – that is, enthralled by his work. In fact, she has been pursuing more important tasks 'hereabout'; this is a local tragedy, and among the 'waterway[s]' visually dredged by the moon may be the same weir which claims two victims in Hardy's *The Return of the Native*. The poet, 'rapt' as he himself seems to be, is oblivious to this nearby suffering. The word 'blinkered' implies a narrowness of vision which might be necessary for the production of great work – a mind which is blinkered will not be distracted from its task – but at the same time seems callous and less than human. His singleness of purpose provokes guilt in the author, who considers the sinister possibility, in the poem's final lines, that he should take responsibility as a perpetrator of further violence. The poet who uses the drowned man in his work 'drown[s] him too', and all for the sake of a poem. Yet even self-incrimination is a disguised form of self-indulgence, as Hardy's rhyming repetition of 'me' (overwrought me'/'thought me') hammers home. This is a poem focused – like the moon's 'full gaze' – on the poet himself, for whom wars and suicides are simply more subject matter. Ethical doubts about the writing of poetry are exploited as the inspiration for another poem.

Lacking any such anxieties, Kipling wrote about the war with a freedom which eluded Hardy. This was the result of fundamentally different attitudes to art. He had always placed his gifts at the service of important military causes: the social imperative to improve the treatment of soldiers and their wives and families; the incompetence of British generals and the urgency of army reform; the dangers of complacency across an empire increasingly menaced by German and Russian ambitions. Kipling therefore remained unmolested by agonies over the appropriateness of writing verse as he dedicated all his energies to the war effort. Yet such overt politicking had made him a bitterly divisive figure: Sir Edward Grey, the Liberal Foreign Secretary, demonstrated self-indulgence of his own when in September 1914 he threatened to resign if the rumour that Kipling might be sent to the United States as a goodwill ambassador turned out to be true.[34] Even without this role, Kipling's influence in the States still proved valuable, as he pressed his friend Theodore Roosevelt to campaign for U.S. intervention. When the United States made its belated entry into the war in April 1917, Kipling congratulated it for having 'at long last subscribed to the elementary decencies'.[35] But his warmth towards his wife's native land did not survive President Wilson's sermonising. Kipling told one correspondent that, as a latecomer in the vineyard, Wilson had spent his time tactlessly holding forth on 'the Principles of Viticulture and the Horrors of Intemperance'.[36] His poem 'The Vineyard' (probably 1919) warmed to this theme, complaining of the figure who 'portioned praise or blame / To our works before he came'.[37]

Poetry was only one means by which Kipling could contribute to the war effort. He devoted himself tirelessly to the Allied cause by speaking at recruitment rallies, visiting France (1915) and Italy (1917) as a war reporter, and accepting a number of commissions on behalf of the War Propaganda Bureau and the Navy. Attempts have been made to sentimentalise Kipling's attitudes to the war by claiming that he softened his hatreds after becoming overwhelmed with guilt at the death of his son, John (who, like Sorley, was killed at Loos in 1915). Yet his work demonstrates that subsequent grief inspired no recantation, and tragedy was never voiced in terms of personal loss. Whereas Hardy responded to the death of his second cousin in battle with a conventional elegy commemorating one whose name would not 'fade on the morrow' ('Before Marching and After'),[38] Kipling publicly mourned not as an individual but as a conduit for his country. His 'Epitaphs' is an attempt to bring to national consciousness all those killed in war for the Allied cause, from Hindu sepoys to Voluntary Aid Detachment nurses; in doing so, Kipling describes a vast geographical and cultural range which reminds the reader that these were victims of a *World* War. But it was as a recorder of the war at sea that Kipling seemed most distinctive. 'My Boy Jack' (1916) is the poem most commonly misinterpreted as his expression of private grief:

> 'Have you news of my boy Jack?'
> *Not this tide.*
> 'When d'you think that he'll come back?'
> *Not with this wind blowing, and this tide.*
>
> 'Has any one else had word of him?'
> *Not this tide.*
> *For what is sunk will hardly swim,*
> *Not with this wind blowing, and this tide.*[39]

His son John was never known as Jack. The poem's inspiration and occasion were clear from the circumstances of its first appearance in print, when it accompanied Kipling's prose account of the Battle of Jutland: 'Jack' was Jack Tar, the sailor counterpart of Tommy Atkins.

Kipling's tendency to subsume his own emotion into a communal grief conspicuously differentiates his work from Hardy's. Many of Hardy's war poems begin by situating the poet as an agent within them: 'I journeyed from my native spot', 'I dreamt that people from the Land of Chimes / Arrived', 'I walked in loamy Wessex lanes', 'I met a man when night was nigh', 'I looked up from my writing'.[40] In these cases, Hardy insists on his own presence as if writing a kind of retrospective experiential poetry, even when that experience happens to be imaginary and fantastic. The first person voice offers a stay against propaganda, a supposed proof of the poem's validity. Without this authorial self-projection, Hardy's war poems can sound hectoring, as demonstrated by the imperative which opens the sonnet 'A Call to National Service': 'Up and be doing, all who have a hand / To lift'.[41] The sestet's insistence that, were it not for his advanced years, the poet would himself 'serve with never a slack', epitomises the kind of silver-haired swashbuckling deplored by Bertram Lloyd. Kipling's strength, by contrast, comes from self-forgetfulness, even self-effacement. 'My Boy Jack' is an elegy for any grieving parent, Kipling included. A still greater poem, 'The Children' (probably 1916), has all the authority of a writer who, knowing whereof he speaks, becomes spokesman for a nation of mourners who share his knowledge and pain:

> That flesh we had nursed from the first in all cleanness was given
> To corruption unveiled and assailed by the malice of Heaven –
> By the heart-shaking jests of Decay where it lolled in the wires –
> To be blanched or gay-painted by fumes – to be cindered by fires –
> To be senselessly tossed and retossed in stale mutilation
> From crater to crater. For this we shall take expiation.
> *But who shall return us our children?*[42]

It is hard not to read this passage in the light of John Kipling's fate, as a soldier not just killed but lost, his body unrecovered. The parent stares unflinchingly at the corpse's treatment on the battlefield: the 'flesh' nursed through infancy is now discoloured by mustard gas, burnt, mutilated, disregarded. Is there anything more horrible in the war's literature than that image of the body 'senselessly tossed and retossed in stale mutilation / From crater to crater'? The chorus – *'But who shall return us our children?'* – laments the dead adult and the child he once was, and it seems charged with particular pain for a parent such as Kipling who unsuccessfully sought for so long his son's remains. Even so, the specific circumstances of John's death never dominate; the poet is one among countless grieving parents, and his suffering becomes indistinguishable from theirs.

In a diary entry, Kipling's wife Carrie reported the couple's response to news of the declaration of the Armistice: 'Rud and I feel as never before what it means now the war is over to face the world to be remade without a son'.[43] Kipling's own writings, for the remaining years of his life, became preoccupied with issues of mourning and healing, commemoration and expiation. Hardy's later reflections on the war at times sound flippant compared with such unshifting grief, as in 'Christmas: 1924' when he notes sardonically that 'After two thousand years of mass / We've got as far as poison-gas'.[44] But Hardy did manage one great set-piece poem on the signing of the Armistice. '"And There Was a Great Calm"' focuses on the moment when the firing stops:

VIII

Thenceforth no flying fires inflamed the gray,
No hurtlings shook the dewdrop from the thorn,
No moan perplexed the mute bird on the spray;
Worn horses mused: 'We are not whipped to-day';
No weft-winged engines blurred the moon's thin horn.

IX

Calm fell. From Heaven distilled a clemency;
There was peace on earth, and silence in the sky;
Some could, some could not, shake off misery:
The Sinister Spirit sneered: 'It had to be!'
And again the Spirit of Pity whispered, 'Why?'[45]

This reduces the great dramatic agony of Kipling's later work to a throwaway line: 'Some could, some could not, shake off misery'. For all his emphasis on pity, Hardy remains more detached and more interested in universal forces. The spirits who compete in the poem's final lines are abstractions whose backward-looking exchange promises little insight into the causes of war or the possibilities for establishing peace. Rather, Hardy describes a Romantic landscape which had been 'perplexed' and 'blurred' by war: 'the dewdrop on the thorn'; 'the mute bird on the spray'; 'the moon's thin horn'. This marks the biggest difference of all between Hardy and Kipling: while Hardy the nature poet welcomed the opportunity to return to his proper subject once more, Kipling the politicker and parent never forgot, and never forgave.

NOTES

1 To A.E. Hutchinson, 10(?) August 1914, in W.R. Sorley ed. *The Letters of Charles Sorley, with a chapter of biography* (Cambridge: Cambridge University Press, 1919), 222.
2 *The Years Between* (London: Methuen, 1919), 21.
3 To A.J. Hopkinson, October (?) 1914, ibid., 232.
4 To Ian Colvin, 5 October 1916, in Thomas Pinney ed. *The Letters of Rudyard Kipling, Vol. 4: 1911–1919* (Basingstoke: Palgrave, 2004), 405.
5 *The Years Between*, 157, 158.
6 Florence Hardy, *The Later Years of Thomas Hardy, 1892–1928* (London: Macmillan, 1930), 162. Although Hardy's two-part biography was published in his wife's name after his death, it is generally considered to have been written by Hardy himself.
7 *Moments of Vision, and Miscellaneous Verses* (London: Macmillan, 1917), 230.

8 *The Personal Notebooks of Thomas Hardy*, ed. Richard H. Taylor (London: Macmillan, 1978), 291.

9 'The Captive', *Traffics and Discoveries* (London: House of Stratus, 2001), 20.

10 *The Later Years of Thomas Hardy, 1892–1928*, 162.

11 See Nicholas Murray, *The Red Sweet Wine of Youth: The Brave and Brief Lives of the War Poets* (London: Little, Brown, 2010), 41–2.

12 *Moments of Vision*, 229.

13 Thomas Hardy, *The Complete Poems*, ed. James Gibson (London: Macmillan, 1976), 538.

14 *The Later Years of Thomas Hardy, 1892–1928*, 164.

15 To Professor and Mrs Sorley, 30 November 1914, in *Letters*, 246.

16 To K.W. Sorley, n.d., ibid., 253.

17 'War Poetry', in *Poetry and Drama* II, 1914, 250.

18 *Harold Monro and Wilfrid Gibson: The Pioneers* (London: Cecil Woolf, 2006), 23.

19 'Introduction', *The Muse in Arms* (London: John Murray, 1917), xiv.

20 'Preface', *The Paths of Glory: A Collection of Poems written during the War 1914–1919* (London: George Allen and Unwin, 1919), 8.

21 Edmund Blunden, *War Poets 1914–1918* (London: British Council, 1958), 11.

22 Quoted in Peter Keating, *Kipling the Poet* (London: Secker and Warburg, 1994), 54.

23 'In Partibus', *Abaft the Funnel* (New York: B.W. Dodge, 1909), 216.

24 Major General Sir George Younghusband, quoted by E.B. Osborn, 'Introduction', *The Muse in Arms*, xii.

25 Ibid.

26 Ibid., xiv.

27 To Florence Henniker, 11 October 1899, in Richard Little Purdy and Michael Millgate eds. *The Collected Letters, Vol. 2: 1893–1901* (Oxford: Clarendon Press, 1980), 232.

28 To Professor and Mrs Sorley, 30 November 1914, *Letters*, 247.

29 To J.W. Haines, 2 June 1919, in R.K.R. Thornton ed. *Collected Letters* (Ashington and Manchester: Mid-Northumberland Arts Group and Carcanet Press, 1991), 486.

30 To John Galsworthy, 4 August 1918, in Richard Little Purdy and Michael Millgate eds. *The Collected Letters, Vol. 5: 1914–1919* (Oxford: Oxford University Press, 1985), 275.

31 *The Later Years of Thomas Hardy, 1892–1928*, 173.

32 *Time's Laughingstocks, and Other Verses* (London: Macmillan, 1909), 186.

33 *Moments of Vision*, 248–9.

34 See Andrew Lycett, *Rudyard Kipling* (London: Weidenfeld and Nicolson, 1999), 608.

35 To Andrew McPhail, 14 April 1917, in *The Letters of Rudyard Kipling, Vol. 4: 1911–1919*, 436.

36 To Henry Cabot Lodge, 15 March 1919, ibid., 540.

37 *Debits and Credits* (London: Macmillan, 1926), 51.

38 *Moments of Vision*, 236.

39 *The Years Between*, 61.

40 *Moments of Vision*, 225, 228, 230, 246, 248.
41 Ibid., 240.
42 *A Diversity of Creatures* (London: Macmillan, 1917), 130.
43 Quoted by Lycett, *Rudyard Kipling*, 659.
44 *The Complete Poems*, 914.
45 *Late Lyrics and Earlier, with Many Other Verses* (London: Macmillan, 1922), 58.

14

CHRISTINE FROULA

War, Empire and Modernist Poetry, 1914–1922

'New masses of unexplored arts and facts are pouring into the vortex of London', Ezra Pound reported shortly after the European powers declared war – 'things which are in seed and dynamic'.[1] Symbolists; Futurists; Imagists; Cubists; Vorticists; Post-Impressionists; Fenollosa's China and Japan; the Noh theater; Bloomsbury and the Omega Workshop; *Blast* and the Rebel Arts Center; Elizabeth Robins and Ibsen; Bergson and Proust; Stravinsky and Diaghilev's Ballets Russes; the Poets Club at the Café Tour Eiffel; Frida Uhl Strindberg's Cave of the Golden Calf; suffragist demonstrations in the streets; critics of empire from Yeats, Joyce and Casement to Morel, Conrad and Tagore; Freud on dreams, the unconscious and psychoanalysis; ragtime, music halls and Marie Lloyd; the cinema and Charlie Chaplin; warmongers and pacifists; home-grown Fabians and Vladimir Ilyich Oulianoff (aka Lenin) reading Marx and plotting the overthrow of world capitalism amid the treasures of the British Museum: from seeds blown into the London vortex from all corners of the world sprang the flowering of art and thought known as Anglo-American modernism. 'London, deah old Lundon, is the place for poesy', Pound declared in 1909.[2] By 1914, poets were transmuting these international influences into new aesthetic languages that neither waited for the war nor required it but primed retorts to the guns of August from vantages unbounded by nation and empire.

While the war inspired every kind of poetry, Pound and T.S. Eliot, expatriate Americans who had 'modernized' their work by 1914 and spent the war years as civilians in the imperial metropolis, confronted Europe's cataclysmic technological and economic civil warfare from within its social and cultural surround.[3] In Pound's *Cathay*, *Homage to Sextus Propertius* and *Hugh Selwyn Mauberley* and Eliot's *Prufrock and Other Observations*, *Poems* and *The Waste Land*, these poets deploy a versatile internationalist poetics that London's insular 'Georgian' establishment met with ridicule akin to that which Roger Fry's 1910 Post-Impressionist exhibition inspired. Their works register a crisis of poetic voice – and poetic silence – as they grapple with the moral contradictions of this 'tragic and unnecessary war'.[4]

All voices took on new inflections after 4 August 1914: soldiers', civilians', protesters', state powers', not least, those of civilian resident aliens from the empire's provincial margins. The coming of war shifted the battle-lines for non-combatant foreigners Pound and Eliot and put these barbaric transatlantic poet-challengers with their nascent internationalist program at sudden risk of false positions. As the fighting dragged on, state censorship led to silence, self-censorship and everyday constraint – felt changes in who could speak of the war's unspeakable horrors and how, in what one could say and to whom. The slow emergence of a new poetics – allusive and historically resonant, polylingual, multivocal, technically sophisticated and adventurous, radically inventive in style, prosody and voice – converged in Pound's and Eliot's work with the difficulty of forging public voices to oppose belligerent nationalisms, imperial domination and the manipulative public language that implemented Britain's liberal government's war policy, drowning out witness and critique.[5]

Walter Benjamin observed in 1936 that modern machine warfare reduced soldiers who 'had gone to school on a horse-drawn streetcar' to traumatized silence. The state-sponsored contradiction of 'strategic experience by tactical warfare, economic experience by inflation, bodily experience by mechanical warfare, moral experience by those in power' left combat veterans 'poorer in communicable experience' and impoverished 'the art of storytelling'.[6] The immense corpus of Great War literature qualifies this picture of soldiers stunned to silence by incessant 'torrents and explosions' of unprecedented magnitude, and the moral experience of 'the tiny, fragile human body' against the power that deploys it haunts war literature from the *Iliad* forward. Still, the question remains: how to represent this technologically advanced, state-sponsored instance of mutual slaughter? Rupert Brooke's soldier sings patriotic sacrifice. Amid escalating battlefield horrors, Sassoon, Owen, Rosenberg and others bear eloquent witness to inconscient powers at home. Yeats's Irish Airman speaks with quiet, existential irony from a country enlisted to fight for the freedom of imperial states that hold it in bondage. H.D. limns an inexorable Imagist 'Helen', a silent avatar of war whom 'All Greece hates'.[7] Virginia Woolf brings the war home in veteran Septimus Warren Smith, whose anguished lyric consciousness traces a broken prose poem through *Mrs Dalloway*'s post-war elegy. David Jones's *In Parenthesis* questions the war's meaning through transhistorical epic warrior Dai Greatcoat and frames Welsh infantryman John Ball's war within a pagan-Christian eschatology whose nature deity honors the war dead.

Whereas Jones grounds his representation of combat in an English world-view not at all at odds with public policy, Pound and Eliot wrestle with deep contradictions between the actualities of international war and its public representations. For modernist writers, the Great War was a complex symptom of 'a botched civilization', 'the spectacle of Europe committing suicide'.[8] The colonial wars, rivalries and alliances of European empires had prepared its political, technological and moral ground. By an accident of timing that caused him chagrin, just as Britain declared war on Germany, the ex-provincial Pound published in his native land a rude, crude parody of a Georgian poet suffering a certain moral distortion at the hands of British imperial power. In 'Abu Salammamm – A Song of Empire', addressed 'To my brother in chains Bonga-Bonga', this inane poet depicts himself fettered by King George to Buckingham Palace's 'resplendent' fountain with its 'young gods riding on dolphins' beneath the hoop-skirted late Queen, there plied with 'beef bones and wine', 'women and drinks', in exchange for wooden praise songs.[9] The war immediately complicated such anti-imperial protests. Setting out to write a 'Planh for Louvain' after the city's savage destruction by the German army in August 1914, Pound instead produced – and suppressed – a prosaic 'War Verse (1914)' admonishing civilian poets, primarily himself: 'Be still, give the soldiers their turn,/ And do not be trying to scrape your two-penny glory / From the ruins of Louvain/ And from the smouldering Liege,/ From Leman and Brialmont'.[10] He did not heed this advice. Longenbach traces his stumbling search for a footing from which to speak of a war he does not directly witness, from '1915: February', which allies humanity with artists as 'outlaws./ This war is not our war,/ Neither side is on our side', to the heroic sublime of 'The Coming of War: Actaeon' (*Poetry*, March 1915) and the extraordinary collaboration 'Poem: Abbreviated from the Conversation of Mr. T.E. H[ulme]', a quasi-cinematic pan of the Front published under Hulme's name in 1915 and under Pound's in 1920 after Hulme was killed in 1917.[11] He considered enlisting: 'they wont have Americans in the English Army yet', he wrote his parents, and: 'if I should want to go to france I must show that "I have been American for 3 generations"'.[12]

The war lent new dimension to the lyric personae of Pound's *Cathay* (April 1915), in which William Carlos Williams found 'perhaps a few of the greatest poems ever written'.[13] Pound attuned the ancient Chinese poems' modalities of loss – leavetakings, homesickness, exile, loneliness, lament, desolation – to *Cathay*'s wartime moment.[14] Originating in a faraway time, place, language and culture yet time traveling, border crossing and enduring; vivid, singular, expressive, yet impersonal and choral, *Cathay*'s plaints resounded in London's wartime vortex. In 'South-Folk in Cold Country', a southern-born 'horse neighs against the bleak wind' and 'Flying snow bewilders the barbarian heaven./ ... Hard fight gets no reward'. Li Po's frontier guard's lament seems to echo from the Western Front:

> There is no wall left in this village.
> Bones white with a thousand frosts.
> High heaps, covered with trees and grass;
> Who brought this to pass?
> Who has brought the flaming imperial anger?
> Who has brought the army with drums and with kettle-drums?
> Barbarous kings.
> A gracious spring, turned to blood-ravenous autumn,
> A turmoil of wars – men, spread over the middle kingdom ...
> Sorrow to go, and sorrow, sorrow returning.[15]

'The poems depict our situation in a wonderful way', wrote French sculptor Henri Gaudier-Brzeska from the battlefield.[16] Eliot's Symbolist Prufrock of 1910–11 – published in *Poetry* (June 1915) and again in 1917 through Pound's energetic offices – gained similar fortuitous resonance when he at last appeared in London's half-deserted streets, visiting rooms where 'women' come and go, pusillanimous in war as in love.[17]

Blast 2 appeared in July 1915 with poems by Pound and Eliot, Gaudier-Brzeska's 'Vortex (written from the Trenches)', and a death notice: 'MORT POUR LA PATRIE. Henri Gaudier-Brzeska ... on June 5th, 1915'.[18] Documenting this young genius's short life and prodigious work in *Gaudier-Brzeska: A Memoir*, Pound noted, 'It is part of the war waste. Among many good artists, among other young men of promise, there was this one sculptor already great in achievement at the age of 23, incalculably great in promise'.[19] The preface broaches the insoluble paradox of world peace enforced by violence: Pound takes as axiomatic that 'no nation has any longer the right to make a war of offence against any other' and foresees an internationalist future in which 'it would be as much an outrage ... for one European nation to attack another, as ... for Kent to make war upon Wessex'; yet failure to defend world peace by military strength would be as 'ignominious' as belligerent aggression.[20]

Witnessing a civilization making cannon fodder of its artists, Pound came to see war as 'the enemy' of 'the civilizing intelligence'; and art, artmaking and the life of the mind, especially the creative deployment of critical sensibilities, as modes of war resistance.[21] Redrawing the battlelines in this way entailed not a refusal to mourn – *Gaudier-Brzeska* animates the elegy's resources[22] – but a refusal to let war, loss and mourning blight the vitality of thought and art. Pound's epistolary pupil Iris Barry moved to London in January 1917 and attended his weekly dinners at inexpensive restaurants. There, to wailing air-raid sirens, we younger ones heard for the first time of Proust and the Baroness Elsa von Freytag Loringhoven, of Negro music and Chinese poetry, of the Oedipus complex and Rousseau the Douanier and Gertrude Stein. ... [S]omething that mattered very much had ... rather miraculously been preserved round that table when so much else was being scattered, smashed up, killed, imprisoned or forgotten. It was as though someone kept reminding us that the war was not perpetual (as it certainly seemed by then) and that it was in the long run more important that there should be new music and new and fresh writing and creative desire and passionate execution ... It was, for the hours the gathering lasted, less important that so many were being killed and more that something lived: possible to recall that for every Blenheim there is a Voltaire and that the things that endure are not stupidity or fear.[23]

Barry, who would become a pioneering film critic and found the film department of New York's Museum of Modern Art, felt that 'It has never been sufficiently recognized what heavy and important work he did for letters at that time'.[24]

Pound's heavy work that year included efforts to preserve fellow artists from Gaudier-Brzeska's fate in a war in which 'Neither side is on our side' and contradictions abounded. 'Certainly the bosche must be beaten', he wrote, yet, himself 'too old tew fight', he felt it 'indecent' to 'flag-wave' and 'go about shouting magniloquently about the glory of war'.[25] By 1918 he understood the imperialist war machine as a tool of 'international capital', to be trained 'upon any section of the planet which too daringly attempted to interfere with, tax, or restrict the actions of Capital'.[26] Still, he hoped some shards of 'civilization', that violently contested idea, might survive. Eliot, whose studies in Marburg were disrupted by the war, perceived 'great moral earnestness on both sides' and rejected any 'wholly partizan [sic] attitude', yet 'I should certainly want to fight against the Germans if at all'.[27] After America entered the war in April 1917, Eliot had to register with the St. Louis military board and angled for a commission in Naval Intelligence or the Quartermasters. Pound proposed to the American embassy on Eliot's behalf that 'if it was a war for civilisation (not merely for democracy), it was folly to shoot or have shot one of the six or seven Americans capable of contributing to civilisation or understanding the word'.[28]

That summer Pound's provisional 'Three Cantos' appeared in *Poetry*. An *in vivo* experiment in shoring cultural fragments against an imploding civilization, they open with Pound's brash 'I', half-confessional half-professorial, at center stage. But Pound was deep in study of the French Symbolists, his tonal range broadened and tempered by Gautier, Corbière, Jammes and Laforgue, Eliot's model in his Paris days. He had searched in vain for a good English Propertius and offered to 'rig up' something for Iris Barry.[29]

Suddenly, mutually amplifying ironies in Laforgue and Propertius converged to spark one of the era's most original, beautiful, provocative anti-war poems, the *Homage to Sextus Propertius*. Pound found in both poets a quality he named logopoeia, 'the dance of the intellect among words' – a sort of verbal forehand slice that undercuts 'habits of usage', 'the context we *expect* to find with the word'. The 'ironical play' of a supple, inventive sensibility, logopoeia is untranslatable 'locally', although one may catch the poet's 'attitude' and seek a 'derivative or equivalent'.[30] Earlier Pound had noted one touchstone line of Propertius, 'Ingenium nobis ipsa puella fecit' ('my genius is only a girl').[31] Now, against the martial drumbeat of imperial Britain – once a client kingdom of Augustan Rome, now its geopolitical heir – the songs of this Latin poet struck him afresh. Make love, not war; at least, make poems. The *Homage*, he later explained, 'presents certain emotions as vital to me in 1917, faced with the infinite and ineffable imbecility of the British Empire, as they were to Propertius ... when faced with the infinite and ineffable imbecility of the Roman Empire'.[32]

Steeped in empire, capital-driven war and irony-infused love songs, Pound created neither a translation nor an adaptation but a new poem that springs as much from imperial London as from imperial Rome; a Latin-English Propertius, a kindred spirit inspired by Rome's ex-provincial poet-lover, his witty, sceptical sensibility as startlingly contemporary as *Cathay*'s. Leaving the empire's prospective 'distentions' (*finem imperii ... futura*) to compeers Virgil and Horace, this confessedly empire- and war-averse Propertius counters bombastic belaurelings of Roman military conquests and reputations with urbane litotes: 'But for something to read in normal circumstances? / For a few pages brought down from the forked hill unsullied? / I ask a wreath that will not crush my head' (I).[33] In elegiac meters that gave Roman readers 'the shock of a new revelation' and still 'open a new world of sound',[34] he sings of Cynthia, love, death, poetry, empire, war and (Pound detected) the politics thereof.

Pound freely selects, arranges, translates, paraphrases and plays with passages from Propertius's four books to make not a syntactic and semantic translation, but a Cubist collage, a neo-Propertian sensibility bodied forth by a dazzling avant-garde technique. The 'curve of speech'[35] floats on the poem's long line, embracing colloquial anachronisms ('erasers' at the ready, 'devirginated young ladies', 'frigidaire patent', 'Q.H. Flaccus's book-stall' [I, II]), slapstick parody ('I guzzle with outstretched ears' [IV]), deadpan doggerel ('My little mouth shall gobble in such great fountains / "Wherefrom father Ennius, sitting before I came, hath drunk"' [II]), and freestyle interlingual puns: 'Like a trained and performing tortoise [*testudo*: lyre; tortoise], / I would make verse in your fashion' (XII), in tones that modulate from tenderness ('The moon will carry his candle, / the stars will point out the stumbles' [III]) to mock-epic irony ('The Parthians shall get used to our statuary / and acquire a Roman religion' [VI]). An overlay of modern Britain upon ancient Rome, Pound's 'composite character' distills exiled Ovid and expatriate Pound into 'the spirit of the young man of the Augustan Age, hating rhetoric and unde-ceived by imperial hog-wash'[36] – rankling, too, from Octavian's confiscation of his family's Umbrian lands to pay his army: 'behold me, small fortune left in my house. / Me, who had no general for a grandfather!' (XII). Opposing love and poetry to warmaking and empire building, parodying official cant and wartime pieties, the *Homage* stands as a civilian counterpart to the iro-ny-saturated war poems of Rosenberg, Owen and Sassoon.

Pound's ravishing virtuoso of the conversational sublime deploys the exuberant cacophony of a sociable, intimate, chatty Roman world against empire and war through a scintillating play of voices, rendered through every kind of rhetorical sleight-of-hand: invocation, apostrophe, address, dialogue, storytelling, ventriloquized speech (real and imaginary). In late 1917, as Pound was orchestrating these voices against war-making impe-rial powers, he was reading *Ulysses*'s early episodes. In 1922, he described Joyce's use of this signal mode of critique: the variegated speech 'of small boys, street preachers, of genteel and ungenteel, of bowsers and undertakers, of Gertie McDowell and Mr Deasy' depicts 'Ireland under British domina-tion' – and 'the whole occident under the domination of capital' – so vividly that even 'a denizen of the forty-first century' could grasp 'the scene and habits portrayed'.[37]

As *Ulysses*'s voices mount a dialectical critique of imperial capital, the *Homage* opposes a polyvocal counterforce to civilization's enemies. Cross-cutting between past and present, potentates and poets, mortals and immor-tals, imperial wars and imperious Cynthia, Pound's Propertius summons the legendary Greek elegists who inspire him – 'Shades of Callimachus, Coan ghosts of Philetas, / It is in your grove I would walk' – against Roman poetasters outwearying Apollo with 'Martian generalities' and the mutual admiration societies of provincial and metropolitan celebrities (I). He soliloquizes entertainingly, mutters *sotto voce* asides and conjures a quasi-novelistic world of characters: his *innamorata* Cynthia, his slave and com-panion Lygdamus whose tact in reporting her doings ('things which you think I would like to believe' [IV]) earn ironic boons ('Much conversation is as good as having a home' [IV]), his duplicitous 'friend' Lynceas who seduces Cynthia, his stern patron Maecenas ('you ask on what account I write so many love-lyrics' [V.2]), underworld gods 'Persephone and Dis' (IX.2), the 'august Pierides!' (V.1) and Augustus himself, whom he offers a 'large-mouthed product' on 'the affairs of your cavalry' (V.1). Many talk back. Virgil, 'Phoebus' chief of police', wanders by in cartoonish cameo: 'Make way, ye Roman authors, / clear the street, O ye Greeks, / For a much larger Iliad is in the course of construction / (and to Imperial order)' (XII). Cynthia, Lygdamus, the gang of Cupids who waylay him to drag him to her bed talk to him; even his future tombstone intones a lover's epitaph: 'HE WHO IS NOW VACANT DUST / WAS ONCE THE SLAVE OF ONE / PASSION' (VI). From the empyrean, Apollo – god of poetry – commands lyric while honey-voiced Calliope presses epic duties. '"You idiot!" [*demens*]' Apollo chides, finding him hanging about Helicon. 'Who has ordered a book about heroes? / You need ... not think / About acquiring that sort of a reputation. / Soft fields must be worn by small wheels, / Your pamphlets will be thrown, thrown often into a chair, / Where a girl waits alone for her lover; / Why wrench your page out of its course?' (II). Calliope (who in Propertius cedes to his lyric vocation) hands him 'with face offended' a white feather: 'Content ever to move with white swans!/ Nor will the noise of high horses lead you ever to battle' (II).

If poets who can talk to gods flaunt their poetic power,[38] Propertius goes them one better, ventriloquizing deities calling him to his lyric vocation and stamping his 'deathless' words with divine authority. Thus anointed, he can neglect worldly things: 'My cellar does not date from Numa Pompilius'. For words outlast stone:

> Happy who are mentioned in my pamphlets,
> > the songs shall be a fine tomb-stone over their beauty.
> > But against this?
> Neither expensive pyramids scraping the stars in their route,
> Nor houses modelled upon that of Jove in East Elis,
> Nor the monumental effigies of Mausolus,
> > are a complete elucidation of death.
> Flame burns, rain sinks into the cracks
> And they all go to rack ruin beneath the thud of the years.
> Stands genius a deathless adornment,
> > a name not to be worn out with the years. (I)

Tutoring his father on the *Homage,* Pound thought he had 'perhaps over-emphasized the correspondences between Augustan Rome and the present'; 'still there is a great deal unchanged, and some of its most modern lights are the most literal in their interpretation of the latin'. He hoped it would 'give as much Rome as Cathay gave China' and remind his readers of Ovid's exile 'for no published reason. General flood of official rhetoric, as now flood of journalism. Ovid and Propertius really up against the thing very much as one is now – and similarity does not apply to any other known period'.[39]

The *Homage* has influenced much work on Propertius, but the modernist comrades whose work Pound promoted did not reciprocate. Joyce, whom he had hoped to amuse, said nary a word. Eliot, too, remained mute until Pound 'stood over him with a stick', and then, with 'no sign of exhilaration', wrote 'a dull but valuable puff', leaving Pound to 'struggle out from under the enormous weight' of these 'granite laurels' to wonder whether Eliot 'has or has not found' the poem 'enjoyable?'[40] It seems not: Possum pronounced it 'a necessary prologomena [*sic*] to the Cantos' but omitted it from *Selected Poems*, doubting 'its effect upon the uninstructed reader, even with my instructions'.[41] Twenty years later he allowed, 'Certainly, I should now write with less cautious admiration of "Homage to Sextus Propertius"', although he did not actually do so.[42] Playing dead, Eliot left classicists to pile on, readers to make of the poem what they could, and obscure critics to allege that Pound was ignorant of Latin, mute without a mask, was not and would never be a poet. Neither May Sinclair's recognition of the poem's 'reality', its 'modernity', 'the voice of a live man … you might meet in Piccadilly today', nor *Dial* publisher James Sibley Watson's plaint 'Is nobody aware that a contemporary writer', 'a poet, with the rarest gift for translation', 'is actually giving a course on the Comparative Literature of the Present?' could counterweigh Possum's ponderous dubiety.[43]

A silence was falling. The age demanded something else entirely. In *Hugh Selwyn Mauberley* (1920), Pound carves, as if from 'granite laurels', a 'sepulchre' for 'E. P'. in sardonic parody of the Georgian establishment's damning judgment: 'For three years, out of key with his time / He strove to resuscitate the dead art /of poetry; to maintain "the sublime"/ In the old sense. Wrong from the start – / No, hardly, but … Better mendacities / Than the classics in paraphrase!' (Ode, II).[44] Yet rumors of E.P'.s death are greatly exaggerated. In III he asks, 'What god, man, or hero / Shall I place a tin wreath upon!' In the war elegies IV and V, whose disrupted quatrains and strong, expressive rhythms break the poem's tight prosodic sendup of Georgian versifiers, these 'tin' ($\tau\acute{\iota}\nu'$ $\acute{\alpha}\nu\delta\rho\alpha$, $\tau\acute{\iota}\nu'$ $\H{\eta}\rho\omega\alpha$, $\tau\acute{\iota}\nu\alpha$ $\theta\varepsilon o\nu$) laurels metamorphose into a somber funeral wreath for the soldiers – 'Charm, smiling at the good mouth, / Quick eyes gone under earth's lid' – who were, 'in any case', sacrificed by public lies and public silence:

> These fought, in any case,
> and some believing,
> > pro domo, in any case …
>
> Some quick to arm,
> some for adventure,
> some from fear of weakness,

some from fear of censure,
some for love of slaughter, in imagination,
learning later ...
some in fear, learning love of slaughter;

Died some pro patria,
                    non 'dulce' non 'et décor' ...
walked eye-deep in hell
believing in old men's lies, then unbelieving
came home, home to a lie,
home to many deceits,
home to old lies and new infamy [...].

Mauberley is often misread as a failed poet's verse scrapbook along-side Prufrock's failed lover. Even Possum professed, 'I am quite certain of *Mauberley*, whatever else I am certain of'.[45] Yet the sequence presents a diagnostic study of the contradictory, and consequential, predicament of English poetry around the war years: critique disabled, satire silenced, words marketed, bought and sold; a gap, fatal for combatants and civilians, between public rhetoric and the war's actualities; prostitution of and by art ('Yeux Glauques'); Arnold Bennett's advice to the young poet visiting his yacht: 'Don't kick against the pricks, / Accept opinion', 'And give up verse, my boy,/ There's nothing in it' ('Mr Nixon'). Moving between 'anaesthe[tic]' medallion making and the aestheticized eros Pound had satirized in 'Fratres Minores' (*Blast 1*), Mauberley makes 'no immediate application' of his constricted sphere 'to relation of the state / To the individual' ('Mauberley [1920]' II). As if he were the speaker of 'Abu Salammamm' redivivus, he acquiesces to poetry's sidelining: 'Nothing, in brief, but maudlin confession / Irresponse to human aggression' ('The Age Demanded'). Vitiated and defanged, he abdicates the vital role of public witness and truthtelling and his prey escapes: 'Mouths biting empty air' ('Mauberley [1920]' II). Pound's 'Rome-London Diptych' – the brilliant, sociable *Homage* and the eerily hermetic *Mauberley*, sealed in stanzas and rooms more silent than Prufrock's[46] – stages an analytic drama of poetry's impotence faced with the countermanding of a civilization's moral experience by modern states' war-making powers, deployed through words no less than money and mechanized arms.

Eliot played possum on his own behalf, too, as, slowly exuding *Observations* and *Poems*, he negotiated wartime constraints on thought and voice. He liked describing London 'at the beginning of the war' but resented the 'check' of 'always finding oneself running up against subjects which it is wiser not to mention, and everything seems to lead to such subjects now'. Annoyed that 'political topics are barred in letters ... as I am violently interested in the subject', he could only '"lay down" bottles' in his mind.

Meanwhile, 'The war has at least brought *variety* into our lives. I am at present combining the activities of journalist, lecturer, and financier'.⁴⁷ His work at Lloyds, which interested him, involved settling Germany's pre-war debt. He deplored the Versailles Treaty as 'obviously a bad peace' whereby 'the major European powers tried to get as much as they could, and appease or ingratiate ... the various puppet nationalities which they have constituted and will try to dominate'; he judged its 'reorganisation of nationalities' – 'the "Balkanization" of Europe' – a 'fiasco' and recommended 'an important book', Keynes's *Economic Consequences of the Peace*.⁴⁸ The same year, Eliot charged Emerson among other American philosophers with failure to be 'a real observer of the moral life'; he elaborated in 'Sweeney Erect': 'The lengthened shadow of a man / Is history, said Emerson / Who had not seen the silhouette / Of Sweeney straddled in the sun'.⁴⁹ *Poems'* voices arise from the banker-poet's 'intensely serious' observations of everyday contradictions, cross-purposes, betrayals and delusions of 'the moral life' during and after Europe's convulsive war.⁵⁰

If Eliot felt his imagination forced underground, he found ways to project voices and stances that cut through public cant and sentiment. Disappearing into French in 'Petit Epître', he parodies censorious inquisitors:

> 'Il se moque de l'égalité?'
> --'Mais c'est un vrai réactionnaire'.
> 'Il dit du mal de nos ministres?'
> --'Mais c'est un saboteur, le cuistre'.
> 'Ici il cite un allemand?'
> --'Mais c'est un suppôt de Satan!'
> ...
> 'Ne nie pas l'existence de Dieu?'
> --'Comme il est superstitueux!'
>
> ['He ridicules equality?'
> --'But he's a true reactionary'.
> 'He speaks ill of our ministers?'
> --'But he's a saboteur, the prig'.
> 'Here he quotes a German?'
> -- 'But he's Satan's henchman!'
> ...
> 'He doesn't deny God's existence?'
> --'How superstitious he is!']⁵¹

In 'Airs of Palestine, No. 2' he privately satirizes (his own) jingoist editors, whose 'viscid torrents' make readers with stomach to 'swim' them feel 'Cleansed and rejoiced in every limb, / And hate the Germans more and more'.[52] In 'A Cooking Egg', composed in 1917 and published in 1919 and again in *Poems* (which echoes *Prufrock*'s dedication, 'For Jean Verdenal, 1889–1915 *mort aux Dardanelles*'), a silent thinker who once 'wanted Peace here on earth' contemplates a 'Heaven' of ironic compensations – Coriolanus, Sidney, Lucrezia Borgia, Madame Blavatsky, Dante's Piccarda – for a sold-out ordinary life. There he will not 'want' 'Honour', 'Peace', 'Society', even Pipit's affection, or – as if in fleeting self-parody of the banker-poet in bed with financiers who indentured Europeans to private wealth to pay for the war – 'Capital': 'I shall not want Capital in heaven / For I shall meet Sir Alfred Mond; / We two shall lie together, lapt / In a five per cent Exchequer Bond'. Suddenly the real world punctures this painted paradise – the loss, or state theft, of ordinary people's everyday hopes in an overburdened, war-ravaged world:

> But where is the penny world I bought
> To eat with Pipit behind the screen?
> The red-eyed scavengers are creeping
> In Kentish Town and Golder's Green;
>
> Where are the eagles and the trumpets?
>
> Buried beneath some snow-deep Alps.
> Over buttered scones and crumpets
> Weeping, weeping multitudes
> Droop in a hundred A. B. C's.[53]

The outlier line that slashes through the neat quasi-Georgian quatrains foregrounds the pointless, inglorious sacrifice borne by grieving people to feed the monstrous 'scavengers' of their vanished penny worlds. No less subject to the economy of war and empire than the speaker in 'Abu Salammamm' or 'maudlin' Mauberley, this wolf-in-sheep's-clothing seer infuses satire with pathos, at no loss of diagnostic power.

'Gerontion' – the silent soliloquy of an old man who did not himself fight at the hot gates or in the salt marshes but who (his despair of 'forgiveness' suggests) betrayed a younger generation to war – sounds early intimations of the symphonic *Waste Land*.[54] '[D]riven by the Trades / To a sleepy corner', he seems an aged echo of Sassoon's caricatured 'Bishop' or 'They', Owen's 'you', Pound's 'liars in public places' or the international financiers of the Hell cantos. His '[t]houghts of a dry brain in a dry season' arise from a defeated post-war landscape strewn with '[r]ocks, moss, stonecrop, iron, merds'. Amid tattered remnants of Christian ethics flapping in 'windy spaces', no victory 'sign' appears: 'Christ the tiger' springs 'in depraved May' – Verdenal's death month – 'Us' to 'devour'. His decrepit rental signifies not just 'London'; a pre-war Europe that once seemed safe as houses has fallen to ruin in Antwerp and Brussels too, and in his faded memory shadowy international figures form tableaux, as if auditioning for *The Waste Land*: a Mr Silvero in Limoges, Hakagawa among the Titians, a proto-Sosostris, Madame de Tornquist in a darkened room, the liminal Fraulein von Kulp, De Bailhache, Fresca, Mrs. Cammel. Agency, will, courage, fear and foresight wither before 'History', whose 'many cunning passages' manipulate 'ambitions' and 'vanities' to perverse, unchosen ends: heroism fosters 'unnatural vices', 'impudent crimes' enforce 'virtues'. Futile as 'tears ... shaken from the wrath-bearing tree', his thoughts gust like gull feathers on sea wind, dissipated into an indifferent nature.

Eliot told E.M. Forster in 1929 that *The Waste Land* 'might have been just the same without the War'.[55] In those censored 'bottles' laid down in wartime there fermented a broad critique of modern civilization, one to set beside Yeats' prophecy in 'The Second Coming' and the jeremiads of Lewis – that '"orang-outang of genius"' – in *Blast* and *Tarr*, with the war its suicidal symptom.[56] Eliot had troubles aplenty to inspire 'a personal ... grouse against life', 'a piece of rhythmical grumbling',[57] and by 1929, his sense of Europe's corrupted moral life telescoped back to Dante. But if war does not circumscribe the poem's lamentation of death by modernity, Lil's 'demobbed' husband Albert and the pub curfew anchor the poem in wartime London; and many of its elements – topical and timeless – evoke that catastrophe: the Austro-Hungarian aristocrat, the burial of the dead, fortune-telling, death in life, 'rats alley / Where the dead men lost their bones', drowned Phlebas, declining empires (ancient and modern): 'Falling towers / Jerusalem Athens Alexandria / Vienna London'.[58] Its rough-hewn draft emerged from *miglior fabbro* Pound's less-is-more editorial genius shorn of half its bulk, with Tiresias its über-consciousness, its sections streamlined and ordered into phantasmagoric stations of Europe's ancient Grail quest made new. Caught in expressionist stony deserts, rat-infested cityscapes, and claustrophobic interiors, hollowed-out souls thirst for regenerative 'water', their spiritual longing only intensified by the oily trash-bearing river, the tantalizing water-dripping song, the memory of sailing gaily on the sea. Raising *Poems*' poignant voices to the grandeur of public elegy, *The Waste Land* animates *Ulysses*'s 'mythical method' to give 'a shape and a significance to the immense panorama of futility and anarchy which is contemporary history'.[59]

This poem first titled 'He Do the Police in Different Voices' multiplies and disperses Gerontion's singular voice into a cloud of voices issuing from actual and mythic locales – rooms, pub, London streets, riverbank, bridges, churches, desert, plain, 'Ganga' – and netted into the formal idea, almost the afterthought, of impersonal Tiresias. 'Vocative? vocative??' Pound queried of addresses to 'Unreal city' and 'London' and cautioned 'personal'; 'Pruf[rock]' – bringing to the fore, as a reader of the then-unfinished but technically stunning poem, the central question of the nature, locus and tone of its elusive voice.[60] The 'voice' mourning post-war Europe must not be Eliot's, the poet's or any 'personal' speaker's; it must belong to many, must float unhoused and disembodied – issue now from here, now there. Nor, of course, can it be English: its untranslated citations evoke an Indo-European mind, a shattered Europe whose cosmopolitan ideal persists amid desolation. Gathering and surpassing the spectral dialogue technique of 'Prufrock', the *Homage*'s teeming voices, *Mauberley*'s silent stanzas and the monologic 'Cooking Egg' and 'Gerontion', *The Waste Land*'s sound collage encompasses voices human and inhuman; the colloquial, popular and everyday and the literary and oracular; the onomatopoetic dry grass singing and the enigmatic Thunder, to end in a Sanskrit incantation – Shantih, the peace that passeth understanding – that at once evades and evokes an English word corrupted to the core by the 'bad peace' instated at Versailles.[61] Its salvaged – or scavenged – shards of language, wrecked on modernity's rocks, are 'spelt into' – on second thought, 'shored against' – ruin by a voice that is no one's and everyone's.[62]

The Great War did not make modernist poetics, but it did make modernist poems whose voices echo down history's corridors. It also left deep scars on their creators. In 1949, when his *Pisan Cantos* won the Bollingen Prize, Pound flagged 1918 as the year he 'began investigation of causes of war, to oppose same'.[63] For decades he lived self-exiled in France and Italy, where he lies buried on Venice's Isola San Michele; for thirteen years he was a prisoner of his own government. In 1958, as would-be foreign correspondent of the *Virginia Quarterly Review*, he complained that a press official 'suspects me of wanting to write about art (I ax you ART) instead of politics'; he recalled Admiral Beatty's remark that the Americans were heading home and the politicians to Versailles to prepare the next war, and he invoked the betrayal of Poland and the Tirol.[64] If Pound never forgave England the war and its aftermath, Eliot made England home. He worked at Lloyds until 1925 and thereafter at Faber, publishing many important writers. In 1927 he converted to Anglicanism and took British citizenship; in 1948 he received the O.M. and the Nobel Prize; he rests in Poets' Corner. Yet in 1959 he reflected that his poetry had 'more in common with my distinguished contemporaries in America than with anything written in my generation in England. ... It wouldn't be what it is ... if I'd been born in England, and it wouldn't be what it is if I'd stayed in America... But in its sources, in its emotional springs, it comes from America'.[65] Pound must surely have agreed. In London, 'the place for poesy', two young American poets plunged into a vortex whose roiling violence made them and unmade them as observers of modern 'moral life'.

NOTES

1 'Affirmations VI: Analysis of This Decade,' *New Age* 16:15 (11 February 1915): 411.

2 D.D. Paige ed. *Selected Letters of Ezra Pound, 1907–1941* (New York: New Directions, 1950), 7. Hereafter abbreviated as *SL*.

3 *SL*, 40.

4 John Keegan, *The First World War* (New York: Knopf, 1999), 3.

5 See Vincent B. Sherry, *The Great War and the Language of Modernism* (New York: Oxford University Press, 2003), especially chap. 1.

6 'The Storyteller: Reflections on the Works of Nikolai Leskov' in Hannah Arendt ed. *Illuminations,* trans. Harry Zohn (New York: Schocken, 1969), 83–4.

7 H.D., *Heliodora and Other Poems* (Boston and New York: Houghton Mifflin, [1924]), 24.

8 Ezra Pound, *Hugh Selwyn Mauberley* in *Selected Poems of Ezra Pound* (New York: New Directions, 1957), 61–77, section V. Hereafter *Selected Poems* abbreviated as *SPND*; *Hugh Selwyn Mauberley* cited by section. Wyndham Lewis, 'Early London Environment' (1948) in Hugh Kenner ed. *T.S. Eliot: A Collection of Critical Essays* (Englewood Cliffs, NJ: Prentice-Hall, 1962), 33.

9 'Abu Salammamm – A Song of Empire', *Poetry* 4:5 (August 1914): 176–7. Pound regretted its timing but feared apologies would draw undue attention (James Longenbach, *Stone Cottage: Pound, Yeats, and Modernism* [Oxford: Oxford University Press, 1991], 115).

10 Longenbach, 115–6.

11 Longenbach, 122–5.

12 Mary de Rachewiltz, A. David Moody and Joanna Moody eds. *Ezra Pound to His Parents: Letters 1895–1929* (Oxford: Oxford University Press, 2010), 347, 352 (23 May 1915, 10 September 1915). Hereafter abbreviated as *EPPL*.

13 Zhaoming Qian, *Orientalism and Modernism: The Legacy of China in Pound and Williams* (Durham, NC: Duke University Press, 1995), 114.

14 Ronald Bush, 'Pound and Li Po: What Becomes a Man' in George Bornstein ed. *Ezra Pound among the Poets* (Chicago: University of Chicago Press, 1985), 36f.

15 *Cathay: Translations by Ezra Pound ... from the Chinese of Rihaku, ... the Notes of the Late Ernest Fenollosa, and the Decipherings of the Professors Mori and Ariga* (London: Elkin Mathews, 1915), 16–7.

16 Ezra Pound, *Gaudier-Brzeska: A Memoir* (London: John Lane, 1916), 63. Hereafter abbreviated as *GBM*.

17 *Prufrock and Other Observations* (London: Egoist [Ezra Pound], 1917), 10.

18 Wyndham Lewis et al., *Blast 1: Review of the Great English Vortex* (London: John Lane/The Bodley Head, 2 July [20 June] 1914); *Blast 2: War Number* (15 July 1915): 34.

19 *GBM*, 3.

20 *GBM*, 1–2.

21 A. David Moody, *Ezra Pound: Poet: A Portrait of the Man and His Work, I: The Young Genius 1885–1920* (Oxford: Oxford University Press, 2010), 261. Hereafter abbreviated as Moody.

22 Christine Froula, '*Gaudier-Brzeska*: Abstract Form, Modern War, and the Vicissitudes of Elegy' in Hélène Aji et al. eds. *Ezra Pound and Referentiality* (Paris: Presses Universitaires de Paris-Sorbonne, 2003), 119–31.

23 Iris Barry, 'The Ezra Pound Period', *Bookman* 74:2 (October 1931): 168.

24 Barry, 162.

25 *EPPL*, 402.

26 'Studies in Contemporary Mentality. XVIII', *New Age* 22:10 (3 January 1918): 193; Moody 340.

27 Valerie Eliot and Hugh Haughton eds. *The Letters of T.S. Eliot Vol. 1: 1898–1922*, (London: Faber, 2009), 62. Hereafter abbreviated as *Letters*.

28 Moody, 342.

29 *SL*, 91.

30 'How to Read' (1929), *Literary Essays* (New York: New Directions, 1968), 25. Hereafter abbreviated as *LE*. Pound revisited this moment: 'Unless I am right in discovering *logopoeia* in Propertius', Laforgue 'invented logopoeia' or at least 'found or refound it' (33).

31 *The Spirit of Romance* (1910; New York: New Directions, 1968), 96.

32 *SL*, 231.

33 *Homage to Sextus Propertius* (1917, 1919), poem cited by section from J.P. Sullivan's bilingual text, edited in consultation with Pound, in *Ezra Pound and Sextus Propertius: A Study in Creative Translation* (Austin: University of Texas Press, 1964), 107–71. Cf. *Personae: The Collected Shorter Poems of Ezra Pound* (New York: New Directions, 1971), 205–30.

34 J.W. Mackail, *Latin Literature* (New York: Scribner's, 1909), 124. Pound sent Mackail to Barry, noting, 'Propertius for beautiful cadence, though he uses only one metre' (*SL* 87); after composing the *Homage*, he noted that MacKail missed Propertius's irony – 'read him entirely through Burne-Jones, Vita Nuova, Victorian slosh and Xtn sentimentality' (*EPPL* 347).

35 Hugh Kenner, *The Poetry of Ezra Pound* (London: Faber, 1951), 151.

36 *SL*, 150.

37 'Ulysses,' *Dial* 72:6 (June 1922); *LE* 404–6.

38 Cf. Jonathan Culler, 'Apostrophe' in *The Pursuit of Signs* (Ithaca, New York: Cornell University Press, 1981), 135–54.

39 *EPPL*, 438.

40 *SL*, 151; 'Mr. Pound and His Poetry', *Athenaeum*, 4670 (31 October 1919): 1132. Eliot pronounced the *Homage* 'one of the best things Mr. Pound has done'; 'a new *persona*, a creation of a new character, recreating Propertius in himself, and himself in Propertius' and 'probably a truer interpretation ... than Professor Mackail's'; observed that an assemblage of passages from Propertius's corruption-riddled text rearranged into a twelve-section English poem is no 'translation'; and judged that although 'no other poet living ... could justify such a method ... Mr. Pound has succeeded' ('The Method of Ezra Pound', *Athenaeum* 4669 [24 October 1919]: 1066). He relegated his enjoyment of the poem outside 'public interest; *his non plebecula gaudet* [commoners do not enjoy such things]' (*Athenaeum*, 4671 [7 November 1919]: 1163; cf. *Letters*, 414).

41 T.S. Eliot ed. *Selected Poems of Ezra Pound* (1928; London: Faber, 1959), 18. Hereafter abbreviated as *SPF*.

42 *SPF*, 21.

43 Eric Homberger ed. *Ezra Pound: The Critical Heritage* (London and Boston: Routledge and Kegan Paul, 1972), 183, 193.

44 See note 8.

45 *SPF*, 21.

46 *Mauberley*'s only 'you' is the poet briefly addressed by Mr. Nixon and 'Bloughram's friend'; the poem has but two apostrophes, the appeal to Apollo to say what contemporary merits 'tin' laurels and the envoi.

47 *Letters*, 257, 182.

48 *Letters*, 404–5, 425, 428.

49 'American Literature', *Athenaeum* 4643 (25 April 1919): 237; Ronald Schuchard, 'Burbank with a Baedeker, Eliot with a Cigar: American Intellectuals, Anti-Semitism, and the Idea of Culture', *Modernism/Modernity* 10:1 (January 2003): 3.

50 *Letters*, 441.

51 Christopher Ricks ed. *Inventions of the March Hare: Poems, 1909–1917* (New York: Harcourt Brace, 1996), 86–7.

52 *Inventions*, 84–5.

53 *Poems* (New York: Knopf, 1920), 23.

54 *Poems*, 13–6. Eliot proposed 'Gerontion' as 'prelude'; Pound advised against it (*Letters*, 630).

55 Schuchard, 6.

56 '"Orang-outang of genius"': Eliot characterizing Lewis; Sherry, 195.

57 Valerie Eliot ed. *The Waste Land: A Facsimile and Transcript of the Original Drafts Including the Annotations of Ezra Pound* (New York: Harcourt Brace, 1971), [1]. Hereafter abbreviated as *WL*.

58 *WL*, 138, 145.

59 '*Ulysses*, Order, and Myth', *Dial* 75.5 (November 1923), 483.

60 *WL*, 42, 44, 106.

61 Cf. citations of Eliot's wartime letters (220 above) and note 48.

62 *WL*, 80.

63 *SPND*, [vi].

64 Jon Schneider, 'Ezra Pound: Foreign Correspondent', *Virginia Quarterly Review* 84:2 (Spring 2008): 219–37.

65 Interview with Donald Hall, *Paris Review* (Spring-Summer 1959); www.theparisreview.org/interviews/4738/the-art-of-poetry-no-1-t-s-eliot.

PART IV

Afterlives of First World War Poetry

15

FRAN BREARTON

'But that is not new': Poetic Legacies of the First World War

> And I remember
> Not the war I fought in
> But the one called Great
> Which ended in a sepia November
> Four years before my birth.[1]

Vernon Scannell's 'The Great War', first published in 1962, is perhaps the most explicit articulation of a legacy, felt at different times in different degrees, bequeathed to poets across the twentieth century: the inherited 'memory' of a war they did not experience. An historical, literary and cultural legacy, it is also in some ways an unaccountable one. In *Poems of the First World War* (1988), Martin Stephen points out that:

> The Second World War killed roughly five times as many people as did the first, brought untold destruction to civilian populations, and in its final throes unleashed a horror that could – and still can – wipe out life on earth. The facts, and logic, dictate that if any images dominate poetry they should be those of Hiroshima, Dachau, and Stalingrad. Certainly these images appear frequently in modern writing, but it is far easier to find the images of the Great War ...[2]

Stephen's historical 'logic', for anyone writing poetry post-1945, seems irrefutable. Nor is the legacy straightforwardly attributable to the literary reputations of its frontline combatants and their subsequent influence on an Anglophone poetic tradition. If one looks to the 'bigger' war historically, one might also look for the 'bigger' and more influential names of modern literature. As Paul Fussell puts it: 'The roster of major innovative talents who were not involved with the war is long and impressive. It includes Yeats, Woolf, Pound, Eliot, Lawrence, and Joyce – that is, the masters of the modern movement. It was left to lesser talents ... to recall in literary form a war they had actually experienced. Sassoon, Graves, and Blunden are clearly writers of the second rank'.[3]

Yet the facts speak for themselves – in the war's pervasive presence through the literature of the last century; in a continuing fascination with

Owen, Rosenberg, Thomas and other literary casualties of 1914–18; and in the seemingly insatiable appetite for more work on the subject that the war still generates. As Stephen goes on to note, 'The Great War seems to exert a terrible and perhaps terrified fascination over the modern imagination, and not only in terms of poetry'. The more the Great War is explicated, rationalised and demythologised by historians, literary critics, writers, filmmakers, journalists et alia who feel the compulsion to 'go over the ground again'[4] – often to fight over it – the more manifest becomes an extraordinary 'fascination' above and beyond the 'facts', an enactment of the very cultural phenomenon that is also under scrutiny.

Paul Fussell's equation of 'involvement' with combat experience, and his almost exclusively male roster of writers in *The Great War and Modern Memory*, serve to equate the 'war poet' with the 'soldier-poet'. By extension, therefore, the custodian of memory is the 1914–18 veteran. And yet his choice of the word 'recall' is suggestive beyond the combatant (trench warfare) experience his seminal study habitually privileges as embodying the 'memory' of war. To recall is 'to remember'(*Oxford English Dictionary*); but first and foremost, it is 'to call back', 'to bring back'. In his closing chapter on 'Persistence and Memory', he notes that 'Everyone fighting a modern war tends to think of it in terms of the last one he knows anything about. [...] The act of fighting a war becomes something like an unwitting act of conservative memory, and even of elegy'.[5] Keith Douglas, for example, the Second World War poet killed in action in 1944, three days after D-day, consciously reflects on the 'tautology' inherent in articulating the experience of a subsequent war in 'Desert Flowers':

> Living in a wide landscape are the flowers –
> Rosenberg I only repeat what you were saying –
> the shell and the hawk every hour
> are slaying men and jerboas, slaying
>
> the mind: but the body can fill
> the hungry flowers and the dogs who cry words
> at nights, the most hostile things of all.
> But that is not new.[6]

The poem is both elegy (for Rosenberg) and self-elegy, anticipating as it does his own fate as 'not new'. Douglas's desert war, seemingly remote from Flanders' fields, nevertheless reinvokes the familiar landscape of 1914–18 – the rats, Rosenberg's 'poppies whose roots are in man's veins', the continual bombardment, a hostile 'enemy' other than the opposing army (in the Great War, rats, lice, mud). The years 1939–45 are 'remembered' through 1914–18. Paul Fussell himself – as critic and cultural historian – exemplifies the argument he propounds that the Great War has 'become Great in another sense – all-encompassing, all-pervading, both internal and external at once, the essential condition of consciousness in the twentieth century'.[7] A veteran of World War II, who fought with American forces in France in 1944, he is nonetheless haunted by World War I. *The Great War and Modern Memory* (1975) is powerful and compelling even where it is controversial, one of the most influential texts on war to have been published in the decades since 1945; its 'companion' volume – the subsequent study of the war he fought in, *Wartime: Understanding and Behaviour in the Second World War* (1989) – much less so.

Poems that draw on, respond to and 'remember' the Great War are numerous (if not as numerous as they once were, of which more anon); but my focus here is on a handful of poems by poets in whose oeuvres the war is particularly compelling, for reasons familial, experiential and generational (and, therefore, historically specific, coinciding with and in part accounting for – in the 1960s and 1970s – one of several 'revivals' of interest in the Great War).[8] That is, those whose fathers and uncles fought in the war and survived to share memories directly, or those who have served in the army – those, in other words, for whom the war has been part of their social and cultural landscape, a still-living memory around them. For poets such as Ted Hughes (1930–98) or Michael Longley (b.1939), the act of 'Recalling War', as Robert Graves puts it in 1935, in one of the few of his post-1918 poems to address his own war explicitly, is 'A sight to be recalled in elder days / When learnedly the future we devote / To yet more boastful visions of despair'.[9] It is a remembering forwards as well as backwards. Graves, recalling war at a point in the 1930s when the mood had already shifted from being 'post-war' to 'pre-war', acknowledges the anachronisms, the 'antiqueness of romance' in wartime ('old importances came swimming back … A weapon at the thigh, surgeons at call …') as against a harsh reality, and anticipates, in 'boastful visions of despair', the cyclical repetition of history and its motifs – what Douglas later finds to be 'not new', and what Longley too, following on from Douglas, finds himself 'nearly repeat[ing]' in the 1970s.[10]

For Vernon Scannell, a veteran of World War II (who fought in the Middle East and Normandy, and who deserted twice), it is the earlier war that liberates his poetic voice in the 1960s. His reputation as a war poet is founded on collections such as *Walking Wounded* (1965) and *Epithets of War* (1969), in which are evident the profound influence of Sassoon, and the Great War's landscape and motifs, on his own wartime experience. 'The Great War', from 1962, is formally slightly unusual in his oeuvre in that it breaks up its own instinctive pull towards (rhymed) iambic pentameter, but the 'default' setting still shadows the lines as his memory, too, habitually returns to a default setting on the 1914–18 Western Front:

> Whenever war is spoken of
> I find
> The war that was called Great invades the mind:
> The grey militia marches over land
> A darker mood of grey
> Where fractured tree-trunks stand
> …
> These things I see,
> But they are only part
> Of what it is that slyly probes the heart …[11]

The poem is pulled towards the traditional, even the clichéd; its landscape is learned from literary and cultural representation, not experienced directly; what 'invades the mind' here is less the war than inherited memory of it. The poem draws on all the expected Great War elements – 'iron brambles', 'corpses on the wire', 'Duckboards, mud and rats', the 'bugle's hoarse, sweet cry', 'grey earth', 'crimson flowers' – to end, tellingly, with the war's own end in a 'sepia November'. If the poet is not wearing rose-tinted spectacles, he is nonetheless aware of the 'sepia' tint of memory, the lure of nostalgic images that both soften and preserve.[12]

Scannell, in some respects a relatively slight poet, here acknowledges that which 'probes the heart': the seductiveness of the 'tunes' – '*A long, long trail, The Rose of No-Man's-Land, / Home Fires* and *Tipperary*' – that 'creep into the mind' (like a creeping barrage); the emotional haunting wherein 'reason darkens'. 'The Great War' is not a poem that reverberates much beyond the fact of emotional identification, although it may trigger that emotion in its reader, too. In contrast, a darker haunting is ever present in the imagination of Ted Hughes, for whom the First World War is part of his childhood landscape – and at the core of the primal, sometimes apocalyptic, thrust of his poems. Hughes's father was one of only seventeen survivors of a regiment of the Lancashire Fusiliers slaughtered at Gallipoli, and would sometimes share stories of the war with his son; William Hughes was also, as Elaine Feinstein notes, 'so shattered by the experience' that 'nightmares had him calling out in his sleep'.[13] The war's effect on the life of the Yorkshire valley in which he grew up was such that Ted Hughes would later write of his home ground:

> The people are not detached enough from the stone, as if they were only half-born from the earth, and the graves are too near the surface. A disaster seems to hang around in the air there for a long time. I can never escape the impression that the whole region is in mourning for the First World War.[14]

Hughes's mud, blood and violence in the 1950s and 1960s are less stylised and sepia-tinted than they are visceral and immediate: in 'Six Young Men', the photograph of local men doomed to die in the Great War that inspires the poem may be 'faded and ochre-tinged', but it becomes the site of 'contradictory permanent horrors' that 'shoulder out / One's own body from its instant and heat'.[15] 'Bayonet Charge', another poem which shows his debt to Owen, is a nightmare reliving, over and over again, of trauma, another 'permanent horror[s]': 'Suddenly he awoke and was running – raw / In raw-seamed hot khaki, his sweat heavy...'.[16]

In his introduction to Keith Douglas's poems, Hughes writes:

Owen carried about, in his pocket, photographs of trench horrors which he would evidently have liked to see magnified and put on public display in London, his idea being to shock his non-participant fellow-citizens into an awareness of the new day dawning in the trenches. One can't help wondering how much of this passionately formulated but frustrated motive diverted itself into the graphic focus and massive, direct appeal of his poetry. When he declared 'The Poetry Does Not Matter' what he also meant was that in the poems nothing mattered but truth to the facts, the deepest possible grasp of the human implications of the facts, and expressiveness – irresistible communication on the most private, the most affecting level. The poetic style which he bred ... the basic simplicity, the shocking directness, the colloquial flexibility ... was a means to this end ... After perfecting this means, and producing a few examples of what could be done with it, Owen died and bequeathed it to others.[17]

In 'Wilfred Owen's Photographs' (the title not obviously explicable from the body of the poem), confrontation with the 'human implications of the facts' serves as an indictment of those abstract 'virtues' – patriotism, glory, honour, pride – also subverted and redefined by Owen. The poem recounts Parliament's resistance in the 1870s to a call for the abolition of flogging in the British Navy. In a manner reminiscent of the Battle of Waterloo, 'Parliament / Squared against the motion': the 'old school tie' mentality satirised in the poem sees the institutionalised brutality as 'No shame but a monument – / Trafalgar not better known'. Yet when the 'cat-o'nine-tails' itself is brought into the house and 'The gentry finger[ing] its stained tails', then 'quietly, unopposed, / The motion was passed'.[18] The 'stained tails' of the whip are also, in a sense, the bloodstained hands (tails) of the gentry (now between their legs). As Gifford and Roberts note, Hughes has sometimes been criticised for a 'poetry of violence', yet that 'impression' may be 'outweighed by poems that react with horror to human violence',[19] and to human suffering. Hughes's reading of Owen (as also of Douglas) marks continuities with his own aesthetic; his early war poems illuminate and critique a human capacity for political violence as telling and as discomforting as that offered by his precursors. The 'shocking directness' characteristic of Hughes's style is expressed in a diction, dense and alliterative, that bombards the reader with an extraordinary energy: in 'Bayonet Charge', we are 'dazzled with rifle fire', 'Bullets smacking the belly'; in 'Out', the poet's father is 'recovering / From the four-year mastication by gunfire and mud / Body buffeted wordless ... His memory's buried, immovable anchor / Among jaw-bones and blown-off boots, tree-stumps, shellcases and craters ...).[20]

For Hughes, the Great War landscape expands to underwrite an exploration of man's place in the world, his control over, or control by, the forces of nature. In this, he partly follows Robert Graves (from whom he is otherwise remote in style). Graves's recalling war is also a coming to terms with the experience of war through the evolution of a complex mythological belief system, outlined in *The White Goddess* in 1948. In the introduction to *The White Goddess*, he argues that that poetry was 'once a warning to man that he must keep harmony with the family of living creatures among which he was born ... [but] is now a reminder that he has disregarded the warnings, turned the house upside down by capricious experiments in philosophy, science and industry, and brought ruin on himself and his family'.[21] In a passage added to a revised edition of 1952 (the edition read by Hughes), the Cold War and the capability for destruction, evident in the atomic bombs that devastated Hiroshima and Nagasaki in 1945 and confirmed by the post-1945 development of the infinitely more powerful thermonuclear or hydrogen bomb,[22] inform a Gravesian vision that verges on the apocalyptic: 'we have come to be governed, in practice, by the unholy triumvirate of Pluto god of wealth, Apollo god of science, and Mercury god of thieves. To make matters worse, dissension and jealousy rage openly between these three, with Mercury and Pluto blackguarding each other, while Apollo wields the atomic bomb as if it were a thunderbolt'.[23]

The summer of 1914 is often perceived as a watershed, the point in history that marked the beginnings of a new, modern, ironic sensibility, or as Larkin puts it, 'Never such innocence again';[24] the brutalities of modern warfare in 1914–18 were such that they set the terms for responses to war in 1939–45, for what was not 'new'. But post-war poets drawn to the First World War write from a context where total annihilation, not simply total war, is possible, in which apocalyptic visions are scientifically achievable realities – and that *is* new. Although Hughes writes a number of poems directly about the Great War, its landscape and images spill out into other poems about nature – as if it has become as uncontainable as the forces of violence unleashed in the century that followed it. 'November' is a poem in which the war is unmentioned, but everywhere present:

> And again the rains' dragging grey columns
>
> Smudged the farms. In a moment
> The fields were jumping and smoking; the thorns
> Quivered, riddled with the glass verticals.
> [...]
> The hill where the hare crouched with clenched teeth.
> Rain plastered the land till it was shining
> Like hammered lead, and I ran ...[25]

The poem is in part derivative of Owen's 'Exposure', where 'war lasts, rain soaks' and 'Dawn ... Attacks once more in ranks on shivering ranks of grey', or of 'Spring Offensive' where 'the sky burned / With fury against them'.[26] Its language intimates the moments immediately before and during a trench-warfare attack; the tramp in the ditch is taken 'for dead'; the 'keeper's gibbet had owls and hawks / By the neck'. The war becomes more than the sum of its parts in Hughes, here less an 'instrument of policy' that must 'bear its character ... measure with its scale', as Clausewitz defined war,[27] than a life/death struggle with the 'predatory, destructive character of nature', of which man is yet still a part.[28] The sheer size of Hughes's oeuvre, and the growing epic ambition of his poem sequences, are also telling: the poet rains down death and violence, blood and dismemberment, the verbal excess of the poems encompassing both the darkness and a resistance to it, as if the language itself is a counter-blasting life force. In 'Scapegoats and Rabies', the 'dead millions' of ghost soldiers are:

> Marching in their boots, blindfold and riddled,
> Rotten heads on their singing shoulders,
> The blown-off right hand swinging to the stride
> Of the stump-scorched and blown-off legs
> Helpless in the terrible engine of the boots.[29]

Trying to explain the incommunicability of the Great War experience in language, Robert Graves observed that 'you can't communicate noise. Noise never stopped for one moment – ever'.[30] That noise is the sound of death; but to hear it is to be among the living, not the dead. If one is tempted, amidst the sometimes cacophanous verbal din of such poems by Hughes, to cry 'enough', yet to be bombarded with more, that may be part of the point.

Hughes is one of the most war-haunted of post-1945 British poets (along with Geoffrey Hill and Christopher Logue). In Ireland, the Great War is a subject which Michael Longley has, in the context of the Northern Irish 'Troubles', and in a politically fraught climate, made peculiarly his own. Like Hughes, Longley is the son of an English First World War veteran; for both, an imaginative preoccupation with the Great War informs their writing about the natural world. However the similarities really end there: at odds with Hughes's 'graphic focus', primal energies, and flaunting excess is Longley's elegiac mode and restrained style. (It is to over-simplify of course, but where Hughes reveals a considerable stylistic and thematic debt to Owen, Longley's more obvious Great War precursor, and the subject of a number of his elegies, is Edward Thomas.) Where Hughes, in 'Out', characterises his four-year-old self as his father's 'luckless double', in a poem from the mid-1960s, 'In Memoriam', Longley posits his origins, metaphorically, twenty years before his birth, in the landscape of the Great War:

> But, as it was, your proper funeral urn
> Had mercifully smashed to smithereens,
> To shrapnel shards that sliced your testicle.
> That instant I, your most unlikely son,
> In No Man's Land was surely left for dead,
> Blotted out from your far horizon.
> As your voice now is locked inside my head,
> I yet was held secure, waiting my turn.[31]

The landscape becomes, in Longley's poetry, the origin of much that follows in the twentieth century, as the historical fault lines of the Great War period continue to haunt Irish history. Yet as 'In Memoriam' makes clear, it is the private rather than public utterance here – the grief for a father 'lingering in the hall, your bowels on fire, / Tears in your eyes, and all your medals spent' – which gives the poet his elegiac voice. For Longley, as for Hughes, the Great War is an enduring legacy, one which increases in significance through his own development; but in contrast to Hughes, it does not become the archetype for a Manichean struggle between the forces of light and dark. Rather, it is a testing ground for poetry's capacity both to remember honestly and potentially to heal. As he was 'held secure' by the past, that past, it is intimated, will be 'secure' with him as a custodian of memory. At the close of 'In Memoriam', it is the poet's role 'To summon' imaginatively for his dying father the 'lost wives', 'chorus girls and countesses' of his post-war love affairs to accompany and shield him 'Underground': 'On the verge of light and happy legend / They lift their skirts like blinds across your eyes'.

That his father's 'old wounds woke / As cancer' in 'In Memoriam' resonates on other levels, too. War experience is not left behind in 1918; its survivors 'go over the ground again' – emotionally, even physically. History takes us over the ground again, too, since in Northern Ireland, 'old wounds' resurfaced in 1968 to devastating effect. In 'Wounds', one of the most powerful of all post-war Great War poems, Longley sets 'two pictures from my father's head' of the Western Front beside the deaths in Northern Ireland of 'teenage soldiers, bellies full of / Bullets and Irish beer', and a 'bus conductor' who was:

> ... shot through the head
> By a shivering boy who wandered in
> Before they could turn the television down
> Or tidy away the supper dishes.
> To the children, to a bewildered wife,
> I think 'Sorry Missus' was what he said.[32]

The 'landscape of dead buttocks' in 'Wounds' over which his father followed for 'fifty years' is a permanent condition: past and present are telescoped into a terrifying continuity. War is no longer something incomprehensible and 'elsewhere' since it encroaches on domestic, private space. So from its private, familial beginnings, the Great War has expanded, looking forwards as well as backwards, to become the direct subject of more than twenty of Longley's poems, indirectly informing many more – the elegies for Troubles victims, such as 'Wreaths'; poems about World War II and the Holocaust (as in 'Ghetto'); poems from Homer's *Iliad* (notably 'Ceasefire'). In 'Edward Thomas's Poem', he describes Thomas as 'The nature poet turned into war poet as if / He could cure death with the rub of a dock leaf'.[33] The poem qualifies ('as if') any claim that might be made for what war poetry can or cannot do, in its curative or consolatory aspirations; at the same time, the memory work these poems undertake is a means of understanding a contemporary condition, and their care and precision with language is a felt ethical responsibility as well as a stylistic trait. '[A]s Wilfred Owen stated over 50 years ago', he writes, 'it is the artist's duty to warn, to be tuned in before anyone else to the implications of a situation'.[34]

Longley, and other poets writing out of conflict, look to the Great War, and to the example set by poets in the Great War, as a means of evaluating their own role and responsibility. And they understand them differently: witness the divergent readings of Owen by Hughes, Longley or Seamus Heaney. In *The Government of the Tongue*, Heaney's reflections on song and suffering lead him to describe 'Wilfred Owen, and others like him in the trenches of Flanders' as 'among the first of a type of poet ... who looms as a kind of shadowy judging figure above every poet who has written subsequently ... [who] represents poetry's solidarity with the doomed, the deprived, the victimized, the under-privileged'.[35] Yet ultimately, he eschews the aesthetic he attributes to Owen, drawn instead to Mandelstam and the poets of Eastern bloc countries whose 'situation', he argues, 'makes them attractive to a reader whose formative experience has been largely Irish'.[36] In contrast to Longley, the Great War does not haunt Heaney's imagination. If this might seem surprising in a Troubles elegist of Heaney's calibre, it does suggest that the poetic legacy of the Great War is not separable from its political legacy in a way more readily apparent in Ireland than in England, and that an Irish (or indeed English) 'formative experience' can be infinitely variable. As John Horne noted recently:

> ... [The Great War] contributed decisively to the major turning-point of twen-tieth century Irish history, 1913–1923, which saw a polarisation and realign-ment of national and political identities that has lasted to the present. Since divergent versions of the war experience lay at the heart of those opposed identities, it is not surprising that the war's legacy should have proved so con-tested nor that Irish war experiences – North and South, male and female, military and civilian, unionist and nationalist – should so rarely be placed in a common framework.[37]

In the only poem in which he addresses the Great War directly, 'In Memoriam: Francis Ledwidge', Heaney struggles with a legacy he cannot reconcile with subsequent 'realignment[s]'. Ledwidge, the Irish Catholic nationalist poet and British army soldier killed in 1917, is for Heaney 'our dead enigma' in whom 'all the strains / Criss-cross in useless equilibrium'.[38] Competing histories converge on the poem, as on the Great War battlefields, and they get stuck there; the poem's only resolution (with an echo of Owen's 'Strange Meeting') is that both Protestant and Catholic dead 'consort now under-ground'. It is as if the legacy left by Ledwidge has become culturally unintel-ligible to a writer of Heaney's particular experience; at the same time, the poem takes on the burden of a legacy it does not understand to perform its own act of recovery.

'The doddery English veterans are getting / Fewer', Longley writes in 1994, 'and point out to fewer doddery pals / Hill Sixty, Hill Sixty-one, Poelkapelle'.[39] The last British combat veteran of the Great War died in 2011; the last survivor of trench warfare in 2009. No one now can have the privilege, or pain, of firsthand memories from the Great War shared with them, and the effect that may have on the war's legacy as it has manifested itself thus far is as yet unknown. Yet some changes are evident. In *The Great War and Modern Memory*, in 1975, Fussell writes:

> The whole texture of British daily life could be said to commemorate the war still. It is remembered in the odd pub-closing hours, one of the fruits of the Defence of the Realm Act ... The Great War persists in many of the laws controlling aliens and repressing sedition and espionage. 'D'-notices to newspapers, warning them off 'national-security matters', are another legacy. So is Summer Time. So

are such apparent universals as cigarette-smoking, the use of wristwatches [...] Egg and chips became popular during the war because both bacon and steak were scarce and costly. It ... remains a staple of public menus [...] A sign of the unique persistence of the war in England is literally a sign, above a large section of shelves in Hatchard's Bookshop, Piccadilly. I have seen nothing like it in any other country. It reads: 'Biography and War Memoirs', in recognition of a distinct and very commonly requested English genre. [...] The current economic bankruptcy of Britain is another way it remembers. From 1914 to 1918 its gold reserve diminished dramatically. The beneficiary was the United States ...[40]

Such passages now commemorate not only 1914–18, but aspects of 'British daily life' that have disappeared in the decades since the 1970s. If egg-and-chips remains popular, and the clock changes endure for practical reasons, the 'odd pub-closing hours' have gone; so too has 'cigarette smoking' as a 'universal' (it is now, indeed, a prohibited activity in public places); the sign in Hatchard's has long disappeared – no one there remembers it; media culture has been transformed since the 1990s, in large part through technological developments; the global financial situation of the last decade, and the shifts in economic power, render his argument historical too. The world Fussell describes was still relatively familiar through the 1980s, but it has become less recognisable to a generation born since then, and is now itself the stuff of nostalgia.

A number of centenaries loom in which the Great War will be commemorated by a society for whom it stands now at the same remove the 1815 Battle of Waterloo stood for its participants. That the Great War's literature will endure seems certain; whether the war will prove in the future, and for a new generation of poets, as hauntingly pervasive a 'remembered' presence in the fabric of British and Irish verse as it has been through the twentieth century may be less so. Yet as more and more images of the early twentieth century emerge, they can still, it is apparent, '[f]resh images beget'.[41] For Sinéad Morrissey in 'Electric Edwardians' (2008), a poem inspired by the 1901–6 films of Mitchell and Kenyon, the long-dead wave their handkerchiefs with a poignant immediacy from the recovered footage 'at whoever may prove their witness: / themselves, their wives, coal miners, tram conductors, / Boer War veterans ... not to mention the unthinkable yet-to-be-born, / not to mention me'.[42] It is also, in its collapse of time and space, past and future, an elegy for the not-yet-dead of the Great War:

> children linger longest in the foreground,
> shoving, lampooning, breaking the line,
> or simply staring back at us, across the lens's promise,
>
> as though we still held Passchendaele in our pockets
> and could find a way to save them.

Their fate foreshadowed in the broken 'line', the ghost children 'staring back at us' are emblematic of a century's victims, from the Great War through the Holocaust and into the present day, for whom the 'promise' of the future is broken, too. They cannot now be saved, yet insisting from beyond the grave on their presence in the 'foreground' of the mind, and stored in the poem's memory, they 'linger longest'.

NOTES

1 Vernon Scannell, 'The Great War', *Selected Poems* (London: Allison and Busby, 1971), 40.
2 Martin Stephen ed. *Poems of the First World War: 'Never Such Innocence'* (1988; London: J.M. Dent, 1993), 289.
3 Paul Fussell, *The Great War and Modern Memory* (London: Oxford University Press, 1975), 313–14. Hereafter abbreviated as *The Great War*.
4 The phrase is Edmund Blunden's. See the 'Preliminary' to *Undertones of War* (1928; London: Penguin, 1982), 8.
5 Fussell, *The Great War*, 314.
6 Keith Douglas, *The Complete Poems*, intro. Ted Hughes (Oxford: Oxford University Press, 1987), 102.
7 Fussell, *The Great War*, 321.
8 The first of these popularly begins with the publication of E.M. Remarque's *All Quiet on the Western Front*, followed by a stream of war memoirs in the late 1920s and early 1930s; the second, in the 1960s, is marked by such productions as *Oh What a Lovely War*, together with new histories and anthologies of Great War poetry; the third might be placed in the late 1990s/early 2000s, and the respective 80/90 year Armistice commemorations, the last for which any British wartime veterans were still alive.
9 Robert Graves, *Complete Poems: Vol. 2*, ed. Beryl Graves and Dunstan Ward (Manchester: Carcanet, 1997), 92.
10 See Michael Longley, 'Bog Cotton', *Collected Poems* (London: Jonathan Cape, 2009), 136.
11 Scannell, *Selected Poems*, 39–40. Although it is to speculate about numerology, the broken pentameter brings the number of lines in the poem to forty-five, marking the end of the second war, and 'terror ticks on wrists at zero hour' on line 14, the date the first war began.
12 The function of sepia in photography was to help prevent black and white images from degrading over time, as well as rendering them less stark visually.
13 Elaine Feinstein, *Ted Hughes: The Life of a Poet* (London: Weidenfeld and Nicholson, 2001), 6.
14 Quoted in Keith Sagar ed. *The Achievement of Ted Hughes* (Manchester: Manchester University Press, 1983), 10.
15 Ted Hughes, *Collected Poems*, ed. Paul Keegan (London: Faber, 2003), 45–6.
16 Ibid., 43.
17 Hughes, 'Introduction' to Keith Douglas, *Complete Poems*, p. xxvi.
18 Hughes, *Collected Poems*, 78–9.

19 Terry Gifford and Neil Roberts, *Ted Hughes: A Critical Study* (London: Faber, 1981), 13.

20 Hughes, *Collected Poems*, 43, 165.

21 Robert Graves, *The White Goddess* (London: Faber, 1948), 11–12.

22 This was tested by the United States and USSR respectively in 1952 and 1953. The hydrogen bomb worked by fusing atoms rather than by splitting them (as with the atomic bomb), and had the potential to 'make real Clausewitz's vision of a total and therefore purposeless war'. John Lewis Gaddis, *The Cold War* (London; Penguin, 2005), 61–3.

23 Robert Graves, *The White Goddess*, rev. ed. (1948; London: Faber, 1952), 468.

24 Philip Larkin, 'MCMXIV', *Collected Poems*, ed. Anthony Thwaite (London: Faber, 2003), 99.

25 Hughes, *Collected Poems*, 81–2.

26 Jon Stallworthy ed. *The Poems of Wilfred Owen* (London: Chatto & Windus, 1990), 162, 169.

27 Carl von Clausewitz, *On War* (1832) trans. J.J. Graham and ed. Anatol Rapaport (London: Penguin, 1982), 410.

28 See Gifford and Roberts, *Ted Hughes*, 14.

29 Hughes, *Collected Poems*, 187.

30 Quoted in Fussell, *The Great War*, 170.

31 Longley, *Collected Poems*, 30–1.

32 Ibid., 62.

33 Ibid., 307.

34 Michael Longley, 'Introduction', *Causeway: The Arts in Ulster* (Belfast: Arts Council of Northern Ireland; Dublin: Gill and Macmillan, 1971), 8.

35 Seamus Heaney, *The Government of the Tongue* (London: Faber, 1988), p.xvi. Heaney's affinity with Owen lies more in what he describes as Owen's 'violent assault ... upon the genteel citadel of English pastoral verse' (p.xiv), given that his very early poems, mediated by the powerful influence of Hughes, follow this line, too.

36 Ibid., p. xx.

37 John Horne, 'Introduction', *Our War* (Dublin: Royal Irish Academy/RTÉ, 2008) 14.

38 Seamus Heaney, *Field Work* (London: Faber, 1979), 59–60.

39 Longley, 'A Pat of Butter', *Collected Poems*, 224.

40 Fussell, *The Great War*, 315–7.

41 W.B. Yeats, 'Byzantium', *Collected Poems* (London: Macmillan, 1950), 281.

42 Sinéad Morrissey, *Through the Square Window* (Manchester: Carcanet, 2009), 55–6.

16

JAY WINTER

Beyond Glory: First World War Poetry and Cultural Memory

Why is it that a selection of British war poetry written during or about the 1914–18 conflict still serves, a century later, as a cultural archive of popular images and phrases associated not only with that war, but with war as such?[1] Archives are always selective, and this one is no exception. By no means was all war poetry written by trench soldiers, and by no means did all trench poetry enter the canon. But over time, a loosely-defined set of such poems took on a metonymical function; the part stood for the whole.

One reason that this small selection of soldiers' war poetry became iconic is that it struck then, as now, a popular chord. It captured a wide-spread sense, although not universally shared after the Armistice, that the war was an exercise in futility and that older languages of grandeur and glory had been recast in the light of what soldiers saw and felt during that war. That recasting is the achievement of war poetry. In effect, what the British war poets did was to clean up the English language, degraded by propaganda and civilian euphemism concerning events and cruelties most people at home could hardly imagine. War poetry brought the language of industrialized war down to earth, down to the muddy terrain of the Western Front, and thereby provided a specifically British poetic pathway beyond glory.

In no other country did the vast array of poetry produced during the war yield such a discrete body of materials which came to constitute for Britain what Jan Assmann has termed a repository of 'cultural memory'. Here is his understanding of the term: 'Cultural memory has its fixed point; its horizon does not change with the passing of time. These fixed points are fateful events of the past, whose memory is maintained through cultural formation (texts, rites, monuments) and institutional communication (recitation, practice, observance). We call these "figures of memory."'[2] In countless cities, villages and towns in Britain and Northern Ireland, such 'recitation, practice and observance' time and again has linked the words of the war poets with public remembrance of the Great War. It is in this sense that we can speak of a body of poetry written by soldiers of the Great War as having provided a kind of 'cultural memory', a timeless register of terms and images through which later generations still frame their understanding of the 1914–18 war and its aftermath.

Why then is there voluminous poetry about the 1914–18 conflict scattered throughout the world, but 'war poetry', understood as a compound noun, a discrete corpus of writing, only in Britain? A journey across the Irish Sea may offer some hint of an answer to this question.

In 1936, William Butler Yeats explained the omission of the poetry of Wilfred Owen from his *Oxford Book of Modern Verse* in these terms:

> I have a distaste for certain poems written in the midst of the great war; … The writers of these poems were invariably officers of exceptional courage and capacity, one a man constantly selected for dangerous work, all, I think, had the Military Cross; their letters are vivid and humorous, they were not without joy – for all skill is joyful – but felt bound, in the words of the best known, to plead the suffering of their men. In poems that had for a time considerable fame, written in the first person, they made that suffering their own. I have rejected these poems for the same reason that made Arnold withdraw his "Empedocles on Etna" from circulation; passive suffering is not a theme for poetry. In all the great tragedies, tragedy is a joy to the man who dies; in Greece the tragic chorus danced.[3]

When he learned that some were shocked at the exclusion, he elaborated on his Olympian disdain for Owen, calling him 'all blood, dirt & sucked sugar stick' and judging him to be 'unworthy of the poets' corner of a country newspaper'. He famously concluded: 'There is every excuse for him but none for those who like him'.[4] I want to suggest that the 'excuse' for him and for those who admired him in Britain was that Owen's work operated within a linguistic grammar and register of emotion different from that of Yeats and many other writers in Ireland and on the continent. This is not to say that there was only one voice in which either Yeats or other Irish poets spoke on this subject; it is rather that the shadings of meaning read into war differed in Ireland and in Britain, for the simple reason that their histories diverged in important ways. The same is true of French writers. The point here is to highlight what was particularly British by stepping outside of its literary and historical boundaries.[5] When we do so, we can see that the British register of what came early on to be termed 'war poetry' moved 'beyond glory', or in Yeats's language, beyond the 'tragic joy' he believed to be at the heart of poetry.[6] 'Tragic joy' was not the register of Owen or of much of British war poetry, because life in the trenches had blown such notions to pieces.

Yeats' choice highlights the character of much of British poetry of the Great War and the reasons why a socially constructed corpus of work became central to the way later generations in Britain have imagined the 1914–18 conflict. The war poets pointed to a way beyond glory, at the very moment the word had lost its purchase in describing the fate and fortune of the men who had fought in the Great War. That was their achievement, and the reason their work has had such resonance among generations of readers.

The significance of this poetic archive of the war is independent of the representative character of the writers or of their views. Much ink has been spilled unnecessarily in challenging the view of the war poets' words as misleading in constructing the way 'ordinary soldiers' saw the war.[7] Skeptics argue that Owen and company did not share the working-class attitudes of the overwhelming mass of soldiers who served in the ranks. Such men, they hold, had lived difficult lives, and living in a ditch in Flanders was not fundamentally different from living in urban or rural poverty before 1914. They were proud of their war service, and did not shrink from boasting about it. Whether or not these claims are true is beside the point. What matters is that the words of the war poets reverberated; and millions of readers have been drawn to their work, still in print long after the Armistice. What the Germans term *Rezeptionsgeschichte* matters.[8] Cultural archives are selective by nature; inclusion and exclusion are arbitrary. And unlike the 'Auden generation'[9] or artistic circles like the Fauves or the impressionists, many war poets died before they could have had a say about being placed in a group of fellow soldier-writers. That the British war poets have entered the English-language cultural archive is indisputable. The question remains why there and not elsewhere?

One answer is that the British war poets spoke a certain kind of English, a poetic language which was precisely that – English, rather than French or German or Irish or American English. In this part of his work, Yeats, who after all wrote his own war poetry and spent a good deal of the war in London, nonetheless inhabited a poetic and literary space closer to that found in France than to that found in Britain during and after the war.[10] Many Irish and French writers still saw 'glory' in war, in part because both adapted a revolutionary rhetoric to the issues of the day, and in part because Roman Catholicism kept the notion of 'glory' alive among communicants and freethinkers alike in both civil war Ireland and Republican France. When Yeats wrote of the men of the 1916 insurrection, he claimed that 'a terrible beauty is born'. In doing so, he was speaking out of a romantic tradition of nineteenth-century insurrections not only in Ireland, but also in France. Here is Victor Hugo's paean to glory in his 1831 poem 'Chants du crépuscule', honoring those who died in the revolution of the previous year:

> Ceux qui pieusement sont morts pour la patrie
> Ont droit qu'à leur cerceuil la foule vienne et prie.

Entre les plus beaux noms leur nom est le plus beau.
Toute gloire près d'eux passe et tombe éphémère;
Et, comme ferait une mère,
La voix d'un peuple entier les berce en leur tombeau.[11]

Those who piously have died for their country
Have earned the right that the masses come to their tomb and pray.
Among the most beautiful names, theirs is the most beautiful.
Alongside them, all other forms of glory pass and fade away;
And, as a mother would do,
The voice of the people as a whole rocks their cradle.

That revolutionary language had little resonance in Britain, nor did the Catholic romanticism of Patrick Pearse and his brethren. War poetry in England had the room to move beyond glory because British political, religious, military and literary traditions created an entirely different cultural environment out of which poetic and prose reflections of the Great War emerged.

Let me add some statistical evidence in support of my argument about British attitudes toward and reference to 'glory'. Together with a consortium of universities, Google has created a unique statistical database, composed of 6,000,000 books produced between 1800 and 2000, every page of which has been scanned in machine-readable form. We can search these two-billion words easily, through Google N-grams, or graphs, where N means the number of occurrences in print of a particular word in a particular year. User-friendly software enables us to compare the frequency of the use of different words over time in a very large corpus of published books.[12] I present two comparisons: one for the word '*gloire*' in French over the period 1900–30, and a second for the word 'glory' in British English books over the same period. The upward inflection in the recourse to '*gloire*' contrasts strikingly with the slow decline in the use of the word 'glory' in British English. In the second set of graphs, the contrasts show the same pattern, although set against the years 1900–2000. The peak of '*gloire*' in French in the whole of the twentieth century is during the Great War; in contrast, 'glory' in British English has declined in virtually a linear fashion from the Victorian years to the present. To be sure, the presence of a word in a book does not describe its weight or its significance, but these data are consistent with my argument that language patterns vary over time and in different linguistic spaces, and so do the way different languages encode widely disseminated messages both about war in general and about the Great War in particular (see Figures 11–14). In a nutshell, language frames memory.

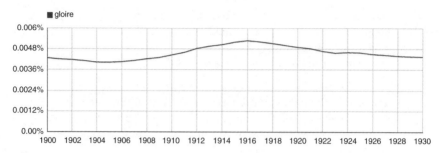

Figure 11 Google N-gram of the word 'gloire' in French 1900–1930

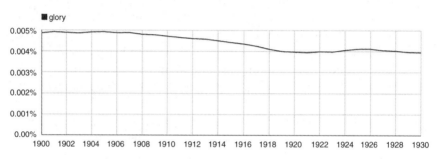

Figure 12 Google N-gram of the word 'glory' in British English 1900–1930.

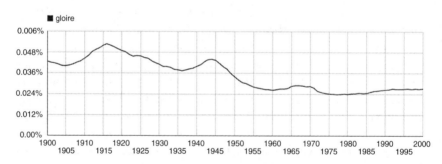

Figure 13 Google N-gram of the word 'gloire' in French 1900–2000.

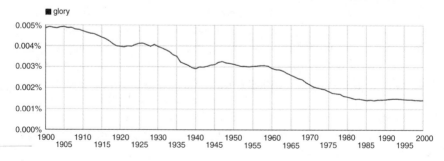

Figure 14 Google N-gram of the word 'glory' in British English 1900–2000.

My argument, then, is that the war poets created a new non-glorious lexicon about war. The ground had been prepared for them to do so. 'Glory be to God for dappled things', wrote Gerard Manley Hopkins in 1883. The word 'glory' almost always operates in a sacred register. The war poets took the language of the Bible and turned it to new uses in their meditations on war. They did not turn away from Scripture, or from romantic tropes, but refashioned them in order to frame an angry indictment of those who let the war go on.[13]

In 1914, the King James Version of the Bible was imbedded in the British vernacular. It had no equivalent in France, and only a family resemblance to Luther's German translation of the Bible. Soaring over the contested terrain of the English reformation and the Civil War, it trumpeted, with Shakespeare, the unique cadences of British English.

Nothing like the King James Version exists in France, where a divided nation shared two robust yet contradictory traditions – the Catholic and the French Revolutionary tradition. Each had its own rhetorical life in nineteenth-century France, and each had its own version of glory at its core. In contrast, by 1900, despite pride in the empire, and the literature of the Raj, glory was becoming an outmoded, even an archaic, word in England, conjuring up martial images, to be sure: those of Crispin Crispian's day in *Henry V*, of Gloriana, the first Elizabeth, and the Glorious Revolution. All once glorious perhaps, but hardly the signature (outside of Protestant Ireland) of a trading nation without a standing army, and whose powerful navy had the great advantage of doing her work at sea and abroad. Perhaps the Crimean War had knocked the stuffing out of the word 'glory', despite Tennyson's six hundred; the first war photographs and reports of the shocking sanitary conditions of army encampments in *The Times* trampled on notions of 'glory', as did much of Kipling's words about Tommy Atkins. There were many words one could use about the Boer War of 1899–1902, but glory or glorious is not one of them, except in the gentle mockery of Gilbert and Sullivan about who was or was not an Englishman. In the Edwardian period, conscription was the mad dream of a small group of conservatives, and military service in no way constituted a pillar of citizenship, as it did in France. When Elgar and Benson wrote 'Land of Hope and Glory' in 1902, they were trying to revive a set of images and impulses slowly but surely fading away.

The glacial character of the slow-moving history of the two countries lay behind the fact that the French word '*Gloire*' is not in any meaningful sense the equivalent of the English word 'Glory'. In 1914, the two words carried different associations and had very different echoes. True, the Royal anthem spoke of the King as 'happy and glorious', but I suspect that that choice of words arose out of finding a suitable partner to 'victorious'. In addition, church rhetoric was fading as political rhetoric grew in Britain. There was in late-Victorian and Edwardian Britain a movement away from church atten-dance which caused the Anglican Church no end of worry. There was a similar decline in the number of parishioners taking mass in France every Sunday; but in Britain, the language of politics was less and less about reli-gious sentiment and more about social class.[14] The Dreyfus affair – when most Catholics defended the Army and most Republicans defended an inno-cent man who was unjustly convicted of treason – ensured that Catholicism and Republican values remained at war until 1914.

These subtle cultural differences may help us to account for the fact that although there is a substantial corpus of poetic works written by French soldiers during and after the war, there is no such thing as a group of 'war poets'. Fighting on French soil, French writers remained within the orbit of glory. Some British poets went beyond it.

In the tradition of Reinhard Koselleck and *Begriffsgeschichte*, or the his-tory of concepts,[15] I will stake my claim that 'glory' and '*gloire*' operate in different semantic systems, redolent with images and emotions arising out of different revolutionary and religious contexts. The literary and mental fur-niture British soldiers brought with them to the Front was not the same as that carried by French or German soldiers. True enough, British soldiers had a reservoir of swashbuckling tales of imperial conflict from which to draw, and many could recite Kipling's verse 'though I've belted you and flayed you, by the living God that made you, you're a better man than I am Gunga Din'. However, the Raj was a long way from the Somme and Passchendaele; 'glory' was the stuff of other times, other places, other nations, with other histories and other sacred texts.

The war poets saw the worst of the war, and that was on the Western Front between 1915 and 1918 and at Gallipoli in 1915. It is important to note a slow and uneven evolution of trench poetry, from that written during its first year to that reflecting the great offensives of 1916–18. The poetry of Rupert Brooke, Julian Grenfell and Patrick Shaw Stewart antedated the failed attempts in the last two bloody years of the war to break through German lines in Picardy and in Flanders. Shaw Stewart helped bury Brooke on Skyros, and wrote 'Stand in the Trench, Achilles', a phrase harder to swallow on the Western Front, which formed the setting for much of the work of the later war poets – Owen, Sassoon, Rosenberg, Gurney.

This development from early to later war poetry is not uniform; language does not march in step over time. And yet, with some notable exceptions, it is apparent that 'glory' got a bad name during the war, and British war poetry was in part responsible for that. Yes, Brooke's 'The Dead' is a coun-ter-example. His verse is unambiguous: 'He leaves a white/Unbroken glory, a gathered radiance'. In contrast, Julian Grenfell does not use the word 'glory' even once in 'Into Battle', where we would expect such a word. He praises 'courageous hearts', 'nobler powers', the 'joy of battle', but not glory. The word is absent in Hardy's 'Men Who March Away'.[16] Owen uses the word 'glory' several times, perhaps most memorably in 'Dulce Et Decorum Est'. We all know his appeal 'To children ardent for some desperate glory', to turn away from the old lie and to stare at the ugliness of war. Less celebrated, but equally powerful, is his account in 'Smile, Smile, Smile', of the reaction of 'half-limbed men' reading a press report from Westminster, where, Owen imagines, they say: '"We rulers sitting in this ancient spot / Would wrong our very selves if we forgot / The greatest glory will be theirs who fought"'. Reading this nonsense, disabled men 'smiled at one another curiously / Like secret men who know their secret safe'. And yet, Owen also wrote in 'Apologia Pro Poemate Meo' of the faces of dying men. 'War brought more glory to their eyes than blood / And gave their laughs more glee than shakes a child'. But, Owen insists, theirs was a private language, beyond the rest of us:

> ... except you share
> With them in hell the sorrowful dark of hell,
> Whose world is but a trembling of a flare
> And heaven but a highway for a shell,
>
> You shall not hear their mirth:
> You shall not come to think them well content
> By any jest of mine. These men are worth
> Your tears: You are not worth their merriment.[17]

In a misogynistic vein, Sassoon wrote that women were not worth their merriment, either. In 'Glory of Women', he scoffed: '... you believe / That chivalry redeems the war's disgrace' and need to keep notions of heroism alive, without the slightest inkling of what a dismembered corpse smelled like.[18] Glory was not imbedded in war; it lived, if at all, only in the fellowship of those who suffered together, and who shared the horrors of combat.[19] War poetry was a language of bereavement and of separation, from the dead and from an older, archaic language of glory in the process of fading away.

This move beyond 'glory' in war poetry marks a boundary between British and continental poetic responses not only to the Great War, but to other wars. In France twenty years later, there was Resistance poetry, which had a collective character, in part arising out of the strength of the Communist party and the role it played in the *Maquis*. But in 1914–18, even when the invasion of France gave every reason for Frenchmen to view the war as a calamity inflicted on them by Germany, there still was no outburst of soldiers' poetry which turned into a collective body of work.

Part of the reason is that dissent was much more muted in France than in Britain. With military service as the price of citizenship from 1848 on, refusal to serve was tantamount to betraying the sovereign people. Not so in Protestant Britain, where the strength of the call to arms in 1914 and 1915 was that it was voluntary. And when the need for men made conscription necessary, provision was made for those who could not in conscience bear arms and take the lives of other men. Here, too, we find a distinct contrast between British and French military practices and traditions. In France, the notion of conscientious objection was virtually unknown in 1914, and remained so throughout the century. In Britain, the dissenting tradition was robust, and in both world wars, objections on grounds of conscience were duly recognized in law when they arose from undisputable transcendental or clear religious convictions.

The war poets were dissenters in another sense – one which arose out of moral considerations rather than religious ones. In a secularizing nation, the war poets reconfigured conscience outside of conventional faith. Their secular beliefs and their eyes led them to indict the war and the men who allowed it to go on for fifty bloody months.

It is important to note that the war poets were not pacifists; if they had been, they would not have been in uniform. Their active service gave them the moral authority to denounce that war and the suffering it caused. Their references to shell shock are part of their dissenting legacy. A war which, by its very industrialized nature, drove perfectly sane men mad was one which had redefined what bravery and honor meant. A new 'anatomy of courage', in the words of Charles Moran, had to be composed, and the war poets did so, bearing in mind the faces of those 'whose minds the Dead have ravaged', in Wilfred Owen's phrase. War poetry helped introduce the term 'shell shock' into the lexicon of war, where it remains to this day. Not so elsewhere. Iconic language is language which finds a niche in the vernacular. What better instance of this is there than the British war poets' reference to the awkward, puzzling, frightening and stigmatized category of psychological injury in war? Revealingly, there is no equivalent French poetic or other literary response to the recognized medical category of *choc traumatique* in France. Once more, we see how important it is to place poetry in a wider cultural framework in order to understand its meaning and its echoes.

It is also important to repeat the injunction that Owen, Sassoon, Gurney and Rosenberg did not write as a group. Furthermore, none of the war poets had the slightest idea they were writing canonical texts; that was not the way they were written, but it is the way they have been read, taught, mastered, set to music and passed on to younger generations. Even in the twenty-first century, after every single soldier who fought in the war had died, the war poets still are quintessentially English figures. They are indeed among Assmann's 'figures of memory': the sentinels of the two-minute silence of Armistice Day. They seem to stand guard over the nation's acknowledgment, or active knowledge, its re-cognition, its eternal return to and remembrance of the catastrophe of 1914–18.

One puzzling question is why the Second World War did not produce its own company of British war poets? There were those who wrote poetry of great power and technical skill, but the collective 'war poets' we have described emerging out of 1914–18 has no British analogue for the Second World War. One explanation is that poetry is a form of commemoration, and British commemoration after 1939 suffered from a particular problem. First World War writing and commemorative sculpture was bathed in the language of never again; those who gave their lives did so in order that their children would not have to do so in their turn. And then Hitler made 'never again' vanish into thin air. 'Never' lasted twenty-one years, and thereafter, war casualties were heavier among civilians in Britain than in the military, at least until D-Day in 1944.

This sense of a disappointed anti-war spirit may help us understand why Second World War commemoration, and English poetry within it, returned to the Great War poets. Therefore, it was perfectly natural that when Benjamin Britten, a pacifist composer, wrote his *War Requiem* for the re-consecration of Coventry Cathedral in 1962, he turned to the poetry of Wilfred Owen to complement and renew sacred texts. In the midst of *Requiem aeternum*, right at the start, we hear a tenor rendering 'What passing bells for these who die as cattle? /Only the monstrous anger of the guns'. Then in the *Dies irae*, the baritone recites: 'Bugles sang, saddening the evening air; / And bugles answered, sorrowful to hear'. In the *Offertorium*, we find Owen's Abraham, whose hand was not stayed by an angel, 'but slew his son, and half the seed of Europe one by one'. In the *Libera me* we hear Owen's 'Strange Meeting' with 'the man he killed'. This braiding together of the Latin *Missa pro defunctis* with fragments of Owen's poetry was not only extraordinarily powerful, but it gave a new impulse to the afterlife of the 'war poets', just in time for the run-up to the fiftieth anniversary of the outbreak of war in 1914, a moment from which a new 'memory boom' devoted to the Great War was about to take off.[20]

On Armistice Day 1985, a plaque was placed in Poets' Corner in Westminster Abbey to sixteen men who wrote war poetry about and during the Great War (Figure 15).[21] What better representation is there of the canonization of the war poets? School curricula have ensured that the younger

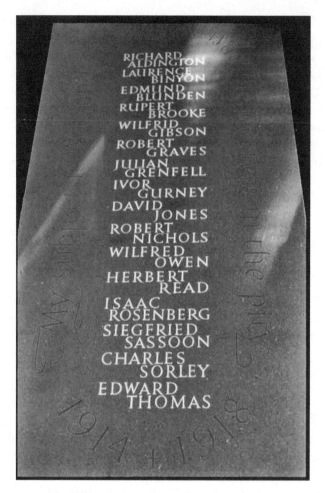

Figure 15   The War Poets at the Poets' Corner, Westminster Abbey,
London. Personal photograph.

generation has the chance to be exposed to this 'cultural archive' of the
nation's past. In 2012, one of the four awarding bodies responsible for the
advanced-level course in English literature offered students 'World War One
literature' as one of four options from which they could choose for the
examination.[22] Web sites of sixth-form colleges present syllabi and reading
materials for those who make this choice.[23] Many similar instances can be
cited. To be sure, a common education may be a body of learning we have all
forgotten over time. However, it is the music of the words, the cadences of
the poems, which linger – at times subliminally, at times with direct effect –
long after school days. Those sounds and gestures, half remembered, half
forgotten, help us to see how deeply imbedded the poetry of the Great War

is in the ways substantial numbers of men and women think about their country's past.

In conclusion, it may be useful to tie some of these threads together and to speculate yet again on the peculiarities of the English. One explanation for the English *Sonderweg* is the extent to which the classics and literature dominated elite education in the period prior to the Great War. Rhetoric, usually classical rhetoric, was more central to the curricula of the public schools of England than to the great *Lycées* of France or the *Gymnasia* of Germany. In France, the Third Republic added geography and history as focal points of the school curricula, and thereby lessened the time and space left for the classics. In Germany, the sciences had a position in the school curricula and in university life that was superior to that of her competitors'.

However, there is a more directly political matter which may have been decisive. The outcome of the war and its staggering human costs left deeper and more lingering doubts in Britain as to the meaning of victory. Frenchmen and women had little doubt as to the justice and necessity of expelling from their land an invading army which treated the captive population the way all invading armies had done before. The meaning of victory was less troubling too in parts of the dominions. Soldiers who had fought for Australia and Canada by fighting for Britain retained their laurels as the founding fathers of their allied, although more fully independent, nations. Among defeated countries, the meaning of the war was hardly ambiguous. Two million German soldiers had died for nothing; the same was true for one million men who died while serving the Austro-Hungarian monarchy. Italian nationalists were outraged at their treatment at Versailles, where, despite the loss of 600,000 men, their territorial ambitions were thwarted. In other cases, as in post-Ottoman Turkey, defeat led to a heroic new lease on national life.

Only in Britain did the debate about what the war had achieved stimulate such ambivalent attitudes. To Ted Hughes, the war was a defeat around whose neck someone hung a victory medal. The shock of war losses was so severe that the notion of a Pyrrhic victory made sense. No nation could survive another such episode in gallant sacrifice. And once the early economic troubles of the 1920s turned into the interwar depression, once the brotherhood of arms turned into the embitterment of the General Strike of 1926, then what possible benefit the British people had gained from their victory became a question without an answer. War poetry expressed this ambivalence. It was proud, elegiac, angry and dedicated to protecting from trivialization the memory of men pushed beyond the limits of human endurance in a war which placed metal against men and assured that the men would lose. It offered a semi-sacred epitaph to the Lost Generation, and offered it up to the nation not only as a memorial, but as a powerful if vague explanation of why Britain, once a great power, had become a country with a great future behind it. War poetry was pessimistic history, nostalgic history, elegiac history – written in a language which has endured. It is in no sense the only register in which images of war have been passed on from generation to generation, but it is there, still. It has provided generations of schoolchildren with a language for family history, their family's history, a history of pride and of wounds – wounds which have never healed. It is to war poetry that we must turn to understand why commemorating the Great War in 2014, a century after the outbreak of the conflict, still has a taste as of ashes to it.[24]

NOTES

1 The terms 'British war poetry' and 'British war poets' are here used to refer primarily, although not exclusively, to popular 'English' war poetry and the 'English' war poets. I retain the term 'British' to indicate the mixed ancestry of poets such as Sorley, Owen, Thomas, Rosenberg and Sassoon and their conflicted relation to 'Englishness', as discussed in the 'Introduction', 25–26. However, 'British war poetry' is here used, as in popular cultural perception, to indicate a largely English tradition, distinct from Irish war poetry which, as I discuss, has a different trajectory indeed from Welsh or Scottish war poetry.

2 Jan Assmann and John Czaplicka, 'Collective Memory and Cultural Identity', *New German Critique*, 65 (Spring–Summer, 1995), 125–33.

3 W.B. Yeats ed. *Oxford Book of Modern Verse* (Oxford: Oxford University Press, 1936), xxxiv.

4 *Letters on Poetry from W.B. Yeats to Dorothy Wellesley* (London: Oxford University Press, 1940), 113.

5 Thanks are owed to Sarah Cole for her comments here and elsewhere.

6 Roy Foster, *W.B. Yeats. A Life. The Arch-Poet*, ii (Oxford: Oxford University Press, 2003), 555–8.

7 Corelli Barnett, 'A military historian's view of the Great War', in *Essays by Diverse Hands. The Journal of the Royal Society of Literature* cvi, 3 (1978), 1–30.

8 Gunter Grimm, *Rezeptionsgeschichte: Grundlegung einer Theorie: mit Analysen und Bibliographie* (München: W. Fink, c1977).

9 Samuel Hynes, *The Auden Generation: British Writing in the 1930s* (London: Penguin, 1988).

10 I am grateful to Nicholas Allen for his advice on this point. See his *Modernism, Ireland and Civil War* (Cambridge: Cambridge University Press, 2009).

11 Victor Hugo, *Œuvres complètes: Les Feuilles d'automne. Les Chants du crépuscule. Les Voix intérieures. Les Rayons et les Ombres* (Paris: Ollendorf, 1909), vol. 17, 203–4.

12 Jean-Baptiste Michel, et al., 'Quantitative analysis of culture using millions of digitized books', *Science*, 331 (2011), 176ff.

13 Jay Winter, *Sites of Memory, Sites of Mourning: The Great War in European Cultural History* (Cambridge: Cambridge University Press, 1995), chapter 8.

14 Gareth Stedman Jones, *Languages of Class: Studies in English Working Class History, 1832–1982* (Cambridge: Cambridge University Press, 1983).

15 Reinhart Koselleck ed. *Historische Semantik und Begriffsgeschichte* (Stuttgart: Klett-Cotta, 1979).

16 Ian Parsons ed. *Men Who March Away: Poems of the First World War* (London: Heinemann, 1965), 164, 38–9, 33.

17 Jon Stallworthy ed. *The Poems of Wilfred Owen* (London: Chatto and Windus, 1990), 117, 167, 101–2.

18 Ibid., 97.

19 Thanks are owed to Santanu Das for his suggestions on this point.

20 Jay Winter, *Remembering War: The Great War between Memory and History in the 20th Century* (New Haven, CT: Yale University Press, 2006).

21 In alphabetical order: Richard Aldington, Laurence Binyon, Edmund Blunden, Rupert Brooke, Wilfrid Gibson, Robert Graves, Julian Grenfell, Ivor Gurney, David Jones, Robert Nichols, Wilfred Owen, Herbert Read, Isaac Rosenberg, Siegfried Sassoon, Charles Sorley and Edward Thomas.

22 January 2012 1741/2741 English Literature A (AS and A2), http://www.aqa.org.uk/qualifications/a-level/english/english-literature-a.php.

23 Just one instance among many:http://www.tomlinscote.surrey.sch.uk/documents/6thFormCoursesBooklet-Sept2012.pdf.

24 As, at long last, it finally does in Ireland. See Sebastian Barry, *On Canaan's Side* (London: Penguin, 2011); John Horne ed. *Our War* (Dublin: Royal Irish Academy, 2010).

MICHAEL LONGLEY, ANDREW MOTION AND JON STALLWORTHY

WAR POETRY: A CONVERSATION

Edited By Santanu Das

SD: 'We must go over the ground again' (Blunden). What has been drawing you to that 'ground' for so many years?

ML: My father's central, really, to my preoccupation with the First World War. He joined the London-Scottish Regiment in September 1914 and miraculously survived the war. He was wounded at High Wood. He died before I was twenty. So I've always regretted not talking to him more and, in a sense, my own urge to write about the Great War is ... I simply want to go on talking to my father. In my late teens and early twenties, a number of things came together: a growing admiration for the poems of Owen, Sassoon and Rosenberg which I'd first encountered at school; then my father's distinguished service in the Great War (he was awarded a Military Cross for gallantry and became a Captain by the time he was twenty); then discovering the glorious songs from the trenches (Seamus Heaney loaned me a recording of Joan Littlewood's *Oh, What A Lovely War!*). At Trinity College Dublin, at the beginning of my relationship with Edna [the literary critic Edna Longley], we treasured the little blue Faber hardback of Edward Thomas's poems. For decades, Edna has been profoundly engaged with Thomas. He now haunts our lives, an illuminating ghost. We have travelled to his grave in Agny twice and we have visited his three Hampshire homes. Over the years, I have written seven or eight poems about Thomas, footnotes to Edna's monumental annotated edition of his *Collected Poems* (2008). I also remember as a student a handsome Chatto and Windus *Collected Poems* of Wilfred Owen (1963) edited by Cecil Day Lewis. For me the work produced by the war poets is an inexhaustible well. And that's why I keep returning to it, not only as a reader, but also as a pilgrim to the battlefields and cemeteries of northern France. We last visited the war graves in 2010, along with Isaac Rosenberg's nephew and Edmund Blunden's daughter. At Rosenberg's grave I read to a group of fellow pilgrims 'Dead Man's Dump' and found myself saying that it was one of the greatest poems I knew – like a chorus from Aeschylus or Sophocles. I now believe that's true. I feel the same about Owen's 'Insensibility' and 'Exposure'. My reading of the poem was followed by this epiphany: out of the bus window I watched Rosenberg's nephew kneeling by his uncle's grave and placing a pebble on the headstone. The Great War keeps generating epiphanies like that.

JS: I had an uncle who was killed at Gallipoli, and a cousin of his who was wounded there. So my first visit to that ground was for personal reasons. At school – in the 1940s – our lives were soaked in the First World War. Of the masters who taught me, one had lost half his face in the trenches and was a terrible sight. Another had a steel plate in his head. Every Armistice Day, sun or rain, we had the Armistice Service in front of a tall stone school cross engraved with eighty-three names of boys and masters killed in the First World War. But of course, that was when another war was on, so I grew up with the radio. The airwaves were clogged with news of war. And at school, almost every week, someone's mother would come wearing black clothes. So for me, there was the entirely subjective First World War from my schooldays, and then as I began to grow up, the first poem I remember writing was a bad ballad about a British pilot shooting down a Japanese Zero fighter plane.

AM: I came to this through my grandfather's involvement – my grandfather fought in Palestine from 1915 until 1917 and then went to France and ended the war fighting in France, with never a scratch on his body. And also through my father's involvement: he enlisted in 1944, landed on Gold Beach in Normandy on D-Day, fought through France and Germany until the end of the war, then stayed in the Territorials until the mid-1960s. But while a lot of my early memories of him are memories in which he's wearing a uniform, he very rarely spoke about his experiences as a soldier. In fact, his silence on the subject was a powerful kind of presence – until the end of his life, when he began speaking a little more freely. His memories were all there, intact. Like the little plastic folder he'd been given on D-Day, with a phrasebook and a map in it, that he kept in his desk until the last ... So yes, that was one way into my thinking about the war. The other was reading the war poets at school, in my teenage years. I came from a very un-bookish background, and these poems were crucial for me. I suspect the same is true for a lot of people – maybe boys especially. For good and for ill, they shaped my idea of what all war poetry could and should be like. My ideas have modified a good deal since then, of course.

SD: What then is 'war poetry'? When does a poem become a 'war poem'? Are there particular pressures in writing war poetry?

ML: First of all, it has to be a *good* poem. Tens, hundreds, thousands of poems were written in 1914–18, and most of them are ghastly. So that's the first thing, really.

JS: Yes, more than 2,000 poets – most of them were hopeless. I think we make too much of some of the minor poets of the First World War because they were fine courageous people. But not all their poems are as good. Many are less good than those of the underrated poets of the Second World War.

AM: Sure, I agree, although for a lot of people, war poetry remains, essentially, First World War poetry. It's about trench fighting, it's the reversal of the pastoral tradition in which the old comforts of beautiful landscape, birdsong, poppies, flowers are found to have lost their consoling powers. Second World War poetry, by contrast, tends to be broader in its types and varieties – and is often not about fighting itself, but about being frightened, or displaced, or bored. It's perhaps too neat a way of putting it, but for me, these differences are well-summarised by the difference between 'I parried; but my hands were loath and cold' in Owen's 'Strange Meeting', and 'Now in my dial of glass appears/ the soldier who is going to die' in Douglas's 'How to Kill'. One is hand-to-hand – and the other is detached. Like Michael, Edward Thomas has been very important to me, as a way of understanding what these differences might be (I wrote my graduate thesis on his work in the 1970s, and subsequently published it as a book). Even though Thomas wrote all his poems wearing a uniform, he wrote next-to-nothing in France – and has consequently loosened-up my idea of what war poetry can be. I imagine that, as life goes on, other kinds of loosening will occur too, because our experience of war changes as time passes – as combatants and non-combatants (as non-combatants because we read about it all the time, see it on telly, and so on). There are dangers associated with this I think, from a writer's point of view. I mean, there's a temptation to aggrandise yourself by associating with an extreme subject; a danger that you'll end up parading your sensitivity.

JS: Well, remember the most unpopular poem in American poetry written during the Vietnam War – by Anthony Hecht:

> Here lies fierce Strephon, whose poetic rage
> Lashed out on Vietnam from page and stage;
> Whereby from basements of Bohemia he
> Rose to the lofts of sweet celebrity,
> Being, by Fortune, (our Eternal Whore)
> One of the few to profit by that war
> A fate he shared – it bears much thinking on –
> With certain persons at the Pentagon.[1]

An awful lot of those poets stayed comfortably at home and made a great deal of money. Poems about bullets whacking through the thatch, written in flats in Harvard and Princeton, seem to me obscene, in a way.

I think the term 'war poetry' may have outrun its use. War poetry, as you extend it, generation by generation, now includes the Home Front, and women, and very rightly, but it used to mean a poem about combat. It can no longer do only that. It's become so elastic now that I think one has to use it in sort of quotation marks.

ML: Well, the example of Edward Thomas means one uses the term without quotation marks, because he wrote all his poems in England. If the cosmos of a poem is the Great War, then that's it. And it doesn't matter if it's a woman writing, or Edward Thomas writing in England. War turns everything upside down, and redefines poetry. The quality of the best poems continued through from 1914–18 to Keith Douglas in the Second World War.

JS: Absolutely. And I think Edward Thomas is a particularly interesting case because his are intensely, beautifully made, very moving poems by someone who hasn't even seen a trench. But he's aware of what the war is doing to England, and the pastoral world that he so loves. And I think you can translate that experience into the American experience in Vietnam, where there are some poets who wrote very movingly about what the war was doing to *America*, which they knew about, rather than the bullet whacking through the thatch, which they didn't know about.

AM: That's absolutely it. There are two things to add perhaps – to be specific. One is that time needs to pass, and things need to mulch down. And the other is that poems often benefit from approaching their subject through the side door or the back door or the roof, and not through the front door.

JS: Not full-frontal, yes, I agree. It seems to me that to write well about a war that you've only seen on the television, or read about in the newspapers, there has to be a sort of subjective way in. When you're thinking about the great war poems, by people who never saw a battle – for example, 'The Charge of the Light Brigade' – it's because Tennyson had spent his life thinking about chivalry, men on horseback, charging, that the story of the charge of the Light Brigade was an extension of an Arthurian story. What flows into it is all he's been reading and imagining for years. And similarly, Hardy's 'Drummer Hodge':

> Young Hodge the drummer never knew –
> Fresh from his Wessex home –
> The meaning of the broad Karoo,
> The Bush, the dusty loam,

And why uprose to nightly view
Strange stars amid the gloom.[2]

Hardy cycled down to Southampton to see the troops leaving for South Africa, and he'd spent his life thinking about Wessex, and countrymen like young Hodge, and home and so he was able to identify with Hodge as Tennyson with the soldiers of the Light Brigade. It's very hard to do that, and to write a poem as good as these, unless you have that sort of personal connection.

AM: There's got to be that engine, hasn't there? For you, Michael, it's your Dad; for you, Jon, it's your relatives – and for me, it's my Dad. That's how it works. In my own poems about war, I've tried to use this personal element as a way of preventing myself from grandstanding. And by doing something else as well. By writing poems that collaborate with soldiers and others; by writing 'found' poems. 'The Five Acts of Harry Patch' (2008) is a good example. I used some of Harry's own words, wrote my own, and listened to my father's heartbeat.

ML: A bad poem is a big enough offence, but a bad poem about the suffering of one's fellow citizens really is a sin against the light. Like other Irish poets I have approached the Troubles obliquely – and still do. I dislike the notion that the Troubles might be subject matter for art, or that art might provide solace for those damaged by the violence. Having said that, I would like to add that I have received from people bereaved in the Troubles some warm letters in response to my elegies. When my elegy 'The Ice-cream Man' was first published, I received a letter of thanks signed 'Loretta Larmour, the Ice-cream Man's Mother'. That alone makes the poetic enterprise seem worthwhile.

SD: **War poetry, it is often alleged, is too weighted towards war and politics. How important is the role of aesthetic form to war poetry?**

JS: There are those who know that war's a confusing experience and think that if you're going to write about it, you have to have a confusing form – and that I think is nonsense. Someone like Owen or Blunden used form which is what people of that time expected if they read a poem, and then they gave it a violent twist. They set up a sort of lyric pastoral expectation, but then delivered a shocking sting in the poem's tail.

AM: Completely right. First World War poetry is literary, however visceral it might also be. Literary because the people writing it had the sort of the education that was beginning to diminish by the time the Second World War started. Metaphorically and sometimes actually, soldiers of the First World War had all kinds of book-culture in the knapsacks: stuff they took for granted. The Classical tradition. The English inheritance. And the Bible, of course.

ML: And they test the English lyric. The whole war experience tests it, and shows how sturdy it remains. The Keatsian, the Wordsworthian tradition (and all the way back to Homer and Virgil). 'Insensibility' is Sophoclean: it's war poetry reaching way beyond what we normally think of as war poetry: it seems to touch on everything. I remember asking you, Andrew, why you didn't include in your war anthology Sassoon's 'The Dug-Out':

> Why do you lie with your legs ungainly huddled,
> And one arm bent across your sullen, cold,
> Exhausted face? It hurts my heart to watch you,
> Deep-shadow'd from the candle's guttering gold;
> And you wonder why I shake you by the shoulder;
> Drowsy, you mumble and sigh and turn your head...
> *You are too young to fall asleep for ever;*
> *And when you sleep you remind me of the dead.*[3]

If Sappho had written those last two italicised lines, they would automatically be considered immortal. But here they are, the work of a poet who has been dismissed as lacking transcendence. But that seems to me an extraordinary moment in English poetry, not just in Sassoon's work. The whole poem's marvellous. And I love 'Everyone Sang'. It moves me to tears every time I read it. It has the transcendental note.

JS: I wonder whether you know Sassoon's poem, never published in his lifetime, called 'Christ and the Soldier'. It was written one month after he had seen the first day of the battle of the Somme. It's interesting in that, at the end of his life, Sassoon entered the Roman Catholic Church, and I suspect he didn't publish it because he had doubts about whether it would be seen as blasphemous. You have the soldier kneeling before a crucifix, so religion is right there from the start:

> The straggled soldier halted – stared at Him –
> Then clumsily dumped down upon his knees,
> Gasping, 'O blessed crucifix, I'm beat!'
> And Christ, still sentried by the seraphim,

And here's the natural world:

> Near the front-line, between two splintered trees,
> Spoke him: 'My son, behold these hands and feet'.

Now the poem has these two voices: the soldier, and Christ. And Christ is completely out of touch. He says, 'I made for you the mysteries,/ Beyond all battles moves the Paraclete.' The soldier would think, what the hell's a paraclete? A parachute? He would have no idea. Sassoon does this deliberately, to show you how out of touch Christ is. And the soldier answers him:

> 'I was born full of lust,
> With hunger, thirst, and wishfulness to wed.
> Who cares today if I done wrong or right?'
> Christ asked all pitying, 'Can you put no trust
> In my known word, that shrives each faithful head?
> Am I not resurrection, life and light?'

In part three of the poem, at the third time of asking, the soldier says:

> 'But be you for both sides? I'm paid to kill
> And if I shoot a man his mother grieves.
> Does that come into what your teaching tells?'

Not surprisingly, the figure on the Cross is silent and the soldier has the last word:

> 'Lord Jesus, ain't you got no more to say?'
> Bowed hung that head below the crown of thorns.
> The soldier shifted, and picked up his pack,
> And slung his gun, and stumbled on his way.
> 'O God,' he groaned, 'Why ever was I born?'
> The battle boomed, and no reply came back.[4]

ML: That's very formal. By and large the Anglophone poetry of the Great War is at its best when it's formal. In fact, war poems would not be as interesting as they are, if they were formally less complex.

AM: This is an extremely interesting poem. It's a lyric debate – similar to the kind of thing Larkin does. And about the question of form: taking images in nature which have traditionally been used to help us enjoy and endure our experience as humans, and showing that either they don't work anymore, or have been forced into some ironical relationship with new brutal material, seems to me the default strategy in an awful lot of First World War poetry. And nobody does it better than Owen, as in 'Spring Offensive':

> Hour after hour they ponder the warm field
> And the far valley behind, where buttercups
> Had blessed with gold their slow boots coming up ...[5]

JS: I think that's so moving because it calls into mind a time when buttercups did cover the feet of children, and happy picnics with parents. And I think the same goes for form. If you ask whether there's a tension between the subject form and the lyric mode, I would say not necessarily.

ML: Owen keeps changing, doesn't he? There are so many Owens. 'The Send-Off' is about all the send-offs, isn't it? It is a symbolic poem.

JS: And it would do for any war. It would do for Afghanistan.

AM: It's my favourite of all his poems, as a whole poem, even though it's in some ways un-typical of him. While most of his greatest poems are set in the trenches, this is not: it's behind the lines somewhere or other. So the angle of entry to the subject is surprising and different. And as a result, this business we're talking about – about the pastoral tradition and what's being done to it, about how it's being brutalised and discredited or undermined – becomes very fascinating:

> Down the close darkening lanes they sang their way
> To the siding-shed
> And lined the train with faces grimly gay.
>
> Their breasts were stuck all white with wreath and spray
> As men's are, dead.

Here nature (the dust, the 'wreath and spray') has become memorialising the soldiers, rather than being something that fortifies them. And this point of view is strengthened by the non-combatant observers:

> Dull porters watched them, and a casual tramp
> Stood staring hard,
> Sorry to miss them from the upland camp.
>
> Then, unmoved, signals nodded, and a lamp
> Winked to the guard.[6]

Though it's only a little poem, the world suddenly opens and shows us the hinterland of things: the emotionlessness of natural objects, and of man-made objects (the 'unmoved' signal). Or the way they conspire with death, rather than bringing comfort (the lamp 'winking').

JS: Not 'moved', as a watcher might be moved.

AM: Precisely. 'So secretly, like wrongs hushed-up, they went'. This idea of their being *wrong* … Well, of course, we know it's *wrong* because war is *wrong* in some fundamental way, but that's -

JS: And hushed up, too -

AM: Exactly, the idea that this is all being swept under the carpet – the whole thing is done guiltily. Everybody really knows this is all a terribly bad idea. But they're not saying so.

JS: It does have a political thrust there, actually.

ML: For all its documentary propulsion, it's a very mysterious poem. And the drift of the different line lengths, the short and the long, emphasises that. It comes in by the sidedoor. It's a poem about mortality.

AM: Absolutely. And then there's that business of the 'wells':

> Shall they return to beating of great bells
> In wild train-loads?
> A few, a few, too few for drums and yells,
>
> May creep back, silent, to village wells,
> Up half-known roads.[7]

It always reminds me of Hardy – of that moment in *Jude the Obscure* when he identifies the well as the *omphalos* of the village. It's the essence of the place, and so it is here. But what we're being told in this poem is that not many people are going to come back, and even for those who do, the well may not (so to speak) know them. Because the place will have changed – and so will the people. Horribly changed by the war.

JS: The poem also comes around in circles: they *sang* their way down the darkening lane, now they *creep* back, maybe on two legs, maybe not on two legs, *silent*, no singing. To village wells -

AM: Wells, wells up, tearfulness – all these things come into it. And speaking about this reminds me very much of what Thomas says about watching the clods crumble and topple over *for the last time* in 'As the team's headbrass':

> The horses started and for the last time
> I watched the clods crumble and topple over
> After the ploughshare and the stumbling team.[8]

He's telling us here that the landscape has changed for reasons which are not only to do with the war, but with agricultural changes. You go to fight the war to defend the country that you love, but when you come back, oh! It's not quite the same.

JS: There's a brilliant ambiguity in that, because the plough is going up and down, and it goes up for the last time – so, just the last time today, but there is another last time which we hear behind that.

ML: *Multum in parvo.* The 140 poems he wrote in the last two years of his life are a miracle – one of poetry's great mysteries. Nowadays Thomas's presence seems to be everywhere: 'the past hovering as it revisits the light'.

SD: **Auden famously wrote that 'poetry makes nothing happen'. Is this true of war poetry?**

JS: One of the things that makes Auden's claim so vitally interesting and significant is its context, his great elegy 'In Memory of W.B. Yeats'. The Irish Archpoet died in January 1939, the month in which Barcelona, the last Republican stronghold, fell to Fascist Nationalists in the Spanish Civil War, and the banners of Hitler's Third Reich were preparing to advance across Europe. Auden, believing that poetry could help democracy to happen, had been one of many British and European poets to have gone to Spain and written in support of the Republican cause. So, profoundly disillusioned in 1939, he ventured to take issue with Yeats who, by contrast, had long believed that the arts in general, and poetry in particular, *made* history happen. In his great late poem, 'The Statues' (written in 1938), he had argued that it was the ancient Greek artists – sculptors, in particular – who created the culture, the society that shaped and inspired the citizen sailors who defeated the Persian navy at the battle of Salamis. In the same way, he claimed it was the artists of the Irish Renaissance – poets (like himself) in particular – who reintroduced the mythology that inspired the Irish Republican Brotherhood gunmen, whose Easter Rising against the British had led to Ireland's Home Rule.

It's an argument that artists – and poets, in particular – find attractive. Myself, I think Auden and Yeats are *both* right: poetry makes nothing happen in the short term, but has in the past had long-term results. Poetry from Homer to Brooke presented a view of war that led young men to take up arms. And, by contrast, I would argue that it was the anti-war poetry of Owen, Sassoon and others – in which British schoolchildren have for half a century been steeped – that helped make the protest marches in London against the Iraq War so much larger than those in America (where war poetry is seldom on a school syllabus).

ML: Poetry gives things a second chance. It helps to make sure that victims are not forgotten. Good war poems escape the category 'war poetry'.

JS: Yes, war poems should be *good* poems. I think bad ones are sometimes not so much harmless as harm*ful* in that, like bad journalism, they numb nerves which the best poems (only the best) of Owen, Sassoon, Rosenberg and Thomas reach and still retain the voltage to shock.

NOTES

1 Quoted in Philip Hoy ed. *Anthony Hecht in Conversation with Philip Hoy* (London: Between the Lines, 2001), 76.
2 Thomas Hardy, 'Drummer Hodge' in James Gibson ed. *Complete Poems* (London: Macmillan, 1976), 91.

3 Siegfried Sassoon, 'The Dug-Out' in Rupert Hart-Davis ed. *The War Poems* (London: Faber, 1983), 129.
4 Sassoon, 'Christ and the Soldier' in *The War Poems*, 45–46.
5 'Spring Offensive' in Jon Stallworthy ed. *The Poems of Wilfred Owen* (London: Chatto, 1983), 169.
6 Owen, 'The Send-Off', *Poems*, 149.
7 Ibid.
8 Edward Thomas, 'As the team's head-brass' in Edna Longley ed. *Edward Thomas: The Annotated Collected Poems* (Tarset: Bloodaxe, 2008), 124.

GUIDE TO FURTHER READING

Compiled by Santanu Das and Alice Kelly

Military History

Banks, Arthur. *A Military Atlas of the First World War*. London: Leo Cooper, 1997.
Keegan, John. *The Face of Battle: A Study of Agincourt, Waterloo and Somme*. Harmondsworth: Penguin, 1978.
  The First World War. London: Hutchinson, 1998.
Strachan, Hew. *The First World War: Volume 1: To Arms*. Oxford: Oxford University Press, 2001.
  The First World War: A New Illustrated History. London: Simon & Schuster, 2003.

Art, Cultural and Social History

Barham, Peter. *Forgotten Lunatics of the Great War*. New Haven: Yale University Press, 2004.
Barrett, Michele. *Casualty Figures: How Five Men Survived the First World War*. London: Verso, 2008.
Bond, Brian. *The Unquiet Western Front: Britain's Role in Literature and History*. Cambridge: Cambridge University Press, 2002.
Bourke, Joanna. *Dismembering the Male: Men's Bodies, Britain and the Great War*. London: Reaktion, 1996.
Brockington, Grace. *Above the Battlefield: British Modernism and the Peace Movement, 1900–1918*. New Haven; London: Yale University Press, 2010.
Cooke, Miriam and Angela Woollacott, eds. *Gendering War Talk*. Princeton: Princeton University Press, 1993.
Cork, Richard. *A Bitter Truth. Avant-Garde Art and the Great War*. New Haven and London: Yale University Press, 1994.
Cooper, Helen M., Adrienne Auslander Munich and Susan Merrill Squier, eds. *Arms and the Woman: War, Gender, and Literary Representation*. Chapel Hill: University of North Carolina Press, 1989.
Das, Santanu. 'India, Empire and First World War Writing' in Elleke Boehmer and Rosinka Chaudhuri, eds. *The Indian Postcolonial: A Critical Reader*. London: Routledge, 2010.
Das, Santanu, ed. *Race, Empire and First World War Writing*. Cambridge: Cambridge University Press, 2011.

Doan, Laura. *Disturbing Practices: History, Sexuality, and Women's Experience of Modern War*. Chicago: Chicago University Press, 2013.

Eksteins, Modris. *Rites of Spring: The Great War and the Birth of the Modern Age*. London: Bantam, 1989.

Field, Frank. *British and French Writers of the First World War: Comparative Studies in Cultural History*. Cambridge: Cambridge University Press, 1991.

Fussell, Paul. *The Great War and Modern Memory*. Oxford: Oxford University Press, 1975.

Goebel, Stefan. *The Great War and Medieval Memory: War, Remembrance and Medievalism in Britain and Germany, 1914–1940*. Cambridge: Cambridge University Press, 2009.

Gregogy, Adrian. *The Last Great War: British Society and the First World War*. Cambridge: Cambridge University Press, 2008.

Higonnet, Margaret R., Jane Jenson, Sonya Michel, and Margaret Collins Weitz, eds. *Behind the Lines: Gender and the Two World Wars*. New Haven: Yale University Press, 1987.

Horne, John, ed. *A Companion to World War I*. Chichester; Malden: Wiley-Blackwell, 2010.

Hynes, Samuel. *A War Imagined: The First World War and English Culture*. London: Bodley Head, 1990.

Jackson, Ashley. *Distant Drums. The Role of Colonies in British Imperial Warfare*. Brighton: Sussex Academic Press, 2010.

Jeffery, Keith. *Ireland and the Great War*. Cambridge: Cambridge University Press, 2000.

Leed, Eric. *No Man's Land: Combat and Identity in World War I*. Cambridge: Cambridge University Press, 1979.

Leese, Peter. *Shell Shock: Traumatic Neurosis and the British Soldiers of the First World War*. Basingstoke: Palgrave, 2002.

Malvern, Sue. *Modern Art, Britain and the Great War. Witnessing, Testimony and Remembrance*. New Haven and London: Yale University Press, 2004.

Meyer, Jessica. *Men of War: Masculinity and the First World War in Britain*. London: Palgrave, 2008.

Ouditt, Sharon. *Fighting Forces, Writing Women: Identity and Ideology in the First World War*. London: Routledge 1994.

Women Writers of the First World War: An Annotated Bibliography. London: Routledge, 2000.

Paris, Michael, ed. *The First World War and Popular Cinema: 1914 to the Present*. Edinburgh: Edinburgh University Press, 1999.

Parker, Peter. *The Old Lie: The Great War and the Public School Ethos*. London: Constable, 1987.

The Last Veteran. Harry Patch and the Legacy of War. London: Fourth Estate, 2009.

Roper, Michael. *The Secret Battle: Emotional Survival in the Great War*. Manchester: Manchester University Press, 2010.

Roshwald, Aviel and Richard Stites, eds. *European Culture in the Great War. The Arts, Entertainment and Propaganda 1914–1918*. Cambridge: Cambridge University Press, 1999.

Shephard, Ben. *A War of Nerves: Soldiers and Psychiatrists, 1914–1994*. London: Jonathan Cape, 2000.

Thompson, Alistair. *Anzac Memories. Living with the Legend*. Melbourne: Melbourne University Press, 1994.

Todman, Dan. *The Great War: Myth and Memory*. London: Continuum, 2005.

Vance, Jonathan F. *Death So Noble: Memory, Meaning and the First World War*. Vancouver: UBC Press, 1998.

Williams, David. *Media, Memory, and the First World War*. Montreal and Kingston: McGill-Queen's University Press, 2009.

Winter, Jay. *The Great War and the British People*. London: Macmillan, 1985.

   Sites of Memory, Sites of Mourning: The Great War in European Cultural History. Cambridge: Cambridge University Press, 1995.

General Literary Criticism

Bergonzi, Bernard. *Heroes' Twilight: A Study of the Literature of the Great War*. London: Constable, 1965.

Booth, Allyson. *Postcards from the Trenches: Negotiating the Space between Modernism and the First World War*. New York; Oxford: Oxford University Press, 1996.

Buitenhuis, Peter. *The Great War of Words: Literature as Propaganda 1914–18 and After*. London: Batsford, 1989.

Carden-Coyne, Ana. *Reconstructing the Body: Classicism, Modernism, and the First World War*. Oxford: Oxford University Press, 2009.

Cecil, Hugh. *The Flower of Battle: British Fiction Writers of the First World War*. London: Secker & Warburg, 1995.

Cohen, Debra Rae. *Remapping the Home Front: Locating Citizenship in British Women's Great War Fiction*. Boston: Northeastern University Press, 2002.

Cole, Sarah. *Modernism, Male Friendship, and the First World War*. Cambridge: Cambridge University Press, 2003.

   At the Violet Hour: Modernism and Violence in England and Ireland. Oxford: Oxford University Press, 2012.

Das, Santanu. *Touch and Intimacy in First World War Literature*. Cambridge: Cambridge University Press, 2005.

Einhaus, Ann-Marie. *The Short Story and the First World War*. Cambridge: Cambridge University Press, 2013.

Gerster, Robin. *Big-Noting: The Heroic Theme in Australian War Writing*. Melbourne: Melbourne University Press, 1987.

Gilbert, Sandra M. and Susan Gubar. *No Man's Land: The Place of the Woman Writer in the Twentieth Century*. 3 Volumes. New Haven: Yale University Press, 1991.

Goldman, Dorothy, with Jane Gledhill and Judith Hattaway. *Women Writers and the Great War*. New York: Twayne, 1995.

Harvey, A.D. *A Muse of Fire: Literature, Art and War*. London: Hambledon Press, 1998.

Higonnet, Margaret. 'Not So Quiet in No-Woman's Land' in Miriam Cooking and Angela Woollacott, eds. *Gendering War Talk*. Princeton: Princeton University Press, 1993.

Howlett, Jana and Rod Mengham, eds. *The Violent Muse: Violence and the Artistic Imagination in Europe, 1910–1939*. Manchester: Manchester University Press, 1994.

Kerrigan, John. *Archipelagic English: Literature, History and Politics, 1603–1707*. Oxford: Oxford University Press, 2008.

Marcus, Jane. 'Corpus/Corps/Corpse: Writing the Body in/at War'. Afterword. *Not So Quiet ... Stepdaughters of War*. By Helen Zenna Smith. New York: The Feminist Press, 1989.

McLoughlin, Kate, *Authoring War: The Literary Representation of War from the Iliad to Iraq*. Cambridge: Cambridge University Press, 2011.

   ed. *The Cambridge Companion to War Writing*. Cambridge: Cambridge University Press, 2009.

Parfitt, George. *Fiction of the First World War: A Study*. London: Faber, 1988.

Piette, Adam and Mark Rawlinson, eds. *The Edinburgh Companion to Twentieth-Century British and American War Literature*. Edinburgh: Edinburgh University Press, 2012.

Potter, Jane. *Boys in Khaki, Girls in Print: Women's Literary Responses to the Great War, 1914–1918*. Oxford: Clarendon Press, 2005.

Raitt, Suzanne and Trudi Tate, eds. *Women's Fiction and the Great War*. Oxford: Oxford University Press, 1997.

Sherry, Vincent. *The Great War and the Language of Modernism*. Oxford: Oxford University Press, 2003.

   ed. *The Cambridge Companion to the Literature of the First World War*. Cambridge: Cambridge University Press, 2005.

Smith, Angela K. *The Second Battlefield: Women, Modernism and the First World War*. Manchester: Manchester University Press, 2000.

Tate, Trudi. *Modernism, History and the First World War*. Manchester: Manchester University Press, 1998.

Tylee, Claire M. *The Great War and Women's Consciousness: Images of Militarism and Womanhood in Women's Writings, 1914–64*. Basingstoke: Macmillan, 1990.

Whalan, Mark. *The Great War and the Culture of the New Negro*. Florida: University Press of Florida, 2008.

Select Primary Texts (Mainly by Poets)

Aldington, Richard. *Images of War*. London: George Allen and Unwin, 1919.

Barbusse, Henri. *Under Fire*. Trans. W. Fitzwater Wray. 1918. London: Dent, 1965.

Blunden, Edmund. *Poems 1914–1930*. London: Cobden-Sanderson, 1930.

   Undertones of War. 1929. Harmondsworth: Penguin, 2000.

Borden, Mary. *The Forbidden Zone*. 1929. London: Hesperus, 2008.

Brittain, Vera. *Poems of the War and After*. London: Victor Gollancz, 1934.

   Testament of Youth. 1933. London: Virago, 1999.

Brooke, Rupert. *Collected Poems*. 1918. London: Papermac, 1992.

   The Letters, ed. Geoffrey Keynes. London: Faber, 1968.

Cannan, M.W. *In War Time*. Oxford: B.H. Blackwell, 1917.

Dennis, C.J. *The Songs of a Sentimental Bloke*. Sydney: Angus and Robertson, 1916.

Eliot, T.S. *Collected Poems 1909–1962*. New York: Harcourt Brace, 1968.

Inventions of the March Hare: Poems 1909–1917, ed. Christopher Ricks. New York: Harcourt Brace, 1996.

Farjeon, Eleanor. *Sonnets and Poems*. Oxford: Blackwell, 1918.

Gellert, Leon. *Songs of a Campaign*. Angus & Robertson: Sydney, 1918.

Graves, Robert. *Poems about War*, ed. William Graves. London: Cassell, 1988.

The Complete Poems, ed. Beryl Graves and Dunstan Ward. Manchester: Carcanet, 1995.

Good-bye to All That. 1929. London: Penguin, 2000.

But It Still Goes On: An Accumulation. London and Toronto: Jonathan Cape, 1930.

On Poetry: Talks and Essays. Garden City, New York: Doubleday, 1969.

Gurney, Ivor. *Collected Poems of Ivor Gurney*, ed. P.J. Kavanagh. Oxford: Oxford University Press, 1983.

Collected Letters, ed. R.K.R. Thornton. Manchester: Carcanet, 1991.

Hardy, Thomas. *The Complete Poems*, ed. James Gibson. London: Macmillan, 1976.

Housman, A.E. *A Shropshire Lad and Other Poems*, intro. Nick Laird. London: Penguin, 1995.

Islam, Kazi Nazrul. *A New Anthology*, trans. and ed., Rafiqul Islam. Dhaka: Bangla Academy, 1990.

Jones, David. *In Parenthesis*. 1937. London: Faber, 2010.

The Anathemata. London: Faber, 1952.

Epoch and Artist: Selected Writings, ed. Harman Grisewood. London: Faber, 1959.

Dai Great-Coat: A Self-Portrait of David Jones in his Letters, ed. René Hague. London: Faber, 1980.

Kettle, T.M. *The Ways of War*. New York: Charles Scribner's Sons, 1917.

Kipling, Rudyard. *The Years Between*. London: Methuen, 1919.

Debits and Credits. London: Macmillan, 1926.

War Stories and Poems, ed. Andrew Rutherford. Oxford: Oxford University Press, 1990.

Lawrence, D.H. *Bay: A Book of Poems*. London: Beaumont Press, 1919.

Ledwidge, Francis. *Selected Poems* ed. Dermont Bolger and intro. Seamus Heaney. Dublin: New Island Books, 1992.

Lee, Joseph. *Ballads of Battle*. London: John Murray, 1916.

Lewis, Wyndham. *Blast*. Issue 2 (War Number). London: Bodley Head, 1915.

Macaulay, Rose. *Three Days*. London: Constable, 1919.

MacGill, Patrick. *Soldier Songs*. London: Herbert Jenkins, 1917.

McCrae, John. *In Flanders Fields and Other Poems*. London: Hodder and Stoughton, 1919.

Mew, Charlotte. *Collected Poems and Selected Prose*, ed. Val Warner. Manchester: Carcanet Press, 1997.

Nichols, Robert. *Ardours and Endurances*. London: Chatto and Windus, 1917.

Owen, Wilfred. *The Complete Poems & Fragments*, 2 vols, ed. Jon Stallworthy. London: Chatto and Windus, Hogarth and Oxford University Press, 1983.

The Poems of Wilfred Owen, ed. Jon Stallworthy. London: Chatto and Windus, 1990.

Wilfred Owen: Collected Letters, ed. Harold Owen and John Bell. London and Oxford: Oxford University Press, 1967.

Postgate, Margaret. *Poems*. London: Allen and Unwin, 1918.

Pound, Ezra. *Hugh Selwyn Mauberley, Selected Poems of Ezra Pound*. New York: New Directions, 1957.

    Personae: The Collected Shorter Poems of Ezra Pound, eds. Lea Baechler and A. Walton Litz. New York: New Directions, 1990.

Read, Herbert. *Selected Poetry*. London: Faber, 1966.

Rosenberg, Isaac. *The Collected Works of Isaac Rosenberg: Poetry, Prose, Letters, Paintings, and Drawings*, foreword by Siegfried Sassoon, ed. Ian Parsons. London: Chatto and Windus, 1979.

    The Poems and Plays of Isaac Rosenberg, ed. Vivian Noakes. Oxford and New York: Oxford University Press, 2004.

Sassoon, Siegfried. *War Poems*, ed. Rupert Hart-Davis. London: Faber, 1983.

    Collected Poems, 1908–1956. London: Faber, 1983.

    Sherston's Progress. London: Faber, 1936.

    The Complete Memoirs of George Sherston. 1937. London: Faber, 1952.

    Siegfried's Journey. London: Faber, 1945.

    Memoirs of An Infantry Officer. 1930. London: Faber, 1965.

    Diaries, 1915–18, ed. Rupert Hart-Davis. London: Faber, 1983.

Service, Robert. *The Rhymes of a Red-Cross Man*. London: T. Fisher Unwin, 1916.

Sorley, Charles Hamilton. *Marlborough and Other Poems*. Cambridge: Cambridge University Press, 1916.

    Collected Poems, ed. Jean Moorcroft Wilson. London: Cecil Wolf, 1985.

    The Letters of Charles Hamilton Sorley, ed. Jean Moorcroft Wilson. London: Cecil Woolf, 1990.

Thomas, Edward. *The Annotated Collected Poems*, ed. Edna Longley. Tarset: Bloodaxe, 2008.

    The Diary of Edward Thomas: 1 January-8 April 1917, intro. Roland Gant. Andoversford: Whittington Press, 1977.

    A Language Not to Be Betrayed: Selected Prose of Edward Thomas, ed. Edna Longley. Manchester: Carcanet, in association with Mid-Northumberland Arts Group, 1981.

    Edward Thomas: Selected Letters, ed. R. George Thomas. Oxford: Oxford University Press, 1996.

Yeats, W.B. *Collected Poems*. London: Macmillan, 1950.

Anthologies

Baetz, Joel, ed. *Canadian Poetry from World War I: An Anthology*. Oxford: Oxford University Press, 2009.

Barlow, Adrian, ed. *Six Poets of the Great War*. Cambridge: Cambridge University Press, 1995.

Brophy, John and Eric Partridge, eds. *Songs and Slang of the British Soldier: 1914–1918*. 1930. London: Scholartis Press, 1965.

Buelens, Geert ed., *Het lijf in slijk geplant: gedichten uit de Eerste Wereldoorlog*. Amsterdam: Ambo, 2008.

Cross, Tim, ed. *The Lost Voices of World War I: An International Anthology of Writers, Poets and Playwrights*. London: Bloomsbury, 1988.

Dawe, Gerald, ed. *Earth Voices Whispering: An Anthology of Irish War Poetry, 1914–1945*. Belfast: Blackstaff Press, 2008.

Featherstone, Simon, ed. *War Poetry: An Introductory Reader*. London: Routledge, 1995.

Gardner, Brian, ed. *Up the Line to Death: The War Poets, 1914–1918: An Anthology*. Foreword by Edmund Blunden. 1964. London: Methuen, 2007.

Haughton, Hugh, ed. *Second World War Poems*. London: Faber, 2004.

Hibberd, Dominic and John Onions, eds. *Poetry of the Great War: An Anthology*. London: Macmillan, 1986.

The Winter of the World: Poems of the First World War. London: Constable, 2007.

Higgins, Ian, ed. *Anthology of First World War French Poetry*. Glasgow: University of Glasgow French and German Publications, 1996.

Higonnet, Margaret, R. ed. *Lines of Fire: Women Writers of World War I*. New York: Penguin, 1999.

Hollis, Matthew and Paul Keegan, eds. *101 Poems Against War*. London: Faber, 2003.

Jeffcock, John, ed. *Heroes: 100 Poems from the New Generation of War Poets*. Croydon: Ebury Press, 2011.

Kendall, Tim, ed. *Poetry of the First World War: An Anthology*. Oxford: Oxford University Press, 2013.

Khan, Nosheen, ed. *Not With Loud Grieving*. Lahore: Polymer Publications, 1994.

Laird, J.T. *Other Banners. An Anthology of Australian Literature of the First World War*. Canberra: Australian War Memorial and Australian Government Publishing Service, 1971.

Motion, Andrew, ed. *First World War Poems*. London: Faber and Faber, 2003.

Nichols, Robert, ed. *Anthology of War Poetry, 1914–18*. London: Nicholson and Watson, 1943.

Noakes, Vivien, ed. *Voices of Silence: The Alternative Book of First World War Poetry*. Stroud: Sutton, 2006.

Page, Geoff, ed. *Shadows from Wire: Poems and Photographs of Australians in the Great War*. Victoria: Penguin, 1983.

Parsons, I.M., ed. *Men Who March Away: Poems of the First World War*. London: Chatto and Windus; Heinemann Educational, 1965.

Powell, Anne, ed. *A Deep Cry: First World War Soldier-Poets Killed in Northern France and Flanders*. Thrupp: Sutton, 1993.

Reilly, Catherine W., ed. *Scars Upon My Heart: Women's Poetry and Verse of the First World War*. Preface by Judith Kazantzis. London: Virago, 1981.

Royle, Trevor, ed. *In Flanders Fields: Scottish Poetry and Prose of the First World War*. Edinburgh: Mainstream, 1990.

Silkin, Jon, ed. *The Penguin Book of First World War Poetry*. Middlesex and London: Allen Lane, 1979 [rev. edn. Harmondsworth: Penguin, 1981].

Stallworthy, Jon, ed. *The Oxford Book of War Poetry*. Oxford: Oxford University Press, 1984.

Anthem for Doomed Youth: Twelve Soldier Poets of the First World War. London: Constable, 2002.

Stallworthy, Jon and Jane Potter, eds. *Three Poets of the First World War: Ivor Gurney, Isaac Rosenberg and Wilfred Owen*. London: Penguin, 2011.

Stephen, Martin, ed. *Never Such Innocence: A New Anthology of Great War Verse*. London: Buchan and Enright, 1988.

Taylor, Martin, ed. *Lads: Love Poetry of the Trenches*. London: Constable, 1989.

Van Wienen, Mark W., ed. *Rendezvous with Death: American Poems of the Great War*. Urbana: University of Illinois Press, 2002.

Walter, George, ed. *The Penguin Book of First World War Poetry*. London: Penguin, 2006.

Poetry Bibliography: Biographies and Critical Studies

Anderson Winn, James. *The Poetry of War*. Cambridge: Cambridge University Press, 2008.

Blissett, William. *The Long Conversation: A Memoir of David Jones*. Oxford: Oxford University Press, 1981.

Blunden, Edmund. *War Poets, 1914–1918*. Harlow, London: Longmans, Green for the British Council and the National Book League, 1958.

Brearton, Fran. *The Great War in Irish Poetry: W.B. Yeats to Michael Longley*. Oxford: Oxford University Press, 2000.

'A War of Friendship: Robert Graves and Siegfried Sassoon'. In Kendall ed. *The Oxford Handbook of British and Irish War Poetry*.

Bridgwater, Patrick. *The German Poets of the First World War*. London: Croom Helm, 1985.

Buck, Claire. 'Reframing Women's War Poetry'. In Jane Dowson ed. *The Cambridge Companion to Twentieth-Century British and Irish Women's Poetry*. Cambridge University Press, 2011.

Caesar, Adrian. *Taking It Like a Man: Suffering, Sexuality, and the War Poets: Brooke, Sassoon, Owen, Graves*. Manchester: Manchester University Press, 1993.

Campbell, James. 'Combat Gnosticism: The Ideology of First World War Poetry Criticism'. *New Literary History*. Volume 30, Number 1, Winter 1999, 203–15.

Corcoran, Neil, ed. *The Cambridge Companion to Twentieth-Century Poetry*. Cambridge: Cambridge University Press, 2007.

Curtayne, Alice. *Francis Ledwidge: A Life of the Poet (1887–1917)*. London: Martin Brian and O'Keefe, 1972.

Das, Santanu. 'War Poetry and the Realm of the Senses: Owen and Rosenberg'. In Kendall ed. *The Oxford Handbook of British and Irish War Poetry*.

Dilworth, Thomas. *The Shape and Meaning in the Poetry of David Jones*. Toronto: University of Toronto Press, 1988.

Egrement, Max. *Siegfried Sassoon: A Life*. New York: Farrar, Straus, Giroux, 2005.

Featherstone, Simon. 'Women's Poetry of the First and Second World Wars'. In Kendall ed. *The Oxford Handbook of British and Irish War Poetry*.

Fenton, James. *The Strength of Poetry*. Oxford: Oxford University Press, 2001.

Goldie, David. 'Was there a Scottish War Literature? Scotland, Poetry and the First World War'. In Kendall ed. *The Oxford Handbook of British and Irish War Poetry*.

Graham, Desmond. *The Truth of War: Owen, Blunden, Rosenburg*. Manchester: Carcanet, 1984.

Hassall, Christopher. *Rupert Brooke: A Biography*. New York: Harcourt, Brace, World, 1964.

Hibberd, Dominic. *Owen the Poet*. Basingstoke: Macmillan, 1986.

The Last Year, 1917–1918. London: Constable, 1992.

Wilfred Owen: A New Biography. London: Wiedenfeld and Nicolson, 2002.

Hibberd, Dominic, ed. *Poetry of the First World War: A Casebook*. London: Macmillan, 1981.

The First World War (Context and Commentary Series). Basingstoke: Macmillan, 1990.

Higonnet, Margaret. 'The Great War and the Female Elegy: Female Lamentation and Silence in Global Contexts': *The Global South*, Vol 1:7, 2007, 120–36.

Hipp, Daniel. *The Poetry of Shell Shock: Wartime Trauma and Healing in Wilfred Owen, Ivor Gurney and Siegfried Sassoon*. Jefferson, NC; London: McFarland, 2005.

Hollis, Matthew. *Now All Roads Lead to France: The Last Years of Edward Thomas* London: Faber, 2012.

Howarth, Peter. *British Poetry in the Age of Modernism*. Cambridge: Cambridge University Press, 2006.

Cambridge Introduction to Modernist Poetry. Cambridge: Cambridge University Press, 2011.

Hurd, Michael. *The Ordeal of Ivor Gurney*. Oxford: Oxford University Press, 1978.

Johnston, John H. *English Poetry of the First World War: A Study in the Evolution of Lyric and Narrative Form*. London: Oxford University Press, 1964.

Kendall, Tim. *Modern English War Poetry*. Oxford: Oxford University Press, 2006.

Kendall, Tim, ed. *The Oxford Handbook of British and Irish War Poetry*. Oxford: Oxford University Press, 2007.

Kerr, Douglas. *Wilfred Owen's Voices: Language and Community*. Oxford: Oxford University Press, 1993.

Khan, Nosheen. *Women's Poetry of the First World War*. New York and London: Harvester Wheatsheaf, 1988.

Lane, Arthur E. *An Adequate Response: The War Poetry of Wilfred Owen and Siegfried Sassoon*. Detroit: Wayne State University Press, 1972.

Larkin, Philip. 'The War Poet', *Required Writing*. London: Faber, 1983.

Lehmann, John. *The English Poets of the First World War*. London: Thames and Hudson, 1981.

Longley, Edna. *Poetry in the Wars*. Newcastle upon Tyne: Bloodaxe, 1986.

'The Great War, History, and the English Lyric'. In Vincent Sherry ed. *The Cambridge Companion to Literature of the First World War*. Cambridge: Cambridge University Press, 2004.

Lyon, Philippa. *Twentieth-Century War Poetry*. London: Palgrave, 2005.

Marsland, Elizabeth A. *The Nation's Cause: French, English and German Poetry of the First World War*. London: Routledge, 1991.

Martin, Meredith. *The Rise and Fall of Meter: English Poetry and National Culture, 1860–1930*. Princeton, NJ: Princeton University Press, 2012.

Montefiore, Jan. '"Blind Mouths": Oral Metaphor, Literary Tradition and the Fantasy of the Mother in Some Women's Elegies of the Great War'. *Paragraph: A Journal of Modern Critical Theory*, 21.3 (1998): 376–90.

Moorcroft Wilson, Jean. *Isaac Rosenberg: Poet and Painter*. London: Cecil Woolf, 1975.

Charles Hamilton Sorley: A Biography. London: Cecil Woolf, 1985.

Siegfried Sassoon: The Making of a War Poet: A Biography (1886–1918). London: Duckworth, 1998.

Siegfried Sassoon: The Journey from the Trenches: A Biography (1918–1967). London: Duckworth, 2003.

Motion, Andrew. *The Poetry of Edward Thomas*. London: Hogarth, 1980.

Murray, Nicholas. *The Red Sweet Wine of Youth: The Brave and Brief Lives of the War Poets*. London: Little, Brown, 2010.

Owen, Harold. *Journey from Obscurity: Wilfred Owen, 1893–1918: Memoirs of the Owen Family*, 3 vols. Oxford: Oxford University Press, 1963–5.

Parfitt, George. *English Poetry of the First World War: Contexts and Themes*. New York and London: Harvester Wheatsheaf, 1990.

Perloff, Marjorie. '"Easter 1916": Yeats' First World War Poem'. In Kendall ed. *The Oxford Handbook of British and Irish Poetry*.

Plain, Gill. 'Great Expectations: Rehabilitating the Recalcitrant War Poets'. *Feminist Review* 51 (1995), 41–65.

Potter, Jane. '"The Essentially Modern Attitude Toward War": English Poetry of the Great War'. In Piette and Rawlinson, eds. *The Edinburgh Companion to Twentieth-Century British and American War Literature*. Edinburgh: Edinburgh University Press, 2012.

Puissant, Susanne Christine. *Irony and the Poetry of the First World War*. New York: Palgrave Macmillan, 2009.

Ramazani, Jahan. *Poetry of Mourning: The Modern Elegy from Hardy to Heaney*. Chicago and London: University of Chicago Press, 1994.

Rawlinson, Mark. 'Wilfred Owen'. In Kendall ed. *The Oxford Handbook of British and Irish War Poetry*.

Reilly, Catherine W. *English Poetry of the First World War: A Bibliography*. London: George Prior, 1978.

Ricketts, Harry. *Strange Meetings: The Poets of the Great War*. London: Chatto and Windus, 2010.

Rogers, Timothy, ed. *Georgian Poetry, 1911–1922: The Critical Heritage*. London: Routledge and Kegan Paul, 1977.

Sherry, Vincent. 'The Great War and Literary Modernism in England'. In Sherry ed. *The Cambridge Companion to the Literature of the First World War*.

'The Great War and Modernist Poetry'. In Kendall ed. *The Oxford Handbook of British and Irish War Poetry*.

Silkin, Jon. *Out of Battle: The Poetry of the Great War*. London: Oxford University Press, 1972.

Spear, Hilda D. *Remembering, We Forget: A Background Study to the Poetry of the First World War*. London: Davis-Poynter, 1979.

Stallworthy, Jon. *Poets of the First World War*. London: Oxford University Press in association with the Imperial War Museum, 1974.

Wilfred Owen. London: Chatto and Windus, 1974; Oxford: Oxford University Press, 1980.

Survivors' Songs: From Maldon to the Somme. Cambridge: Cambridge University Press, 2008.

Stephen, Martin. *The Price of Pity: Poetry, History and Myth in the Great War*. London: Leo Cooper, 1996.

Street, Sean. *The Dymock Poets*. Bridgend: Seren, 1994.

Thomas, Edward. 'War Poetry', *Poetry and Drama*, II, No. 8, December 1914.

Vandiver, Elizabeth. *Stand in the Trench, Achilles: Classical Receptions in British Poetry of the Great War*. Oxford: Oxford University Press, 2010.

Van Wyk Smith, Malvern. *Drummer Hodge: The Poetry of the Anglo-Boer War*. Oxford: Oxford University Press, 1978.

Webb, Barry. *Edmund Blunden: A Biography*. New Haven, CT: Yale University Press, 1990.

Welland, Dennis. *Wilfred Owen: A Critical Study*. London: Chatto and Windus, 1978.

Williams, Merryn. *Wilfred Owen*. Glamorgan: Seren Books, 1993.

Web Sites

The 'First World War Poetry Digital Archive' (http://www.oucs.ox.ac.uk/ww1lit), hosted by the University of Oxford, is a major web resource, and is linked to other important sites (including the Wilfred Owen Multimedia Digital Archive). It has substantial primary material on Blunden, Brittain, Graves, Gurney, Jones, Leighton, Owen, Rosenberg, Sassoon and Thomas. It has an online collection of several thousand items of texts, images, audio and video files.

Other important web resources include:

'War Poetry' (http://war-poets.blogspot.co.uk)

'Lost Poets of the Great War' (http://www.english.emory.edu/LostPoets)

'War Poetry Website' (http://www.warpoetry.co.uk)

'War Poets Association' (http://www.warpoets.org)

'War Poets Collection' (http://www2.napier.ac.uk/warpoets)

INDEX

Owen, Wilfred, 6, 8, 19, 20, 25, 40, 52, 55,
    62, 69, 82, 85, 117–27, 144, 145,
    161, 167, 186, 211, 216, 230, 233,
    237, 243, 244, 248, 249, 250, 257,
    258, 261, 266
  and A.C. Swinburne, 122–23
  and Alfred Tennyson, 120
  "Anthem for Doomed Youth", 57, 122
  "Apologia Pro Poemate Meo", 17, 249
  Britten's *War Requiem,* work quoted in,
    251
  and civilians, 62
  colonial troops in the writing of, 25
  "Dulce Et Decorum Est", 14–17, 45, 118,
    125, 249
  "Exposure", 45, 126, 235
  "Futility", 10, 20
  "Greater Love", 122, 123
  health (physical and mental), 16, 60, 62,
    82, 97
  and Henri Barbusse, 125
  homosexuality and homoeroticism, 17,
    62, 117
  "I Saw His Round Mouth's Crimson", 17,
    108, 123
  and John Keats, 117, 118–19,
    121, 124
  letters to his mother, 10, 55, 118, 122
  "Maundy Thursday", 9
  "Mental Cases", 60, 124
  "Miners", 62, 100
  and Percy Bysshe Shelley, 119, 120
  "Preface", 6
  and R.F. Brewer, 52
  and Rabindranath Tagore, 25
  and Seamus Heaney, 237–38
  "The Send-Off", 264–65
  "The Sentry", 60, 124
  "The Show", 125
  and Siegfried Sassoon, 4, 55, 57, 95, 97,
    121
  "Smile, Smile, Smile", 62, 124, 249
  and sonnet form, 118
  "Spring Offensive", 62, 126–27, 235,
    263
  "Strange Meeting", 62, 118, 120, 123,
    124, 259
  and Ted Hughes, 233
  "A Terre", 120, 121, 123
  therapy. *See* Brock, Arthur
  and W.B. Yeats, 88, 243
  women in the poetry of, 23

Oxenham, John
  "Christs All!", 19
Oxland, Nowell, 69

Parsons, I.M.
  Men Who March Away, 6
Passchendaele, Battle of, 129, 239, 248
pastoral form, 8, 20, 21, 36, 39, 91, 101,
    107, 118, 119, 169, 170, 189, 190,
    194, 259, 261, 264
  anti-pastoral, 126, 186, 192
patriotism, 7, 19, 58, 69, 71, 74, 107, 134,
    167, 178, 180, 200, 201, 202–3, 211,
    233
peace, 7, 35–36, 62, 88, 138, 140, 186, 190,
    192–93, 194–95, 213, 221, 223,
    See also Armistice Declaration, the.
    Brooke, Rupert: "Peace"
photography, 23, 55, 121–22, 125–26, 247
Picasso, Pablo
  Les Demoiselles d'Avignon, 111
Poems of the Great War (anthology, 1914),
    7, 69
Poetry (Chicago), 110, 213, 214
Poets' Corner, 82, 251
Pope, Jessie, 23, 125, 185
Postgate, Margaret (Margaret Cole), 23,
    186, 193–95
  "Afterwards", 194–95
  "Epitaphs", 194
  Poems, 193
  "Recruited", 193
  "Rest", 193
  "Spring Song, 1917", 194
  "The Veteran", 194
Post-Impressionism, 210
Pound, Ezra, 7, 46, 82, 110, 210–11,
    212–19, 222, 223, 229
  "Abu Salammamm – A Song of Empire",
    212, 219
  anti-imperialism of, 212
  Cathay, 59, 210, 212–13
  "The Coming of War: Actaeon", 212
  "Fratres Minores", 219
  Gaudier-Brzeska: A Memoir, 213
  Homage to Sextus Propertius, 7, 46–47,
    210, 215–18, 223
  Hugh Selwyn Mauberley, 210, 218–19, 223
  and Jacques Laforgue, 215
  and James Joyce, 216
  and modernism, 21, 210, 212, 223
  "1915: February", 212

Cambridge Companions to...

AUTHORS

Edward Albee edited by Stephen J. Bottoms

Margaret Atwood edited by Coral Ann Howells

W. H. Auden edited by Stan Smith

Jane Austen edited by Edward Copeland and Juliet McMaster (second edition)

Beckett edited by John Pilling

Bede edited by Scott DeGregorio

Aphra Behn edited by Derek Hughes and Janet Todd

Walter Benjamin edited by David S. Ferris

William Blake edited by Morris Eaves

Brecht edited by Peter Thomson and Glendyr Sacks (second edition)

The Brontës edited by Heather Glen

Bunyan edited by Anne Dunan-Page

Frances Burney edited by Peter Sabor

Byron edited by Drummond Bone

Albert Camus edited by Edward J. Hughes

Willa Cather edited by Marilee Lindemann

Cervantes edited by Anthony J. Cascardi

Chaucer edited by Piero Boitani and Jill Mann (second edition)

Chekhov edited by Vera Gottlieb and Paul Allain

Kate Chopin edited by Janet Beer

Caryl Churchill edited by Elaine Aston and Elin Diamond

Coleridge edited by Lucy Newlyn

Wilkie Collins edited by Jenny Bourne Taylor

Joseph Conrad edited by J. H. Stape

H. D. edited by Nephie J. Christodoulides and Polina Mackay

Dante edited by Rachel Jacoff (second edition)

Daniel Defoe edited by John Richetti

Don DeLillo edited by John N. Duvall

Charles Dickens edited by John O. Jordan

Emily Dickinson edited by Wendy Martin

John Donne edited by Achsah Guibbory

Dostoevskii edited by W. J. Leatherbarrow

Theodore Dreiser edited by Leonard Cassuto and Claire Virginia Eby

John Dryden edited by Steven N. Zwicker

W. E. B. Du Bois edited by Shamoon Zamir

George Eliot edited by George Levine

T. S. Eliot edited by A. David Moody

Ralph Ellison edited by Ross Posnock

Ralph Waldo Emerson edited by Joel Porte and Saundra Morris

William Faulkner edited by Philip M. Weinstein

Henry Fielding edited by Claude Rawson

F. Scott Fitzgerald edited by Ruth Prigozy

Flaubert edited by Timothy Unwin

E. M. Forster edited by David Bradshaw

Benjamin Franklin edited by Carla Mulford

Brian Friel edited by Anthony Roche

Robert Frost edited by Robert Faggen

Gabriel García Márquez edited by Philip Swanson

Elizabeth Gaskell edited by Jill L. Matus

Goethe edited by Lesley Sharpe

Günter Grass edited by Stuart Taberner

Thomas Hardy edited by Dale Kramer

David Hare edited by Richard Boon

Nathaniel Hawthorne edited by Richard Millington

Seamus Heaney edited by Bernard O'Donoghue

Ernest Hemingway edited by Scott Donaldson

Homer edited by Robert Fowler

Horace edited by Stephen Harrison

Ted Hughes edited by Terry Gifford

Ibsen edited by James McFarlane

Henry James edited by Jonathan Freedman

Samuel Johnson edited by Greg Clingham

Ben Jonson edited by Richard Harp and Stanley Stewart

James Joyce edited by Derek Attridge (second edition)

Kafka edited by Julian Preece

Keats edited by Susan J. Wolfson

Rudyard Kipling edited by Howard J. Booth

Lacan edited by Jean-Michel Rabaté

D. H. Lawrence edited by Anne Fernihough

Primo Levi edited by Robert Gordon